T0367698

A Philosophy and a Sensible Alternative .

Entrepreneurism

for the Market Economy

Entrepreneurism

A Philosophy and a Sensible Alternative •

for the Market Economy

Raymond W. Y. Kao
McMaster University, Canada

Kenneth R. Kao
Memorial University of Newfoundland, Canada

Rowland R. Kao
Oxford University, UK

Imperial College Press

Published by

Imperial College Press
57 Shelton Street
Covent Garden
London WC2H 9HE

Distributed by

World Scientific Publishing Co. Pte. Ltd.
5 Toh Tuck Link, Singapore 596224
USA office: Suite 202, 1060 Main Street, River Edge, NJ 07661
UK office: 57 Shelton Street, Covent Garden, London WC2H 9HE

Library of Congress Cataloging-in-Publication Data
Kao, Raymond W. Y.
    Entrepreneurism : a philosophy and a sensible alternative for the market economy /
Raymond W. Y. Kao, Kenneth R. Kao, Rowland R. Kao.
        p. cm.
    Includes bibliographical references and index.
    ISBN 1-86094-312-8 (alk. paper) -- ISBN 1-86094-313-6 (alk. paper)
        1. Entrepreneurship--Moral and ethical aspects. 2. Values. 3. Common good. I. Kao,
Kenneth R. II. Kao, Rowland R. III. Title.

HB615 .K3629 2002
174'.4--dc21   2002068579

British Library Cataloguing-in-Publication Data
A catalogue record for this book is available from the British Library.

Printed in Singapore by Mainland Press

Preface

"It is 95% likely that the world's remaining oil resources will last at least another 63 years, but only 5% likely that it will last another 95 years."

The American Petroleum Institute

There is an interesting concept found in Generally Accepted Accounting Principles or "GAAP." It is the principle of the "going concern." This means that a balance sheet or operating statement can only be considered true and fair, if it applies to a business, which is a going concern. If the business is not a going concern, then no balance sheet, no matter how meticulously kept, can be considered to be a true and fair representation of the company's financial state. When this concept is extended to the level of our planet, if mankind consumes all of the Earth's petroleum resources, whether in the next 65 years, or the next 1000 years, then such resources exploitation is not profitable as it cannot be considered a "going concern." We would simply be borrowing against the future to finance the present. How does this help us to attain sustainability for our economic future?

We present here the most serious challenges humanity has ever faced, those resulting from over-running our planet. We often hear people speak of "the market economy." What is the market economy? In fact, in this world in which we live, there is not just one market economy, but four, listed here in order of decreasing affluence:

(1) Western market economy
(2) Transition market economy
(3) Survival market economy, and
(4) Benevolent or begging market economy.[1]

---

[1] In some places, such as Calgary, Alberta, beggars require a license to beg!

The Western market economy is comprised of nations populated by approximately one-sixth of humanity, and it contains the world's most affluent societies, consuming 75% of the world's energy. If its kindhearted members have it in mind to bring the remaining world population to their level of "prosperity," then we shall need at least four more planets to accommodate us as we stand right now. So what are our options?

With our level of knowledge and technological expertise, we have three of them. In the first option, we accelerate the work on the American-led space program, land on Mars, and in the words of Star Trek's Captain James T. Kirk, let any natives, or "aliens" know that "We come in peace." The second is that we sensibly allocate and utilize our resources, both renewable and non-renewable, and address the challenge of defining the making of "profit." The third option is that we innovate and create new ideas and new technology, not just out of self-interest, but also for the common good.

For the time being, the first option is nothing more than science fiction. While research continues on a future mission to Mars, the difference between exploration and exploitation of the Red Planet is a matter of at least several decades. There is no way we have the resources to either send enough of the population off-planet, or bring back enough resources to make the burden on Mother Earth more bearable. Who would be crazy enough to sell us the travel insurance? The other two options are really inter-related; to create and innovate both in self-interest and in the interest of humanity requires knowledge of what true profit is, in order to keep Earth a going concern. Taking from the future to pay for the present is undesirable, but we need to use at least some of the Earth's resources in order to survive. How much is enough? How much is too much? Therein lies the difficulty.

All humans are driven by two fundamental desires: the desire to own and the desire to create. Ownership is not just the titular holding of property — physical, intellectual or otherwise — but the right to make decisions, or put another way, the right of free choice. The desire to create is the desire to take that which is there, and to alter its form to suit our purposes bringing into being something that did not exist before.

These desires can be twisted to make that which is good, into that which is evil. Vandalism and the urge to destroy are deviant expressions of the desire for ownership — if I can destroy something, then I claim mastery over it. Destruction is also a perversion of creation — for in order to create, I must change that which already exists. The difference is that destruction leaves behind nothing but a vacuum that others can fill but which I do not fill myself.

These needs and desires are so fundamental that we sometimes forget they belong to all of us. We are born to create. We are born with it in us to procreate, and with the desire to raise children. That is creation. To watch a child grow up and develop is surely one of the greatest joys in life. The life of a newborn baby is entirely under our control as we regulate how and when it eats and sleeps. But we all watch our children eventually grow up, mature and leave home to start their own families. In this, we have the ultimate expression of ownership — owning the choice to create something and let it go.

Communism has and is failing precisely because it makes the mistake of removing ownership from the individual. Pure capitalism will also fail, because it erroneously equates creation with acquisition.

The key is to determine what profit really is, and how to measure it. Loosely speaking, profit must be real gain. If accumulation of wealth is to the detriment of others and contributes to the ultimate destruction of our planet, then this would be an impairment of capital, which ignores important costs without giving returns for it. In this case, it would not be a "profit," but a residual before unpaid costs, which should be included in the cost of operation.

Humanity in general and the business sector in particular must come to realize that for a sustainable future we must be creative and innovative. We must use sensibly clean and appropriate technology, while organizing different combinations of people, places and ideas, which work not just for self-interest but also more importantly, the interest of humanity. Fundamentally, we must deal most of all with "human technology," and re-assess the meaning of profit. Profit cannot be determined without taking into consideration everything — people, environment and the resources needed by our descendants. This mindset must become second nature to us, or it is all too easy to follow the old, selfish ways.

The book is centered on four concepts: Creativity, Innovation, Wealth and Value. By wealth, we mean wealth for the individual, and by value, value to society. These are definitions that we first advocated in a publication on Innovation Management in Manchester, U.K. in 1994. In the first part of the book, we discuss the fundamental issues of self-interest and the common good, and "Profit and Cost." We then build on these fundamentals with applications to economic activities including the meaning of having one's own business, the two sides of family business, corporate power, its mission and management, and entrepreneurship for charitable organizations. "Profit" and the "market economy" have been the focal point of our efforts. It is not our intention to dispute the notion of profit or question the importance of the market economy at work. Rather, we seek wisdom and facts to help us improve our understanding of what real profit is, what "profit" can do to the people and the environment, and how is it possible through creation and innovative activities to create wealth for the individual and add value to society.

This is not a book about the environment. It is a book about Entrepreneurism. However, as you the reader will see, one of the great driving forces behind this book is an awareness of poverty and environmental devastation resulting from overuse and criminal inequality of resources distribution. Thus a variety of examples are given to provide the setting for this work. Some of these examples, for which the original citations are given, were first read by the authors in "The Little Earth Book"[2], a thought provoking collection of short essays on topics ranging from the Kyoto accord on global warming, to the recent (and at time of writing, ongoing) epidemic of foot-and-mouth disease in the U.K. *The Little Earth Book* asks many questions for which we believe Entrepreneurism provides a sensible alternative to the market economy.

This book was the product of many sleepless nights, much sweat and tears, and much frustration as we looked over the state of the world today. How long can we blind ourselves, living only for the purpose of making

---

[2]Bruges J., *The Little Earth Book*, 2nd ed. (Alastair Sawday Publishing, U.K., 2001).

money or profit without knowing the meaning of it? We are not owners of the planet earth, but merely its stewards. Our stewardship does not give us the right to take everything just to satisfy our selfish desires. Ultimately we shall be judged, not just in heaven, but here on earth, by those as yet unable to speak for themselves: the unborn children of tomorrow.

Raymond W. Y. Kao
Kenneth R. Kao
Rowland R. Kao

Contents

A hero returns victorious from war. When he arrives home, he announces to his son: "We won! It was glorious. We didn't lose a single ship." The son responds joyfully: "That's great, but how about the other side?"

In war, there is no victory without casualty. Similarly, in business, there is no profit without sacrifice. In each case, there is one true question to be answered: Whose casualties? Whose sacrifice?

"On the 11 September 2001, terrorist attacks in New York City and Washington D.C. gave us a clear signal that we are living amongst two kinds of people: Those (terrorists) who would sacrifice their own lives to destroy the lives of others; and others (New York fire fighters and New York City police) who selflessly gave their lives to save the lives of others."

Rev. R. Sukhram

"Our problems are man-made, therefore, they may be solved by man. No problem of human destiny is beyond human beings."

John F. Kennedy

Section I. The Pillars and the Foundation

"Man is part of nature, and his war against nature is inevitably a war against himself."

Rachel Carson, in a CBS interview in 1963,
Time, 29 March 1999, p. 117

"If I give a man a fish, then I feed him for a day. If I teach a man to fish, then I feed him for life. If I teach a man to fish responsibly, then not only do I feed him, but the rest of his village as well, for generations to come."

Raymond W. Y. Kao, 1993

Chapter 1

Introduction: How Have We Managed?

There is a world of difference between ownership and stewardship. Entrepreneurism is all about making human proprietary decisions: Exercising ownership rights on the one hand, and assuming stewardship responsibilities on the other.

1.1 The Evolution of Business Management Thought

Business and management are as old as human history. Chinese business management has existed as a body of knowledge since well before Christian times. Similarly Japanese management philosophy, so trendy in recent years in the West, has foundations that are centuries old. Western thinking can be linked to a history passed on from the early civilizations of the Near East, through ancient Greece, Rome, the Middle Ages right down through the Reformation and development of the Protestant work ethic, and ultimately the Industrial Revolution. It was here that management shifted from a culturally influenced endeavor, to a more organized factory system.

The concept of the "social man" was a breakthrough in management knowledge, and its widespread practice has some very tangible results. For example, although the relationship between management and labor remains confrontational, it has certainly improved from the days when labor had no representation, or when any confrontation was a violent one. One result has been a focusing of management thought on the ideas of organizational humanism and the search for harmony within the organization. Now we are faced with the challenge of separating the legal entity of business, originating from economists advocating the micro theory of the firm, from the social entity, while recognizing the stake of the community in the business. Business cannot escape its social responsibility. Where once the financial benefit of its investors was the only consideration in business thought, in

Table 1.1 The evolution of business management thought.

Sequential development	Management thought	Proponents (not comprehensive)
The early period: prior to the factory system	Search for new harmony; call for new moral order	Robert Owen (1771–1858)
Scientific management	Improving and reforming based on fact	Frederick Winslow Taylor (1856–1915)
The gospel of efficiency	The task and bonus system Graphical aids Motion and fatigue studies Efficiency through organization	Carl Barth (1860–1939) H. L. Gantt (1861–1919) Frank Bunker Gilbreth (1868–1924) Lilian Bunker (1878–1972) Harrison Emerson (1853–1931)
The human factor	Industry psychology	Hugo Munsterberg (1863–1916)
Social man	Sociology as a field of inquiry-economics and society	Vilfredo Pareto (1848–1923)
Administrative theory	The man and his career	Henri Fayol (1841–1925)
Union and management relations	Union-management cooperation	Many noted individuals
Entrepreneurism	Through entrepreneurial applications, to create wealth for the individual and add value to society	Authors of this book

recent years the idea of an entrepreneurial approach emerged in management concerns, and has broadened entrepreneurship to include ideas of wealth creation and the value adding process — both for the individual and the common good. The early development of management thought is illustrated in Table 1.1.

As a recent development, there has been some thoughts in respect to innovation management, technological management which is essentially the use of the capital budgeting model, and is traditionally referred to as "project management," and the use of net present value or NPV as the basis of evaluation. It has no "knowledge" origin, but is an application of a technique.

1.2 Frozen in a Changing World — Management in the Later Twentieth Century

Charles Babbage's mechanical calculator was the world's first computer, patented in 1822. While his original designs were not practicable, the theory eventually led to the invention of the Burroughs accounting machine. Further advances in the use of calculating devices for business purposes would await the mathematical ideas of Alan Turing, which led to the development of the first large scale electronic computing device in 1944 by Howard Aiken, under the company then known as International Business Machines. Since then computers in business, personal computers, the Internet and all the other developments of information technology have completely altered the world we live in. Similar stories of fantastic breakthroughs and advances can be told across the board of scientific and technological disciplines.

Mainly due to these technological changes, trade has become increasingly global, and resulted in vast uncertainties in the future course of the world economy. In response, the World Trade Organization has been set up to facilitate the flow of resources. Implementation of any such program is hampered by the existence of extreme wealth and poverty, for as long as such discrepancies exist, there can never be a free flow of resources between two peoples. These difficulties are accentuated by the sharp differences between the island and continental economies, each with problems requiring different solutions, especially while they experience the upheavals of the technology driven market environment.

All these changes have drastically changed the environment of business management. For example, improved storage and access of information through widespread adoption of modern information technology has resulted in near instantaneous transmission of business information anywhere in the world. However, this has not necessarily resulted in improved management quality. In fact it may come as a surprise to some, that since the 1940s, there has been little or no progress in organization and business management to accompany the striking changes in the tools with which management practice is conducted.

Management by objective was a concept conceived in the years immediately following the Second World War. Soon after, it was followed by the ideas of management control systems, management by exception and goal congruence (congruence with the goals of the firm, not the goals of the firm in congruence with those of the individual). The profit center and cost center ideas came next, both originating in management accounting (the use of the contribution approach, which is a variant on cost accounting) and then the concepts of team work and the quality cycle. Since this initial spurt of ideas, management theory has virtually stood still.

Of course, there are always new ideas. One idea which has been around for a few decades is "intrapreneurship," which attempts to infuse the spirit of entrepreneurship into the corporate world. It is basically a decent idea, confronting the problems of corporate control and standardized reporting which often stifle the entrepreneurial spirit. However, it has encountered a number of problems which have proven difficult to solve within its framework, including a lack of provision for ownership of spin-off companies, and distribution of equity; parent companies are rarely willing to part with more than 51% of equity holdings of the spin-off companies.

More recently, "Total Quality Management" and "Total Quality Management and Beyond" have been all the rage in some professional circles. Unfortunately, they are little more than a new coat of paint slapped on the ideas of "consumer driven," "market driven," "system thinking" and "organizational learning," failing to address corporate purpose, corporate governance, or global competition.

Improvement of management quality requires not just improved information, but improved information processing, and that requires human decision-making and a re-direction of the manager's mindset. Without this, development in business management will never catch up to the technological revolution. Worse yet, the danger is that the tool will become the master, as we spend more and more time trying to cope with technology, frightened to steer our own path and relying on access to information, rather than knowledge and wisdom. While at best technology will lead to a better world, at its worst it will merely make us more efficient at exploiting and destroying it, for the benefit of the privileged few. This brings us to the looming concern of today: resources depletion and the destruction of the environment.

1.3 The Environmental and Economic Crisis of Today

As the deterioration of our environment reaches critical levels, human misery due to improper distribution of wealth continues to cause conflicts that push people further apart. In 1992, 1670 scientists, including 110 Nobel Prize winners in Science, issued the "World Scientists' Warning to Humanity," which included the following statement:

> *We are fast approaching many of the Earth's limits. Current economic practices which damage the environment cannot continue. Our massive tampering could trigger unpredictable collapse of critical biological systems which are only partly understood. A great change in our stewardship of the Earth and the life on it is required if vast human misery is to be avoided and our global home on this planet is not to be irretrievably mutilated.*[1]

This environmental catastrophe in the making, is matched step-by-step by human misfortune that can be seen and experienced on our own doorstep, no matter where we are in the world. Following are a few examples:

---

[1] *http://www.ucsusa.org*

- The United States is the richest and most influential nation in the world. Meanwhile, in sight of Washington D.C.'s Capitol Hill are areas with some of the highest crime rates in the world.
- Canada is widely recognized as one of the most desirable and prosperous countries to live in, yet native Canadians live in Third World conditions and the homeless exist in such numbers that the federal government has recently appointed a "Minister for The Homeless" for the first time in history. Its leading city, Toronto, has been rated as the number one city in which to live in the world,[2] yet it seems that the number of beggars increases every year. A quick body count taken on a sunny day in September 2000 found two or three persons begging on every downtown block in the city core, although in the city mayor's words "they aren't Torontonians, they come from outside."
- Costa Rica is known as the only successful Western democracy in Central America. Generally reputed to be a peaceful, environmentally conscious nation, some wealthy residents feel the need for razor-wire fences, dogs and security guards with automatic weapons to safeguard their homes. The country has double digit inflation without any relief, and inflation taxes the poor more than the rich. Free trade with other countries in the Americas may give the rich more to consume, but it needs the hardworking common people to work even harder, in order to earn the exchange to satisfy the "rich" who want their "wants" to be satisfied more and more as the days pass by.
- Despite its recent economic problems, Japan is one of the most resounding success stories of the post-war period. Its influence is such that one might say that it has replaced its military imperialism of WWII, with a business one. However, behind a harmonious facade numerous terrorists acts and a high teen suicide rate are symptoms of a troubled society.

---

[2]While Canada has been considered by some to be the best place in the world to live, in July 2001, the Canadian television network CTV National News and others reported that Canada had slipped down to the number three position as a place to live, trailing Norway and Australia.

- Myanmar (formally Burma) lies in the fastest growing economic region in the world — Southeast Asia. It is here that some of the largest problems are seen, with environmentally devastating projects proliferating as this country attempts to catch up to and overtake their more developed neighbours.[3]
- Malaysia is rich in natural resources, and is a leading exporter of tin, rubber, palm oil and tropical hardwood. It was once considered to be a country with great potential for economic growth, however it has concentrated excessive effort on a number of "non-productive," attention-getting projects such as the world's tallest building, longest bridge, and largest airport. Indiscriminate borrowing has drained available resources for "real economic-growth purposes" and in 1994 the value of the Malaysian Ringgit dropped precipitously, taking with it Malaysia's economy and real growth potential.
- In poverty-stricken Indonesia, the country's president has urged people to sacrifice one meal a day, so the grain saved can be used to trade for foreign exchange.
- In Russia the transition from a command economy to market system was supposed to trumpet the superiority of capitalism over communism, yet the vast majority of its people have been plunged into a life of disease and poverty. Meanwhile, a few individuals have managed to carve out for themselves vast financial empires, and government officials including former President Yeltsin have passed out state enterprises to their close friends.[4] Meanwhile President Yeltsin continued to urge Western countries and the IMF to support Russia's economic reforms with loans and hard currency. After Yelstin's retirement, the situation seems to have improved, and the new government of Vladimir Putin seems determined to crack down on corruption. However, there is still a long way to go before the people of Russia can gain the economic freedom promised by their own politicians and leaders of the West.

---

[3]*Toronto Star*, 6 August 1996.

[4]Charlie Rise, New York Harvard Institution for International Development on the CTV National News, Canada, 14 July 1998.

- In Korea, the recent Hanbo scandal has shocked the world. In President Kim Yong San's address apologising for the Hanbo collapse, he said:

> Whatever the reason... all this is due to a lack of virtue on my part. I am responsible. With humility, I am willing to accept whatever reproach and criticism you make. As President, I express my sincere apology for the Hanbo case. The Hanbo case showed the shocking fact that CORRUPTION and the COLLUSIVE LINK BETWEEN POLITICS AND BUSINESS REMAIN DEEPLY ROOTED IN SOME PARTS OF OUR SOCIETY.[5]

These iniquities in the world have long been recognized, at least by a few. And some have always had the noble idea of one world, one people. To help make this dream into reality, the World Trade Organization (WTO), and the International Monetary Fund (IMF) were designed to help build a world with a free flow of goods, resources, capital, technology and most importantly people. Unfortunately, the noble idea has become an opportunity for those already rich to make themselves richer and richer. The Utopian world which the WTO and IMF were given a mandate to create is becoming an increasingly distant dream, a dream as distant as the gulf that separates the very rich from the very poor; the 225 richest people in the world (including the founder of Microsoft, Bill Gates, worth US$78 billion alone) own assets worth the entire annual income of half of the world's population.[6]

1.4 The Management Challenge for the New Millennium

In the world of today, business strategy often revolves around attracting investment and pursuing profit in the interest of the few. Because of this, rate of return on investment (ROI) is attractive because it is conceptually simple and easily measurable, and provides a recognizable standard by which

[5]Gough L., *Asia Meltdown, The End of the Miracle* (Capstone, Oxford, 1998), p. 112
[6]Carley and Spapens, *Sharing the World*, Earthscan, 1998 (ISBN 1-85383-463-7).

outside investors can assess the business. The business management students in MIT were so involved in this idea that ROI is the marquee title of their official publication.

As most managers live in fear for their jobs, they focus their efforts on earning a desirable ROI. This is often the first, last and only focal point of business management, and is customarily referred to as the bottom line approach to business management. Under the current wisdom, it is the single most important motivator in managing a business.

"Human resources management" is a phrase that reflects the sad fact that people are treated like raw material by many corporations. They are used, then thrown out like disposable tissues to pay the price for downsizing, restructuring, mergers and acquisitions. Layoffs involve not just a few people, but by tens of thousands, such as when IBM enacted its global layoff or General Electric put 130,000 people in the street. These are just two of the more dramatic instances. Attempts at global solutions are hampered by extensive trade restrictions and national chauvinism.

Despite the environmental and economic disasters around us, there is serious doubt that the majority of humanity perceives the potential disasters that await us, from immediate problems such as a lack of potable water in some critically overpopulated urban centers, to the long term effects of global warming, and the exhaustion of non-renewable resources.

The problems listed above can be viewed as merely symptoms of the problem of the perception and utilization of business profit. Business profit may not be profitable for society, since we cannot add substance to the earth. The production process is one that merely makes combinations of different resources, thus increasing utility for human consumption. Despite its conceptual flaws, profit is the principle motivator for businesses and managers, sometimes to the exclusion of other factors. The destruction of biodiversity around the world is a typical result of the short-sighted desire for immediate profit at the expense of long term viability. The profit driven market economy has no concern for the common good. In the name of profit, virtually anything can be justified. For example, at the beginning of 1999, it was reported that unsafe drinking water and poor sanitation claim between three to five million people a year, and that over one billion people drink unsafe water in the world.[7] Yet pure capitalism would make even water a commodity to be sold for the largest return. Those who cannot afford it, well, too bad for them. In this capitalist heaven, government's only role would be to prevent the sale of unpotable water. It is all for the good of society, after all. Anyone who thinks this scenario is far-fetched should bear in mind that a liter of bottled water is now more expensive than a liter of gasoline in most countries.

Just about anyone who sees these figures would agree that there is a problem here. What then is the solution? Unfortunately, the problem does not lie just with profit and the managers. There are other culprits as well:

- Economists have been unable to close the gap in economic theory between micro and macro economics. The concept of the common good is not considered to be the concern of business (with a few exceptions).
- Accounting is bound by professional restrictions, and virtually no attempt has been made by the profession to confront the divergence between financial income concepts and economic profit, although there has been some moderate improvement in disclosure practice. The concept of opportunity cost has entered into our judicial system, but there have been no signs of incorporating it into financial reporting. Incorporating environmental cost is not even on the horizon, even though the idea was advanced years ago by Nobel Prize winner Paul Samuelson.
- No one, not economists, accountants, managers, CEOs or entrepreneurs have realized that business is an integral part of the earth, and nothing more than the management of energy. An understanding of the role of science and nature in business, and the role of business in nature, is essential to the development of a mature business philosophy.
- Capitalism must be seen as part of the economic development process, and not the purpose of economic development.

There is an old Chinese saying: "place two silver dollars closely over your eyes, and you will see nothing but two silver dollars." Similarly, a

---

[7]*The Globe and Mail,* 15 March 1999.

business manager concerned only with profit, will see only profit. Productivity for profit. Marketing strategy for profit. Human resources development for profit. Polluting the environment for profit. Depletion of non-renewable resources for profit. This includes the practice of business and also business education, research and the development of business management thought. The business manager is chained in a cave, seeing only the shadows of the real world reflected off cave walls covered all over with the word "profit" in ten foot tall letters. Business managers must remove the coins. They must unchain themselves, so they can see the rest of the world as well. Responsible profit is good; profit for profit's sake, with no added value to society, is not.

The problem is not just one of short and long term profitability. More importantly it is about stealing from the future for short term "wants" satisfaction. Put simply, management practice of today bears an uncomfortable resemblance to the strategy of a scavenging rat or a lethal disease, as opposed to the long term mutual strategy of many social insects. Following this ecological analogy, some relatively far-sighted businesses operate commensally; that is, they operate on principles of "harvestable resources." For example, most forestry companies nowadays plant new trees, but only the minimum to replace what they have taken. Companies that sell tuna in tins advertise themselves as "dolphin friendly" because they use nets that do not trap dolphin, but do not contribute to dolphin survival.

We propose that business must strive for a "mutual" relationship, which is what an "entrepreneurial" activity should be — one where individuals, society and the environment benefit. Business must address the question of the responsibility of the individual who pursues business profit. The concept of responsibility is illustrated in this quote:

> *If I give a man a fish, then I feed him for a day. If I teach a man to fish, then I feed him for life. If I teach a man to fish responsibly, then not only do I feed him, but the rest of his village as well, for generations to come.*[8]

---

[8]Kao R. W. Y., *Entrepreneurship, a Wealth Creation and Value Adding Process* (Prentice-Hall, Singapore, 1993), Preface.

This is the challenge to business managers in the new century: to make profit responsibly. That is of course, if there can be defined such a thing as profit.

There is no doubt that businesses require profit, but not necessarily the profit with which we are currently familiar. The focus must be directed towards a more caring, humanistic approach accompanied by sensible management of the environment and resources. This approach must consider both the present and the future, creating wealth for the individual as well as adding value to society. There is little life left in ROI, though we hope that there is plenty of life left beyond it.

1.5 Breaking Away from Knowledge Barriers and Approaching the Frontiers of Knowledge

1.5.1 What is a business?

Business, which is concerned with the exchange of goods and the development and processing of resources must be placed in the larger context of the exchange of matter and energy in the universe. A business is a tool through which energy is directed, monitored and controlled by human beings. By combining or exchanging resources, the interest of the individual and of humanity is advanced.

1.5.2 Business is a small part of a great system

The universe defies human comprehension, in any way but through abstract mathematical concepts. Within the universe, our galaxy is only one of billions, and within our galaxy, our sun is only one of billions again. Yet the solar system encompasses the sum total of human activity, and the earth the vast majority of that. Of human activity, business is only a small part. Yet the impact of business activities on our existence is far out of proportion to its importance. Understanding this context is critical to understanding the meaning of business, and failure to understand it results often in the sometimes wilful ignorance of the potential impact of business endeavors outside of their boundaries.

1.5.3 Technology drives business and science drives technology

It would be almost impossible to describe a major realm of human endeavor that is not affected by technology. Genetic modification of foods is one of the most controversial subjects of today, even though modification through selective breeding of crops and domestic animals is as old as agriculture. Medical technology has eliminated smallpox and controlled numerous other diseases, while antibiotics and modern birth control spawned the sexual revolution. Plastics overtook steel as the principal manufacturing material in the 1970s. Nuclear weapons have changed the nature of human conflict forever. All these technologies are founded in scientific discoveries of the past century, and are the foundations of multibillion dollar industries.

Technology has increased our ability to impact nature in the pursuit of profit, but also increased our responsibility for it. While science tells us about nature and how nature works, it is business that manages our interaction with nature to increase its utility for the living and for those yet to be born.

1.6 Business Managers' Concern for the Environment

In the name of "profit," we have defaced the earth's surface, emptied its interior of metals and fossil fuels, and contaminated its water and air. Even though some countries now impose rigid regulations to prevent further environmental damage, businesses have simply moved to pastures that are greener both in the state of their natural resources, and in their eagerness for cash and willingness to compromise their environmental well-being.

Though we cannot undo the damage that has gone on before, corrective action and protection are within the means of business management. To make meaningful and appropriate decisions requires understanding of both economic and ecological impact. For example, is paper packaging better than Styrofoam? Is hydroelectric power a better option than nuclear? Are the chemical wastes from washing and reusing glass bottles worse than the cost of recycling them? These questions cannot be answered without at least understanding that they must be asked. Management must be responsible for the asking, even if science is responsible for seeking the answers.

1.7 Resources and People

The challenges of managing resources and people are complicated by other changes occurring in political and economic structures around the world today.

The countries of the Pacific Rim have gone from world-beating economic growth in the early nineties to a sharp downturn, pushing the world economy into recession in the last few years. The economies of this region are typified by small areas, high population densities and few natural resources, often called "island economies." Periods of high growth, are typified by rapid capital accumulation and capital investment from the resources rich "continental economies" of the West, resulting in high returns. Slowing of economic growth results in investors from the "continental economies" pulling out their investments, moving them to safer or higher yield investment regions, exacerbating any downwards trends. This "in" and "out" phenomenon has made living in the island economies an economic roller coaster ride. Meanwhile, poorer continental economies such as China, India and Russia also compete to attract capital investment, always in light of their ever diminishing resources.

Under these circumstances, managing a business is not just about making money for the few, and a global view of business activities and capital investment is insufficient. The scope of business thought must encompass the learning of all cultures and civilizations, and responsibility to all of them, and the earth itself. Anything less would be a disservice to all of us. On the micro scale, businesses are still living with the "residue" concept, and employees in the organization lack motivation. As noted by Peters and Waterman (1982), "We desperately need meaning in our lives and will sacrifice a great deal to institutions that provide meaning to us. We simultaneously need independence, to feel as though we are in charge of our own destinies, and to live in those in the institutions?"

Companies want their employees to be creative, innovative and entrepreneurial, yet through their need for short term profitability, the game is to give their employees as little as possible, while getting the most back. This does not create entrepreneurially inclined individuals, but followers without initiative or the will to make changes. What's there to motivate people to make change, if there is no life beyond ROI?

1.8 The Philosophy of Entrepreneurism

1.8.1 Entrepreneurship and entrepreneurism

Entrepreneurism is a relatively new word and a new doctrine as well. Although not easily found in the dictionary, academics have used the word in place of entrepreneurship, or in association with the creation of a new venture. One such example is a book authored by Jones and Elsaesser (1987) which consists of nine topics from "why you might soon be leaving your job" to a series of venture creation processes including control, delegation, and among other things, costs and return of independence.

Contemplation of new venture creation is part of the entrepreneurial process. Entrepreneurism on the other hand, is an "ism," a philosophy or body of learning with far greater leverage on human behavior and practice. It involves adherence to a system of principles, including:

- the need to create and innovate;
- the desire for ownership; and
- the need to make proprietary decisions for self-interest and the common good.

Entrepreneurism is an ideology in which an individual is a creative and innovative agent with a desire for ownership and the right to make proprietary decisions. As a body of knowledge, it pre-supposes the involvement of three independent yet inter-related entities: the state, business entity and individuals:

(1) **The state: entrepreneurial government**

Under entrepreneurism, the state is the infrastructure consisting of individuals committed to serving people for the common good that will facilitate individuals to realize their economic freedom, their right to acquire ownership for the harvest of their labor, and their right and obligation to protect the natural environment.

(2) **The individual: entrepreneurial person**

An individual is the center of the economy, and as a stakeholder in any undertaking is responsible to him/herself. This individual views entrepreneurship and working as an entrepreneur as a way of life.

(3) **The business entity: entrepreneurial entity and entity entrepreneurial managers**

Entrepreneurship on the other hand, is a process of doing something new (creative) and/or doing something different (innovative) for the purpose of creating wealth for the individual and adding value to society.[9] Through entrepreneurship, the doctrine of Entrepreneurism reigns over all economic endeavors. The entrepreneurial approach is applicable to business management in general, including the creation of new ventures, managing one's own business, business with family members, government and public institutions, charitable and not-for-profit organizations as well as professionals and professional organizations. It goes without saying that the entrepreneurial approach to corporate management is an integral part of entrepreneurial contemplation.

1.9 The Business Entity: How the Entrepreneurial Management Process Differs from Management Tradition

As Entrepreneurism focuses on people, the environment and promoting sustainable enterprise growth, it differs from traditional management in the fundamentals of management philosophy, and thereby in the process as well. The following is a summary designed to highlight the differences

---

[9]Kao R. W. Y., Entrepreneurship, *A Wealth Creation and Value Adding Process* (Prentice-Hall, Singapore, 1993).

Table 1.2 Relative differences between traditional management practice and entrepreneurial approach to business management.

Management practice	Traditional	Entrepreneurial
Economic system	Market economy: capitalistic	Market economy: entrepreneurial
Ownership	Private ownership. Capital accumulation, and ownership augmentation.	Individual ownership. Enterprise creation, personal dedication and pursuit of entrepreneurial value.
Value system	Individuals benefit from the harvest of their efforts. Satisfy consumer needs (sometimes generated through advertising).	Individuals create wealth for themselves and add value to society. Concern for the common good.
Business culture	Maximization, guided by marginal theory. System approach.	Optimization, guided by personal belief. Judgement approach. Self-reliant where ever and whenever feasible.
Mode of managing	Serving investors' need for return on investment. Market driven.	Driven by entrepreneurial need to create and innovate.
Rules for managing	Management separate from ownership. Employees serve the interest of capital investors.	All individuals assume decision-making responsibility. Individuals perceived as stakeholders, with or without capital investment.
The goal of the business entity	To make money.	Re-invest for development and growth.
Management practice decision guide	Maximization principle.	Optimization principle.

Table 1.2 (*Continued*)

Management practice	Traditional	Entrepreneurial
Attitude toward resources	Resources are for exploitation.	Resources are limited. Consideration of future generations.
Attitude towards the environment	Satisfaction of legal responsibilities.	Satisfaction of moral responsibilities.
Attitude toward people	A replaceable and manageable resource.	The source of innovation and creativity. They make or break the business.
Attitude toward innovation and creativity	ROI comes first.	Improvement through innovation.
Attitude toward risks	No risk no loss.	No risk no gain.
Profit computation	Deduct all costs from revenue (accounting method).	Residual, taking into account opportunity cost and cost to the environment.
Profit distribution	To shareholders, with bonuses to top executives.	Residual, to shareholders.
Individual's remuneration	Contractual agreement through collective bargaining between the firm and its employees.	Conciliatory, possibly with worker participation in management.
The role of government	The less the better.	Responsible for matters of the common good, where the market system cannot serve public interest.

Table 1.2 (*Continued*)

Management practice	Traditional	Entrepreneurial
Education	Professionalism and specialization. Serve corporate interests.	Develop creativity and independent thought.
Profession and professionals	Uphold professional standards.	Manage professionally, but without professional managers.
Human resources management	Employment based on short term contracts. Good soldiers.	Relationships built on mutual loyalty. Risk takers.
Human resource performance	Judged by superiors.	Judged in the marketplace.
Attitude toward the presence of opportunity	Cost and benefit analysis.	Make it happen.
Deal with crisis	Seek responsibility. Investigative approach.	Resolve crisis. Firefighter's approach.
Action orientation	There are always more opportunities.	Seize the day.
Tasks	Problem solving.	Identify and pursue opportunities.
The bottom line	Accounting profit and ROI attainment.	Sustainable growth and tasks accomplished.

between traditional and entrepreneurial approaches to management. This does not suggest that there is absolutely no entrepreneurial element in the traditional management process, nor claim that the entrepreneurial approach has no traditional management influence. More often than not, differences address the style of management rather than the structure.

1.10 About this Book

People are driven to act by psychological and physiological needs and wants. They are usually influenced by environmental factors. These include information provided by the media, through personal contacts and countless other sources of input. The psychological needs and wants of the authors that spurred them on to write this book are complex and difficult to express. However, we'll try!

Why this book?

We all live in a market economy, whether in communist countries under dictatorship (we may now consider this to be a transitional market economy), or in capitalist democracies. This means supply and demand turning the wheel of human life. This is illustrated in the following real examples.

(A) *They can drink water from the tap and risk their lives, or not have any water to drink at all and die from thirst.*

In an academic seminar on pricing, one participant reminded the group that the price of bottled drinking water is often higher than the price of gasoline (referring in this case to Malaysia but equally applicable to many other countries). If the trend continues, he remarked, some people would not have clean water to drink. One American professor argued that he saw nothing wrong with this; it would stimulate the discovery of new sources of water, create new opportunities through greater competition and promote entrepreneurship. Another gentleman replied: "What happens if the price of bottled water is driven to a higher level, say as much as $1000 a bottle?" The professor responded: "The higher the better. The more profit, more competition, and eventually competition would drive the price down." The gentleman then asked: "Still, what if some people just cannot afford it? The professor replied: "They will just have to make more money, so they can afford to buy bottled water to drink. Otherwise, they'll drink water from the tap. If it makes no difference to them, they can either drink tap water and risk their lives, or not have any water to drink at all and die from thirst."

(B) *Let the future take care of itself, as we have done for all of our lives.*
The Reagan era is now a part of history, but "Reaganomics" is still very much active in some people's minds. Hardliners will insist that each generation will take care of itself, and that we are not keepers for the future. Future generations may even be more creative and innovative than we are. There is always the question: if we continue to take from the future to provide for the present, what's there for the future to create and innovate? And even in this time of prosperity, the rich still get richer and the poor still get poorer. Will it ever occur to some that perhaps the luxuries we have belong to others?

(C) *Milton Friedman's corporate social responsibility.*
Milton Friedman published his view of corporate social responsibility in the *New York Times Magazine* (1970). In it, he made it clear that: "In a free-enterprise, private property system, a corporate executive is an employee of the owner of the business. He has direct responsibility to his employees. The responsibility is to conduct the business in accordance with their desires. Which generally will be to make as much money as possible while conforming to the basic rules of the society, both those embodied in law and those embodied in ethical custom." He further claims that "…the doctrine of 'social responsibility' involves the acceptance of the socialist view that are political mechanisms, not market mechanisms." Consequently, he argues that corporate executives spending money on social purposes would be in fact taxing the corporate owners…. . Then, the executives of the corporation will no longer be agents who supposedly serve the interest of their principal. They in fact become public employees. Therefore, in his view, the social responsibility of business is to increase its profits. Aside from his misconceptions about profit and the private property system, the single most misleading doctrine is his belief that contribution to society is not a corporate (business) responsibility but a

government one. Yet his laissez-faire economics also advocate that the government should do nothing, and unemployed people are simply lazy individuals.

(D) *Immoral, but legal.*

In the late 1990s, in San Jose, Costa Rica, there was a television program, interviewing executives of the country's largest pharmaceutical company about drug prices. The company's sales manager was asked why, when people were in need of medical drugs, were the prices so high that the average Costa Ricans could not afford to buy them, while the company made huge profits. "Don't you think this is immoral?" he was asked. The sales manager replied: "Yes, it is immoral, but it is legal."

This book attempts to address issues described above and countless other happenings in our world. It is not a book about entrepreneurship nor does it tell people how to start-up a business. Rather it is about a way of thought and a way of life, that is about creativity and innovation and which uses the market as a measure of commercial success. It is more importantly, for people to think. Albert Einstein said that as humans have the capacity to think, we need to think and must think. Entrepreneurism is intended to bring out the social economic value of entrepreneurship, a philosophy that will help us to appreciate our creative and innovative nature, for both our self-interest and the good of humanity. Modern technology gives us needed information to make decisions, but the decision itself is still up to the individual. If we fail to use our brains to think, then our mental capacity will eventually be limited to the intelligence of the software our computers use.

This book consists of 20 chapters. The earlier chapters will be directed to the development of Entrepreneurism as a way of life based on our inherent creative and innovative desires. The second part of the book will address entrepreneurship — its socio-economic value and in particular, its contributions to people who make decisions that affect others. In the case of corporations, this means the management, which must also learn to get a reasonable rate of return on investment for their shareholders, and other contributors as well. Last but not the least, the third part will look at management of resources and the environment, to ensure the future of the human beings yet to be born.

The structure of the book will be like that of a house: after the ground is laid out in this introductory chapter, there is a solid foundation of ideas, followed by the pillars on which the structure of the book will be supported, and finally the bricks of the house — the applications.

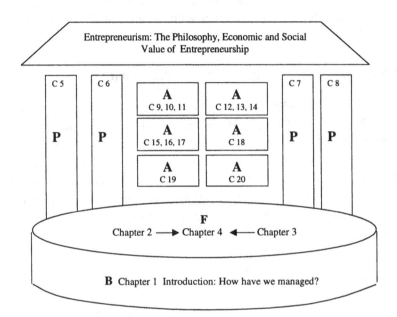

B   The **Beginning** of the beginning
        Chapter 1   Introduction: how have we managed?
F   The **Foundation**
        Chapter 2   The thoughts
        Chapter 3   The motivation
        Chapter 4   The profit
P   The **Pillars**
        Chapter 5   The value
        Chapter 6   The cost
        Chapter 7   The people
        Chapter 8   The culture
A   Applications
        Chapters 9, 10 and 11   New venture creation

Notes on questions listed at the end of each chapter

At the end of each chapter, there will be questions listed for discussions. There is no need to seek right or wrong answers. Rather, the questions are to be taken as starting points to look at the deeper meanings in the text. There might not be perfect answers, but through discussion, there will be better answers, expanding horizons of knowledge and stimulation of thought. Seeking answers from the worldwide web is good, but we still need to think, or we shall be limited by the "brain power" of programmers. We've all got brains — let's use them!

Questions for discussion

1. In a management text, it states that the purpose of management is to utilize resources under the management's trust to achieve the objective(s) of the corporation. Discuss.

2. Assume "resources under their trust" is in fact referring to a corporation that has assumed a stewardship role. What are those resources under the management's trust? The purpose of a corporation is to fulfil a need in the market. In doing so, it is rewarded by consumers' preference of buying its goods and/or services. The prices they pay should be sufficient to recover all "costs" and provide the corporation with needed profit. This is the earned profit that the corporation is working for its shareholders. They rightly expect the corporation to work in their interest, namely to get a decent return on their investment. This is the corporate purpose, and management is rewarded by its receiving adequate remuneration commensurate to the work they have done for their shareholders. Comment!

3. Consider the following: Nortel stock went down from $130 per share in July 2000 to $20 per share at the end of March 2001, but the CEO of the company was still being paid at the rate of CAN$1.35 million annually. Reasons for the drop in Nortel stock price are of course, numerous: a slow economy is one, bad overall performance for all tech stocks is another, but there are also causes directly related with Nortel, such as failure to meet profit objectives, and lay-off of thousands of employees. On top of all those, it was learned that the company's customers were also withheld their purchases. It was considered to be bad news and more bad news. Some shareholders questioned the company's management: why does the CEO continue to receive his hefty remuneration? Why do the CEO as well as other executives not take responsibility for the shareholders' losts? Comment!

4. In the capitalistic driven market economy, we seem to drop economic freedom, Western democracy and capitalism into the same melting pot, equating each one with the others. The most unfortunate part of it is that it all seems to be directly associated with making monetary profit. Profit is a powerful motivation. It motivates managers working for the "bottom line," as well as to those who could not make themselves available for the American dream of becoming one of the contestants for the show "who wants to be millionaire," or make a small fortune through the "dot.com's." It also motivated some who took their answer to the profit question from history: the slave trade, to be specific. They ventured into poor villages of West Africa, telling parents that they would educate their children to be better equipped in the "Capitalistic world," and in the market economy. Pressured by poverty and need for the green bag," some of those parents sold their children for as little as $20, and the "traders" (we cannot call them entrepreneurs) got hold of those kids, packed them in a freighter, abusing some of them, and subsequently resold to the market as sex slaves and/or servants. The whole "modern slave trade" would have gone unnoticed if not for the efforts of a few to bring the criminals to justice, and most especially the Red Cross and UNICEF.[10] This is the 21st century, and with all the

---

[10]*CTV National News*, 16 April 2001.

knowledge, skills and technologies we have, how is it possible that we are still haunted by the same evils of 200 hundred years ago? Is this what the Capitalistic ideal has done to us? Is "making profit" a God given right? Discuss.

5. How should a manager discharge his or her stewardship responsibility? As a traditional manager? As an entrepreneurial manager? If you do not see the difference, then, explain why.

Chapter 2

From the Entrepreneur to Entrepreneurism: The Evolution of Entrepreneurial Thoughts

In the context of idea evolution, Entrepreneurism is not a modern version of capitalism, since capitalism advocates the accumulation of private property and personal wealth through capital accumulation; while Entrepreneurism encourages the creation of wealth and adding value to society through innovation and creativity. It is an alternative to socialism on one hand, and capitalism of the other.

Entrepreneurism is not just about making money, nor is it merely about starting-up a venture or owning a small business. It is a way of life, and a need driven desire to create and innovate. It is in the essence of every human being.

In essence, as a knowledge driven discipline, the term "Entrepreneurship" has its roots in four segments:

(1) Entrepreneurism, an ideology proposed as a sensible alternative to capitalism on the one hand, and socialism on the other.

(2) Entrepreneurship, a process of innovation and creativity through commercialization for the purpose of self-interest and adding value to society.

(3) Entrepreneurial, any creative and/or innovative activity that will create wealth for the individual and add value to society.

(4) Entrepreneur, a person who undertakes innovative and/or creative activities for self-interest, adding value to society.

As we come upon this new millennium we are faced with many of the same problems of old, such as war, poverty, famine and disease, now mixed in with new ones such as global resource depletion and environmental catastrophe. We are approaching what appears to be a crisis point in human civilization, and we must take the responsibility to free every human from servitude and poverty. And yet our old solutions are failing. The socialist experiment failed in the latter part of the 20th century, and capitalism, unchecked and unaltered is doomed to a similar failure. The 21st century is a century for us to realize that we can no longer afford to maximize benefit to the individual with no regard for the common good.

To change capitalism without destroying it, we need to develop the creativity and innovative desire inherent in all of us. This is what "Entrepreneurism" is all about. In the rest of this chapter, we shall outline its historical development, starting from early ideas of the entrepreneur, to the growth of "Entrepreneurship," and finally show how the philosophy of Entrepreneurism can be the hope of our future.

2.1 From the Beginning of the Beginning

If we were to agree with Schumpeter (1934), "Entrepreneurship is ...the finding and promoting of new combinations of productive factors." If this is the case, then entrepreneurship is as old as humankind, as old as the first hominids that made simple stone, bone and wooden tools to hunt and fish. If this is the case, then we are born into entrepreneurship and entrepreneurship will always reflect our desire to take that which is available to us, and recombine it into something new that satisfies our needs and wants. If this is the case, then Schumpeter's definition should be applicable to all human endeavors, and not just academic pursuits, economics and public policy. In the early days, we lived a simple stone-age lifestyle requiring only the simple satisfaction of basic needs, as described by the Confucian ideals of food and sex. Later, "advances" in civilization led us to Maslow's more complicated hierarchy of needs, which recognized both the lower-level physiological needs and higher level needs of love, esteem and actualization. Today, we have a society which some would say views the attainment of "greed" as its highest ideal; many of us might remember Oliver Stone's movie "Wall

Street," where the character Gordon Gecko utters the immortal phrase, 'Greed is Good." This certainly complicates the simple definition of entrepreneurship. One could easily see how a graduate student working on the meaning of the word "entrepreneurship" could develop it into a Ph.D. dissertation, how a college instructor could make it into a lecture or a course, a full university professor might write a book about it, and the dean of a "B" school could build a career or a department on it. Entrepreneurship has become the fox on the hunting ground of any academician or scholar with an opinion, and this includes the authors of this book.

2.2 Misconceptions About Entrepreneurship

Almost as a matter of course, entrepreneurship is linked directly with making profit or money. Here are a few examples that the senior author recalls:

- At a public lecture he gave at the University of Canterbury in New Zealand in 1982, the topic was "Entrepreneurship as an agent of creation." One of the first questions he fielded after the lecture was from one gentleman who asked, "Can you tell me how to make more money?"
- At the 1992 International Small Business Conference held in Toronto, he was the conference chair. In an "Entrepreneurship" discussion session, a businessperson seemed very angry with the group, and with the group leader in particular. In a hostile tone, he shouted at the audience: "I didn't understand a thing about what you guys were talking about; all I can say is, how is it possible that I come to this convention to find out how to make more money, yet you guys waste so much time talking about how to develop entrepreneurship. You haven't mentioned anything about how to make more profit. Don't you guys know that making profit is what entrepreneurship is all about?"
- At the 1st Chinese Entrepreneur Convention held in Singapore 1989, a plenary session participant from South Africa screamed at the panel of speakers: "Look, I am coming here because I want to make more money. I want to make money, that's the reason why I sent my children to school in Israel, so they could learn more about how to

make more money. I don't want you academics to tell me and treat me like a school child and telling what is or is not entrepreneurship."

Incidents such as this are far too common in the capitalist world of the market economy. It indicates a lack of understanding of the nature of entrepreneurship. Making money or profit in the market economy may be a driving force for creation and innovative activities, but it is not the only one, and it is this all-inclusive mindset that causes a great deal of confusion. Reflecting and compounding this confusion is the lack of consensus on a definition of entrepreneurship itself. In the next section, we examine a number of definitions which have been made over the years.

2.3 The "Entrepreneur": A Parade of Definitions

Entrepreneur has its origins in the French word "entreprendre," meaning "to undertake." Not much remains of its original meaning nowadays, and certainly it would be uncertain how to apply it to real life. As its meaning has wandered from its origins, there have been a number of attempts to define it, beginning in the early 18th century, and continuing on to the present day. A number of key definitions are listed here, together with their advocates:

- As a self-employed person with uncertain returns (Richard Cantillon — 1730).
- As a manager, coordinator and risk taker (Abbe Nicollas — 1767, Jean-Baptiste Say — 1803 and 1810, Frank Knight — 1921 and J. E. Stepanek — 1960).
- As a person in need of high achievement and autonomy (D. C. McClelland — 1961 and Oris F. Collins — 1964).
- As a person possessing a variety of attributes, including risk taking, tolerance for ambiguity, leadership, determination and decisiveness.
- As a person with perseverance and an internal locus of control (Robert L. Budner — 1962, W. D. Litzinger — 1965 and J. B. Rotter — 1976).
- As an arbitrageur (Israel Kirzner — 1979).
- As a person who is able to identify opportunities and develop small enterprises (Edith Penrose — 1959).
- As a creative innovator (Joseph Schumpeter — 1910).

The above are only a few definitions. Many others exist, reflecting the realities in which the candidate entrepreneurs ply their trade. Though it is difficult for members of a capitalist society to see how this can work in a socialist country, there is a Chinese restaurateur from Chunqong who calls himself a "Red Entrepreneur." According to him, he and his wife took the risk of starting up a small restaurant, which has developed into a giant operation on its way to becoming China's "hot pot McDonald's." In another case, quite some years ago in British Hong Kong, drug traffickers made themselves out to be "criminal entrepreneurs" (this is likely to be true for many operators of illegal businesses). While perhaps exuding a certain glamour in Hong Kong, these "criminal entrepreneurs" if caught for similar activities in a country such as Singapore, for example, could be executed for their self-styled entrepreneurial activities.

Some would agree that the Chinese "Red Entrepreneur" has a case for himself, but hardly anyone could agree with the drug trafficker's self-delusion. Yet how do they differ? After all, they both operate as independent businessmen. The difference is in their impact on the society in which they live. To be meaningfully considered entrepreneurial, human endeavors must be of benefit to society. Whether you like his food or not, the Red Entrepreneur provides a service to society, whereas the drug traffickers are lawbreakers who supply a product which ultimately only destroys its customers. Criminals are not entrepreneurs because their activities are wholly selfish, whatever claims they may make about the benefits they provide to society.

2.4 Entrepreneurship: Who Says What?

The question "who is an entrepreneur?"[1] has generated much debate; on the other hand, far fewer people are interested in the question: "what is entrepreneurship?" It is commonly acknowledged that entrepreneurship is directly linked with money-making, however a formal definition is not found until

---

[1]Kao R. W. Y., *Entrepreneurship, A Wealth Creation and Value Adding Process* (Prentice Hall, Singapore, 1993), p. 71.

1871, when Carl Menger said that entrepreneurship consists of "obtaining information" to anticipate future wants and needs, "economic calculation," to ensure the technical efficiency of production, "the act of will" which entails purposeful production and "supervision of the execution of the production plan," so that it may be carried through as economically as possible."

More modern definitions have been offered by Joseph Schumpeter (1911), Harvey Leibenstein (1970), Israel Kirzner (1979), W. Ed McMillan and Wayne A. Long (1990) and Howard H. Stevenson (1992). Among these definitions, in the author's opinion only Schumpeter gives a clear notion that entrepreneurship involves activities that are new — the making of different combinations. This is also seen in a more specific definition given at the latter part of the 20th century (Timmons, 1977): "Entrepreneurship is the ability to create and build something from practically nothing. It is initiating, doing, achieving, and building an enterprise or organization, rather than just watching, analysing or describing one. It is the knack for sensing an opportunity where others see chaos, contradiction and confusion..." However, it should be noted that an essential criterion in Timmons is the matter of achieving. This is also implicit in most other definitions. A person can be called an entrepreneur through entrepreneurial activities, but entrepreneurship must generate financial success or recognition from the society. In other words, a person who invents but fail financially or does not benefit society may be an entrepreneur, but is not practising "entrepreneurship."

2.5 Bridging Self-Interest and the Common Good: Fostering Entrepreneurship as Job Creation Strategy

In its programme "Fostering Entrepreneurship" (1998), the Organisation for Economic Co-operation and Development (OECD) noted that entrepreneurship is "a dynamic wealth-creating process of identifying economic opportunities and acting upon them,"[2] an elusive concept, involving the

---

[2]Organization for Economic Cooperation and Development (OECD), *Fostering Entrepreneurship*, 1998, p. 11.

ability to marshal resources to seize new business opportunities, and thus is central to economic growth. This is a rather broad approach in explaining the nature of entrepreneurship.

Although the pursuit of business opportunities is up to the individual's initiative, the creation of business provides job opportunities, so the OECD considers "Fostering Entrepreneurship" to be a job creation strategy. This is perhaps the only definition of entrepreneurship that links the individual's interest in creating a new venture or the micro, and the state policy of fostering entrepreneurship, or the macro.

The OECD's effort to bridge the gap between individual self-interest and public policy creates a further twist in the issue of entrepreneurship: government sanction. It would be totally unthinkable for public policy to encourage or even tolerate criminal activities no matter how well they fit the definitions of entrepreneurship, how creative they are, or how many jobs result. Entrepreneurial activities must operate within the framework of law.

The lack of a clear definition has itself caused problems. In the learning environment, for example, entrepreneurship has not been recognized as an established discipline such as economics, behavioral science or social studies, nor as a functional subject such as marketing, finance, or human resources development. More often than not, it is treated as an offspring from marketing, business strategy, or small business management. In fact, to this day, entrepreneurship is usually considered to be part of small business management, or only slightly better, part of new venture creation. There are number of reasons:

(1) Many respected definitions have evolved from definitions for entrepreneur: Richard Cantillon, Edith Penrose, Jean-Baptiste Say, Frank Knight and W. D. Litzinger have clearly linked the entrepreneurial "person" with venture creation and managing an enterprise under personalized supervision or direct control.

(2) Many of the advocates of entrepreneurship have been closely associated with small business. For example, the high profile U.S. Small Business Administration was created towards the end of WWII. It was designed originally to assist smaller companies to bid

for government contracts and its offices were the source of a series of programs that helped small companies to grow. In Canada, the Minister of Small Business is a cabinet post that was designed to oversee legislative matters relating to the benefit of small business. There have also been private sector initiatives, including the founding of the American Federation of Independent Business and Canadian Federation of Independent Business. These organizations and similar ones in other countries acted as small business/independent business advocates as early as in the 1960s. In the academic community, the creation of the International Council for Small Business marked a concerted effort in promoting academic research, curriculum development and the teaching of small business and "entrepreneurship." There have of course been similar activities around the world, such as "Rencontres de St. Gall" in Switzerland. Later a coalition of existing larger businesses, governments, academia and associations founded a powerful instrument known as the International Small Business Congress, which has contributed to small business development around the world. All these have been champions of entrepreneurship, but unfortunately, this has also helped to foster the close association of entrepreneurship with the development of small businesses. Under this definition, any small business activity (including the creation of a new venture and the management of a small business) is consistent with entrepreneurship.

(3) In the 1970s the British Steel Corporation (BSC) in the U.K. made notable efforts to contribute to the "common good" through new venture development activity — perhaps a first for a large corporation. Concerned steel industry executives saw the start of unprecedented closures in heavy industry, and fought to put jobs back into devastated steel communities by helping businesses to create jobs (Usher, 1989). In essence, the BSC effort had a dual purpose; first, as an entrepreneurial undertaking, it provided assistance to laid off workers by allowing them to start small businesses on their own — a solution designed to help resolve human tragedies of possible unemployment caused by a depressed industry at that time, and second, as a linkage between entrepreneurship on the part of stee

workers as well as the British Steel initiative. However, the creation of small businesses was not by British Steel, but laid off workers. This inseparable relationship certainly gives the matter of entrepreneurship definition an unnecessary complication.

There are other reasons to link small business with entrepreneurship. This is largely related to creativity, as the founding of a venture is undoubtedly an act of creation. But if a small business exhausts its entrepreneurial drive, depletes its capital cost, and eliminates most of its employment capacity, would the particular small business still be an entrepreneurial undertaking? Would the owner/manager still be an entrepreneur? It would certainly be difficult to fit it into some of the definitions stated above. Yet if the business would continue to serve its community, and the owner/manager makes a living and perhaps even provides a part-time job or two, does it really matters whether the definitions fit or not?

2.6 The Merging Reality: Small Business and Beyond

It was perhaps in the early to mid-1980s that the word "entrepreneurship" became more commonly used. Universities had entrepreneurship chairs that never existed before. In Canada, the Small Business Secretariat, Canada's official agency within the Federal Department of Industry and Technology, changed its name to the Office of Small Business and Entrepreneurship. The government of the Canadian province of Ontario recognized the importance of entrepreneurship to the nation's economy, especially in the context of youth education, and in the early 1980s introduced a set of Entrepreneurship curricula for senior students in the province's secondary schools. This was when the senior author renamed the *Journal of Small Business — Canada* to the *Journal of Small Business and Entrepreneurship*. Later, the Swiss Small Business Research Institution, Switzerland also renamed itself: as the "Swiss Small Business and Entrepreneurship Research Institute." Yet as Chell, Haworth and Brearly (1991) suggested: "…the problem of identification of an entrepreneur has been confronted by the fact that there is no standard, universally accepted definition of entrepreneurship."

2.7 The Corporate Spin-Off: Intrapreneurship

In the 1980s, some large corporations (as well as institutions) began to take interest in what entrepreneurship could do to help them achieve their profit objectives. These corporations included big names such as 3M, IBM and Motorola. They all sought to induce "entrepreneurial spirit" into their organizations, especially in the areas of research and development. For this purpose, one approach was to encourage their technical personnel to take inventions or patented products out of the corporation and form small companies as spin-offs. Corporate investment of 51% or more of the required capital for the spin-off company was common, and management assistance was often provided. The subsidiary company would be subjected to parental control and standardized reporting requirements. Such a structural arrangement was termed a "profit center," or more factually corporate entrepreneurship. In the academic community, "Intrapreneurship" is commonly used, though the term is yet to be added to the dictionaries.

The problem with this approach is that the essence of entrepreneurship includes ownership. Without proprietary decision-making rights, the managers of spin-off companies cannot be considered to be practising entrepreneurship, as they neither have the stake nor the creative control necessary to fit the minimum criteria. The lack of independence is the antithesis to the spirit of entrepreneurship. Nevertheless, intrapreneurship is one of the earliest attempts to apply the creativity and innovation of entrepreneurship in the corporate environment. Further attempts to foster corporate entrepreneurship were observed by Schollhammer (1982):

- *Administrative entrepreneurship.* The company engaging in this form of corporate entrepreneurship is taking a step beyond a traditional research and development (R&D) department. There is a philosophy of corporate enthusiasm for supporting researchers, accompanied by the provision of extensive resources to make the new ideas commercial reality (commercializing technology and research).
- *Opportunistic entrepreneurship.* The company encourages champions to pursue opportunities for the company, and through external markets. Quard!/Graphics, the company that prints U.S. News & World Report Inc. and Newsweek, for example, permits its managers to develop

computerized printing technology and even sell it openly to anyone on the market (Holt, 1992).

- *Acquisitive entrepreneurship.* The corporate managers are permitted to seek new opportunities outside of the company. These may include mergers, acquisitions, new technologies and strategic alliances.
- Imitative entrepreneurship. This form of entrepreneurship is epitomized by Japanese firms in their study and reverse engineering of others' products.
- *Incubative entrepreneurship.* Semi-autonomous new venture development units are formed that provide seed capital, give access to corporate resources, freedom of independent action and responsibility for implementation from venture concept to commercialization. The picture here is one of an in-house incubator. This form of entrepreneurship is much the same as intrapreneurship described earlier, except labeled differently.

2.8 Entrepreneurship's Illegitimate Children

In the marketplace, a new product or new idea can explode onto the scene at any time, so long as there are no overwhelming factors preventing it, such as an obstructive monopoly. Similarly, "Entrepreneurship" is not an established discipline like economics, sociology or psychology. At most it might be called a branch of social science, or an interdisciplinary body of knowledge, awaiting classification. The demand for a comprehensive definition is there, but the supply is insufficient to meet it, and consequently, numerous new initiatives have been developed to define certain economic functions in the marketplace, all springing from the original entrepreneurship concept.

"Intrapreneurship" was described in the previous section. "Interpreneurship" and "Technopreneurship" soon followed. "Intrepreneurship" may be another, but the authors are not familiar with it, so we shall have to give Intrepreneurship an "honourable mention." If this were not enough, "Technopreneurgist" was a term used by one keynote speaker at the International Council for Small Business International Conference held in Singapore in 1997, to describe government officials who are creative and innovative individuals that incorporate entrepreneurial spirit in their endeavors. We are sure that there are probably many other terms we have not even heard of. In the following paragraphs, we shall summarise briefly the two most important ones, and put them in the entrepreneurship context.

2.8.1 What is "interpreneurship?"

As with intrapreneurship, interpreneurship will not be found in the Oxford Dictionary. It is used to describe how the entrepreneurial environment and activities are found in family business or family member managed business. Within a business primarily managed by family members, there is expected to be a continuing entrepreneurial drive inherited from the founders of the business. This spirit may evolve over time, and from generation to generation. Nevertheless through continuing effort to innovate and create new niches, products, services and technologies growth of the family business is sustained.

2.8.2 The commercialization of technology: technopreneurship

Technopreneurship is obviously associated with technology. The commonly acknowledged description is the "commercialization of technology." To expand the use of this term, it also implies the "commercialization of research" and "commercialization of scientific discovery." Also common is the concept of technologically based entrepreneurship. Perhaps as early as the 1940s and 1950s, universities offered programs such as "Engineering Business" which were designed for students who wished to embark on careers in business that require an applied science and technology background. In 1975, Professor David Watkin presented a paper on technologically based enterprise at Rencontres de St. Gall in Switzerland, and followed it with a series of workshops held at Manchester University which were all about Technopreneurship.

An interesting application of the concept is the city state of Singapore where Technopreneurship is effectively the national strategy which they hope will give them a competitive edge over the rest of Southeast Asia and the world, and will lead the country through the 21st century. Although Technopreneurship is not new, it does sound impressive. While technological achievement may be considered an entrepreneurial undertaking, only if it is seen to be commercially successful will it be considered to be Entrepreneurially successful. In the market economy where everyone sees only dollar signs, it is no surprise that even a superior technological innovation would be considered a failure if it disappoints commercially. On the other hand, financial success makes the developer of even an inferior product an entrepreneurial hero, as anyone familiar with the story of Apple Computers and Microsoft will know.[3]

Other economic concepts such as "innovation management" and "innovation and change" are also associated with entrepreneurship. Innovation management involves capital budgeting techniques, and selection of decision-making criteria, while "innovation and change" is an all-inclusive phrase for any management and decision-making challenges that involve changes and innovations in an economic entity.

2.9 Entrepreneurship Defined

We have seen how the entrepreneur is someone who innovates, and how entrepreneurship is about fostering innovation and creativity. Yet none of the definitions above adequately reflect the way that entrepreneurship can fill these fundamental human desires or their broad applications in practice. On this basis, we utilize the following definition (Kao, 1993):[4]

> *Entrepreneurship is the process of doing something new (creation), and/or something different (innovation) for the purpose of creating wealth for the individual and adding value to society.*

---

[3]Cringely R. X., *Accidental Empires: How the Boys of Silicon Valley Make their Millions, Battle Foreign Competition and Still Can't Get a Date*, 1996.
[4]The definitions were first published in *Creativity and Innovation Management*, Vol. 1 (Blackwell, London, March 1993), pp. 69–71.

An entrepreneur is a person who undertakes a wealth-creating and value-adding process, through developing ideas, assembling resources and making things happen.

Here, we recognize that entrepreneurship is a process applicable to all wealth-creating and value-adding economic undertakings. This of course includes small businesses. However, owning a small business does not automatically make for an entrepreneurial undertaking unless it continues to update its service and improve its operations.

The definitions of both entrepreneur and entrepreneurship exclude criminals and criminal activities. On the other hand, merely lying within the framework of the law does not make normal business activities entrepreneurial. For example, "acquisitive entrepreneurship" is often not entrepreneurial at all. Mergers and takeovers cannot be viewed as entrepreneurial if they are merely corporate strategies to weed out competition and improve corporate profit. Usually this implies lost employment, reduced service, damage to the environment and depletion of resources, all in the name of corporate greed. This may be legal, but it is not entrepreneurial. It must be clear that this does not ignore the importance of law, rather it reinforces it. Law is essentially reactive, while entrepreneurship implies individual initiative and is proactive. The essence of law is the protection of the *status quo*. Of course no sane society can exist without some change, however the role of the law is in allowing what would otherwise be restricted, rather than developing what is new. For example, tax breaks for developing ideas is really about giving back money (income tax) that the tax laws first of all took away. On the other hand, entrepreneurship is all about fostering the new, and turning "revolution" (destruction due to dissatisfaction with the *status quo*) into "evolution" (the development of new ideas to change the *status quo*).

2.10 From Entrepreneurship to Entrepreneurism

Entrepreneurship has no formal definition earlier than the 19th century. Yet the seed of entrepreneurship has been part of humanity since the earliest days. Entrepreneurship is neither all about money-making, no merely the domain of starting-up a venture and owning a small business. It is a gift of nature seeded in the birth of every human being, and a vehicle to economic freedom. Under this definition, the earliest toolmakers practised entrepreneurship long before we had the concept of money, and no doubt entrepreneurship will continue to be part of us even long after we leave money behind. However, to make the spirit of innovation and creation into a philosophy of life, entrepreneurship must lead into entrepreneurism.

2.10.1 The ideology of entrepreneurism is seeded in the broad application of entrepreneurship

In practice, the spirit of entrepreneurship is applicable in all economic endeavors. It is the entrepreneurial drive that often prompts individuals to pursue business opportunities. The same entrepreneurial drive can be cultivated, nurtured, supported and developed in family businesses, large corporate entities, "not-for-profit" organizations, government, and indeed the home environment as well. Therefore, entrepreneurship helps us to attain both wealth creation for the individual and contribute to the common good at the same time. Of course, wealth need not merely be the accumulation of "money," but can be interpreted in its broader sense, to include public recognition, a well-rounded family life, attainment of knowledge or wisdom, or spiritual development. Entrepreneurship is interdisciplinary, and an obvious consequence of this is that it can and does feed off of other disciplines, including virtually all branches of social science. Its tools are the tools of practical management. In particular, the shaping of the way we see, derive and appreciate the true meaning of profit. Naturally this includes management information. This is understandable; as we have seen, entrepreneurship has historically been closely tied in to the notion of capital, cost, profit, business and management. However, one of the greatest challenges of our time is to improve our relationship with the environment. This is true on every level, from the banks who try to convince us they are doing it all for us even when they are making record "profits," to the petroleum companies who try to convince us with mottos such as "We are here to explore, not to exploit," and to the healthy 25 year old who chooses to drive rather than walk to the corner store for a liter of milk. We all treat non-renewable resources as if they were unlimited, so can we honestly say we are not exploiters?

There are at least three areas of learning that contribute to cultivating, nurturing and enhancing entrepreneurship: skills (what we learn), behavior (how we act) and attributes (who we are). These apply everywhere. For example, risk taking is an attribute needed in sports, investing and even your personal life, such as in marriage. It is this broad application of entrepreneurship and the entrepreneurial spirit that leads us to entrepreneurism.

2.10.2 What is entrepreneurism?

As with many of the other terms discussed in this chapter, entrepreneurism is a word that you are unlikely to find in a dictionary. It has been used in the academic community to describe undertakings, especially the founding of a small business. This narrow interpretation does not represent the comprehensive nature of entrepreneurism, especially when viewed in terms of the comprehensive nature of terms where the suffix "ism" is used. For example, capitalism, catholicism, liberalism and socialism; these all reflect life-changing philosophies.

> *Entrepreneurism is not just a way of conducting business; it is an ideology originating from basic human needs and desires: the need to create wealth for oneself and to add value to society. In practice, entrepreneurism can be considered as the application of ingenuity for self-interest and for the common good. This entails discovering the new, while changing, adapting and preserving the best of the old. It champions the rights of the individual to acquire ownership through the freedom to make decisions. Although capital will always be an important factor, entrepreneurism is unlike capitalism which facilitates capital accumulation and delivers ownership to the rich. Likewise, although the community and the good of the state are key concepts, entrepreneurism is unlike communism, which provokes class struggle through revolution, taking ownership away from the individual and giving it to the state.*

Table 2.1 The evolution of entrepreneurial thought.

Period	Featuring	Contributors and definitions	Remarks
Early thoughts	Not a definition for entrepreneurship, rather describing who is an entrepreneur.	Richard Cantillon (1730); (entrepreneur) self-employed person with uncertain returns.	After more than 270 years, still is viewed a good definition; clearly refers to the owner managed venture and specifies the risk bearing attribute of entre-preneurial undertakings.
Incubation	Entrepreneurship is still considered a branch of business practice.	Carl Menger (1871); obtaining information, calculating value, acts of will and the supervision of production to efficiently satisfy needs.	Activated the thinking of those interested in clarification of entrepreneurship, and its meaning to the individual and society.
Growth of ideas	New thinking: entrepreneurship not confined to domain of self-employment and small business.	Joseph Schumpeter (1910); finding and promoting new combinations of production factors.	A very comprehensive yet simple definition, that can be applied to all human endeavors.
A confusing proliferation of ideas	Entrepreneurial function clearly extended beyond self-employed entities.	Harvey Leibenstein (1970); the reduction of organizational inefficiency and the reversal of organizational entropy.	Drive for efficiency, can be part of "make changes to the old," but entrepreneurship has much great scope than organizational efficiency.
		Long and McMullan (1990); the building of new organizational growth.	A broader approach at the organizational level. However, organizational growth may not be entrepreneurial unless "sustainable" is added.

Table 2.1 (*Continued*)

Period	Featuring	Contributors and definitions	Remarks
Consolidation	Action orientation.	J. A. Timmons (1989); the ability to create something from nothing. Initiating and building rather just watching, analyzing or describing; sensing an opportunity where others see chaos, and confusion.	A good definition that includes both enterprise and organization
Maturation	Fostering entre-preneurship as a job creation strategy; entrepreneurship central to economic growth.	OECD (1998); the ability to marshal resources to seize new business opportunities.	Bridging the individual's initiative and the common good.
	The socio-economic value of entre-preneurship. Development into an ideology.	R. W. Y. Kao (1993, 1997); creating wealth for the individual and adding value to society through new and innovative undertakings.	An ideology as an alternative to capitalism and communism.

In a society under entrepreneurism, every individual would be encouraged to be self-reliant, and an agent of creation and innovation. This spirit would pervade all economic entities including the government, corporations and all other human institutions.

Questions for discussion

1. Under Capitalism, individuals and groups are able to accumulate wealth for themselves, how then does the accumulation of personal wealth add value to society?

2. When should governments intervene to correct improper market behavior? For example, should they prevent mergers and acquisitions in the name of preserving a competitive environment? Would measures taken by the government to prevent corporate concentration help entrepreneurship development?
3. More people have defined "Entrepreneur," but not with the same dedication devoted to the definition of "Entrepreneurship." Why?
4. In your opinion, what are essential criteria needed to consider "Entrepreneurism" as an academic discipline?
5. Human conflicts are more often than not caused by struggle for ownership. On the other hand, the need for ownership may not necessarily involve resources, rather ownership decision. The right of making proprietary decisions seems to be the real issue. The downfall of Communism at the end of the 20th century in many countries was not the failure of ideology, rather, people under Communism were not given the right to make proprietary decisions. This caused its demise both in the East and the West. In your opinion, how does Capitalism facilitate giving individuals the right to make proprietary decisions? Would it be the same under Entrepreneurism?
6. Assume that you are the newly appointed CEO of a medium size corporation. The company enjoys the rare privilege of patent rights giving a monopoly of 15 years by the government for its inventions. It has been a profitable operation for the past five years. The right has five more years to go, but no one has any idea what will happen when the time comes.

   On account of its success, the former CEO instituted both an employees' ownership participation plan (5% of common shares) and profit sharing scheme (1% of sales). As the new CEO, you sense that all employees (including senior management staff) are relying on the Company's good fortune, and have absolutely no drive. To put it bluntly, they are just "company-reliant deadwood, living off the birthright of the company's researchers of the past."

   The board of directors gave you a specific task: to turn this place from a money making machine, to a community of entrepreneurs within the next three years. What would you do?

Chapter 3

Beyond Maslow's Hierarchy of Needs: The Need for Ownership

> The greatest challenge of the 21st century is to appreciate the nature of ownership and the nature of profit. The greatest fear for the capitalist-based democracy is not communism or socialism, but poverty. The seeds of communism did not take root in the prosperous nations of the Western world. It took root in countries where accumulation of property reached obscene levels, and poverty drove a desperate population to extreme measures. As long as "poverty" remains in the dictionary, the fear of communism will always be there.

3.1 The Ownership Struggles of Rich and Poor, Past and Present

The idea of ownership is simple, but achieving it is a life-long struggle. It involves taking responsibility for possessions and assuming a proprietary position. It does not have a single profile, but takes many different forms. The irony is that we cannot take ownership with us to the grave. No one lives forever. We all know that, but we have come up with at least three distinct views on how to deal with it:

(1) We belong to nature, and so we follow the laws of nature. If there is anything more than that, it is beyond our control.
(2) We can fight against nature, and try to establish mastery over it. Maybe one day, we can become immortal, but for now, all we can do is to struggle.
(3) What we have on earth, is merely a preparation for a better life, so let's do our best to get there.

The ancient Egyptians thought they could take worldly wealth with them to the afterlife. Even today, we hear stories like that of the Japanese gentleman who wanted his art collection to be buried with him. In the meantime, we do everything possible to accumulate as much personal property as possible.[1] Life is less about a search for excellence as it is about a search for ownership. For instance, on 12 July 1969, the first man to land on the Moon planted a U.S. flag on the Sea of Tranquility. While it was certainly a "giant leap for mankind," was it not also the first claim of extraterrestrial ownership for humanity?

The struggle for ownership is a fact of life. Human history may be inscribed in stone or written in blood, but underneath it all lies the struggle for ownership. A popular piece of folk humor wryly says: "He who dies with the most toys wins." There is a litany of historical events tied to ownership. The colonization of the world by the European nations was about taking ownership from the local inhabitants and cultures, just as the various wars of independence of the last two centuries have been about returning it. Similarly, the capitalist revolutions of the 19th century were about the accumulation of ownership in the hands of the few, while the communist revolutions of the 20th century were about putting it back in the hands of the people. Finally, the religious struggles of one faith against another throughout history have been about the most important ownership of all, the ownership of our souls. The lesson to be learned from these experiences is that all of humanity, at the individual, family, community and national level have been drawn directly or indirectly into bitter struggles of exploitation, or defence against exploitation.

The need for ownership is a basic need of humanity. It is the universal driving force behind the growth of civilization. Maslow's Theory of Needs is really about what is needed by the human soul. We require different things on different levels. Once the basic needs are satisfied, our "need to need" does not change, but the target of our needs does. However, Maslow's theory does not include in its list a need for ownership, even though this is fundamental to the satisfaction of all needs, most importantly the basic

---

[1]But remember to bring some money to grease the palm of the doorman to the Pearly gates, otherwise, you may be refused entry!

survival needs of food, water, clothing and shelter. Without ownership, a human may survive, but only at the mercy of God.

3.2 The Story of the Theory of Needs

In a series of publications from 1943 to 1969, Abraham Maslow established himself as the founder of needs theory. His categorical set of human needs was established in 1970, and it still occupies an important place in the academic community. Supposedly, recent evolutions of business management practice (such as "Total Quality Management" or TQM, and "Total Quality Management and beyond") are mainly an extension of Maslow's Needs Theory. But then again, even Maslow's theory is an example of the old becoming new again. Some two thousand years ago, a certain philosopher by the name of Confucius coined a simple phrase that really forms the basis of needs theory: "Food and Sex are human nature."

Though not new, Maslow's theory forms the basis of modern motivational theory. In a nutshell, it lists needs in a series of increasing sophistication. consisting of the following:

- physiological needs
- need for safety
- need for love
- need for esteem
- need for self-actualization
- need for self-accomplishment

This list remains relevant in both research and education, though most work concentrates mainly on the "higher" needs such as self-actualization which were later viewed as "the need for growth," while all other needs were considered to be "deficiency needs."

Other noted contributors in needs theory include David McClelland (1948) and Clayton Alderfer (1972). Through his achievement motivation theory, McClelland and his students investigated the relationship between hunger and the degree to which food imagery dominates thought processes. The investigation subsequently prompted the study of motives of human behavior, extending to such primal forces as the needs for power, aggression sex, fear and achievement. Alderfer's theory can be viewed as a modification and extension to Maslow's thought. For example, Alderfer's "existence needs" correspond to physiological needs and safety needs of the material type.

The contributions of Maslow, Alderfer, McCelland and others are now extensively applied in practice. Management strategies deal with human situations and are without exception based on the needs of people. Needs are motivational factors; they drive people to think and act either for self-interest and/or for the interest of others as well — or the "common good" as we call it. However, while Maslow's needs theory has been center stage since his work was first known, nothing has really addressed the human need for ownership. At the risk of becoming repetitious, we ask, "How is it possible for anyone to satisfy any needs in today's economy, including the basic ones such as food and shelter, without ownership?"

3.3 Why Ownership?

One of the markers of the development of civilization is some form of statutory governance. Without exception, these statutes recognize "owner-ship" as the right to make decisions about the utilization of the resources over which ownership is claimed. Ownership should imply stewardship, but this is not necessarily the case, and when absolute power is involved, ownership is often corrupted. In China, a Tang Dynasty emperor once claimed ownership over his son's wife. In the mid-1800s, the dowager Empress of China used an entire navy budget to build an immovable stone boat. These are both clear examples of selfish ownership.

Whether we are defending our freedom, defending our faith, defending our honor, or preserving our culture, so much of our suffering comes down to ownership. History is marred by evidence of the endless struggle for ownership. Conquerors use their power to crush weaker nations and subjugate them. Subjugated people then fight to reclaim their land, or their heritage, or simply to impose their will on their former oppressors. Our past is filled with stories of the glory of war, of honor and duty, but really underneath it all is the sacrifice of human blood, usually in the name of noble causes, but almost always with the ultimate aim of ownership. How often have we fought for the right to take something? How often have we fought for the right to give something away? In the American Civil War, the North did not fight to free the slaves, they fought to maintain ownership over the South. The Crusades were not fought to free the Holy Land, but to deflect the grumbling of the feudal nobility in Europe, curb the influence of the Moslems and maintain the power of the Pope. The first Crusaders themselves were mostly younger sons of nobility, out to carve names and territories for themselves in foreign lands. Beginning in the 16th century, the European nations, once terrorized by warriors from the steppes, and in awe of the power and majesty of the Eastern civilizations, began to assert themselves and to colonize and subjugate the rest of the world, a process that continued well into the last century. Everywhere around the world — in Asia and Africa, in the Americas and even in Europe, ownership was enforced behind the muzzle of a gun. Resources were stripped from the land, the people were enslaved and those who did not submit were killed. Colonial imperialism reached its apogee under the glory of Queen Victoria's Britannia, over which it could be rightfully claimed that the sun never set. Even in this century, countries have dispatched their troops to troubled places such as Korea and Vietnam, and for what? To defend democracy? Why did the Western nations respond so quickly to Saddam Hussein's invasion of Kuwait, when they watched for so long the self-destruction of Yugoslavia? Nevertheless, it is still the same story of "ownership," as one country or corporation seeks the power to control another.

We can look back over the last hundred years, and while the 20th century has witnessed many stunning achievements, it is also painted with human blood spilled in the cause of "ownership." Table 3.1 is a short list of only some of the major human conflicts of the last century.

The 20th century has now passed, but the wars continue. Palestine. Chechnya. Kosovo. Rwanda. Zimbabwe. The Israeli–Palestinian conflict seems to continue without foreseeable peaceful resolution. The newest war in the newest century, the war against terrorism, is only in its infancy and nobody knows how and when it will end. Ownership is and always will be the major cause of human conflict, and a driving force to push individuals' attributes to behave and act either for self-interest or for the interest of society.

Table 3.1 A short list of wars of the last century involving more than one country (adapted from Mollica, "Invisible Wounds," *Scientific American*, June 2000, with some additions).

Major Conflict	Years of Conflict
Spanish–Cuban	1895–1902
Spanish–Cuban–Filipino–U.S.	
Filipino–U.S.	
British–Boer	1899–1902
Russo–Japanese	1904–1905
World War I	1914–1918
Russian Civil	1917–1921
Russo–Polish	
Chaco (Bolivia-Paraguay)	1932–1935
Spanish Civil	1936–1939
Sino–Japanese	1937–1941
World War II	1939-1945
Franco–Vietnam	1945–1954
U.S.–Vietnam	1963–1973
Arab–Israeli	1948–1949
	1967
	1973
Korean	1950–1953
Belgian Congo	1960–1965
Angolan–Portuguese	1961–1975
Angolan Civil	1975–1995
Mozambique–Portuguese	1965–1975
Mozambique Civil	1975–1995
Bangladesh–Pakistan–India	1971
Soviet–Afghanistan	1979–1989
Iraq–Iran	1980–1988
Iraq–Kuwait–U.N.	1990–1991
Serbia–Croatia–Bosnia	1991–1995
Russia–Chechnya	1994–1996
	1999
"America's war on Terrorism"	2001–?

While the wars continue, for the most part economic imperialism has taken the place of military conquest. Ownership is won and lost in the boardroom rather than on the deck of a battleship. For the individual, the struggle for ownership is more or less a daily routine. A table reservation at a restaurant, a "no trespassing" sign, front row tickets at a concert or football game, or even the spot in front of the monkey cage to take a picture — all these things are forms of proprietary claims or ownership. Throughout one's life, a person will encounter many ownership challenges. Yet sometimes, it is difficult to understand the importance of ownership rights. The following are a few examples from the authors' own experiences:

(1) **"Your fence is one foot inside my property!"**

Some years ago in the small town (now city) of Markham, Ontario, Canada, a new subdivision had just been built. The Kao family had just moved in, as had a Mr. Steinrod and his family. Fearing property line confusion, Mr. Steinrod immediately began to erect a wooden fence around his property. As soon as the fence was erected, his neighbor Mr. Brown jumped over the fence, screaming at Steinrod, saying "Take your bloody fence out of here, you've got it one foot into my property." Steinrod refused, and Brown continued to scream, getting more and more angry until he had a heart attack, dying right on the spot.

(2) **Even beggars fight for ownership**

Bali is a beautiful resort island in Indonesia and a paradise for people who can afford such luxuries. A few hundred meters away from the five star beach hotel, there are small shops and vendors to serve the tourists, but the neighboring area also houses families in dried-out sewers. The people use bits of discarded cardboard for shelter and privacy. A miserable life to the typical reader of this book, yet even here the struggle for ownership is in evidence; families and individuals frequently fight for ownership over the best sewer spots. Similar incidents also occur in other parts of the world, including in the most affluent countries. Even in Toronto and San Francisco, often quoted as among the most desirable cities in the world to live, homeless people jostle to claim strategic places to beg.

(3) **The ERMO story**

In Toronto, Canada, on 25 September 1998, the local publicly funded television station, Television Ontario or TVO, aired a Chinese movie. The title of the film was "ERMO." It is a story about Ermo, a noodle maker, who worked very hard, unimaginably so by Western working standards, to make enough money for her to buy an expensive TV, so she could impress her family and friends. She eventually achieved her goal and realized her dream of owning a giant television that attracted virtually all of the local villagers. Soon the crowds began to pack into her bedroom, one of only two rooms in her tiny house. She and her family, however, got nothing out of it, for most of the TV shows were either in English or were programs that were of no interest to them. The show concluded with a scene showing ERMO, her husband and their six-year-old son all sound sleep in front of her giant black box.

Ownership will always be a fundamental driving force for human behavior. In the first incident, defending "ownership" costs a person his/her life. In the second incident, ownership rights were fought over, even at the level of subsistence. Finally, the last incident shows us that sometimes, ownership can result in owning nothing of value at all. The desire for ownership has led to the killing of other human beings as well as ruthlessly exploiting the environment, people and life support belonging to the future. Sometimes we confuse ownership with love, yet in the simple story of King Solomon's wisdom, we see the difference. Two women come before him, each accusing the other of replacing her own living baby, with the other's dead one:

> *The king said, "This one says, 'My son is alive and your son is dead,' while that one says, 'No! Your son is dead and mine is alive!'"*
>
> *Then the king said, "Bring me a sword." So they brought a sword for the king. He then gave an order: "Cut the living child in two and give half to one and half to the other."*
>
> *The woman whose son was alive was filled with compassion for her son and said to the king, "Please, my lord, give her the living baby! Don't kill him!"*

> *But the other said, "Neither I nor you shall have him. Cut him in two!"*

Old Testament, 1 Kings 3:23–26
(New International Version)

Love wants the object of love to survive and flourish, even if we cannot enjoy it directly, while desire for ownership would rather see the thing destroyed, than to let someone else possess it. The greedy acquire ownership for reasons that are inexplicable, since life is a one-way trip with no return ticket.

3.4 Acquiring Ownership

History is defined by ownership. Wars of conquest are the scenes of history's most heinous acts, and what is conquest but the quest for ownership? In World War II, the Japanese invaded China on minimal pretext, and committed such crimes as the Rape of Nanjing. The Germans attempt to control Europe and purify the land of impure peoples led to the death of millions of Jews in horrible circumstances. Sometimes these acts are masked by good intentions, or are the results of good intentions that have been corrupted, but even in these cases, it is often the quest for ownership that causes the corruption. Too often, the causes of religious, political or class freedom are corrupted by those seeking ownership. This does not mean that peaceful ways of acquiring do not exist. In fact, in the pure market economy there is a saying, that "any ownership is negotiable, the only difference is price." This is true enough, or at least people think it is. Otherwise how could Hollywood sell the movie "Indecent Proposal," where a wealthy man buys another man's wife for one night for a million dollars?

3.5 The Ideological Difference of Ownership Acquisition

Global politics in the past hundred years have been dominated by the confrontation of the two ideologies of communism and capitalism. Both of these are concerned with the issue of property ownership; while Communism claims that all property belongs to the state, capitalism champions the right of the individual to private property. This difference in ideology has led to the use of different methodologies to acquire ownership: the capitalists advocate the use of a market system to acquire ownership, mainly through hard work, but also through windfalls such as inheritance, marriage and "gifts from heaven." There are also legal practices such as gambling and (in some places) prostitution, which many would consider immoral and illegal, even while they tacitly accept practices such as cheating the tax system. On the other hand, under the communist system ownership is directly acquired by the state and for the state, initially by the violence of revolution. The sad underlying truth is, that both systems lead to ownership becoming concentrated in the hands of the privileged few, often driving many others to poverty.

3.6 The Ideological Adjustment

Ironically, neither capitalism nor communism satisfies the individual's need for ownership. No matter how much there is, there can never be enough ownership to go around, since so much of greed is not about what we need, but about what others have that we do not. Under capitalism those who do not have, want, and those who have, want more. Under communism, in theory everyone owns everything, but real ownership, i.e. decision-making, is lost. The ownership need-driven process continues. Consequently, both "isms" have made adjustments. In a capitalist society, workers form unions to negotiate and bargain for a share of corporate earnings. Concessions are made to corporate management to allow workers (including managers) to participate in the company's share subscription. Part of the corporate profit is redistributed to workers as a bonus (it may, for instance, be incorporated into an individual's retirement plan).

In communist countries, there was no provision in state-owned enterprises to motivate individuals to high achievement, and thus individual stake-holding has become allowed in a limited way. Even during the Cultural Revolution, China did business with the West, through Hong Kong and in various other ways.[2] In *rural China*, medium and smaller state enterprises allow workers to acquire ownership in a way similar to that practiced in the West. Using various schemes, workers may acquire part-ownership of the enterprise through cash purchase, or payroll deduction, transfer debt from the state to the individual, as a year-end bonus, or in a profit-sharing scheme.

After the break up of the Soviet Union, the transformation of the Russian economy has been marked by worker acquisition of ownership in formerly pure state-owned enterprises. This story has been repeated across Eastern Europe, formerly dominated by the communist ideology. The success of these efforts has varied, however, with the transition more successful in the countries that were already relatively prosperous. For example, Poland has accomplished more in the pursuit of returning ownership to the people by restructuring and privatizing large state-owned companies, but also forming numerous small, privately-owned business enterprises. To some extent, the Polish accomplishments are due to the fact that the Polish people in rural regions had never given up their land ownership.

In Hungary, a form of ownership network developed during the last decade of the 20th century. Limited liability companies that began as "corporate spin-offs" sometimes became linked through ownership ties to more than one share-holding company and, significantly, often linked to other limited liability companies as well. This network of direct and indirect ties between properties, linking entities in a given configuration was called a "Recombinet." The Recombinet is not a simple summation of sets of horizontal and vertical ties rather it represents the characteristics of "horizontal and vertical" integration. The practice of pervasive inter-enterprise ownership and emergence of the Recombinet organizational form means that the actual economic unit of the Hungarian economy is no the individual firm but a network of firms. This setup can now also be found in Western nations. In fact, while "Intrapreneurship," or perhaps

---

[2]In contrast, the Soviet Union attempted to "go it alone," and its business activities were largely done within the Warsaw Pact, and with other countries in the Soviet sphere of influence.

more appropriately, "inter-enterprise" is now a darling of the capitalist west, it is really only Recombinet revisited.

3.7 The Matter of Making Proprietary Decisions

The methods by which workers in various countries acquire ownership and by which state-owned enterprises are privatized vary considerably, as are the ways they exercise their right to make proprietary decisions. In the West, corporate decisions are made based on capital contribution, and almost without exception, on a "one share, one vote" basis.

In the East, and particularly in China, some enterprises recognize both capital and personal contributions. It uses a method practised in cooperatives, combining a corporate vote in accordance with capital contribution plus the "one person, one vote" system. The practice is known as a "Corporate Cooperative" or "Cooperative Corporation." In Hungary for example, it is not uncommon to find a large public enterprise with its shares distributed among 20 or more satellites around the corporate headquarters. These satellites are independent legal entities. The controlling shares over these corporate satellites are normally held by the large public enterprises themselves, but for making major business decisions, their status is semi-autonomous. They even have their own board of directors, with separate accounting.

In Western Europe, workers often participate in high level decisions at shareholders' meetings and vote on the basis of share participation. They can also participate in management operational decision-making processes through their elected representatives on a one person, one vote basis, at management committee meetings.

3.8 The Emerging Reality: From Conflict to Congruence

Is any ideology really evil? In the U.S., Soviet Russia was once called the evil empire, or the "red menace." Yet, Saddam Hussein called the President of the U.S.A. the "Great Satan." And there are many who would believe him. Who is right? Undoubtedly, there are some ideologies that the majority of us would label as evil, such as the National Socialism of Adolf Hitler. Yet, even Hitler has his admirers.

Of course, most reasonable people recognize that there are some things which are truly evil. And one of those things is poverty. When China's Premier visited the U.S. to seek government support for their application to enter the World Trade Organization (WTO), a reporter asked him: "What does China really want?" The Premier replied, "to give our people a decent living." If this is accomplished, how much does it really matter whether China practices communism, socialism or the socialists' version of the market economy?

Ownership participation is becoming increasingly acknowledged in both capitalist market economies and socialist command economies. Does this signify the emergence of a new reality in which recognition of individual ownership is ending the ideological struggle between "East" and "West?" At the very least, it suggests that both capitalism and communism are "processes" for economic progress, and that ownership for the individual is the only end. Even Karl Marx celebrated individual ownership in "das Kapital" as the end of the class struggle. Unfortunately, it was not as clearly presented in his treatise as we would have liked. The significance of this evolutionary process from ideological conflict to goal congruence is that, just perhaps, we are finally learning to live together. What is important is how to facilitate ownership acquisition both for the individual and those in policy-making positions. Individuals need to assume ownership responsibilities by working diligently and earning return for investors, people, resources and our natural environment, all of which have made contributions to the welfare of humanity.

3.9 Entrepreneurship, Entrepreneurism and Ownership

Entrepreneurship is a process of creating wealth for the individual and adding value for society. To acquire ownership is the right of individuals to make decisions for their interest as well as for society. Entrepreneurism is an ideology in which an individual is a creative and innovative agent with the desire for ownership and the right to make proprietary decisions. Businesses or economic entities are not money-making machines, but par of a community of businesses, run by entrepreneurs whose purpose is to create wealth for individuals and add value to society. The state is an agent to facilitate and provide an environment that makes it possible for the individual to create and innovate. Under entrepreneurism, all individuals are owners of their own making, who are entitled to, and able to make, proprietary decisions simultaneously for self-interest and for the common good.

As a society is progressively transformed from either a capitalist, communist or any other system to one that gives individuals entitlement to ownership, it is the owners who must assume responsibility for sustainable economic growth. Sustainable economic growth, however, is not a term easily accepted by many people, especially those with an inquisitive mind.

3.10 A Short Discussion on Ownership, Sustainable Economic Growth and the Problem of World Population

What is sustainable growth? Malthus showed us long ago that a population that continually expands only leads to disaster. Of course, because we are resources-limited there is only a finite population that the world can sustain. Fortunately, it appears that the world's population may be levelling off. Certainly the Western nations are approaching zero or even negative population growth in some cases. And advancements in technology will help, as we find new, better, more efficient and cleverer ways to extract energy and resources from our surroundings. But there are still only limited resources to go around. Even if the population only remains constant, it is inevitable that we shall run out of resources. Sustainable growth then, can only be defined for a limited time frame in terms of improved quality of life for a finite number of people.[3]

Related to sustainable growth is the fundamental issue of ownership. Why do some individuals want to own everything in the world? What good

---

[3]Of course, we shall eventually run out of resources no matter what, as even the Sun's fuel is finite, and beyond that, the Galaxy and perhaps the universe.

will it do for them? After all, we can only use one chair, one car and one shirt at a time! Why must one person own an entire island to holiday on or some people have 30-room mansions? Why must some people own five cars for themselves, or one person own more than 1000 pairs of shoes? The fundamental question is: what are the limits of ownership? Is the sky the limit? An immediate knee-jerk response to this question is: "This is how socialists or communists think!" But is it? What is the justification for unchecked ownership for a few, in a world of limited resources?

The challenge to humanity is not over-population, nor is it who is capitalist or who is socialist. The challenge is to turn our thinking away from one of exploitative ownership, where some persons are driven to accumulate unlimited monetary wealth and expand personal ownership, at the cost of everything else. That is the challenge we must face. A recent article on the value of the world's resources states:

> *Economics is the driving force of today's widespread environ-mental destruction. Markets undervalue the earth's resources and compound their overuse. Since World War II the world has used resources voraciously. The situation can be described as the industrial countries over-consuming resources, which are over-extracted and exported by developing countries and traded at prices that are lower than the social costs. Resources-intensive patterns of growth and trade are inefficient for the world economy, and lead to tragic mal-distribution of the Earth's riches... ."*

Chichilnisky (1996)

What technology provides us does not exist merely to help individuals accumulate more ownership. We need broader thinking, individual wisdom and a knowledge-driven strategy alongside information technology to lead us to the path of sustainable economic growth: we must pay what is due — the cost of resources, land and the lost opportunities of impoverished people.

To a large extent, we are all driven by the need for ownership (rich or poor). But we also need to assume the owner's responsibility and pay our dues for the right to own properties. In particular, large business entities need to extend the responsibility that comes with ownership beyond earning a return for the investors to adequately compensate the contribution of the people, and the cost in resources, and to the environment as a whole.

3.11 The Hierarchy of Ownership Needs

The needs for ownership differ from individual to individual. Figure 3.1 shows the hierarchy of ownership needs, corresponding to Maslow's high and low needs theory, and reflecting the reality of life. We do not include what we would call "forbidden" needs, which involves indisputably destructive activities, such as murder, or wars of conquest, which are both illegal and immoral.

(1) Need for survival

Poverty is the price we pay for civilization as poverty does not exist in "primitive" and aboriginal societies untouched by modern civilization. At

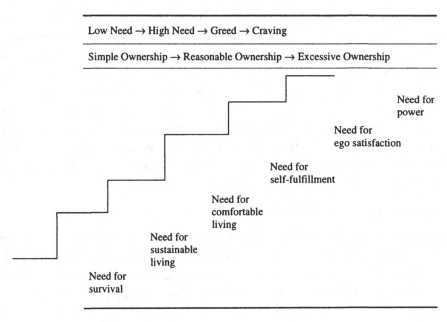

Figure 3.1 The hierarchy of ownership need.

this level, the community lives or dies as a unit. However, in our market economy-based civilization, even the most liveable cities in the world such as Vancouver, Canada, have many people living in poverty. Oxford, England, is known as the "City of Dreaming Spires," home of the university that produces prime ministers and presidents, poets and physicists, and yet one cannot walk ten meters down the central Cornmarket St. without encountering a homeless person. The San Francisco Bay region, home of Silicon Valley and the world's highest concentration of millionaires is considered one of the most desirable and affluent regions on the planet to live in, yet San Francisco's downtown streets are lined with sick and homeless masses. Poverty will always be a fact of life as long as we are at the mercy of a market economy. This is supported by Milton Friedman's monetarism, finance and financial theory, including his non-interventionist private ownership accumulation theory. Thus, our world will always have some people who are on the edge of survival, and who seek ownership to satisfy their basic desire to live.

(2) **Need for sustainable living**

Individuals who need to sustain their living are those on or below the poverty line. Individuals in this category are unlike the homeless, because their essentials are taken care of. They would normally have a place to live, even though it may be subsidized by the government. They are normally wage earners, but their earnings may be at or below minimum wage rates. They include self-employed entrepreneurs with minimal and uncertain revenue, with the amount they receive barely sufficient to meet daily expenditures, and little or no savings for the future. They may also be long term unemployed individuals. Their need for ownership is based on the hope that there will be better days.

(3) **Need for comfortable living**

Need for a comfortable living is perhaps the most common ownership need in an affluent society. They may be wage earners, or possibly self-employed People in this category are usually educated to at least a high school level with the potential to up-grade themselves. Their ownership needs for such things as food, a home, comfortable, perhaps even fashionable clothing and motorized transport are probably already met, and they likely have some security for their retirement needs. These are middle income earners often supporting families, who continue to seek a broader ownership of material goods and services. Their earnings may be supplemented by participation in the investment market to strengthen their financial position and afford themselves a broader ownership base.

(4) Need ownership for self-fulfillment

Individuals who have established themselves at a level of secure comfort, begin to seek ownership at another level. Higher education, artistic expression, learning to play a musical instrument; these are often the result of a need to acquire self-fulfillment.

(5) Ownership for ego satisfaction

Some ownership for ego satisfaction can be acquired through the market system, including status symbols such as works of art, luxury cars, private jets, mansions, real estate and resort estates. More often than not, however, it is not obtainable in the marketplace. It is this type of ownership for ego satisfaction that is difficult to define, and in what is seen and judged by others, it can often be confused with ownership for self-fulfillment. Ego satisfaction can involve many of the same things as self-fulfillment, such as participation in sport, learning music, art, or community involvement, however the motivation is different. Here, approval of the community is required, or perhaps some yardstick by which to compare oneself to others. It can be part of an "exchange economy," involving such things as titles, or public monuments, including streets, buildings or perhaps a university or institution named after oneself.

This type of ownership normally cannot be purchased at a fixed price. On the other hand, $5 million would definitely earn you a university building in your name, and perhaps an honorary doctorate to boot. In a market economy, everything is for sale.

(6) Ownership for power

Ownership for power is typified by Lee Ka-Shing in the Orient, and the Kennedy family in the U.S.A. These individuals are satisfied by nothing less than the ownership of everything there is. To be fair, these people may be in many ways both entrepreneurs and capitalists. They often have an enormous contribution to society, but may also take more than they receive, and quite often, their contributions are not necessarily their original intent but are by-products of selfish desires.

(7) Ownership through legalized theft

Underpinning all these needs is the idea that the actions taken to accomplish them are basically legal, or perhaps outside legality. However, it is often the case that acquisition of ownership is legal, but immoral. Mining companies who think of merely accumulating personal property damage the environment and pollute the air and water, but they continue to do so, because *their operations are legal.* In 1995, the Bre-X corporation, a Canadian mining company, fraudulently engaged in gold prospecting in Indonesia to maximize profit for their operation. Even though there was no gold to be found, they used one of the most damaging but least costly methods, strip mining, for gold exploration. Virtually everybody knows about how the company's owners and many of its wealthy speculators "earned" undisclosed huge profits from countless innocent investors. However, the real tragedy lay in the environmental destruction in the wake of their "conquest," which included deformation of the earth, destruction of wildlife, complete depletion of the usefulness of the land, and impoverishment of a large number of people dependent on the natural environment for their livelihood.

Similarly, in order to avoid offending their home countries' regulations other companies move their operations to developing countries to take advantage of cheap labor and relatively liberal environmental and occupational regulations. This is one of the reasons people protested against the WTO conference held in Seattle in 1999.

3.12 Ownership Seen as Self-Employment

Traditionally, entrepreneurship has been seen as business self-ownership or self-employment. This issue was explored in Chapter 2. The topic of owning one's own successful business is still as popular as ever — it is, euphemistically and traditionally the "American dream." The dream of business ownership is deeply embedded in American culture. From what we are told in various forums and conferences, researchers have suggested that more than 90% of young Americans wish to have their own business. We are also told that this spirit that pursues opportunities had its beginnings with the first pioneers. A pioneer was an individual who battled the forests, native peoples and other environmental hardships to build a home in the wilderness. As time passed, the spirit of this creative and innovative individual was seen to pass on to the small merchant or independent trades person. Since then, entrepreneurship has become the foundation of the business success story in the U.S. This appears to be the reason why entrepreneurship and entrepreneurs have been so closely associated with owning one's own business, being self-employed and/or managing or owning a small business.

Fostering entrepreneurial drive and in particular, the drive to create a business, is the idea that everyone has the right and deserves the opportunity to try to do so. On the frontier, pioneers could build a "homestead" and through agriculture, create something from the land. Today, so few of us have a similar opportunity. Instead, that creative drive is expressed through "entrepreneurship." It is this drive that is viewed as the engine of economic growth and source of employment. This can take many forms. For example, it includes retail shop owners, independent professionals such as general medical practitioners, plumbers or lawyers, computer software and hardware troubleshooters, or building contractors. It is universal, found in people living in all parts of the world. Prior to the monetary crisis of 1997, small business startup was the way of life for the booming economies of East Asia. In China, budding entrepreneurs are driven to gain their economic freedom through business ownership. Technicians, carpenters, painters and individuals in other trades, take their distinct "business assets" — a brush and a can of paint, a handsaw, a set of screwdrivers, cable wires or sharpening stone to the streets. They carry posters, sing and chatter with the public to solicit business that will give them an opportunity to gain the economic freedom they seek. The need for ownership drives entrepreneurship everywhere, not just in the Western world. Nor is need-driven entrepreneurship exclusive to single individuals and small businesses. The entrepreneurial approach is prevalent even in the marketing and organization of large corporations such as Wal-Mart, Starbucks, Home Depot and Federal Express.

To foster entrepreneurship and stimulate individuals to start a business is a challenge that relies both on the personal need for ownership and a favorable environment for the individuals who are willing to take the risk. The environmental factors include:

- Supportive surroundings
- Ease of business creation
- Availability of risk capital
- Continuing financial support
- Low taxation
- Light regulatory burden
- Flexible labor market
- Patent protection
- Availability of relevant technology
- Wide range of public programs

All of the above will be dealt with in a later chapter. The most important motivational factor, however, is that business ownership is the way to economic freedom.

3.13 Ownership Profile

All ownership is temporary. This may be compared with the nature of cost. Given a long enough time, any cost is variable while given a short enough time, the same is fixed. Similarly, given long enough time, ownership is temporary while in a short enough time, ownership is fixed. Ownership can take many forms — let us explore the various profiles of ownership.

(1) Full ownership

Traditionally, in the case of a business, full ownership of a corporation belongs to the corporate shareholders, and the management acts as the agent for the shareholders with all others working in the corporation as employees. This situation no longer holds true. This was clearly reflected in a labor union and management negotiation situation, when the GM management decided to sub-contract jobs to Mexico. The Canadian Automotive Workers (CAW) union boss flatly told the management: "The jobs are ours, you can't take them away from us." The message was clear: the shareholders may own the company, but we own our jobs.

Full ownership means that the exercise of the owners' rights is limited only by the law, as long as the public interest is not jeopardized. For example, many people own their own homes. Usually the owners can renovate or alter their homes as they wish, however endangerment of the public (such as building an unsafe structure) or infringing on your neighbors' rights (for example, blocking their view with another storey on your house) may result in legal action. Any questionable actions may require municipal government approval. Similarly, a sole proprietor of a registered business establishment, and an individual who has 100% shareholding of a limited liability corporation, would have the proprietary right to make decisions and act on these decisions, as long as they are within the legal limits.

Contrary to popular belief, the board of directors and CEO of a corporation have no right to make proprietary decisions for the corporation. They do so only after empowerment by shareholders at the shareholders' meeting. However, almost without exception, directors of the board are normally able to obtain a simple majority support at the shareholders meeting as a form of empowerment to act on their behalf. Furthermore, the directors of the board and the CEO normally assume that they are empowered to operate the corporation in a manner that solely maximizes (or at least optimizes) their return on their investment. The penalty for failure to do so is the withdrawal of the shareholders' investments. Under the shield of needing an adequate earning or to maximize the ROI umbrella, the corporate management is often able to get away with murder.

(2) **Shared ownership**

No one owns the planet Earth, but in a broad sense, the six billion plus human beings are custodians of it, as we are not accountable in this life to anyone else. However, all other living beings are also owners of the Earth. This is shared ownership.

Shared ownership is central to our daily life. We share the roads we drive on. We share the air we breathe. We share our homes with our families. Let's look at the ownership of the road. We drive in self-interest, to get to where we are going, yet we also respect others' shared ownership right — the common good. Each of us has the ability to recklessly endanger the lives of others, yet we do not. It is not merely fear of retribution which stops us from endangering others, but respect for the "common good."

(3) Honorary ownership

The conferral of honorary degrees, titles or medals are all forms of honorary ownership. Often they are a reflection of a more substantial ownership, either historically, such as a knighthood, which was used to confer both responsibility and privileges, but now is just honorary (recently, a Canadian gave up his Canadian citizenship to be knighted by the Queen of England) or concurrently (such as an honorary doctorate). However, these forms of ownership can also confer effective proprietary rights. Anyone whose restaurant reservation has been usurped by someone on the VIP list can attest to that! Honorary ownership is commonly granted to recognize an individual who has made valuable contributions to society in some field of endeavour. However, a substantial monetary contribution to a university, for example, can also result in an honorary degree, or a building, room, or even a chair named in one's honor.

(4) Symbolic ownership

A common example of symbolic ownership can be found in corporations to recognize the founder of the corporation. For example, after retirement the founder, might receive recognition as Honorary Chairman of the Board. Similarly, in universities, respected academicians are sometimes granted the title of Professor Emeritus upon retirement. These are common symbolic ownership expressions. In traditional Inuit society, older hunters were given the ownership recognition when the hunter reached an age of "retirement." The retired hunter claimed his share of the catch simply by placing his hands on the spoils of the hunt.

(5) Ownership for the dead

In as much as we are aware that no human can take anything into the grave, attempts still are made to award ownership to the dead. For example, posthumous medals are awarded for bravery in battle. In China, villagers still practice the burning of paper, clothes, houses, cars and other personal possessions with the hope that the dead can "own" these possessions while in the "other world." Also in China, tourists still have the opportunity to go to Xi An to review the "grand parade" of the Emperor's stone honor guard buried with him when he died.

(6) Inherited ownership

Inherited ownership is a contrary thing in two very different ways. First, this type of ownership does not exist within the market exchange system, but as a transfer of ownership from people of the past to people of the present. The kings and queens of today have all inherited their ownership. Inherited ownership is an expression of the human determination to act against nature. It is nature's intent for us humans to leave everything behind:

Naked I came from my mother's womb, and naked I shall depart.

(Old Testament, Book of Job 1:21)

On the other hand, it is human nature to wish to exercise our proprietary rights, even after death, and so we choose to decree who will own our possessions, even if we cannot enforce it.

(6) Part ownership

Part ownership is similar to shared ownership, except the relationship is more exactly defined, first in terms of the number and identity of the owners, and also in terms of the nature of the sharing. In many Western countries, married couples have part ownership over everything each one of them owns. Business partners are part owners of the business, as are shareholders of limited liability corporations. In the case of a business, part owners' rights to make business decisions are limited by the partnership agreement. In a limited liability corporation, the right of part-owners is limited to the sharing of profit, not to take part in making business decisions. In the case of a limited partnership, limited partners have legal rights, but not decision-making rights for the partnership.

(7) Empowered ownership

Empowerment ownership involves delegation of discretionary decision-making to lower management by upper management, for example.

(8) **Entrepreneurial ownership**

Entrepreneurial ownership need not be formalized. It is based on the fundamental tenet that every individual is a shared owner of planet earth. Under entrepreneurial ownership, individuals assume the responsibility of an owner. Proprietary decisions are made with passion and love as if the whole planet were their own creations. The objective is to create wealth and add value in the interest of the individual and society.

3.14 Ownership Must be Earned, Minimizing Cost to Others and to the Future

Ownership stimulates individuals to create and innovate. The individual's desire and need for ownership is good for the individual and the society. For the poor, ownership represents economic freedom. For the rich, ownership may mean waste. For the bad, ownership might end up in criminal activities. If, through personal effort, ownership is acquired by an individual, there will be passionate love and respect for that ownership. On the other hand, ownership acquired by force or deceit will only result in waste and destruction or neglect.

King Solomon's story is one that gives us the greatest wisdom: two women fought for the ownership of a baby, each pleading for just judgment. It was only the true mother who brought the child into the world who loved enough to put the baby's welfare before her own desires.

Ownership is the root of everything in our society, whether it is in the East, South, North or West. It will not be difficult for anyone to observe that flags, names, markers and signs are symbols of ownership. We all have the right, and indeed the responsibility to be entrepreneurial owners of the world, and we must assume the responsibility to exercise this right while respecting the rights of all other owners. Those who seek entrepreneurship as a way to gain economic freedom, need to appreciate the economic freedom of others.

Ownership will always be a fundamental driving force to human behavior. In the first incident in Sec. 3.3, defending "ownership" cost a person his life. In the second incident, ownership rights were fought over, even at the level of subsistence. Finally, the last incident shows us that sometimes

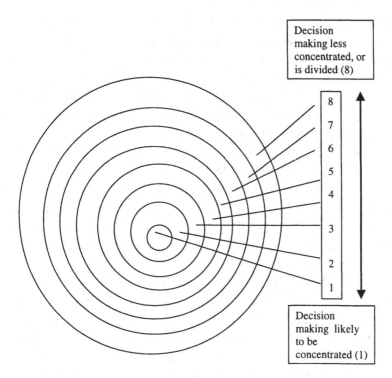

Decision making less concentrated, or is divided (8)

8
7
6
5
4
3
2
1

Decision making likely to be concentrated (1)

Figure 3.2 Relationships amongst different levels of decision-making. All systems with less centralized decision-making contain more centralized cores.

ownership can result in owning nothing of value at all. The desire for ownership has led to the killing of other human beings as well as ruthlessly exploiting the environment, people and life support that belongs to the future.

Questions of discussion

1. Ownership may be the right word to reflect how proprietary interest is preserved and exercised in the interest of the owner. But in fact we do not own anything on this earth. All of us are stewards and all of us have a stewardship responsibility for the planet and the future of humanity. Does this mean we should remove the word "ownership" from all

dictionaries? If not, how is it possible to ask people to take a stewardship responsibility, so we may have a better world to live in, and serve our purpose as humans in the interest of humanity?

2. Explain how some business operations could be conducting legalized theft. Why does a government condone theft, and in particular practices not in the interests of the public, helping some people make a profit, and creating poverty at the same time?

3. Explore justifications to claim ownership in space. For example, ownership over the planet Mars. If we discover that it is suitable for human inhabitation, and we are confronted with other living creatures, what must we do? Do we tell them we come in peace, and help them to be civilized just as we are? Or do we simply shoot them in the name of self-defense? With our past success in civilizing the natives, perhaps it amounts to the same thing.

4. Maslow's Theory of Needs is well known, well cited and has been applied to virtually all studies of human behavior since 1943. However, nowadays we are much more sophisticated than in his time, and it seems to be more fashionable to emphasize "profit" more than needs. Everyone must make a profit including those homeless people who have only their own skin wrapped around their bones. Instead of need driven, perhaps we should say we are all "ownership driven" and "profit driven." Discuss.

5. Where do passion and love stand, in the name of ownership? Discuss.

6. Ownership of the dead is implicit in traditions found worldwide. Is this a practice for the living or for the dead, and what is the meaning of it? Discuss.

Chapter 4

Common Good and the Making of Profit

> *Factors contributing to the common good are "the over-all conditions of life in society that allow the different groups and their members to achieve their own perfection more fully and more easily."*
>
> Second Vatican Council

4.1 Introduction

Why the common good? Or, put another way, why morality? C. S. Lewis says that morality must be from God because it goes against our every instinct.[1] This is also a question which modern science has tried to answer. Is there a scientific reason behind cooperation and selflessness? E. O. Wilson and other sociobiologists would say that there is.[2] Selfless human behavior occurs merely because cooperating beings have a higher reproductive fitness than they would if they were non-cooperative. In other words, selflessness is the expression of selfishness. In "The Selfish Gene," Richard Dawkins goes even further, saying that human behavior stems from the survival instincts of the individual gene. Everything about life, he says, is about the "quest" for survival of this tiny unit of biological information.

Whether you believe it comes from God, or nature, or both, there is no question that "the common good" is a phrase beloved by the politicians, and one that is used by everyone from the Nazis to the Communists, and everyone in between them in the political spectrum. But what does it really mean?

---

[1]C. S. Lewis, *Mere Christianity* (Fount Paperbacks, 1997; first published 1952), pp. 18–22.
[2]E. O. Wilson, *Sociobiology: The New Synthesis* (1975).

As used in this book, *"the common good"* refers to the improvement of the public interest that results when an individual or business undertakes any economic activity. However, in the exchange system, making profit does not necessarily contribute to the common good. If Adam Smith's doctrine of making profit is rigidly observed, it could be the result of a single transaction or a group of transactions over time. *Residual,* on the other hand, reflects entrepreneurial profit. Based on the definitions of entrepreneurship and accounting practice, it is what is left of earnings after returns have been made to all contributors to those earnings. *Added value* is similar to the common good, except that it is more strictly defined in terms of economic activity and thus is more easily recognized and identified, even if it is not always measurable.

4.2 Adam Smith's View on Self-Interest and the Common Good

There is no simple way to determine whether any human activity, business or otherwise, works toward the common good. It is unlikely that the average person would view unbridled self-interest, where the individual's need to succeed far outweighs the desire to give to society, to ever be for the common good. But what if there are beneficial byproducts of the process of doing business — can this be for the common good? In micro profit theory, there is no clear reference to concern for the common good, only maximizing profit for self-interest. Adam Smith and other classic economists begin with the assumption that people pursue their own self-interest. But Smith also advocates that in acting in his own self-interest, he must realize that need to appeal to the self-interest of others.

> *It is in vain for him to expect (help) from their benevolence; only he will be more likely to prevail if he can interest their self-love in his favor, and show them it is for their own advantage to do for him what he requires of them. Whoever offers to another a bargain of any kind, propose to do this.* **Give me that which I want and you shall have this which you want.** *It is not from the benevolence of the butcher, the*

brewer, or the baker, that we expect our dinner, but from their
regard to their own interest that we address ourselves, not to
their humanity but to their self-love.

Adam Smith (1976), *An Inquiry into the*
Nature and Causes of the Wealth of Nations (p. 8)

The result, according to Smith, is the division of labor from which personal and national wealth arises. Similarly, self-interest leads an entrepreneur to maximize the "product of industry," which Smith describes as "What (industry) adds to the subject or materials upon which it is employed. In proportion as the value of this produce is great or small," he says, "so will likewise be the profits of the employer (*ibid.* p. 477). The larger the profits, the greater the benefit he confers on society.

4.3 Common Good, Good for Some and Good for One

If Smith is right about the division of labor, then if each individual acts for the good of the one in the market economy, the completion of a transaction will also be good for others. On the other hand, selling drugs certainly satisfies the customer's self-interest, in the sense that it meets their demands. But very few would argue that this is for the common good, or even the long term good of the one. The answer of course, is that the harm that drugs do to the users cannot be casually dismissed. Thus the death penalty in some countries such as Singapore or Thailand for drug trafficking. On the other hand, "soft drugs" such as marijuana have been legalized in some countries, and may soon be in many others such as Canada.

On Friday, 28 April 2000, a Canadian citizen named Nguyen Thi Hiep was executed by firing squad in Hanoi, Vietnam, following a conviction for drug trafficking. This occurred despite numerous pleas by the Canadian government on her behalf. In response to her execution, the Canadian ambassador was withdrawn, all Canadian aid to Vietnam suspended, and Canada withdrew her support for Vietnam's application for a membership to the World Trade Organization. The Vietnamese government can claim that drug trafficking is immoral and evil, and examples must be made. Canada can claim that to kill anyone for any crime is also immoral and evil. The net result is that one person is dead and much needed aid to an under-developed country does not reach its destination. Both sides can claim to be acting for the common good. Yet what is for the common good, and what is not?

To further our understanding of the relationship between making a profit for self-interest and the common good, four situations are illustrated:

(1) A case of all for the common good.

(2) A marginal situation in respect to self-interest and common good.

(3) A case involving a decision apparently for the common good, but which is in reality, destructive.

(4) A case of virtually complete self-interest which has nothing to do with the common good.

(1) All for the common good

The following case (summarized in Table 4.1) was provided by Victoria Walzak of McMaster University, where she expresses her views on the senior author's definition of Entrepreneurship, Entrepreneurial and Entrepreneur as related to added value and for the matter of common good:

> ...With a new train of thought, I tried to figure out the definition. Entrepreneurship is the process of doing something new, something different for the purpose of creating wealth for the individual and adding value to society. Ahhh — the word wealth almost threw me off again! I will not succumb. To begin, what is wealth? It is personal gain, abundance, knowledge and success in anything that brings satisfaction and personal fulfillment. For some individuals this is indeed monetary. However, this does not necessarily have to be so. In coordination with the definition of entrepreneur, who is a person who undertakes a wealth-creating and value-adding process, through incubating ideas, assembling resources and making things happen.
>
> In reflecting on entrepreneurship in terms of the common good and self-interest, I realized that I know of an individual who optimizes these definitions perfectly, and yet, monetary profit never even enters the equation. Consider this true story of a mother who tragically lost her daughter to a senseless random killing. Through her anguish,

confusion and hurt (the list of emotions are endless), she realized that she could channel her energy into something positive. The mother decided to work to prevent future senseless murders. With the help of caring and supportive friends, she started a non-profit organization with three main areas of focus: crime prevention, a voice for victim's rights and legislative amendments. For nine years, in the capacity of president, she has dedicated her life to the organization, which has become a national voice in Canada. Through her hard work, and the work of others, victims come to have a voice in the judicial system. Legislation is examined and awareness is created.

Is this women an entrepreneur? Has she engaged in the practice of entrepreneurship? You bet! She never received payment for her work and the organization has never made a profit. But the mother worked for the common good of society to prevent terrible and senseless acts from plaguing other families. She was motivated by her self-interest to correct the mistakes in the system that may have contributed to her own daughter's demise.

In examining this case, I have come to understand the meaning of Prof. Kao's ideas. This woman definitely brought about change, added value to society, assembled resources and made things happen. Not everyone clearly understands how an entrepreneur can engage in the process of entrepreneurship without making a monetary profit.

(2) **A marginal situation in respect to self-interest and some applicable common good**

The local supermarket is owned and operated by a multinational corporation. It had served the community's needs for nearly four decades. Prior to expansion, approximately 120 people were employed under its roof, virtually all of them local residents. In the previous 20 years, the store had undergone a series of minor renovations. Displays were changed, old fixtures replaced, and refrigeration units modernized. In response to a community growing in both size and prosperity, the parking lot was expanded and the store front refurbished twice to make it more attractive to the target market.

The typical customer came from a middle class community, was working and was likely part of a two-income household. The only competition was a second supermarket a few miles away. Store performance was good, with earnings of approximately 20% to 25% after taxes the typical return on

Table 4.1 Driven by self-interest, an entrepreneurial initiative as reflected for the common good.

For the common good	Not for the common good
Driven by self-interest, an entrepreneurial initiative creates an organization solely for the common good. There is no financial incentive, and the organization makes no profit.	–0–

head office's capital investment. This was better than other stores in nearby locations, and in the minds of top management, this particular store had earned itself a place in the corporate plans for expansion and added investment.

An expansion plan (capital budget) was approved by the board, and a complete redevelopment with an all-new store appeared to be inevitable. In coping with the overall expansion strategy, corporate management was given the green light to proceed with the development of a greater store that would blend both shopping and entertaining at the one location. Plans were for the store to employ approximately 200 people on the premises, with extended opening hours, Monday to Saturday from 8:30 to 21:00 and 9:00 to 18:00 on Sundays.

Prior to closing for the expansion, store management decided they wanted to create a strong positive impression on the local community, in anticipation of drawing customers away from the competitor's store. Various special events were held, and a strong emphasis was placed on customer service. Employees were encouraged to be more friendly to interact with people and serve customers courteously, above and beyond the usual standards. It worked. The store was an absolute success by any standard and the plans for the new store were "Ready, set and go!" But there was a problem. With the building and expansion project, there would be no employment in the store for at least a year. Though management staff were transferred to other stores in the area, no plans were made for the employees. A few of them sensed the upcoming changes and sought jobs elsewhere but the rest were laid off with no promise of further employment.

Three years later, a brand new "superstore" was launched with a big celebration. It was a major community event; there were decorations, balloons and banners of every description. Dance troupes were hired to perform in the car park, and a live band played in front of the store entrance. Inside, the fashionable café became an instant meeting place for young and old. But despite the celebrations, there was one sad note that was only noted by a few old customers. Not even a single old employee was re-hired to work in the store. The unofficial hiring policy was to recruit young and inexperienced job seekers, who would require only the minimum wage and would have no seniority.

The new store was perhaps the largest in the city, and a point of pride for local residents. It certainly added something to the community beyond just serving shoppers. But how does the company's hiring policy fit in with working for "the common good?" This example is summarized in Table 4.2.

It is clear the expansion has "added value" to the community and is for the common good. However, the laid off individuals, despite some early

Table 4.2 Driven by profit, the common good for some, but not for others: a marginal case.

For the common good	Not for the common good
1. Employing younger workers. 2. Increasing traffic flow, keeping business in the community. 3. Added value to local economy. 4. Better and more food selection. 5. Increasing local property value. 6. More pleasant environment. 7. Added shopping convenience due to additional stores on premise, such as telephone shop, dry cleaning, flower shop, a trendy café with live music, in store bakery etc. 8. Possible improved overall performance, adding value to the supermarket industry.	1. Approximately 200 people laid off indefinitely, creating a small army of unemployed, some of whom would experience hardship in managing day to day living. 2. Laid off individuals claim unemployment benefits from the government.

sympathy, went almost unnoticed in the general excitement. Some of them did find other jobs elsewhere, and between unemployment insurance benefits and the social welfare program, none of the rest ended up on the street. But almost all of them suffered some financial and personal hardship, and of the 200 new employees, not one was from those who worked in the old store. Many excuses could be made, but in truth the decision not to re-hire the old store employees was solely a matter of protecting financial profit. In traditional management strategy under the market economy, humans are disposable.

(3) **A massive fishing enterprise — it may appear to be for the common good, but could be a disaster to both individuals and the entire community**[3]

This is a story of a small town whose existence depends on one of the world's great fisheries: the Grand Banks of the North Atlantic, lying off the coast of Newfoundland. The Grand Banks fishery was once the source of giant cod longer than a man is tall. It may have been the cod that first brought Europeans to North America. Certainly John Cabot when he "discovered" North America, came upon vast Basque fishing fleets off the coast of Newfoundland. This was long before most Europeans had even heard of America. Yet before long, numerous immigrants came not just to fish, but to stay, and a way of life was transported to the western shores of the Atlantic.

In the small town, before the factory fleets came into operation, local fishermen in small fishing boats with simple equipment made a living from their daily catch. The town was peaceful, and even though there were no skyscrapers or luxury tourist hotels, the people led a simple, hard, but satisfying life. From the catch, some fish were sold both in the local markets, as well as exported, earning the fishermen more than enough to give their families a decent living.

In the 20th century, a number of innovations at first slowly, and then more quickly began to change the fishing industry. First bigger, faster, deep

---

[3]Adapted in part from M. Kurlanksy, *Cod: A Biography of the Fish that Changed the World* (Jonathan Cape, London, 1998), paperback edition.

sea ships with more sophisticated catching techniques, and then giant factory ships, employing modern technology and capable of handling every aspect of the fishing industry changed the North Atlantic fishery from a lifestyle to a massive commercial operation.

While the locals resisted, outsiders were quick to exploit the opportunities that the new technology offered. A big city businessman came and set up a company, recruiting a sizable proportion of the local populace to work in his new fishing fleet. With the increased cashflow the fleet brought in, it certainly seemed that there would be better days for at least some people in town. To them, life seemed to have a new beginning, with regular pay cheques, and no uncertainties. Meanwhile, the rest of the townspeople tried to continue on with their traditional lifestyles, hoping that the good times for some would eventually lead to a general upsurge in the town's fortunes.

As CEO of one of the largest fishing fleets on the Eastern Seaboard, our big city businessman was doing ok. Or at least he thought so. Soon he found himself on a treadmill that would not stop turning. His partners had a taste of the big time, and were not about to let it go. They were satisfied with nothing less than a maximized return on their investment. The problem was that the mighty factory ships soon found that the big catches are not so big anymore. The cod, once regularly over four feet long, were getting smaller. The solution? Buy bigger ships, with bigger nets and better equipment. The catches increased for a time, but got smaller again, and worryingly, the size of the fish continue to get smaller as well. More ships. More technology. Bigger catches, and then smaller again.

Let's see how this was viewed from our successful CEO's perspective: his first goals were for himself: top level remuneration, big annual dividends and a handsome pension upon leaving the company. On top of that, he and the rest of his "gang" had an aim to double their investment money within three years. They fished, fished and fished some more, using the most modern fishing technology to get record catches. Their drag nets scraped every last living species off the bottom of the ocean floor, so as not to miss even the least part of their target catch. Soon they achieved their goal of taking the biggest catch in the history of the region (maybe even a world record). Then they sold its harvest to the mainland and to friends "south of the border," making the company huge profits approaching the limits of even their selfish imagination.

The local and national media soon publicized this "fish plus money" story. It was so impressive that our CEO won the local chamber of commerce's "CEO of the year" award, for his role in making the biggest profit in fishing industry history. A year later, the "CEO of the last year" received incontrovertible evidence of declining fish stocks in the region. Quickly cutting his losses, he pulled the company out of the region, and sent local employees back to the town. Many of them went back to the traditional fishing they knew best, but sadly, the fishing factories had virtually destroyed the fishery, leaving them far worse off than they were before modernization. The town ground to a virtual economic halt. Soon most of the old fishermen were relying on government unemployment insurance benefits and welfare. Sadly, many of them were unable or

Table 4.3 Driven by profit, the fish story, all for private interest, nothing for the common good.

For the common good	Not for the common good
1. Private initiative, providing prosperity for a few, stimulating local economic growth, reducing unemployment, and providing added taxes for the local government. All temporary.	1. Massive depletion of fish stock beyond immediate recovery levels. 2. No consideration of other elements of the local ecosystem that may depend on the cod. 3. Long term loss of livelihood for the local fisherman. 4. Loss of morale and sense of community in the local town. 5. No added value to society. 6. Burden of unemployment and welfare benefits paid to out-of-work fishermen and their families. 7. Disillusionment of the young, pushed away from traditional homes and forced to migrate to other cities, with unknown consequences for all.

unwilling to retrain — fishing was the only way they knew. In any case, the town itself had few resources and little industry or commerce to soften the blow that had been dealt to the fishing trade.

Compared to the other cases discussed above, the common good is seriously compromised here. It is really a case of pure private interest. It is legalized highway robbery thinly veiled as modernization and development. Will the fishery ever recover? Did this company ever make the effort to find out? Will the fishermen themselves ever recover? The CEO may be yesterday's man, but the blow of his failure is softened by his money, his happy investors and his award. Sadly, the town and the fish have nothing. Amen.

While this initiative of high-tech fishing would traditionally be viewed as entrepreneurial, it added no value to society (except of course, in making fish more available for consumers), but is a simple profit driven undertaking with no concern for the common good. Our CEO of the year may be a smart profiteer, but he is not an entrepreneur. He may have acted in accordance with the law, but he did nothing for his community.

(4) **Bre-X Minerals Ltd. — The gold diggers: a story of criminal fraud, acting only for profit, with nothing for the common good**

The following is based on a lead story from *Fortune Magazine*:[4]

> It has been labeled the worse mining fraud in history. The Bre-X gold scandal has bilked many investors of their retirement savings and has witnessed several billion dollars of market value disappear. Bre-X Minerals Ltd. is a Calgary-based mining company that claimed to discover a huge gold deposit in Busang, Indonesia. Estimates of the size of the deposit ranged from 71–400 million ounces. As one might expect, the value of the firm's common stock soared when the news of this stupendous find broke. The market value would at one point exceed $4 billion, on a growth rate of 100,000% during the last three years. The company, which was started by David Walsh, a former stockbroker, grew from a basement office to the 30th largest firm in Canada and a spot on the Toronto Stock Exchange (TSE) 300 index (*The Wall Street Journal*, 16 May 1997, pp. C1 and C17)

---

[3]Adapted from *Fortune Magazine*, 9 June 1997, pp. 116–126.

But the bubble was soon to burst. Investigators attempting to duplicate Bre-X's find could not. They were accused of "salting" the core samples with flakes of gold before they were tested. News of the hoax came when Freeport-McMoRan conducted an independent drilling next to Bre-X highest grade holes and found only insignificant amount of gold. The results were then submitted to the Securities and Exchange Commission. The common stock plummeted over 90% on the news. Bre-X has since filed for bankruptcy in Alberta.

It was later learned that Bre-X had never found gold in Busang. It was a pure fraud. The turbulent life of David Walsh came to a peaceful end in a Bahamas hospital, four days after he was stricken by a brain aneurysm. He was 52. However, the media claimed the cause of his death unknown.

As is often the case, greed for maximized profit was at the core of the Bre-X story. The Bre-X corporation was only interested in the maximization of monetary gain. And for a time, it appeared that they had succeeded. In three years, Bre-X stock gained over 100,000%. Then the scandal hit, and that same stock plummeted to oblivion. Many lost, but a few gained. Walsh, his wife and vice-chairman, John Felderhof, between them netted about $50 million before the scandal hit.

Was there anything for the common good in the case of Bre-X mining? The company defrauded investors, small and large. Other companies, acting on the Bre-X "find," sunk useless energy and resources into searching for gold, damaging the environment, wasting vast sums of money, and who knows with what consequences for Indonesia?

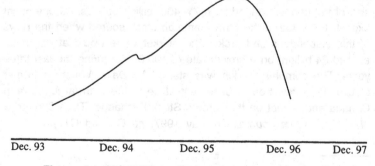

| Dec. 93 | Dec. 94 | Dec. 95 | Dec. 96 | Dec. 97 |

Figure 4.1 Bre-X Minerals Ltd. Stock Performance.

Table 4.4 The Bre-X gold diggers strip mining for gold, with no conception of the common good.

For the common good	Not for the common good
1. Nothing	1. Everything

The Bre-X gold diggers made their fortune by cheating others, and at the cost of small investors, the environment and the people of Indonesia.

Indonesia is a developing country, populated by a culturally advanced people. Its ecosystems are unique in the world. Yet, the profit driven gold diggers had no concern for any of the possible damages to people and nature. The senior author once asked one of the gold diggers who had been involved in the scheme about the fortune he had made for himself, and about how he felt about the harm done to Indonesia? All he said was: "Too bad, but this is business. Anyway, the environmental damage did not happen in Canada."

Bre-X is not the only culprit. For example, one of the biggest beneficiaries of mining in Indonesia has been Canada's Inco Corporation. Inco developed an open-pit nickel mine in Soroako, Sulawesi in 1963. According to Minewatch, the main reason Inco shifted production from Canada to the Third World was because of the Ontario government's scrutiny of its pollution, and increasing criticism of its long history of appalling treatment of workers (according to the environmental awareness company ETAN Canada, Indonesia's environment is threatened). Indonesia at the time was in the midst of civil unrest, and the Sukarno regime of the time was not known for its democratic principles. Despite this, the Canadian Export Development Corporation (CEDC) gave Inco about CAN$57.25 million to convert a once pristine rainforest into a vast mining operation.

Since then Sukarno was overthrown and replaced by General Suharto. Despite an even worse human rights record than his predecessor, Suharto preserved a pro-Western stance, and assistance to Indonesia was provided by the governments of the United States, Britain, Australia, Norway and Japan. Did the CEDC and others count the true cost of their investment? For decision-makers in Western countries, in the Third World is just as good as "out of sight, out of mind," especially since it is often out of the sight of the voters as well. And so it was with Inco's baggage of environmental pollution and worker exploitation. The company made a "profit," many costs were saved, government legal prosecution was not an issue, and the activists were off their backs.

4.4 Making Profit Does Not Automatically Contribute to Common Good, Nor Fulfill a Business' Social Obligation

In all fairness, most human economic activities would be revealed to be simple matters of giving and taking, if scrutinized with sufficient care. If one takes more than one gives, this would not be in the interest of the public, nor would it add value to society or for the common good. Milton Friedman was right when he claimed that the social responsibility of business is to increase its profits. This is no more than a reiteration of Adam Smith's early claim that "...so will likewise be the profits of the employer. The larger the profits, the greater the benefit he confers on society." This is very much Friedman's vein. All well and good, except neither has mentioned cost. Without taking into account all costs, how is it possible to determine the value of the profits? And is there more to the "common good" than simply giving more than you take? Is the common good more than the sum of the individual "goods?" This is a question which we shall address in a later chapter.

To the die-hard capitalist, our market system is best served by minimal public intervention in the marketplace. A business transaction completed in good faith should be to the common good to both parties (those who supply and those who demand). On the other hand, a successful transaction involving illegal drugs would certainly meet the consumer's needs, and certainly is exactly what the supplier wants. By the capitalist definition it meets the needs of the common good. Or does it? We would hope that the gut reaction of most readers is that it is not. Of course, the harm that the drugs do to the users cannot be casually dismissed. In many countries such as Singapore, a person found guilty of trafficking in drugs could be legally executed. In contrast, there is some ground to consider the legalization for medical use of some hallucenogenic drugs. Canada is one of the countries considering this. Using the legal system as a basis for determining the common good would then seem to be a worry, as how can we base a universal code on such a fragmented and contradictory array of national statutes? Too often, legislation is about money. In 1991, Thailand and South Africa had similar problems with HIV and AIDS. Perhaps fearing the loss of its lucrative sex trade, Thailand instituted a variety of stringent control measures and now HIV prevalence is extremely low. In the Republic of South Africa, with no such incentive, prostitutes are brought in by the big mining companies to "service" their armies of low-paid mine workers who are unable to see their families for most of the year. It is now estimated that perhaps a third of all South Africans are HIV infected and will die of the disease. To put it simply, it is all about making money.

4.5 Where Do We Draw the Line?

The cigarette industry is massively profitable to the companies involved in it. In a manner of speaking, smoking can even be beneficial to society. Smokers typically suffer little or no loss in productivity compared to non-smokers with otherwise similar lifestyles, and when they do get lung cancer, typically die quite quickly and thus society is saved the expense of medical and disability benefits, and in the long term saves on paying out retirement benefits. On the other hand, if we value life above monetary gain, there is nowadays no question that smoking cigarettes cause cancer to both smokers and those around them. Consequently, the industry as a whole adds no value to society because human lives are at stake. On the other hand, the members of the industry tend to be amongst the best corporate citizens, providing many jobs, contributing greatly to charities, and generously support (through advertising) amateur and professional sports and cultural events. How is it possible to say that the cigarette industry contributes no common good, or adds no value to society? Is it possible to draw the line between "good" and "evil" for what the cigarette industry has done to the individual and society?

Consider Toronto's Jazz Festival. On 23 March 2000, on the 8:45 morning news, Radio station CJRT (a Toronto-based radio station) announced that Du Maurier was to be the major sponsor of Toronto's year 2000 Jazz Festival. The decision was prompted by a personal telephone call from Toronto mayor Mel Lastman to Don Brown, the CEO of Du Maurier, securing an undisclosed contribution from the tobacco company which made it possible for Toronto to host the festival. Prior to this, the organizer of the festival had already decided to cancel the event, due to a shortage of funds. Hearing the announcement, it made one feel that something wonderful was happening:

- The Jazz Festival is an important cultural event not just for Toronto, but for North America, and maybe even for jazz lovers all around the world.
- It is a tourist attraction; it brings dollars and provides jobs.
- It looks really good for Lastman, as a personal triumph.
- It is an excellent piece of PR for Du Maurier, showing their support for the community.

On the basis of the above, who has the right to say that Du Maurier's generous contribution to Toronto's Jazz Festival is not for the common good? Unless, of course, you link Du Maurier's good deed with the promotion of a habit which causes a variety of health problems including cancer and death. In a nutshell, Du Maurier's money comes from the death of individuals. This is summarized in Table 4.5.

The above illustration is by no means complete and there are many consequences which cannot be fully understood here. On the other hand, how is it possible to put a price on human life? Here we must question our value system. How can we explain a government that bans smoking in public places, and discourages the sale of cigarettes, but also takes money from one of the major tobacco producers? The money may not filter directly to the government, but nevertheless it is the mayor who put his full support behind it, and made it happen. Is it acceptable to risk human life for the promotion of culture? It is sometimes difficult to draw a clear line between what is for the common good and what is not. On the other hand, is not that true that there is no price in the world worth a human life? Is this how we should draw the line?

Table 4.5 The pros (value added) and cons (damages done to society) of Du Maurier's money for Toronto's Jazz Festival.

Value added to society and possible financial benefit	Damage to human health, cause premature death to people and financial cost for healthcare
Support of a major cultural event Provide local jobs Promote local tourism Increase spending of tourists while in Toronto Improve Toronto's image as a world-class cultural center Additional tax revenue for all levels of government	Waste of resources to produce tobacco products For smokers and secondary inhalers: Increased risk of bronchitis Increased risk of emphysema Increased risk of stroke Increased risk of lung cancer Increased risk of premature and underweight babies Promotional campaigns reduce impact of anti-smoking programmes

4.6 Micro Theory and the Matter of the Common Good

Prior to Marshall, economic theory provided no clear distinction between micro and macro. It seems that in the academic world, little had changed since Adam Smith said: "...The larger the profits, the greater the benefits he confers on society...." The challenge is a matter of bridging self-interest and common good. In a capitalist's ideal world, an individual makes profits and profits are the fruits of the harvest. The individual simultaneously provides a service through innovation and creation, and thus the benefits are shared with the rest of the society. If this all worked out, wouldn't it be a wonderful world? But this is hardly the reality. How can the micro theory link "profits" with the following news story from Ethiopia, saying: "Hassan (a young boy of about six or seven) lies listlessly on a concrete pad with barely enough strength to brush away the flies".[5]

---

[5]Toronto Star, Wed, 26, 2000 A3.

Or what is the benefit of the nuclear warheads stockpiled around the world: Russia with 20,000, the U.S.A. with 10,500, France with 464, China with 410, Israel with 200, the U.K. with 185, and even latecomers like India (60) and Pakistan (30) with substantial stocks. What are these for? To feed starving Africans, save homeless people from dying on the streets or save animals that are on the brink of extinction? Of course not! How many warheads do you need for "strategic defense?" And of course this is all "in the name of freedom" or perhaps better yet, "in the name of God!" More realistically, and less emotionally, the real reasons form a packet of ideologies, which in Western democracies include defense of the market economy, respect for private ownership, rights to own property and free enterprise, although ultimately the whole idea is "profit." This is perhaps how macro and micro are wedded in holy matrimony. It is no wonder that hardcore conservatives cry so loudly, asking government to stay out of the marketplace, and let the market make its own adjustment.

4.7 Concluding Notes

4.7.1 A note on our challenges: the making of profit and to initiate needed change

Yet despite the triumph of the capitalist way with the fall of the Soviet Union, and even mainland China looking for ways to emulate the American way of the market economy, based on private property rights and capital accumulation, we have a real dilemma. On the one hand, we have booming economies and incredibly high living standards, and on the other, countless people who through no fault of their own, are dying from starvation, domestic violence, crime in the streets, the blight of war, or any of dozens of reasons.

There are two major issues that make it difficult to accept the idea that making a profit will automatically contribute to the common good and add value to society. When there is good for some, but damage to others, or even no benefit to the rest of society, there is no clear-cut line deciding what is beneficial and what is not. The "drug trafficking" case is a case in point. And there is an even more fundamental challenge — the way "profits" are determined. The currently accepted idea of profit does not take into account all the costs. These issues must be addressed and problems resolved. Until then, we cannot consider making a profit to automatically contribute to the common good.

We can apply some common sense to the matter, and perhaps this could be credited to us as wisdom. No doubt every jet traveler will have heard the safety talk at the beginning of the flight, where they always say something like: "In the event the cabin is de-pressurized, air masks will automatically drop in front of you. Always put on your own mask first, before helping your children." The idea here is the same as in business. Just as adults must attend to their own needs before helping their children, so business needs to make profit, a "real profit" which will serve self-interest, contribute to the common good, and add value to society. If a business makes no profit, it will be a dead business, and a dead business is good for nothing. There is no intention on the part of the authors to question whether or not business (or anyone) should or should not make profits. The only questions remaining to be addressed are: (1) Do we realize that the profit we currently use as the indicator for economic growth does not reflect economic reality for humanity as a whole? (2) As we make "profit," are we really aware of how profit will affect ourselves and our future generations? (3) What will profit do to the environment and our life support system in the future?

Our challenge is to encourage businesses to make more "profit," but to be aware that profit must be made through creation and innovative activities, and not just by taking from silent partners and people who have devoted themselves at work, but have no stake in the organization. The notion of residual is not something new, but from this concept that already has some 40 years of history as a starting point, we shall address what we mean by creativity, innovation, wealth and value.

Surely, as intelligent humans, we cannot accept the idea that corporate responsibility to the people and the environment is a rare and unnatural occurrence, nor the thought that making profits, achieving return on investment, and shareholders is the only way of our life. Moreover, by knowing our planet has finite resources, to teach and advocate "profit maximization" is at the least a thoughtless aggravation to human intelligence. If our purpose in life is to allow life to continue, then we must initiate changes, and we must not be scared of attempting to make changes, both in our mindset and practice.

4.7.2   A note on financial democracy and people's capitalism

As a recent development prompted by the rapid advancement of information technology (IT), some people with relatively small amounts of available cash have been successfully investing into stocks through "e-trade," consequently created a new breed of rich, and therefore capitalistic advocates, living in what is contradictorily called a "Financial Democracy and People Capitalism."

What is the meaning of "financial democracy and people capitalism?" In the old days, investing in share stocks of corporations through the stock exchange had been the dominion of people in the moneyed upper classes. Investing required more than just small potatoes. There are many factors that would influence people, some of them quite complicated. In the stock market, the risk bearing attribute was always what made brokering a worthy undertaking. Today, it seems anyone can invest in the stock market with little more than a sum of money, and some computer skill and play the stocks as if it were just a matter of tic-tac-toe. A large number of "small, home-based investors" made their fortune this way, and the do-it-yourself investing atmosphere has given everyone the opportunity to be a "capitalist." In addition, there is clear evidence that many pension fund trusts are investing funds into corporate shares and mutual funds. For example, there was recently a successful acquisition by the Ontario Teachers Pension Fund of a controlling interest in the Toronto Eaton Centre, one of the largest shopping malls in Canada.

General easy public access to the stock market has moved the investment culture and corporate finance away from being the domain of the financial elite. This move to the general populace, has not changed the relationship to the "common good" however. The investors' interest in stocks remains solely in making financial gains. Funds invested in corporations such as tobacco manufacturers or mining companies engaged in questionable ethical practice are still considered good investments, and there are only a few ethical investment companies which refuse to deal with them. The real issue is not how the stock market has strengthened its position in the market economy, or how many millions have been distributed to the middle class through easier access for some people gaining financial success, the issue is how we perceive profit and the contribution of making profit to the common good. This is the subject which will be explored throughout our continuing deliberation.

Questions for discussion

1. "From an economic perspective, the problem (the problem of the ecological and economic significance of biodiversity loss in the current market economy in practice) lies in the fact that while the private benefits of biodiversity loss are captured in the market prices, many of the associated costs are not... ." (*Trends in Ecology and Evolution,* Vol. 11, No. 6, June 1996, p. 270) Comment!
2. Making profit automatically "adds value" to society. Do you agree? Why?
3. A corporate executive addresses corporate employees, and begins his deliberation by quoting Adam Smith:

   "Dear Folks, as your CEO, I represent the corporation and offer a few simple words of wisdom, that come from our grand master of Economics, Adam Smith. He said: 'Give me what I want and you shall have this which you want... .'

   Before he could continue, a employee in the audience raised his hand, and asked him: "Mr. Knight, I figure that your salary and benefit package amount to a quarter of a million dollars a month, but I only get paid $7.50 per hour, is that...?"

   Mr. Knight interrupted him, replying: "What's your name, and by the way, what you can do, is to do what you can to become a CEO like me." Comment on the question and answer.

4. For the interest of the common good, one of the most significant, perhaps single most important measures that the stock exchange

commissions worldwide can do is to enforce full disclosure of corporate environmental care commitment and human resources policy. How would such disclosure practices be implemented? More fundamentally, why should the stock exchange commission assume such a responsibility in the interest of the common good?

5. How far should "for the common good" go? Within a community? A country? Worldwide?

6. A businessperson confused about his business philosophy spoke in front of the participants of a conference on social entrepreneurship. He was wondering about what he should be doing for now, and what to do now for the future? He said: "We know that we could help make the world a better place, but we don't know when it might happen. And if we were dead, we would never get there. Why don't we enjoy what we can and take what we can, maximize our profit and beat our competitors. Maybe they'll enjoy the 'promised land,' but for now, we'll enjoy our life now. The others can do what they want." Comment!

Chapter 5

What Price "Profit?"

Imagine a "primitive" utopian society, where there is no market economy, no poverty, no problems with wealth distribution, nor trouble with unemployment. There is plentiful individual initiative and at the same time, people work together whenever there is a need. The people live in harmony, both with nature and with each other. They enjoy life as it is. What are they missing? Do they miss the "dot.com's" or automobiles or big city buildings? Do they miss television and air travel? They have no desire to satisfy any of Maslow's needs beyond the most basic ones, because they do not know they exist. That is, until someone from outside comes along and "civilizes" them. One need only imagine such a "primitive" society to realize that in many ways it is far more civilized that our society today.

5.1 Introduction

"What is the price of profit?" This is a question that is seldom asked. However, the consequences of profit-motivated activity are often both good and bad. Profit sits like a devil and an angel, one on each shoulder. What makes it most confusing, is that there are times when it seems they are both whispering the same message. As we strive for profit, which one are we listening to? Sometimes it can be hard to tell! Profit is an angel, or a messiah that urges us to excel, to produce products and services that others want and need. Profit is also a devil, a demon that tempts to uncontrolled acquisition, to grab and hold on to wealth, any way that we can, and at whatever cost to others. It is a messiah to resurrect flagging businesses, and a destroyer of humanity, gobbling up everything in its path.

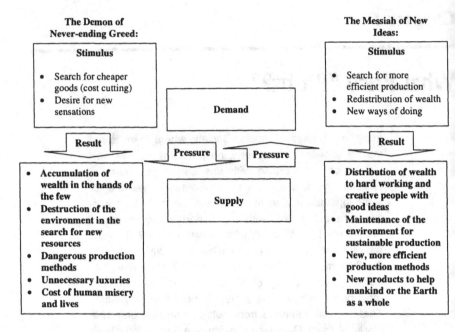

The Demon of Never-ending Greed:

Stimulus

- Search for cheaper goods (cost cutting)
- Desire for new sensations

Demand

Result

- Accumulation of wealth in the hands of the few
- Destruction of the environment in the search for new resources
- Dangerous production methods
- Unnecessary luxuries
- Cost of human misery and lives

Supply

Pressure **Pressure**

The Messiah of New Ideas:

Stimulus

- Search for more efficient production
- Redistribution of wealth
- New ways of doing

Result

- Distribution of wealth to hard working and creative people with good ideas
- Maintenance of the environment for sustainable production
- New, more efficient production methods
- New products to help mankind or the Earth as a whole

Figure 5.1 "What price profit?" Messiah of new ideas or demon of neverending greed?

5.2 When Entities Become Dominant, There is No Room for the Small

Under our market economy, everything is for sale, the only question being price. This seems to be a fact of life for those of us who live in the modern world, with few exceptions. The odd devoted Buddhist or spiritual Christian might reject materialism, or the occasional ascetic living in the desert, but for most of us, we would have to admit that the search for material wealth, and thus "profit" is part of our way of life. Yet we seldom ask: "what price profit?" Advocates of the market economy claim that this system is the most desirable, the most attractive, indeed, even the most just. A form of financial democracy, where the consumer has the ability to choose with their purses and wallets who wins, and who lives out their lives on the bread line. Unfortunately, what these defenders of capitalism often fail to mention is that these voting rights are really only exercised by the rich. How is it possible for the working class to have a decent say, when so many of them live below the poverty line and can only survive in a marginal fashion. This is especially true of persons living in less developed countries, who may spend their lives eking out livings on the edge of starvation, and with no thought or hope for the future? Where is the equality in that?

What follow are some examples of the reality of some human institutions. Ultimately, the cause of these troubles is the finite nature of our resources, suggesting the price that humanity pays for profit.

Everything alive is a part of nature, and there are fundamental laws of nature that govern all life. Every living being is not just an individual but interacts as part of a group. Animals in the jungle have no government, no regulations and no market economy, but they often illustrate behavior that can be illuminating, to say the least. Why do we study nature? No doubt there are many reasons, but certainly one of them is that through study of nature around us, we learn more about ourselves. The following story of a little elephant reflects a cruel reality — the reality of a market economy, in which the "invisible hands" of market forces are also blind, in which financial democracy has no room for the poor, because the poor have no money, and so no votes.

No Disney story, but a story of real life. The little orphan elephant

On a nature programme, there was a story about a little elephant whose mother died during childbirth.[1] He wandered about the wide African plain, a little refugee desperately looking for his mother, calling for his parents in distress, but with no success. Exhausted from heat and hunger, in need of a little protection to shelter him from the hot sun, and maybe a few drops of milk to sustain him in his struggle. He finally found a herd of elephants, and made a great effort to suckle at one of the mature female's teats, but she roughly pushed him aside. He approached the group once more, this time

---

[1]Viewed while the senior author was visiting Bintan Island off Singapore on the Discovery Channel on 12 May 2001.

mistaking a bull elephant's genitals for a source of nourishment. The bull used his powerful trunk, and tossed him away like a rag doll. He got up, apparently in great pain and continued, dragging his small body over the burnt red earth, until he reached an old tree. Thinking it to be his mother's leg, he rubbed himself against its bark. Even when he realised his mistake, the disappointment didn't kill his courage. Continuing his search, he eventually found another group, and again, he approached a female, thinking that perhaps he would find some motherly kindness there. No luck again. Yet the basic needs of food and shelter (and perhaps some love) drove him on. He continued on with trembling calls for help, but all his efforts were in vain. He was helpless. Perhaps he didn't realise that there is no Goddess of Mercy in the real world.

His struggles finally led him to a pond of muddy water, with a large number of elephants in it. Nearing them, he entered the pool, but was trampled, kicked and thrown away as usual. On the land again, he continued, this time meeting a group of young elephants like him. But they were the young of an established herd, protected and cared for, and there was no room for him. The commentator noted that, though sometimes orphaned young will be adopted, when resources are scarce (lack of food or shade, for example) herds protect their own offspring first. This may have been the case here, or perhaps, like the big players in the marketplace, they simply had no room for the weak and the helpless.

With indomitable spirit, the orphan elephant was unwilling to accept the reality of his fate. He continued his struggle and once again found a large group of adults, which he was able to infiltrate into for a short time. But in truth his luck was no better: an adult female used her long and powerful trunk to pick him up and throw him far away from the group. Nowhere was there mercy, but soon there was relief — of a kind, anyway. Detected by hyenas, the little orphan was doomed, he sensed the dangers and desperately tried to escape, but the pack grabbed him, and pulled him down, ripping him apart. His short life over, the hyenas feasted on his flesh, leaving only a skeleton tinged red with blood, lying on the ground.

We can easily relate the African plain to the marketplace, and just as all living things compete for food and shade, all individuals must seek to make their place in the financial world. In both, the big and strong will always have places for themselves. Their offspring will have the bes chance to thrive, and the helpless would rarely survive. But what about the small, the weak and the helpless? How is it possible for the "invisible hands" to feel responsible for them? To have a passion and kindness towards them when they may even find it impossible to reach the market, much less participate in it? Sadly, for us it is often just as it was for the little orphan elephant, dominated by the big elephants on the African plain, and his flesh valued only as food for the hyenas.

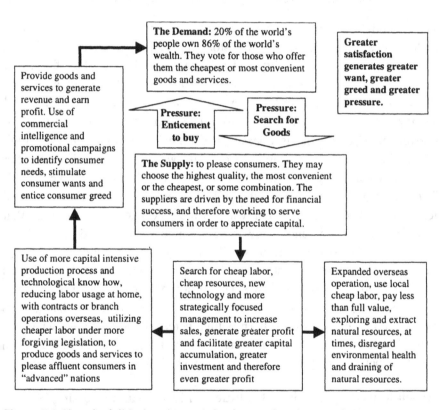

Figure 5.2 How invisible hands work in the marketplace and consumers cast their vote.

The traditional idea of capital and wealth accumulation: the consumers' choice facilitates the generation of profit, profit facilitates capital accumulation, taking from poor to give to the rich through the continued search for cheaper labor and convenient exploitation of resources from the earth.

The hyenas on the savannah made a gain from the "law of the jungle." The adult elephants did not kill the little orphan elephant, but the "law of the jungle" did. We would not call what happened to the orphaned elephant to be civilization, but rather the result of natural animal behavior, but it is the type of behavior that governs us as well. What then does civilization provide us with under the market economy?

5.2 The Market Economy, Profit and Poverty

The essential struggles of civilized man were recognized centuries ago, perhaps even from the dawn of history. In particular, civilization in the West is based on the morality and spirituality of the Christian faith, and here the struggle is well recognized. From admonitions against greed ("No servant can serve two masters.... You cannot serve both God and Money." Book of Luke 16:13) to recognizing the need for taxation ("give unto Caesar what is Caesar's and unto God what is God's." Book of Matthew 22:21), to taking care of what we are given ("Whoever can be trusted with very little can also be trusted with much." Luke 16:10). The Christian faith recognizes the pull of short term satisfaction over long term spiritual aspirations ("For wide is the gate and broad the road that leads to destruction, and many enter through it. But small is the gate and narrow the road that leads to life, and only a few find it." Matthew 7:13,14). Christianity has struggled for two millennia, and other religions for much longer, but Maslow's needs are powerful. There have been teachers and profits in all cultures that have warned about the dangers of temptation, but they have been outnumbered by the profiteers who only care about satisfying their immediate needs. Like the adult elephants in the documentary, they care not a whit about the poor or the needy.

Absolute poverty and life of a little girl in Africa, and a simple exchange economy

There was a CTV national network program with a message from Christian Foundation for Children revealed a story describing what is like in Africa for children. It is re-interpreted here through the eyes of the authors (presented the week of 4 March 2001):

There is a little girl of about seven years of age who lives by herself, in a little hut no bigger than 6' × 4' × 6'. It had no furniture of any kind, save a small mat of straw, rotten and falling to pieces, just big enough to fit under her small body. Every night, she sleeps on this mat, and in the mornings, she rolls it up and goes out of the hut to do her daily chores. What are her chores? Food is necessary to continue living. Previously she lived with her father and mother, until death claimed her father a few years previously, and her mother soon after. She is alone, no parents, no relatives, and so she takes a bucket that seems to be taller than she is, filling it with water and carrying it for her neighbor in exchange for a little food, three times a day.

According to the Christian Fund for Children, we have over 30 million children living in poverty, and approximately 35,000 children who die in poverty every day from a lack of food or shelter or through illness. And some people in our world make profit from the poor and helpless. There is not much of a market system in our story. Just a little girl who needs food, and a neighbor who gains a small comfort from the little girl's labor. It is not for us to judge the neighbor, and yet it is also true that the little girl is totally at her mercy. After all, how is it possible to live without food?

Making profit from human misery and poverty — the extremes

Our market economy is much more sophisticated than the simple portrait of the little African girl. Yet underneath all the sophistication of the stock exchange, generally accepted accounting practices, legal rights and responsibilities, contracts, pensions, department stores, Microsoft, Nortel, General Motors, Honda, Nestle and other corporate giants, there is a simple truth that links the two situations. The sad fact is that there are some individuals who are part of the system, not because they believe in the dream of financial democracy, not because they believe that they too have a chance to be rich, but because they believe that they have no choice.

And so the story of the little girl portrays the most sophisticated and challenging issue today: the close association between "profit" and poverty. The best the little girl had to give was only sufficient to buy her a little food. Where in the market economy is there room to care for those who have little to contribute? There is no mechanism to take care of the needy, as the invisible hands do not recognize the poor. This exchange is a deeply rooted relationship, inseparably tying together the market economy, profit and poverty. In order for some to gain, others cannot gain; in order for some to gain much, others must lose. In order for some to gain greedily, others must lose all.

Our advanced market economy happens to work for and reward less than 20% of the world's population; the remainder have to make do with less than 16% of the resources. Perhaps more seriously, the super rich top 1% in the U.S. have more than the bottom 95% in their own country, the richest on earth. This concentration of wealth can only result in extreme wastage, both of the wealth itself (after all, how much does one man need?), and also of human life.

The middle ground: "what price profit"

The story of the little girl is more sophisticated than the story of the orphan elephant. The story of the market economy is more sophisticated than that. In high powered societies such as Singapore, Hong Kong or Switzerland, standard of living is matched by astronomical cost of living. Most people living there are under extreme pressure to "make it," most especially those in high profile government or business positions, who need a very high income indeed, to match their preferred living style. Consequently, both partners in a typical professional married couple have to work very hard: a condominium for two commands a monthly rent of HK$54,000 or US$10,000, and a town house, HK$66,000 or US$11,000.[2] Domestic help therefore becomes a necessity rather than luxury, particularly for those with preschool children. This constitutes the demand side of the market economy. On the supply send, there are a large number of women

---

[2]*Post Magazine*, Sunday Morning Post HK, p. 22.

(mostly Filipino, mostly young, presumably with an inferior standard of living at home) who are employed as domestic helpers. In both Hong Kong and Singapore, every Sunday there are literally thousands of them congregated in public places to meet their friends and relatives. Some of them gather around singing spiritual songs and songs of hope, saying things such as: "I want to be free, let me be free... Hallelujah," just as the slaves would in some movie or storybook. Here once again, profit contributes to poverty, although it might be argued that profit in this case helps to alleviate poverty. The unfortunate truth is that there are far more little elephants, far more orphan girls, far more desperate young women than there are these marginal positions to fill. The greedy often justify their greed by pointing out that without the jobs they provide, the poor employees would have nowhere to go. Yet the truth is that, while the little girl's neighbor gained little from her "employee," on the other hand she did not give much, and the effort cost the little girl everything that she could give. The Filipino maids certainly escaped their poverty, but the rich gained far more profit from their labor than the laborers do themselves. In fact, "profit" only comes from a recombination of what already exists in nature, in such a way that the value (utility) is greater than the prior existing combination. Unfortunately, under the market economy profit is inextricably linked to "poverty," for example through underpaying labor and exploiting finite resources. Making profit is not a bad thing. In fact, it is a necessity, but only if all costs are accounted for. Excessive profit, built out of the misery of others and at the expense of the environment is in the end no profit at all.

5.3 Profit as Demon

Making profit from human misery, and create poverty

The advanced market economy is increasingly driven by the need of the rich. This form of motivation at times makes one wonder: "What has happened to us?" Are we still claiming to be "civilized" creatures at all?

In the historically-based movie "Amistad," slave traders in the 19th century captured and savagely beat their "human merchandise." Individuals were chained in groups, packed like sardines in the dark, dank cargo-hold, and fed a barely sufficient gruel (no doubt the cost of even that was begrudged). Realizing that they were under-provisioned, the smugglers tied the slaves to heavy stones, dropping them into the sea, but first raping the women and torturing and butchering for pleasure. What was the reason for this? There was not even the justification of war. It was for "profit." The slave traders were making profit from human misery, with no sense of giving back equal value. This situation illustrates what a mockery it is, to say that capitalism will benefit both sides. Which sides? The slave traders and the slave buyers yes, but what about the slaves? What price profit? The price was human misery and death, and one of the darkest marks on human history.

Making a profit on human lives in today's world: sex slavery and human smuggling

As we advance into the 21st century, slavery is still a part of our world. In January 2001, a sex slavery ring in Canada was broken by the police, and it was learned that those unfortunate women, largely Thai, Chinese and Vietnamese, were told that life was better in North America, and the "traders" would help them to arrange visas and jobs. After luring them to Canada, their travel documents were taken, and they were confined to Spartan quarters and forced to "entertain" guests. Threatened with deportation, they were forcibly held, told not to leave or go anywhere because they were in the country illegally.

Another recent story featured the smuggling of "human cargo" from China and other Asian countries to Canada, the U.S. and European countries. People desperate to leave China were packed into cargo containers in an attempt to illegally get them across borders. In one case, approximately 50 people suffocated in a cargo container aboard a ship bound for Vancouver. In another, a driver crossing the English Channel turned off the ventilation in the back of his truck, allowing the people inside to die horrible, lingering deaths. One criminal kingpin, Lai Changxing and his wife, Tsang Mingna, were arrested in Canada to be extradited to Beijing. Lai and his amily pleaded political refugee status to avoid extradition, claiming that hey would face the death penalty if found guilty under Chinese law, omething much more severe than the house arrest in their luxury Vancouver partment in which the Canadian authorities placed them during their earing.[3] Whether or not Lai and his family get their wish, the sheer magnitude to their gall makes it difficult to decide whether to laugh or cry. What a beautiful thought: political refugee status for human smugglers.

All of these are for "profit," and all of these are making profit from uman miseries, from the poor, not the rich. Oh God! How have we rogressed for the past two centuries? Is this how we claim to be civilized? How can we consider people living tribal lives uncivilized and primitive? Surely, our education and civilization condemn our actions even more? The difference between the situations is that the 19th century slave trade pulled people from their homes by force (though our story is based on a Hollywood film, it is substantiated by historical records). The 21st century's human smuggling and sex slavery used the poverty and misery of the victims to ure them into situations that brought the smugglers profit, at the expense of the added misery of the victims.

5.4 "What Price Profit?" Profit, the Angel

People in poverty still require the very basics: food, water (clean water being a luxury), a home and perhaps a few other basic items. These basics do not usually just drop from heaven. In extremis, acquiring these essentials might involve stealing, begging or searching the refuse heaps or trash cans. Begging and scrounging do not belong to the normal segment of market economy. However, homelessness and begging are not inevitable. Given the opportunity and the will, everyone can be self-reliant, creating something, making a "profit" to sustain an enterprise and improve living conditions to get out of poverty.

How many people in poverty are able to make good is not a statistical challenge, or empirically verifiable, because we need everyone out of this

---

[3]*South China Morning Post*, Friday, 18 May 2001, p. 1.

category. Every individual must be counted. Individuals can challenge poverty through their own efforts, if only given the opportunity to be self-reliant, and creative at the same time. Here are three examples:

(1) At the intersection of Yonge and Bloor Streets in Toronto, there usually stands a few fast food vendors, hawking their wares. One day, there was a young man, probably in his mid-20s, selling gourmet hot dogs. What follows is a conversation between the vendor (V) and a customer who happened to be one of the authors (A):

A: "Mmmm... delicious."
V: (responding with a smile) "You like it?"
A: "Yes."

As there were no other customers waiting, the young man was in a conversational mood. He continued:

V: "I like this business. I get to meet people like you, and say good things about my dogs. You know, four years ago, I was still in my teens, a high school dropout from a small town and I came to Toronto to look for a job. My God, it was as hard as trying to get to heaven from hell. Everybody wanted experience. How could I get experience? I never worked before. Even for a waiter's job, they wanted a resume. With nothing in my bag, and hunger driven, I had to beg. Yes, there were people with kind hearts who dropped dimes and quarters into my cup. But some people, even some of those who gave me money, made me feel that I was nothing better than trash, a reject. It felt like absolutely no one cared how I felt inside. Sure, I begged, but I also have pride, perhaps even dignity. Anyway, to make a long story short, one day, I saw some leaflets about a youth venture program, which said that I could get a few thousand dollars via the Ontario youth venture program from the bank. That definitely stimulated me, so I applied. Mind you, even that wasn't easy, but I got the loan. With that little money, I started the hot dog business, making a few bucks to keep me alive. Anyway, summer is good for guys like me. We don't need much. Well, here I am. Now I am an entrepreneur."

A: "Now you are all set."

V: "Not yet, not until I get married, and buy myself a house."

A: "Do you have a girlfriend now?"

V: "That gorgeous girl with the other stand over there? She's the one I'm going to marry; last year we met here, living on the street."

(2) In Beijing, China, there is a "KFC" outlet on a small shopping strip opposite of the Forbidden City. Outside the outlet, an elderly beggar woman was noticed by one of the authors. Rather than give her money, he purchased a dinner (two pieces of chicken and some fries) and gave it to her. Anticipating that she would consume the dinner on the spot, he was surprised when she walked away, took out a pair of chopsticks and sat down for a proper dinner, eating one of the pieces of chicken. She then repacked the other piece and the French fries, walked a few more steps and sold the "trimmed down dinner" to another person for five yuan, making a "profit." What happened in this short real-life play conveys three simple messages:

- The old woman had her pride; she wanted to consume her dinner with dignity.
- She had ownership rights over some property: her chopsticks.
- She evaluated the worth of the dinner, ate what she needed, repackaged what she didn't, and sold it in a way that was attractive to someone else, so she entered the market and made a profit.

This is not to say that, by this example alone, it proves that the woman could use her own efforts to get out of poverty and acquire her own economic freedom, but she maintained the dignity and power of proprietary rights over her own life. The simple equation: two pieces of KFC chicken and French fries equals one meal plus five yuan is not a recipe for success, but it is a start! In this case, is not profit an angel from heaven?

(3) In some Indian cities such as Bombay or Calcutta, there are people living in 21st century and 18th century conditions, right next to each other. On one side of a street, you see tall office towers, with rental costs amongst the highest in the world. The people working in the towers, one would think, own all the wealth

in the world. Yet right next to them, on the sidewalk, "beggar-like" street people attempt to sell homemade jewelry on the streets to the curious tourists.

(4)   In 1949, the senior author was enrolled in the M. Com. programme at the University of Toronto. He had recently arrived from China, leaving just as the Communist People's Liberation Army was about to cross the Yangtze River. He had lost all contact with home, and was a stranger, alone in a strange land with only $50 in his pocket. As a visa student, he was not permitted to work. With no money, or help from any source, pressured by time and coursework, he had no place to turn but himself. The money soon ran out, and after missing two weeks' rent, he found himself homeless. A classmate staying at the YMCA dormitory allowed him to sneak into his room late in the evening. Compared to the sidewalk, a sheet on the floor seemed like a pretty good bed. Attempting to work illegally in a Chinese restaurant, the owner took a look at him and said: "So you are a student. You cannot be a waiter, because you are not handsome enough. Besides you don't speak Cantonese, and you cannot be a dishwasher, because I had a bad experience with students. I remember, a student who used to wash dishes for my restaurant; when my customers complained that the dishes were not clean, and I asked him to do a better job, he told me: "people only eat food from inside of the dish, not the outside." That was the end of his dream of working for a restaurant. Talking to his friend Peter, they decided to form a small venture, working as domestic helpers. The two spent $6.00 to advertise in the Classifieds of the *Toronto Star* newspaper, and called themselves "Varsity Service," offering to do all kinds of chores in and around the house, including painting, cleaning toilets, gardening, snow shoveling, and even babysitting. Priced at $1.00 per hour, plus bus fare. To their surprise, the response was overwhelming. The two responded to the call for services and arranged times for jobs that suited them, and found that they did not have to compromise their classroom hours.

The little enterprise was quite successful. They would normally price a weekend job at a rate of $16.00, but most "clients" would pay $20.00, sometimes more. The weekend earning plus off class odd time jobs gave sufficient money to get the senior

author through his degree. There was no opportunity cost since
he couldn't do anything else anyway. The "profit" was anything
over the $16.00. In his desperate state, this was a grand life,
and the profit, truly a ray of sunshine in the darkness, a gift
from heaven.

These are just some examples of people rising above circumstances to
make a profit for themselves and live their lives with dignity. No doubt
every one of us could find many others.

5.5 Conclusion

"Profit" is a good thing. Making profit is an admirable goal. Ideally, all
human activities should yield a profit, in particular entrepreneurial undertakings, and most especially smaller entrepreneur managed enterprises.
Without profit, it is not possible to make any progress in a world that has
already been formed. Without profit can anyone achieve the self-fulfillment
we all need? Really the issue is not profit, but cost: cost to individuals,
cost to society and cost to the environment. Profit is only possible if all
costs incurred are accounted for. Otherwise, poverty always will be the
cost to humans in the course of making profit.

It is certainly harsh to say that the price for profit is always poverty. Yet
as we currently measure it, this indeed seems to be the case. However,
poverty is a disease of our own making. We can make it disappear, but
only if we realize that our creative and innovative activities must include
concern for the common good. Otherwise all our efforts are simply
spreading the disease. Yet we still put profit before people, value the
accumulation of wealth rather than its distribution. By what magic
putting more wealth in the hands of the few will create wealth for the
many is anyone's guess. Entire continents are filled with "private enterprises"
with the objective for "profit." Privatize. De-mutualize. Acquire. Profit
motivation is viewed as the answer to everything. Healthcare. Sanitation.
Communication. The water supply. Education. Everything is becoming
privatized, becoming a privilege of the rich instead of a human right. In the
Canadian province of Ontario, even the elementary responsibility of water

inspection was contracted to a private company, the result being a disastrous contamination of *E. coli* bacteria in the summer water supply, making the price of profit, in this case, a few dead people. As the trend continues, perhaps the government will also become a corporation, elected on a share basis to govern all other corporations. Consequently, we will have a society of corporations above corporations. Of course, all corporations need "operational resources" (i.e. money), and thus government would have to actively pursue a corporate strategy to make more "profit," facilitating the accumulation of private wealth, so the rich can have more to consume, resulting in less for the poor. Not that there's anything wrong with that; after all, it all adds up to GDP.

Nature gives us orphan elephants, but we are much more creative: sex slaves, human cargo smuggling, people pushed into poverty, and the betrayal of our stewardship of the earth. What can we say, except to quote Charles Dickens' Tiny Tim: "God bless us every one!"

Questions for discussion

1. What is poverty?
2. If we leave the word "exploitation" out of an assessment of business market behavior, where does "Profit" come from?
3. "Small is beautiful," but is "Big" better? Explain!
4. Discuss the criteria for success. What is personal success, society success, a nation's success and the success of humanity as a whole?
5. What is the impact of the theory of the firm on poverty? Does the theory help to create or destroy it?
6. In your opinion, what is the cause (or causes) of "poverty?" Explore and discuss.

Chapter 6

Value and Entrepreneurial Cultural Value

> We need food to survive, real profit to support a business' well-being and sustain its growth, but it is "value" that has enriched our soul, strengthened organizational purpose and made it possible to grow and offer benefits to the individual and society.
>
> Value is a personal, spiritual and organizational property, but more so, a public concern. Although there are value differences among people, and nations alike, it is our value in which we share and where our culture can spread and civilization can flourish.

6.1 What is "Value?"

All humans evolve and live around two sets of values. Sacred value is personal, and more often than not, spiritual. In group situations, individuals express both their own sacred values, but also share through traditions, learning, cultural, religious influences and other forms of knowledge to integrate each individual's sacred value into values of the group and nation.

The other set of values can be referred to as functional values. Utility function is a clear form of functional value. The second is exchange value. It is this set of values that makes the market economy work. While sacred value or spiritual value serves as a guide to a meaningful life for ourselves and others, the second set of values serves as a means to make need and want satisfaction possible. For convenience reasons, the book will use the term "value" throughout, unless it is deemed necessary to make a distinction.

6.2 Sacred Value

6.2.1 Sacred value may not be blindly applied — an illustration

As knowledge has no boundary or entry barriers (it may have "copyright," once it has recognizable "exchange value"), the concept of value can be quite different from one person to another, and one group of individuals to another group of individuals. For example, in the East, the society seems to have a profound sacred value of respecting elders. The perception of such value can also be different from one aspect to another. The simplest and most commonly acknowledged one is that of recognizing the fact that an older person has gone through life "planting trees". The older person had done his/her share of planting trees, so the next generation can enjoy the shade from the trees planted by the elder. On the other hand, there are also many elders who do not comprehend the meaning of tree planting wisdom; they not only have never planted any trees in their lives, but spread their "bodies" as if to occupy every inch of shade provided by the trees others have planted. These people have not helped anyone, but instead continue to keep taking from others. It may seem as if nothing would please them more, than to squeeze blood from a stone. They deserve no respect. Even though they may have placed a deposit for a seat in heaven, they will never achieve that blessing. Being old does not necessarily entitle you to the respect of others. To respect elders is a social value, but it is because the "old" have earned that respect.

Here is a story about a rich man whose life may be completely described by five words: "success," "greed," "unkindness" and "absolute selfishness." His success was based on the result of his greed, using ruthless business strategies to kill his competitors as if they were enemies in a senseless war. He kept everything he took, and used them to harm others, although, in his words: "so what, it's legal, besides, even it is illegal, if I am in trouble, I have friends."

He was called to "final justice" at the age of 75. At a memorial service in his honor, a "friend" rose up and approached the podium to deliver an impromptu eulogy:

A tribute to J. B.: Oh! There is one thing good about you

A "friend" of the late J. B. began his speech by weeping as if his tears would never stop. Finally, he managed to put his feelings in control and looked at the deceased, then, delivered his eulogy which is supposedly in J. B.'s honor... .

J. B., I hope you can hear this, because this is your chance to hear from me about how I feel about you. As far as I can gather we have been through a lot together in the past 15 years. Do you remember when I worked for you? You treated me like a slave. Do you remember my wife? You seduced her, took her away from me and kept her in your penthouse for a year. Then you dumped her for a new favourite. I must admit that you were smart. Your accomplishments in business; as far as I know there is no one who can match your acumen or accomplishments. You had stakes in everything from real estate, mining, the media, fast food joints and retailing, to illegal drugs, gambling and prostitution. There were many people who worked for you, and you were merciless to them. In fact, you treated people like dirt, I remember even in the earlier days, while you were in need of people to help you build your empire. You told me: "people are like the water filling your wash basin; after you use them to wash your hands, you pull the plug, and then let them out the drain and are done with them." You took over my company that I built from scratch and gave me peanuts, just as you did with all your other acquisitions and mergers.

You were an evil man, and you know, what troubled me most in all the years that I knew you, was your hypocrisy. You always acted like you were the "Goddess of Mercy," telling the world: "I am doing all this for the jobs..." The funny thing was our politicians believed in you, and let you got away with murder, but whenever you took over a company, the first thing you did was to lay off people en masse. It reminded me of a small child pouring boiling water on an anthill — indiscriminate destruction. Then you would say, "I had to do it because of the competition; I have to keep costs down and technology up, otherwise, you will all have trouble. It will not only be layoffs, but everyone will have to go, because I would have to close the shop."

There were a few things you knew, because they happened right before your eyes: Bill's suicide, Peter living on the streets, George an alcoholic, all because you forced them out of business, and made them lose everything they had. Then, you said, "I haven't done anything to them, they just can't face reality."

In the late 1970s, you destroyed seven reputable companies by dumping their stocks, companies that were vital to the local economies, companies that employed people who helped to make what you were, but you made the dumping anyway.

I still remember your attitude towards the environment, when the government restricted your operations because of the garbage dumping problem in your chemical plants. You moved them to a developing country and told them it will help their country by creating more new jobs. Pollution was not your concern, as you said: "out of sight, out of mind. Who cares? So my plants will cause some pollution to these countries. A little pollution might affect those people's health, but they will have jobs, live longer, die later. Without me giving them jobs, they will starve and die now."

Certainly you don't know anything about ecology and environmental science, but the truth was, you did not give a damn. I guess you could not recall anything now, let me remind you, when you bought a huge parcel of land in South America used to raise cattle for your fast food joints. The first thing you did was raze the rain forest, destroying the homes of millions of living species. I was still working for you then. I asked you to have some consideration for the ecosystem and go easy with the operation, and you told me: "you are not a bird or monkey, what do you care? They can always find a home somewhere else." Then, you kicked me out.

In short, as far as I know, you have done nothing good for anyone. All through your life, it was not a situation of "one for all," but "all for one." You have done it, not all by yourself, but all for yourself at the cost of others, yet you hardly gave anything back to others in return. You always used to say that everyone cheats, but the truth is, you cheated everyone. J. B., I am here supposedly to pay my respects to you, but I can honestly tell you, you don't deserve it as you have never earned it. But I must admit there is one thing good about you: You are dead.

I want to make this absolutely clear to you. When I look at you lying in this state, I cannot help but weep, not for you, but because of you.

The story of J. B.'s eulogy is fiction, but what has been said in J. B.'s eulogy encompasses many aspects of selfish behavior which, all too sadly, is evident practically everyday.

6.2.2 Respect from others must be earned

We should be proud of respecting elders as part of our heritage, a value system has been with us for so long that it is difficult to trace the origin. For example, in the Inuit community of Canada's north, when an elder in the family becomes too old to go out fishing or hunting for food, all he has to do is to place his hands on the catch and he will share the food with the rest of the family. Respect for the old reflects an everlasting value of humanity. To vacate a seat for the elderly is also a form of respect, but not directly on account of their contribution to society or for personal respect, but simply respect on the basis of the physical evidence that they have experienced long lives. If J. B. was a simple business person, he would have naturally earned a basic respect, because he has proven to be a worthy member of the "human species." He earned his living and made his contribution to society as an honest simple human being.

Most of us shift continuously between two sets of values: inherited value that we either learn from our past, or is part of our inherent nature, and exchange value that arises from pragmatic consideration of our interactions with others and how to satisfy our respective human needs and wants.

6.3 Inherited Value

Inherited values are values that we understand on a child-like level: we believe them because that is what comes naturally, or because that is what we are told, whether or not they appear to benefit us. For example, the senior author was standing in a queue with 20 people to purchase tickets for a Disney movie. A boy of about six or seven years of age jumped from behind to cut the queue where there was a small space between two people. People in the queue had already unknowingly accommodated the boy's move and also allowed room for his mother to cut in as well. However, the mother did not seize the apportunity, instead she called the boy to return to his original position in the line, and said to him: "Peter, come back this minute! You must never try to get ahead of life by cheating others." The mother's angry expression and the tone of voice would have created an unforgettable lesson for the boy, becoming part of the boy's memory — the idea of "one must never try to get ahead of life by cheating others." This is possibly how personal value is permanently implanted in the mind of an individual. It is observed and practiced through interaction with others, and becomes part of the societal value system which we all live in and can proudly pass on as "tradition." It is also clear (as was illustrated in the above example) that the responsibility of personal value of a child rests on the adult. It was the mother who taught the boy not to cheat others in order to get ahead; if on the other hand, the mother had encouraged the boy to cut into the line, the boy may have felt a sense of accomplishment in cheating — the impact on the child as far as personal value is concerned, would be quite different. As a result, the child grows into an adult, his interaction with other adults would also be different if he feels "cheating" in life is part of the game.

Personal (individual) value can be inherited as a natural process; mostly in the form of informal learning from parents, family members, friends and other associates through "human interaction." Formal learning can also take place in schools, churches, temples or places where people congregate, and in organizations wherein the individual is a member. Value can influence group behavior, and over a long period of time, if the value of an individual is persistently presenting itself in the group, it can become a part of group/organizational culture, consequently becoming a cultural bond upon which our civilization is based.

Value may also be based on "natural laws." For example, there are certain principles of morality that we treat as universal, whether or not all humans agree to them. For example, most of us would agree that murder is wrong, even though there are some of us who would commit murder. Whatever one believes the source of inherited values is, they are values that we have or learn without direct reference to the added value they give us, even when they give us added value.

6.4 Chinese Cultural Value and the Doctrine of Confucianism as Related to Entrepreneurial Value

Micro economists tend to the view that profit maximization is the culture for all business undertakings. But this is not necessarily the same as a cultural value. A cultural value is a system developed and nurtured over a long period of time. It integrates the personal value of individuals in the group, similar to an old saying: "The wheels may run on the same road, but not necessarily on the same track." Consequently, nations, societies, territories, regions, social groups and business entities, may have the same culture as for self-interest, but they may not have the same cultural value.

In our civilized world, the cultural values that guide our thinking, behavior and/or actions in the East and those in the West, can be quite different, even though there might be some similarities.

Kirby and Fan (1995) noted 59 Chinese cultural values that have influenced the Chinese over a long history of time. Some of them in the authors' opinion can be viewed as entrepreneurial cultural values and others are applicable for all endeavors (Table 6.1).

Chinese entrepreneurial values have a long history of development. The earliest traceable doctrine tends to associate with the teachings of Confucius more than 2000 years ago, before Christ's time. There are a few placed in China and/or outside of the mainland, such as Taiwan and Singapore, where the very old-fashioned grammar school form of passing down knowledge is still in practice. Some of Confucius' teachings relating to entrepreneurial values are also observed by the Japanese, including the following:

(1) Have a clear vision and objective.
(2) Be able to earn others' trust.
(3) Assume responsibility if things go wrong, and give glory to others, if successful.
(4) Observe the laws of nature.
(5) Help others as you would want others to help you.
(6) Do not aimlessly criticize competitors.

Table 6.1 Chinese cultural values.

	More directly applicable as an entrepreneurial cultural value (Y)
National trail	
1. Patriotism.	
2. A sense of cultural superiority.	
3. Respect for tradition.	Y
4. Bearing hardships.*	Y
5. Knowledge (education).	Y
6. Government by leaders instead of by law.*	
7. Equality/equalitarianism.*	
Interpersonal relations	
8. Trustworthiness.	Y
9. Jen-ai/kindness (forgiveness and compassion).	Y
10. Li/propriety.*	Y
11. Tolerance of others.	Y
12. Harmony with others.	Y
13. Courtesy.	Y
14. Humility (modesty).	Y
15. A close, intimate friend.	Y
16. Observation of rites and social rituals.	Y
17. Reciprocation of greetings, favors and gifts.	Y
18. Repayment of both the good or the evil that another person has caused you.	Y
19. Face (protecting, giving, gaining and losing).	Y
Social (family) orientation	
20. Filial piety.	
21. Chastity in women.	
22. Loyalty to superiors.	
23. Deference to age.*	
24. Deference to authority.*	Y
25. Hierarchical relationships by status and observing this order.	Y
26. Conformity (group orientation).*	
27. A sense of belonging.*	
28. Reaching consensus or compromise.*	Y

Table 6.1 (*Continued*)

	More directly applicable as an entrepreneurial cultural value (Y)
29. Avoiding confrontation.*	Y
30. Benevolent authority.	
Work attitude	
31. Industry (work hard).	Y
32. Commitment.	Y
33. Thrift (saving).	Y
34. Persistence (perseverance).	Y
35. Patience.	Y
36. Prudence (care).	Y
37. Adaptability (flexibility).	Y
Business philosophy	
38. Non-competition.	Y†
39. Not guided by profit.*	Y†
40. Moderation, following the middle way.	Y†
41. Guanxi (personal connection or networking).*	Y
42. Attaching importance to long-lasting relationships not gains.*	Y†
43. Wealth.	Y
44. Resistance to corruption.	Y
45. Being conservative.	Y
46. Long term orientation.	Y
Personal traits	
47. Te (virtue and moral standards).*	Y
48. Sense of righteousness/integrity.	Y
49. Sincerity.	Y
50. Having a sense of shame.	Y
51. Wisdom/resourcefulness.*	Y
52. Self-cultivation.	Y
53. Personal steadiness and stability.	Y
54. Keeping oneself disinterested and pure.	
55. Having few desires.	
56. Obligation for one's family and nation.*	

Table 6.1 (*Continued*)

	More directly applicable as an entrepreneurial cultural value (Y)
Attitude towards environment 57. Fatalism (believing in one's own fate).* 58. Content with one's position in life. 59. Harmony between man and nature.*	

Based on the Chinese Value Survey by the Chinese Culture Connection, *Journal of Cross-Cultural Psychology* **18**(2): 147–148 (1988). Amended and revised by D. A. Kirby and Y. Fan (*) and denoted by R. Kao (Y). Places noted with Y† suggest that these entrepreneurial values do not reflect entrepreneurial values of Westerners.

(7) View others' problems and dealing others' difficulties as if they are your own.

(8) Do not harm others as if you do not wish others to harm you.

(9) Always lend your hands to help others in trouble.

(10) Respect others' responsibility and authority as you would have others respect those of your own.

(11) Say less, do more. Only action counts, not words.

(12) Continue to create and innovate. Always take the lead in innovation and creativity, rather than be a follower and copy what others have done.

(13) Any individual has his/her own strength and weakness, help them to overcome his/her weakness, use and benefit from his/her strength.

Of course, the above are only a few of Confucius' teachings. Both the Japanese and Koreans have dedicated their effort in cultivating the doctrine of Confucius; in China, there is an advanced learning institution devoted to the study of Confucianism, and in Japan, The Confucian Management School (Jyukyo Chuyo Keieiha) is also created to study Confucianism. One of the most important accomplishments is the conclusion drawn from its studies, the relationship between private concern (common good) and private interest which classic economics is unable to offer. There are six conclusions in all. The following three (as listed below) are viewed as the more suitable guidelines for forming and shaping entrepreneurial value:[1]

(1) A group comes first and an individual is willing to sacrifice or deny himself for the group doctrine. The individual who creates group support, generally gains victory in business competition.
(2) The doctrine of Confucianism functions like the spirit of God as the result of the way that both should be taught and recognized.
(3) From the viewpoint of decision-making, harmony (chowa) is a first choice and the virtue of the constant mean must be sought.

6.5 Entrepreneurial Cultural Value of the East as Related to Entrepreneurial

Attributes of the West

The internet, passenger jets and advanced telecommunications have brought human beings closer together than ever before, especially now that the gap between the East and West has narrowed. The Westerners have learned the value of the East, and Easterners have rapidly accepted Western culture as if it is their own. Although they still exhibit some value differences, this is of benefit to each, rather than a hindrance to human interaction.

6.5.1 The links between Chinese cultural values and entrepreneurial attributes

This was examined by Kirby and Fan (1995) based on research findings of entrepreneurial attributes. Related research findings on entrepreneurial attributes by Hornaday (1982), Gibb (1990), Timmons *et al.* (1977 and 1985) and Gartner (1990) were linked with Chinese cultural values, demonstrating remarkable similarities; although there are differences, in particular, in the area of profit orientation. The difference between Chinese cultural values and entrepreneurial attributes found from the West lies in

---

[1]Lee S. M. and Schwendiman G., *Japanese Management* (Praeger, 1982), pp. 108–109.

the fact that the former are mainly guidelines about moral and social norms, about personal values and culture, bearing little relation to enterprising or profit-making activities. The ideal man in ancient China was the one who served the court, the ruler, or father in the family, and orderly conduct was the core value of an individual. However, economic reforms and Deng Xiaoping's remark: "To be rich is glorious" have changed the mindset of enterprising Chinese, although some old, traditional perceived value is still in the minds of the Chinese people. In 1995, the senior author was working in a UNIDO mission in China, when he came across a question posed to the participants of the Training of Trainers Program (TOT): please rank the following individuals in terms of his/her social status. Among six categories, Party workers and government officials are at the top of the list, according to approximately 120 participants.

It should be noted that some of the Chinese cultural values can also be found in people of other Eastern origins. For example, East Indian migrants in Canada also have strong cultural values. In an unpublished paper prepared by Chhinzer of McMaster University, it was reported that some Punjabi cultural values are similar to those values of Chinese origin (as listed in Table 6.1), including "guided by long-term, sustainable growth" and "personal pursuit of contentment and adequacy" (Nos. 42 and 46), "respect tradition" (No. 3), "value family as the highest priority" (Nos. 20 and 56), "think of welfare of the community as ultimate good" (No. 1), and among other things, "trust among community" (No. 8).

Western cultural values by and large are based on the individual's need for personal growth and the "profit driven" corporate culture. As such they formed the cutting edge in a competitive environment, stressing the need for a "win, win and win" situation, which ultimately carries weight in society. However, this "win, win" mentality pushes an individual pursuing personal wealth to form a tree of thoughts associated with the following:[2]

- Freedom of expression
- Accumulation of private property ownership

---

[2]*Asian Wall Street Journal*, 5 March 1996, p. 11.

- Personal freedom within the framework of a society
- Self-reliance
- Individual rights
- Hard work
- Personal achievement

The above and other driving forces (through public display of success models aided by the mass media) have made Western society, particularly in Canada and the U.S.A., impress onto the individual the need to be a rapid financial success. This is typified by the proliferation of television "game shows" all centered around instant wealth. "Who Wants to be a Millionaire?" "The Wheel of Fortune." "The $128,000 question." "The Price is Right." Not to mention lotteries and legalized gambling. This get rich and instant success drive, along with corporate profit drive culture and the need for personal growth, is all for self-interest, but with no mention of the need for common good. As such, the model works well in that government, private profit driven entities and not-for-profit organizations form an interesting triangle, with private profit driven entities on one side, government on the other, and not-for-profit organizations firmly in between to bridge the gap between self-interest and common good.

A triangle with four players:

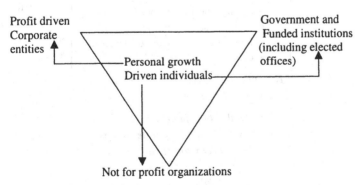

Figure 6.1 The cultural value triangle of the Western world.

Table 6.2 The triangle of Western culture value: further illustration.

The triangle player (3+1)	The player's culture	Entrepreneurial cultural value opportunity
Growth driven individual	Unlimited personal growth potential realization, through: • Hard work • Perseverance • Moderate risk taking • Persistence • Determination • Resourcefulness • Reliability • Others *Negative development in which cultural value may be lost:* • *Personal greed, no regard for common good, can motivate individual to pursue harmful acts on others and the environment*	Encourages innovation and creativity for self-interest and add value to society.
Profit driven private corporate entities	Small may be beautiful, but big is better. Big organization, maximizing profit, through: • R&D • Satisfy consumers' need and wants • Mergers and acquisitions • Innovative and creative marketing • Others *Negative development in which cultural value may be lost:* • *Ruthlessly exploit natural resources for corporate expansion* • *No concern for environmental health* • *Exploit labor* • *Exploit consumers*	Commercializing the result of innovative and creative undertakings for self-interest and add value to society.

Table 6.2 (*Continued*)

The triangle player (3+1)	The player's culture	Entrepreneurial cultural value opportunity
Profit driven private corporate entities (*Cont.*)	• *Erode life support system for future humans* • *Create human conflict* • *Obliterate the balance of market economy*	
Not-for-profit organizations (such as charitable organizations, institutions organized for public interest)	Serving public interest. Bridge a gap between individual's need for self-interest and government's role to provide societal need for the common good, through: • Servicing the needy • Helping those who cannot help themselves • Helping to maintain the balance between those who have and those who absolutely have not *Negative development in which cultural value may be lost:* • *Individuals involved in the undertakings may use the opportunity to work for personal interest, instead of for the common good* • *If the organization gets too large, it will be operated in much the same way as large corporate entities. Although the organization may not be a profit driven entity, it can be a financial gain driven entity, except with no profit responsibility to its members, but can be just as narrowly focused on financial gains rather than real needs*	The idea of serving the needs of society by offering services is innovative, and helping those who cannot help themselves is certainly adding value to society. It is also for self-interest as well. In Canada, one of the nomination criteria for a recipient to the Order of Canada is the person's involvement in community work, e.g. serving on the board of charitable organizations, etc.

Table 6.2 (*Continued*)

The triangle player (3+1)	The player's culture	Entrepreneurial cultural value opportunity
Not-for-profit organizations (*Cont.*)	• *Charitable undertakings are essentially to fill a need where both the private sector and public institutions are unable to provide; charitable work should be an exception rather than a rule*	
Government and publicly funded institutions (including elected offices)	Serving people and using the resources given by people effectively and efficiently for the achievement of the goal of common good, and fully developing an (any) individual to his maximum growth potential, through: • Taxation • Incentive schemes • Regulation and control • Others *Negative development in which cultural value may be lost:* • *If a government is staffed with corrupt individuals, it will harm the common good* • *If the power of control and taxation of people is in the wrong hands, people will be repressed and driven to extremes, resulting in destruction of economic and social balance. All revolutions/ wars, colonization/invasion of other countries and involvement in crimes against humanity are cases in point* • *Others*	Creative thinking leads to creative taxation, not for more taxation, but better taxing system, simplify procedures, tax returns, reducing tax payers' burden, and use tax money for creative and innovative undertakings. Eliminate unnecessary government control amongst other things, effective use of public trust in the interest of common good.

Some of us are more interested in actions than words, but they do not realize that it is "words" and their meaning that will guide us, in particular the use of the words "value," "culture" and "cultural value." As cultural value is a guide to action, "culture" is the consistent behavior of humans while interacting with others, "value" on the other hand is used as a personal strength, a divine right that supports the individual to live through life. A culture without value can be used to justify anything. For example, during the 1980s and 1990s, politicians who were not in power attempted to take an "innovative" approach to form a platform. Some of them felt that governing does not require a high degree of sophistication, therefore, they advocated an innovation slogan: "common sense governing." Once in power, they filled the treasury with dollars (from education cuts, healthcare cuts, social welfare program cuts, etc.), then the culture has been changed to: we need "Great minds for a great future." It should also be noted that sometimes it is difficult to assess the purpose of the government. For example, the gasoline price in Canada is about 78 cents per liter, of which taxes amount to about one half of the price. Why must gasoline tax be so high? The answer is not as simple as it seems. Petroleum is a non-renewable resource. High tax serves at least two purposes, one is to discourage people from getting into the habit of driving, and the other is to use the tax collected to conserve and search for alternative fuel sources. But in reality, gasoline tax is associated with road maintenance and road building. It is understandable that road maintenance is essential, but to build more new roads is not as simple as it seems — for whose benefit? Consumers? Not necessarily, the real reason is perhaps to accommodate the increasing number of cars on the road. The car makers want to make more cars. Is it for the common good? Hard to say, more road takes more useful land away for other meaningful purposes, more cars consume more petroleum, and cause increased level of pollution. Then, whose benefit will it be for?

Humans do not live alone. As a social animal, we live in a cultural bond society, but we rely greatly on self-judgement, behavior and action which make our culture work both for self-interest and for the common good. Negative culture can lead to unexpected and negative impact on the common good. For example, the development of not-for-profit organizations is all for the common good, but once an individual's desire for personal financial incentive overwhelms the purpose to help those who cannot help themselves, it can tarnish the good name of the organization, and individuals involved can be persecuted for fraud and dishonesty.

We need food to survive, and real economic profit to support business well-being and sustain its real growth. But it is the "value" that has enriched our souls, and welded our culture as creative and innovative individuals. Thus, organizational purpose is strengthened and every individual is part of the welding process. Although there are differences exhibited in our behavior, in business conduct or in simple interactions with others, we are all fundamentally driven by our values and living in a big box called the market system. We use our brain power and labor to make different combinations of things and our collective wisdom to offer goods and/or services in exchange for things/services to satisfy individual's needs and wants, but all within the framework of a single value. As Smith says: "Give me that which I want and you shall have this which you want."

Unfortunately, we collectively (and/or individually) seem to be more concerned with "Give me that which I want," and less or not concerned for "you shall have this which you want" thus resulting in unfortunate consequences to others. Throughout human history, we have been continuously taking from nature, and asking nature "Give me that which I want." The silent nature remains (as always) silent, and we take it as "silent consent." We have rarely asked nature: what can we give you which you want? We do the same thing to people. If without a labor union, people will "Give me that which I want," and not give back to others "you shall have this which you want." Even in cases where "people" are not in the position to make decisions for themselves (for some, yes, but not completely), we will take "which I want" and only give back what we *think* is "which you want."

Smith's give-and-take idea is over 200 years old, yet we still do not benefit from this simple value system in our market economy and learn how to take care of people and silent partners and give them what they want?

6.6 Functional Value

Supply and *demand* from economists and debit (*Dr.*) and credit (*Cr.*), from accountants — these are four little words that make the world go around. Supply and demand make one set of functional values, while supply and demand govern all market activities, as these activities all have to be transformed in the language of money. Dr. and Cr. will then speak for these

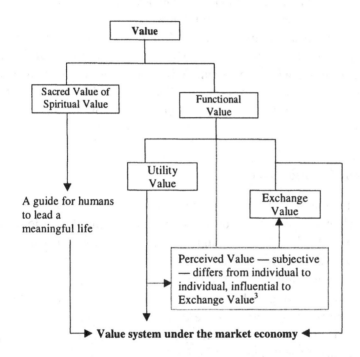

Figure 6.2 The notion of value.

[On 18 September 2001, stock value on the New York Stock Exchange trading lost 687 points, i.e. the single highest loss in one day amounting to trillions of dollars. This does not mean the companies listed and traded in the Exchange lost their assets, revenue or profits, rather the traders perceived a change of value, and the price of stock crumbled. On the other hand, suppose there is one piece of good news, such as Bin Laden had been surrounded and the Al-Qaeda completely destroyed. The price of stock will then be pushed upwards.

transactions and account for who are winners and who are losers. As our history tells us, we have done well, but there are losers who have no idea how to account for their losses, because they are silent suppliers. They silently let us dig into their hearts, scrape their skin, and put them to death (to the animals and other living things in the rainforest) without giving them a trial in a civilized way; sometimes we simply destroy them. They are unable to negotiate or tell us how to recoup their loss, instead they silently bleed until the end when they cannot supply and give us what we want anymore, because we do not know how to account for what they supply and appreciate their "value." If Smith were still alive today, would he be saying to us: "I told you so, '*Give me that which what I want and you shall have this which you want.*' Why don't you give what they want?" Maybe we will tell Smith: "Sorry, we don't know what you want, besides, even if we know what you want, we don't know how to account for what you want."

Questions for discussion

1. "Give me that which I want and you shall have this which you want," is a simple expression given by Adam Smith as a simple wisdom we must all share. Apply Smith's thought to: (a) Free trade and (b) Fair trade. How would you differentiate free trade from fair trade?
2. We live in a cultural bond society, but we rely greatly on value to "self-judge" our thinking, behavior and action which make our culture work both for self-interest and for the common good. How does this cultural bond society work in the market economy where individuals are indoctrinated for "maximization?"
3. Punjabi cultural values are similar to the values of Chinese origin (as listed in Table 6.1), including guidance by long term, sustainable growth and personal pursuit of contentment and adequacy, respect of tradition value family as the highest priority, think of welfare of the community as ultimate good, and among other things, trust among community Explain why.
4. From the viewpoint of decision-making, harmony (chowa) is a firs choice and the virtue of the constant mean must be sought. Based or

your personal experiences, provide situations when decisions had to be made, where harmony was the first choice, and the virtue of the constant mean had to be part of your decision? Explain.

5. What are entrepreneurial attributes? Entrepreneurial culture? How is it possible to develop attributes concurrently with the fostering of the cultural environment in corporate entities?

6. Should a corporation have its own values, how can such values be shared by those working in the organization. Bear in mind, values need not involve substance.

Chapter 7

Cost, Economic Cost and the Notion of Residual

> *Man's capacity for tremendous evil is understandable, but so is his capacity for goodness. "We need to be deeply humble and acknowledge there is in us the possibility of the most enormous cruelty. But the Truth and Reconciliation Commission demonstrated another kind of truth... that we have the most exultant capacity for goodness."*
>
> Archbishop Desmond Tutu
> 14 June 2000, Toronto, Canada

7.1 The Meaning of "Cost"

Cost is a word that, much as with profit, is commonly used in human interactions. Although we normally associate cost with matters that involve transactions under the market economy, cost is not merely an expression of monetary payment. In a more general sense, it represents "suffering" (Webster's Dictionary) and "sacrifice" (Oxford Dictionary) by the party that gives a payment, whether it be money or something of personal value, such as feelings, love, freedom and in the extreme cases, life.

7.1.1 "Cost" as sacrifice

Early in the year 2000, the Vietnamese court sentenced a Canadian woman to the firing squad for a drug trafficking charge (see Chapter 4). But according to Canadian police authorities involved in the investigation, the crime had never been established beyond reasonable doubt. She was executed nevertheless. The execution is an example of the extreme cost being paid. Was the cost of her life worthwhile? The Vietnamese would claim that for justice to be done, the criminal must pay. Yet surely it is injustice to take away a human life for a crime yet to be proven beyond reasonable doubt?

The World Bank is withholding support from India unless it makes progress in privatizing water. Tribals can no longer draw water from an ancient tank in Maharashtra because it is now exclusively used by Coca Cola, who can pay more.

James Bruges,
The Little Earth Book, 2nd edition

What matters here is that the World Bank is concerned only with "privatizing essential services and opening them to foreign companies." The unfortunate thing is it seems neither the World Bank nor the Government of India has any concern for the sacrifice or economic cost associated with the privatization that directly compromises tribals' right for drinking water.

Cost is a sacrifice; indeed, we can consider its broadest definition — that cost embraces all forms of sacrifice. The conventional cost used to measure sacrifices is revenue earned or lost, and therefore profit is only part of cost recognition. Despite having achieved some remarkable technological advancement, we are still unable to account for all the sacrifices made to achieve those advancements, and in particular, non-human costs rendered to serve human interest as well as the usual unquantified human costs.

7.1.2 Different cost for different purposes

Cost and costing are complicated concepts, which most of us address only as we require. However, it is also true that, perhaps because we think about them so little, when the need to address the issues comes, to meaningfully interpret the meanings of cost can be quite frustrating. The following is a collection of cost descriptions, their meanings and applications.

Table 7.1 Different costs for different purposes, all in the name of serving human needs.

Description	Purpose	Cost determination
1. Product	Determines product value. For pricing, planning, control etc.	Inventory cost, manufacturing cost, shop cost, etc.
2. Period, expired and unexpired (for future use)	Costing economic activities over a time period	Period cost, such as monthly rent payment
3. Fixed versus variable	For planning and control on the basis of behavior	Fixed cost — within a certain production period or volume range. Variable costs change with volume, for example
4. Programmed versus committed	Some expenditures are attached to programmes, for a given period, while others are management commitments, binding and unchangeable once a commitment is made	Advertising, or R&D are normally programmed, while costs associated with contractual agreement are viewed as committed
5. Functional	Recognizing cost associated with business operational functions	Commercial cost, agency cost, administrative cost, financial cost etc.
6. Controllable versus uncontrollable	Cost control to ensure spending is within predetermined objectives and within the planned allowance versus spending to achieve a goal, no matter what the cost	Management influenced costs versus unmanageable costs
7. Legal or statutory statutory obligations	Lawsuits involving possible liability, following unfavorable court judgements	Contingent cost

Table 7.1 (*Continued*)

Description	Purpose	Cost determination
8.Cost of product or service responsibility	Honoring product/service to consumers	Based on the extent of commitment to product or service as a contingency for possible future claims
9. Cost of lost opportunity	A cost of choosing a single option from amongst a group of options	Opportunity cost
10. Due payment for ecosystem service	Recognizing ecosystem service for human welfare	Environmental cost or cost for ecosystem service
11. Cost for unrecognized human sacrifices	Recognition for human efforts not compensated for or recognized in the normal systems	Based on human effort, value driven contribution

The above is a partial listing, illustrating the complicated nature of cost and costing. Among listed descriptions in the above table, Nos. 1 to 8 are cost items verifiable in their monetary expressions. No. 9, the opportunity cost, can at times be measured and verified much the same as other costs. It is Nos. 10, 11 and 12 that need judgement. Some costs categorized under these items can be objectively measured and verified once payments are incurred. All things are bearing cost, and can be accounted for, if people want it to be so. For example, what is the cost of a life? The insurance companies could tell you. And now, it seems that not only can we cost life, but we can own it too. The rapid advance in biotechnology has led to the patenting of genes identified for a variety of purposes, and even the patenting of genes for which no purpose is yet known. This is a dangerous precedent — no one can claim to have created anything new, and in fact if the purpose is not yet known, they cannot claim to have increased our ability to utilize it.

Sometimes, we can give costs to what was once free. Water has been and always will be a *natural* resource, available to everyone. In many places in the world, we dump our wastes, both human and industrial willy-nilly into the very water we have always relied on for drinking. Now, extensive processing is often required to keep the water potable, and of course humans control access to that resource. In fact, the water processed by our taxes is often not clean enough, at least for our wealthier citizens, and so we will pay for "pure spring water" bottled and imported from other areas! What else may become a business opportunity? Soon we may be paying for clean air (some of us already do in Tokyo). So who knows? Gradually all aspects of the ecosystem may be priced merchandise. Should this day come, we predict that there will be two classes of people, those who can afford clean air, and those who cannot. Those who can will be in the hands of the market economy. Those who cannot will be in the hands of God.

As extreme as this scenario may seem, it does illustrate a very important point, namely that we take for granted that which is most valuable, and assume that there is no cost because it seems to be an inexhaustible resource. But when it becomes finite it becomes valuable not just in reality but in man's perception, and then we begin to pay for it. Eventually, we shall have to make the effort to sustain the resources that are so vital to our continued existence. But for now, recognizing and costing the contribution from the natural world, is the first step in the right direction.

7.1.3 The complicated nature of cost

Cost is a sacrifice but it must also be a benefit, otherwise it is not cost but waste. For whose benefit? And how should we disclose these costs and make useful judgements about value, both to the individual and to society? These are challenging issues. In the Western tradition, we have been guided by accounting professionals, expressing everything in monetary terms. Yet for some sacrifices we have never been able to assign a true monetary value. One problem of course is that value is very much a matter of perspective. How much is the color of a flower worth to a man who is blind? How much is the love of a man worth to a woman who does not return it? Although the poets give both flowers and love inestimable value, in these two instances, one could argue that they are worthless. Yet in our money-driven society, we nevertheless attempt to give everything a monetary cost. For example, the U.S. courts recently awarded US$145 billion to the families of victims from smoking, for damages caused to them by the tobacco industry. Surely, there were no sure methods available to determine this figure, yet it was done, and in the eyes of the U.S. justice system at least, it was a fair rendering of value.

Throughout this chapter, the issue of opportunity cost will be frequently referred to. All resources under our disposal can have their alternative uses. All our economic activities involve weighing alternatives. The concept of value and value added is invalid unless we realise the impact of opportunity cost on the economy, on people and on the environment. We will begin with an attempt to explore how the opportunity cost concept relates to the cost of our Western style democracy.

7.1.4 The cost of democracy

A report on the spending habits of members of the Ontario provincial parliament (MPP's) revealed extravagance which is totally alien to the average working person, but is likely to be all too familiar to government officials around the world[1]:

- Liberal MPP Dominic Agostino (Hamilton East) spent $23,364 on long-distance telephone calls for the fiscal year ending 31 March 2000.[2] He spent $14,651 for accommodation on days spent at parliament.

---

[1]Theresa Boyle, *Toronto Star*, 15 June 2000, p. A10. All figures are quoted in Canadian dollars.

[2]As a point of comparison, Bell Canada and other competitors offers a rate of 10 cents per minute and $25.00 maximum charge per month for unlimited personal telephone calls to any part of Canada and the U.S., and unlimited use of the Internet with Bell for the sum of $22.95 per month. Moreover, if MPPs decide to phone their constituency after hours, it will cost them at most $0.01 per minute. It should be noted that the cost of business calls is significantly higher, however the point of the report was that the extravagance of a few MPP's was unlikely to be exclusively for fulfilling their role as government officials.

Hamilton is at most a 90-minute drive away from the parliament buildings.

- The Liberal MPP (from Windsor West) attributed $17,389 to long-distance telephone calls on government business.
- Conservative MPP Bill Murdoch (Bruce-Grey) billed $12,732 for travel in his riding.
- New Democratic Party leader Howard Hampton spent $102,386 in travel and accommodation costs and another $258,542 in office and support staff costs.

In the same report, Howard Hampton was quoted as saying that: "Premier Mike Harris and other cabinet ministers can hide many expenses in their ministerial budgets, which are not made public." Harris' expenses, for example, do not show any trips to his North Bay riding. The report also disclosed a sum of $27.1 million on MPPs' expense accounts. Are these MPP's over-spending? It is certainly not our place to say that they are — such a judgement would require more knowledge than these authors have. However, what is undoubtedly true is that a close comparison of all MPP's expenses would reveal serious discrepancies in some charges compared to others. While some of that is no doubt justified, at least some will be due to gross mismanagement or over-spending. It is not a condemnation of Ontario in particular, it is just a fact of life.

Incidentally, coincident to this report, outside of the Ontario Legislature, well over a thousand ordinary people were protesting against poverty, and were involved in a violent confrontation with the police, resulting in 29 injuries. Just this year, it was reported that 15.5% of Canadian children live in poverty. Certainly there is no excuse for this, but there are always reasons, whether we agree with them or not. In a manner of speaking, the reasons are related to cost. In order to allow for reasonable operation of government, any system must rely at least to some extent on the honesty, integrity and responsibility of the persons involved. Too much regulation, too much overseeing, too little security means a government that is unable to function. On the other hand, too little regulation and government officials are too sure that they can "get away with it," thus leading to rampant corruption. The correct question is not to ask if "corruption" is acceptable but rather, what level of corruption is acceptable to allow our government to operate? In other words, what is the cost of government? Ultimately, until everyone has a decent living standard, the answer must always be that one of the costs of government is poverty. However there are different ways of looking at it. Here are three, in decreasing order of abstraction:

(1) The cost of democracy may not be easily expressed in monetary terms, nor quantified, but must be paid to maintain a free society.

(2) The cost to the citizens to pay their legally elected government representatives is possible to quantify, and often can be expressed in monetary terms, for example, the cost of seven deaths in a recent water contamination scandal (the privatization of essential services to the public is a policy decision).

(3) The cost of supporting the extravagant spending of a privileged group is quantifiable, and can be expressed in monetary terms.

Most of us would view (1) and (2) as acceptable, and the costs well worth paying for. On the other hand, (3) would generally be viewed as unacceptable. Yet the three of them are inextricably tied together. Under the umbrella of the macro economy, the expenditure incurred in paying the MPPs' telephone charges, travelling and accommodations are costs of democracy, and costs of having elected representatives to speak on behalf of people, even if some of those MPP's may misuse those privileges. Using what we have learnt from accounting, to recognize the fact of MPPs' spending requires at least three inter-related sets of entries.

Entry set one: At the time the democratic process occurred
Dr. Democracy $258,542
Cr. Tax payers' tax assessment $258,542

Entry set two: At the time taxpayers paid their taxes
Dr. Tax payers tax assessment $258,542
Cr. Cash receipt $258,542

Entry set three: At the time MPPs spent taxpayers' money
Dr. MPPs expenditures $258,542
Cr. Cash payout $258,542

The above constitutes what we normally consider to be "cost" incurred and paid for a consideration. It was one payment, the payment to MPPs telephone charges, but there were three sets of accounting, with each set a consideration. The consideration of taxpayers is fulfilling their obligations as citizens of Canada; the consideration for MPPs is receiving telephones service rendered by the telephone company and the third is the consideration for democracy. It is the consideration for democracy that is of fundamental importance, and the purpose of these transactions. Nevertheless, the cost of Democracy cannot be measured in the same way as recorded in the two other transactions.

In fact, it could be argued that not only is the cost of democracy poorly measured, the aim of democracy is unclear. Every four years, cities around the world vie for the "honor" of hosting the Olympics. Despite recent scandals about bribes and kickbacks to International Olympic Committee members, in 2001 five chosen cities spared no expense to show that their city was worthy of the honor. As most of us know, Beijing has been chosen to host the 2008 Olympics. But what is the cost? The cost of the bid is measured directly, and the cost of the games themselves as well. But the benefits are intangible (city reputation, increased tourism, a shiny set of new sports stadiums) and the detriments are equally difficult to measure (reduced spending on the poor, cost to the environment). How many of our city fathers even have an idea of the cost? What are they really interested in? Creating and running a city for all, or the glory for themselves?

7.1.5 Opportunity cost and the cost of democracy

As mentioned in the previous section, the cost of democracy is extremely difficult to measure. A simple record of expenditure does not explain it. Indeed, "cost of democracy" is an expression that is hardly ever used, but we are all aware that democracy does not drop from the sky. It requires sacrifice and commitment, and many times throughout history — pain, suffering and human lives as well. In ancient Greece, the 13 American Colonies, all across 19th century Europe, and in every continent in the past 100 years, the search for democratic freedom has seen the use of force to overthrow dictatorships at all costs. The question is, can we account for all these costs? Should we cost them in terms of the lost human lives, destruction and prolonged suffering of human beings? Perhaps we could and should, but it would be too difficult. If we were to account for any of these sacrifices, we would have to account for subjective values, even if they can be substantiated by facts. However, one should bear in mind that it is certainly possible that clear evidence for the cost of democracy can be accounted for.

Billions of dollars of financial aid have been supplied by the U.S., other countries and the International Monetary Fund to support Russian democracy and prevent the country from going back to Communism. Let's assume the U.S. Congress has authorized aid to Russia in the amount of US$1 billon, to be used for the installation of a market economy under the democratic system. Then the accounting entry would be:

Dr. Preservation of Russian's Democracy	$1,000,000,000
Cr. Federal Reserve Bank	$1,000,000,000

This is of course not an entry into reality, this is how it should be reflected for the sacrifice made by taxpayers in the U.S. for the preservation of democracy on a worldwide basis.

If democracy is for the good of people in Canada, the U.S., Russia and all around the world, then there must be another set of entries to quantify the Ontario MPPs' spending. The entry should be:

Dr. Common Good	$258,542
Cr. Democracy	$258,542

For the U.S. support for the preservation of Russian's democracy, an entry may be amortized on the basis of probability. Let us assume a straight-line method is used. World democracy will be charged at US$200 million annually:

Year 1 to year 10, an entry of equal amount to be made annually:	
Dr. Global Democracy	$200,000,000
Cr. Preservation of Russian's Democracy	$200,000,000

However, this is not the end. Global Democracy has to be measured by the result, then, there should be another entry to record the result generated. The question is how do we measure it? GDP, GNP, crime rate, employment, healthcare, fiscal responsibility, reduction of corruption, sustainable economic growth, among other things, peace on earth and prosperity to everyone.

In addition to the above, we have also countless human suffering, unaccounted for in the analysis of the impact of policy measures. The UN Security Council military and economic sanctions against Iraq are a case in point.[3] The sanctions were imposed some ten years ago, to curb Saddam Hussein's aggressive policies, but have done little to change Hussein's mind; it is the people in Iraq who pay the price, and in particular, the children. A UNICEF report last year, conducted with the help of the Iraqi government, estimated 500,000 children under the age of five, died between 1991 and 1999.[4] How should we account for the cost of the consequences of UN sanctions?

Why is it that the person most responsible for the cost, should remain untouched by all this, while the innocents suffer and sacrifice their lives for a "cause" they do not yet even understand? Upon examining such a case, it is certainly understandable that some of us would want to throw up our hands in despair, and ask how could anyone ever cost all the human factors in such a complex situation. And yet such is the value in succeeding even in part, that many attempts have been made. As noted earlier, at the macro scale, GNP, GDP have their own contributions to measure a nation's economic growth based on accounting information, and subject to compliance with accounting conventions, and consistent with how economic activities are measured at the micro scale, though of course they cannot account for the cost of democracy and the human factors described here.

---

[3]In December 1996. The UN implemented the oil-for-food program, which allows Iraq to sell oil and buy humanitarian goods. The UN supervised program which approved $10.4 billion (US) worth of goods has not stopped the sharp decline in health and living standards, as Saddam is using the money to build grand palaces and pay off military officials rather than feed his people.

[4]*Toronto Star*, p. A4, 24 June 2000.

7.2 Opportunity Cost

In the above examples, only one side of the costing issue was addressed: the direct cost as a result of the actions taken. There is of course another side to the costing issue: what happens if the allocated was used for other purposes? Authoritarian governance is deplorable, and certainly dictatorship is a word considered to be bad. At least partially because of the allure of the free market system, and because few people seem to believe in the government that can effectively regulate the broad expanse of social and economic life, democracy, American-style, is what the people want. On the other hand, a government can be a democracy in name only, whether it is from unscrupulous manipulation of the democratic process, or simply a flawed system that returns the same people to power, election after election. Dictatorship can happen in any form of governing. It is a matter of leadership style, and how the individual leader acquires decision-making rights. Even in the most democratic of countries, there are unscrupulous politicians whose policies and actions may be self-interested, wasting resources, time and money, and even their own talents which could be used to pursue opportunities of economic benefit and the common good. To illustrate the point, assume that only one half or $13.5 million of $27.1 million of Ontario MPPs' expenditure is needed to meet the necessary expenses incurred for the elected representative, the other one half or $13.5 million is excess, and could instead be used for job creation purpose. From past experiences, approximately $5000 is needed to create a job, and $25,000 to create a small enterprise. Consequently, the number of jobs that could be created is given by the following calculation:

> **Situation 1:** Assume all $13.5 million are used to create jobs directly
> $13,500,000/\$5000 = 27,000$ jobs
>
> Assume each job will add value to society including paying all necessary personal taxes:
>
> **Value added:** 10% (productivity exceeds
> earnings) of $25,000 (wages or salaries)   = $2500
>
> Personal share of contribution to all taxes
> 20% of $25,000   = $5000

Reduction of cost of public support while unemployed $10,000	=	$17,500
Total contribution of each employed or working person $17,500 × 27,000 jobs	=	$472,500,000

In other words, this simple calculation suggests that the reduction of MPP office support expenditures by 50%, and re-allocation of funds to a job creation purpose could create 27,000 jobs, resulting in an annual opportunity cost of the excess expenditures of $472,500,000. While an attractive argument, it can of course, be argued the reverse way as well. Simply telling MPPs to reduce their spending will not necessarily improve their productivity, in fact it may reduce it! Assume a loss of MPP performance through the spending reduction will result in loss of performance, loss of support staff employment and various other forms of loss as well, what would that opportunity cost be? Who knows? Newspapers tend to concentrate on what is simple and makes a good story — thus the article on MPP expenditures concentrates on the dollars spent, not on the opportunity. The point of this exercise is not to solve all the problems of government in a paragraph, but merely to illustrate that the most important losses are sometimes the losses that cannot be easily accounted for.

Determination of opportunity cost is an established practice. It is used widely in the judicial system to determine financial compensation for victims who suffered loss and/or disability caused by another party. As an example, a judgement of US$25 million was awarded to a woman who won a lawsuit against Dow Corning for producing breast implants that caused her pain and physical disability. While we are certainly not privy to the judge's reasoning, this cost was certainly more about the woman's opportunity cost than the cost of the operation itself.

A common area involving judical judgement and determination of opportunity cost is in automobile accident claims. More often than not, the capital budgeting and Net Present Value (NPV) approach are used as a guide. For example, if an auto accident caused personal injury to one party, and another party is determined to be the party who was at fault, such as in a rear end collision, the party responsible for the cause of accident and personal injury could be ordered to pay a sum based on a calculation such as follows:

Property damage (cost of the car repair)	$3000.00 (1)
Car rental during the period while the damaged car was under repair (all inclusive)	$900.00 (2)
Hospitalization medicare and physician's charge	$15,000.00 (3)
Personal injury and long term disability compensation	$3,000,000.00 (4)
Total payment	$3,015,900.00

From the traditional costing point of view, payment items (1), (2) and (3) are costs identifiable through evidence, and normal business transactions, materialized once payments are made. While payment item (4) can be an established cost incurred as the result of an accident, it is not a business transaction payment. Rather, it is based on judgement. These judgements on payment are more often than not based on total estimated earnings over a lifetime, discounted into present value. If there are no actual earnings, lawyers will argue extensively for their clients' ability to earn in the future, to influence judgement in their favor.

For better or worse, opportunity cost has become a part of life, the offspring of damages and injury lawsuits, to become one of the pillars of the North American get rich quick culture. The holy grail of independent wealth, not by personal talent or hard work, but by suing someone who is richer than yourself, or with good insurance coverage. Let a big company's truck hit you, and sue the company for a million. But first back yourself up with evidence for a backache (never mind that you've always had back problems), whiplash, blurred vision, or whatever. And emotional trauma is good too. Just claim for damages of any kind: partial disability, lost of employment opportunity, loss of memory, you name it. The insurance companies are rich, and that's what they are for, after all. It is as good as winning the lottery.

Once a question was posed to a group of MBA students in an informal discussion. "If you can't get rich like Bill Gates,[5] but want to get rich quick, which of the following four options would you choose:

---

[5]Bill Gates, CEO of the Microsoft Corporation, has a personal wealth of US$78 billion at the age of 44.

(1) Play on the quiz show "Who Wants to be a Millionaire?"
(2) Be on the panel of the TV programme: "Greed," or "The Weakest Link."
(3) Stand behind the "Wheel of Fortune," clap your hands, spin the wheel and yell out loud and clear: "Come on, big money, big money!"
(4) Let an expensive car, say, a Jaguar convertible hit you, and then sue the owner and his insurance company?

Strange as it may seem, the vast majority answered No. (4). The reason is simple: option No. (4) is much more probable and controllable.

If these situations do not apply to you, then it is easy to laugh and feel superior to those to whom it does apply. But who is doing the laughing? Most probably it is those who do have plenty — a good education, a good job, a good family background. Most probably it is the people who have "made it" (if you are reading this book, there is a good chance that compared to most people in the world, then you have made it, because you can read, and read in English). We are not trying to imply that there are not legitimate claims for all these damages, but in a land of wealth such as the U.S., where even poor people would be rich if they lived in other countries, why is everyone so concerned with getting "their due?" Is this the model on which the whole world wants to build itself?

7.2.1 Opportunity cost used in making business decisions

Opportunity cost guides people to make important decisions, typically when a decision needs to be made for a choice among options. As an example, an individual may have to choose between working for others at a regular rate of pay, or starting-up a business venture and not knowing what will be the return for his efforts. If working for others would give an annual steady income of $80,000 plus normal fringe benefits, then the opportunity cost for owning one's own business would be $80,000 plus normal fringe benefits. In fact, all business decisions use opportunity cost to some extent as a guide — "do this versus that," "pros and cons, 'weigh all the options," and "don't put all your eggs in one basket," are all expressions related to the idea of opportunity cost.

In more serious situations, opportunity cost suggests the possibility of important losses. For example, if a government is merely concerned about the balancing of budget, it would aimlessly cut essential services to people. This could include closing down schools, eliminating hospitals and cutting back environmental protection measures. The obvious long term consequences include erosion of essential education programs, marginalization of chronic care facilities and environmental damage resulting in health problems, ranging from asthma due to poor air quality to transmission of infection through contaminated drinking water, to poisoning from minerals and industrial waste polluting the soil. All of these are opportunity costs due to inappropriate government policies.

Another interesting example related to the issues of the environment and opportunity cost is a recent attempt by the U.S. military to sell obsolete warships to Taiwan, for defence, mainly with the idea of counterbalancing mainland China's interest in the South China Sea. Without going into the ethics of military spending, we can consider the pros and cons, i.e. the opportunity cost of such a deal. Selling to Taiwan has at least two counts in favor of it: one count of economic benefits related to the revenue generated, and one count of environmental friendliness, because decommissioning will require much expenditure and goes against the principle of the three R's: Repair, Recycle and Reuse. If the warships never end up firing a shot, then this would certainly be a shining example of what a good decision can do for the environment and the economy. The down side, of course, is the potential for military escalation leading to war, with all of its consequences.

7.2.2 Striking examples of opportunity cost of monetary expression

All opportunity costs should be accounted for and used to guide informed and intelligent decisions. Unfortunately, this is not always the case. There are at least two reasons for people not to do so. First, opportunity cost is often subjective, and wide adoption of the opportunity cost concept would require guarantees that costs calculated by and for different entities and in different decision-making scenarios be comparable to each other. After all, how is it possible to determine an entity's "profit," if its financial information cannot compare with others in the marketplace? Second, there is also the problem of filing income tax returns. To account for opportunity cost in the tax return would complicate the entire reporting and tax levy systems both for the government and the economic entity. However, "opportunity cost" cannot be easily dismissed. Does it surprise you to know that a 50-year-old tree, chopped down to make consumer goods, has an opportunity cost of US$194,250? Any one who has an opportunity to visit the Singapore Zoo could see for themselves, a sign hanging outside a shelter. It shows Professor T. M. Das of the University of Calcutta's calculation of the value (opportunity cost) of a 50-year-old tree:

Provide oxygen	US$31,250
Air pollution control	62,000
Soil erosion control and soil fertilization	32,250
Provide water	37,500
Shelter for animals	31,259
Total value	US$194,250
(*Source*: Singapore Zoological Gardens. *Origin*: Updated Forestry, Michigan State University.)	

The above is not complete, missing for example possible fruit for consumption, medicines for health or aesthetic value, but it is an example of the type of calculations we must consider to establish opportunity cost.

Assume a logging company chops down 400,000 50-year-old trees per annum for a period of ten years, then the total opportunity cost of the operation would be US$194,250,000,000. The effect on humanity would be:

$$\$194,250 \times 400,000 \times 10 = US\$777 \text{ billion}$$

Have CEOs of cattle raising, logging and mining companies, or even people in the tourist industry ever thought about calculating the opportunity cost before committing themselves to the operation? While this is only a crude calculation (as the true situation is much more complicated), intelligent use of the opportunity cost concept will allow us to utilize the environment much more sensibly. For example, clear-cutting of forests can result in comprehensive soil erosion and desert where there was once a vibrant ecosystem. Let's face it; we can never really pay back the cost to the environment for the impact caused by humans, because we are part of the environment, and nothing we do will change it. The real question is what is sustainable and what is not? By practising controlled deforestation, we can maintain sufficient forest and still be able to harvest over the long term (see Box 1 at the end of this chapter).

To remind you of the quote from Desmond Tutu at the beginning, humans have as much a capacity for good as evil. Unfortunately, too many of us choose to do evil rather than good, too many who would look only at the short term gain, harvesting whole forests to print up advertisements that most people do not want or read, or destroying coral reefs for the sake of tourism. On the other hand, how is it possible for an individual to determine what is evil and what is good outside of the guiding principles of the law, moral judgement and without the help of religion? There is no simple answer, but to paraphrase Adam Smith: When you get what you want from others, you need to make sure that others also get what they want from you. The only difference is, the others include all our unborn children and the world as a whole.

7.3 Costs Determination

For the purpose of costing and recording transactions, there are different cost concepts and sets of costing for different purposes. Some of these we are familiar with, and others are less so, but nevertheless they are all used in practice. The following is an example for a cost that involves disbursement, where we assume that $50,000 is allocated from the operating budget for the purpose of improving after sales service for an existing product. The expenditure could be viewed as any of the following:

(1) Product cost — product service.
(2) Fixed cost — if the amount is to be amortized over a period of time.

(3) Variable cost — if $50,000 is directly related with number of units of product produced.

(4) Commercial cost — if $50,000 is to be considered as a marketing effort, to create a new product image.

(5) Committed cost — if $50,000 is committed to a certain budget period and an agreement is signed to contract the project to an outsider.

(6) Warranty service cost — if $50,000 is designated as part of product service under product warranty.

It is much the same for an individual. A married man can be viewed as "the man of the house" making the big decisions for his family; a father to his children, providing them with guidance and a good example; a husband to his wife, providing her with love and support in everything she does; a gardener, tending to their garden, a Jack of all trades; and Mr. Fix it, mending cracking walls, repairing computers and trying to catch mice. In business, he can be the CEO, a club member or a team player in the company's squash team. And yet he is still the same man. Similarly, the $50,000 is the same fund, but it can be used for different purposes, largely determined on the basis of how the management wishes it to be used. $50,000 is a definite amount. It is verifiable and can be recorded as the same amount, no more and no less, regardless of what name it bears. It is therefore, a precise measurement for dollar spending, and it is a measurement of money spent, but it is not necessarily an expression of measurement.

Of course, the point is that outside of the measurable, objectively determined cost, it must have a classification, depending on what it is used for. There are also costs that are difficult to determine, including those that may be only in the talking stage, and those that are not talked about at all. They include opportunity cost, environmental cost and cost for unrecognized human sacrifices (see Table 7.1).

7.3.1 Opportunity cost recognition in business and in a legal context

We have seen that there is recognition of the importance of opportunity cost, by professionals, business executives and the legal profession. While it is often difficult to calculate, quantification of opportunity cost is taken seriously: in business, monetary value for the loss of opportunity has been frequently established either through negotiation or based on some conventional procedure. A typical opportunity cost recognition is when one makes a dental appointment and fails to show up for treatment, the patient will still get charged the full amount, even though there was no service performed, as simply by missing the appointment the time (opportunity) has been taken away from the dentist.

In many legal systems, there have been massive court cases involving financial compensation for economic loss that is not easily measured in dollars and cents in accordance with normal commercial transactions. Nevertheless, judges at all levels of courts are passing judgement to determine financial compensation to injured parties and victims of circumstances on a daily basis; no doubt it is because that we now have insurance for everything, with major banking institutions vying to insure us in all aspects of our lives — provided that is, we are under 50 and do not smoke![6]

7.3.2 A rational approach to opportunity cost recognition

The cost of opportunity can be determined and recognized, if it can be placed in the reference frame of sacrifice of the future. Then, the process of rational determination of opportunity cost should not be difficult. For example:

> Sam Lindsay was a computer software developer in a multinational corporation, just as the "dot.com" industries were becoming the fastest developing businesses in the new millennium. With his expertise in computer technology, he decided to enter into the fray. Going into

---

[6]On 16 July 2001 at 3:15 pm, CTV news reported that Phillip Morris had conducted a study on cigarette smoking and how it causes earlier death. The study suggests that early death for smokers is good for the economy, since earlier death would reduce Canada's healthcare cost. Accordingly, the research undertaking is supposed to respond to the claim that cigarette smoking causes cancer, therefore adds to the healthcare cost. If this is true, perhaps cigarette manufacturers and the industry as a whole should file a claim against the government for an enormous health cost saving as the result of early death of cigarette smokers.

business by himself for the first time, and with the risk of not knowing what would be the return on his efforts, he decided to take a minimum amount of salary (say $35,000) to give his venture the best chance to grow. This is sufficient for him to live comfortably, but considerably less than the $85,000 he earned while working for the multinational corporation. The difference between the two salaries of $50,000 will be his forgone income, considered to be his investment into his business. If it is to be prepared as an accounting entry, it will be:

Dr. Administrative salary	$85,000
Cr. Cash	$35,000
Cr. Share capital	$50,000

Sam Lindsay would be subject to a tax levy on the basis of $85,000 rather than actual cash remuneration of $35,000 received. Although the business is incorporated and earning its normal financial income, the business tax rate is higher than Sam's personal tax rate, so in fact he might be better off paying personal income tax.

Opportunity cost can also be determined on the basis of a comparison with similar entities and their CEO's remuneration. For example, if $150,000 would be the typical salary of a CEO with Sam's responsibilities, then this can also be regarded as an opportunity cost established on a $150,000 basis, the rationale being that Sam could continue with his old job and pay someone to manage the business for him. Then the entry would be:

Dr. Administrative salary	$150,000
Cr. Cash	$35,000
Cr. Share capital	$115,000

7.4 Environmental Cost

The topic of environmental cost is a broad one, and it is not possible to adequately cover it in the space of this book. However, it is possible to give an overview of what's available in the way of current thoughts on the matter and make progress as we proceed. For our purposes, we shall consider only the cost of environmental deterioration, the cost of the ecosystem that serves human economic activities, the cost of resources drain (part of ecosystem) and unrecognized human sacrifices.

7.4.1 A simple approach to environmental cost recognition

The recognition of environmental cost can be viewed from two directions:

(1) The cost of environmental deterioration prevention — pro-active measures
(2) The cost of environmental deterioration recovery — reactive measures

Although these costs are not normally seen as part of the commitment and/or are not disclosed in financial information, they do nevertheless involve disbursement. Once disbursement is recognized, then from the traditional costing point of view, there is no problem, as all disbursements are measurable. What is of more concern, is the damage that is unnoticed, unrecognized or unattended. All automakers in every part of the world at least pay lip service to the issues of environmental health, the drain of non-renewable resources and other environmental care issues, and may even have worked closely with environmental care needs as part of their mission statement. However, it is without exception that all automakers promote their products, set sales quotas and act as if the only thing that matters is having more cars on the road. Politicians, and then the government echo the automakers' concern for satisfying consumer needs and jobs, and build more roads to accommodate more vehicles (including luxury cars and mini-vans), and do almost nothing to promote and improve public transport. Perhaps our automakers and the government do not tell lies, when they talk about their concern for the environment, but they also do not reveal the whole truth. It is only their concern after corporate profit has been satisfied, and the government has done what it needs to get re-elected. Then the environment comes first, no question!

Pro-active, the cost of prevention of environmental deterioration

The prevention of environmental deterioration or pro-active measures has been in full swing in Europe for quite some time, however other areas in the world are lagging quite far behind. While it may be that Europeans are simply more environmentally sensitive people, we suspect it may simply be that Europe, heavily populated and industrialized, is simply a vision into the future of other regions, where care for the environment must follow, because otherwise the place would be unliveable. Nevertheless, regulations in Europe, compared with much of the Third World are extremely strict, and some corporations would have to drastically change their operations to comply. They do so by simply moving their factories to developing countries desperately in need of foreign money, technology and industry. These countries have little regard for their environment and are more than willing to take what the developed nations reject. Environmental activists would like very much to levy industries with an environment tax, and use the funds generated from the taxation to sustain environment health. On the other hand, corporations can also initiate their own environmental care programs, as some have already done, making contributions to promote environmental health. One example is the recent proliferation of "fair trade" companies, selling foodstuffs such as bananas, coffee or tea, typically bought at extremely low prices from developing countries. These companies pledge to give decent returns to the farm workers, and promote environmentally sensitive agricultural practices. It is surprising how little extra this costs by the time the products reach the supermarket (as little as 10% to 20%), an indication of just how little of the cost of food goes towards the primary producer! In general, costs of this nature are not difficult to assess, because they are costs incurred in substance and measurable in dollars and cents. One scenario would involve a simple allocation of resources designated for environmental care. In the traditional accounting format, it would be the creation of a "Reserve for environmental care" either from net financial income or non-distributed surplus. There is no need to involve cash disbursement at the time when the reserve is created, but the reserve can be saved for environmental research, conservation programs and health improvement projects.

Re-active measures, include cost of damage control, response to the government actions and/or the pressure applied by environment conservation activists

The re-active measures taken by economic entities or individuals include government fines and penalties for environmental protection, pursuit of legal action, societal pressure and illegal "terrorist" activities of environmental groups. Environmental costs as a result of reactive measures involve disbursement, including cost incurred as fines are paid, cost incurred for repair of environmental damage and compensation to victims of industrial accident and long term exposure to toxins. This includes incidents such as the disaster at the Union Carbide plant in Bhopal, India. However, Union Carbide did not devote the cost to the victims of the accident, rather it liquidated the operation, giving cash to shareholders in a one-time lump sum of dividends instead.

7.4.2 The cost of an ecosystem

An ecosystem is essentially a self-contained community, consisting of a variety of organisms co-existing in an environment, promoting and sustaining life through the flow of energy, materials and information, and existing and surviving as a unit. We can apply these principles to a human "ecosystem," where human activities are in sustained co-existence with nature, to produce goods and services for human welfare. This is a level of cost above environmental cost, because it includes not just the cost to elements of nature, or to a few individuals, but to all of us as a whole. Without accepting this co-existence and working within its boundaries, we can for a short time survive and even prosper, but in the long term, we cannot survive without changing our ways or our expectations for living standards. According to a panel of 12 participating expert organizations, there are 17 identifiable essential services (goods along with ecosystem services):

(1) gas regulation
(2) climate regulation
(3) disturbance regulation
(4) water regulation
(5) water supply
(6) erosion control and sediment retention
(7) soil formation
(8) nutrient cycling
(9) waste treatment
(10) pollination

(11) biological control
(12) refugia
(13) food production
(14) raw materials
(15) genetic resources
(16) recreation
(17) cultural

In total, these 17 services and goods along with the services contribute a total value in the range of US$16–54 trillion, mostly outside of market value and our market economy. Imagine, US$35 trillion as an average, compared to a global GNP of US$18 trillion, is a deficit of US$17 trillion on average. Where is our "Profit?" If this sounds unreal, a simple example can push the point home (Costanza *et al.*, 1997).

Canada is known for its maple trees and the "sugar maple" sap which produces maple syrup. Farmers take the sap for commercial purposes, and maple syrup commands a high price, so to the farmer it is a very "profitable" undertaking. However, if the farmer takes all the sap out of the tree, the tree will die, and there is nothing one can do to revive the tree. Similarly, our ecosystem also has a limited capacity. We can tap into it, but if we destroy it then there is nothing left. The ironic part of costing the eco-system is that most of the services are not marketable as private property in the marketplace, and the economic value assigned to input for production and through supply and demand routines does not apply (for example, "climate regulation" and "water supply"). Although drinking water has a price tag these days, in Canada while petroleum is priced at its highest in recent years at 82 cents a liter, drinking water can be priced as high as $3.50 per liter at a festival, or $1.50 per liter sold in refreshment stands. The same situation, with bottled water commanding a higher price than petroleum, can be found in many other countries around the globe. Still there is no pricing mechanism for the natural water supply; there is a price tag on water only if it is commercialized. Regardless of our technological achievements, breakthroughs in science and accomplishment in all areas of humanity, to deal with the environment, ecosystems and issues relating to life support are still very much in a period of incubation. There are ideas and efforts but none of them touches the fundamental ideas which we have to incorporate in order to understand and incorporate these costs. They are two ideas we have touched on before: (1) Man's capacity for tremendous evil and exultant good, and (2) Adam Smith's concepts of making sure that when you take from others, others also get what they want from you. Both these concepts are in us by virtue of our natures, and really involve the basic issues of self-interest and the common good. In China, some 2000 years ago, Mencius held that: "man (and woman) were caring, good and kind in nature," but only the surrounding circumstances induced and turned them to be creatures of evil. A contemporary Taoist felt differently. He said: "Man is born with an evil character born from self-interest. Only education, discipline and punishment will help him to appreciate decency, the meaning of the common good and how to be an individual of quality." (These are translations made by the senior author directly from old Chinese literature.) In the study of human behavior, there are schools of thought categorizing man in types of X and Y, later Z. Type Y resembles Mencius' idea of "Caring," and type X resembles Troncius' idea. Type Z theory on the other hand, recognizes all individuals can be good as well as evil, and in fact, there is more good than evil. Therefore, what is needed is awareness, caring, understanding and appreciation, along with education and appropriate systems for development and capacity for growth.

Perhaps we can come to the realization that we, like the farmer taking maple syrup, must tap from the earth, but not let it bleed to death. How do the farmers do it? It is a complicated matter, but there are simple solutions. It is nothing more or less than the farmers' creative and/or innovative farming skills and "know-how" based on experience to create wealth for self-interest, and "add value," through sensible practice that benefits the trees and society.

7.6 Environmental Accounting

If accounting is the language of business, environmental accounting can simply be referred to as the language of the ecosystem. It refers to a systematic collecting, assembling, summarizing and interpreting of services provided by the ecosystem, including the materials flow, the flow of energy and any relevant information from natural capital stock (inventory). While accounting is limited to examination of the business entity, environmental accounting has no limit, not even the sky, because the sky is a part of its "costing" and "accounting" involvement.

Naturally, environmental accounting is a great challenge both for system development and system utilization. Like many great things, it may not happen in our lifetime, but if it does it will be a great thing. We recall the voyage of Apollo 11, when Neil Armstrong became the first man to land on the moon, and he said the famous words: "That's one small step for man, one giant leap for Mankind." Here we also make a small step, in the hopes that it will also become a giant leap.

The idea of environmental accounting is based on what is required in accounting practice. Accounting reduces everything to a single denominator, a common expression, that creates uniformity. Then it can be manipulated to serve the business manager for making decisions, and to compare the figures with other available data that relate to business operations. In the case of environment accounting, services provided by the ecosystem cannot be equated with one another. For example, how do we equate soil formation with climate regulation? How much is nutrient cycling worth and can we measure it quantitatively to write regulations and set dollar amounts for services provided by water supply to account for erosion control and sediment retention? It is extremely difficult, if not impossible, to aggregate ecosystem services, perhaps even more difficult than having men land on the moon's surface. However, we simply cannot ignore the reality that we have short-changed our ecosystem, and the cost of environmental service to human welfare must be accounted for.

In the 1970s, British Steel began a campaign with the phrase, "putting something back," a campaign designed to combat the disastrous closures of heavy industry in Britain at the time. This campaign centered on putting something back into the communities, creating new jobs and new businesses. It became a new business in itself, and here we also want to "put something back" but this time not just to the workers, not just to the people, but to the environment as a whole. In business, there has always been a never-ending challenge to create, recognize and measure the worth of "goodwill." The truth of the matter is that goodwill has never had real substance because no price is paid for it, and so no dollar value is assigned. Yet value always has been assigned, and cost attached to it, because it is important. Why not then, the cost of ecosystem services? The easiest thing to do in environmental accounting is perhaps to first create an account entitled: Reserve for the return of ecosystem services with the amount of $1.00 (a symbolic amount for recognition) with an entry into the books of account:

Dr. Retained earnings (or financial income)	$1.00
Cr. Reserve for the return of ecosystem services	$1.00

The next step is to delete the notion of profit and replace it with "residual income," a concept developed in the 1960s for the purposes of recognizing capital contribution to an economic entity. This will be addressed in the next section.

7.7 The Notion of Residual

The development of the residual income concept is the result of the need to recognize "opportunity cost" for capital investment. It is a direct descendent of the distribution theory of production that specifies that all contributions to production deserve their share of "entitlement," including interest on the borrowing capital, rent for the landlord, wages for labor (including management) and capital charge for capital investment.

To our knowledge, the concept of the residual came to the academic world for the first time in the early 1960s, and was related directly with capital charge (*a business practice: to recognize capital contribution is a form of cost. A percentage based mostly on market interest rate as an opportunity cost charged against capital, for example, if a company's capital is $10,000,000, market interest rate is 6%, the capital charge under the circumstance will be $600,000, see also Illustration 1 below*). Once capital charge is levied against corporate financial income, it would make the earnings of a corporation more in accord with the economist's idea of profit. Since a corporation is considered to be an entity, any contribution made to another party would have to be recognized before a corporate profit can be derived. However, the origin of levying a capital charge was not commonly used against corporate financial income, but it was used to deal with corporate investment earning problems in its subsidiaries or profit centers. This was outlined in John Dearden's article "Problems in decentralized profit responsibility."[7] The key concept is that a division must bear the cost of corporate capital (minimum opportunity cost) invested in the division. Put into an accounting format, it would appear, for example, as this illustration:

Illustration 1	
Financial income before income tax	
(use traditional method)	$10,000,000
Income tax (assume to be 46%)	4,600,000
Financial income after income tax	5,400,000
Less: Capital charge (based on 5%	
market interest rate of $30,000,000)	1,500,000
Operating residual	$3,900,000

Note the above illustration recognizes capital contribution to be the same as other contributions such as labor, materials and among other things, money suppliers (such as bank interest on loan). In the traditional view, capital contributors are shareholders and entitled to earn dividends of profit earned. Under the residual concept, capital contributors must first earn their opportunity cost (if they do not invest in the entity, they will deposit funds in the bank earning a going rate of interest of 5%).

If ecosystem services are recognized, their contribution should also be recognized in the process. Using the above $1 reserve as an example, the financial summary may be further expanded as follows:

Illustration 2	
From Illustration 1: Operating residual	$3,900,000
Reserve for return to ecosystem services	$1
Value added	$3,899,999

---

[7] *Harvard Business Review*, May–June 1960.

There are other possible formulations of environmental accounting. The most meaningful one is to create a natural capital account based on the assumption that annual capital assets need to be created based on the estimated services required to support business operations, based on the discretion of management and based on an annual ecosystem service providing for human welfare and equivalent to the sum of total GNP among all nations. It is assumed to be 20% of annual earnings (five year average) in financial income terms. Assume the entity's financial earnings over a five year average are $1,000,000, then an accounting entry can be created as:

Illustration 3	
Dr. Financial income	$1,000,000
Cr. Natural capital	$1,000,000

The natural capital account will be similar to a share capital account, with capital charges and dividends, but only accounting entries. Cash payments will be required, when the entity undertakes environmental care and conservation projects. For example, this would occur when an environment protection project is scheduled to take place and cash disbursements are made. Then the accounting entry would be:

Illustration 4	
Dr. Reserve for return for ecosystem service	$1
Dr. Natural capital (assumed to be $99,999)	$99,999
Cr. Environment care project (a liability)	$100,000

When the environment care project (as a capital project) begins its operation, a separate bank account should be created and cash transferred from the bank's general fund to an environment care project bank account

Illustration 5	
Dr. Environment care project bank account	$100,000
Cr. Cash (general operating fund)	$100,000

Cost is a complicated discipline in the body of knowledge, even more so, if "economic cost" is involved. For illustration purpose, the following is a case in point:

In 1999, four years after the "Common Sense Revolution" swept into power, Ontario's Conservative Government made it known to the public that they fulfilled its mandate of eliminating budget deficit, with a sweetener of a huge surplus that made voters vote them back to office in 1999. Unfortunately, the victory over eliminating the deficit and landing a huge surplus had not been attributed to any added wealth via entrepreneurial initiative on the part of the government; rather it was taken from healthcare (through the closure of some hospitals), the shutting down of schools, the removal of environmental care requirements, as well as the downloading of costs of social housing and public transit subsidies to municipal governments (they in turn levy high property tax to home owners). Although there was no clear information with respect to the use of surplus, one thing had been aired by the media — there will be a 34% salary increase to all MPPs. The entire scheme of "winning the war over eliminating budget deficit and surplus," may be illustrated in the following way:

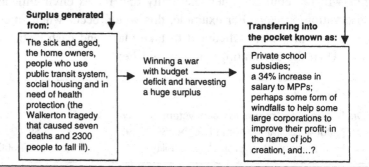

Ontario's economy has not improved; there is no reduction in the rate of unemployment (rather it is at its highest since 1992), retail sales are declining (including the closing down of the legendary Eaton's department store, now mostly taken over by Sears), there are more homeless people on the streets, the number of beggars has increased and the country is at the brink of a deep recession.[8] Workers participate in strikes to fight for an

[8]*CTV News* 11:00 pm 7 September 2001.

increase in wages, creating widespread labor unrest. Despite the strikes, most workers received only a 5% increase over this period, grossly lower than that of the MPPs. On the upward trend, however, is the crime rate and economic costs borne by people — especially the sick and aged, the home owners, and those in need of health protection; not in terms of dollars and cents but rather with regard to welfare of the people and environmental health in the province. How is it possible for the MPPs (with a few exceptions) led by the Conservatives to simply legislate for themselves a pay increase?

(See also Footnotes 9 and 10.)

Questions for discussion

1. What does gross national product or GNP (an indicator of a nation's economic well-being) measure? If the cost of the decline of environmental health and resources depletion are caused by excessive demands on the environment, why are finite resources by humans not included in the determination of the indicator?
2. What if environmental health and depletion of finite resources are not included, but are counterbalanced by the rate of innovation and creativity? Why not include them all in the calculation of costs? Should we assume that as part of economic analysis, that the entire human economic activity is working on the basis of the equation:

   Decline in environmental health + finite resources depletion
   >= total human creativity and innovation?

   Should we add human sacrifice caused by wars, conflict and casualties as the result of the desire of individuals to maximize personal wealth?
3. What is the cost of keeping a loose rein on politicians? What is the cost of peace?

---

[9]*The Globe and Mail*, 28 June 2001, pp. A1 and A7.
[10]*Toronto Star*, 1 September 2001, pp. A1 and A19.

4. Should opportunity be part of the total costs calculation? Who could determine opportunity cost? The legal system? Accountants? Economists? Or people who are victims of circumstances? (Not including those who are dead, because they cannot be included in the discussion!)

5. How should we represent the opportunity cost of declining environmental health and the drain of finite resources resulting from improper behavior in human economic activities.

6. Referring to Q.4, who should represent the unborn children for what we have taken away from them?

7. Why is the concept of residual a better device to determine how we have performed in microeconomic analysis and cost measurement?

8. Two home vegetable gardeners are engaged in a simple conversation.

> Gardener A: "My vegetables are doing really well, but the strange thing is, every year I seem to have to put more and more fertilizer on it. Mind you, I take care of my garden. I weeded out everything that doesn't belong in the garden, and kill all the harmful insects. What's wrong?
>
> Gardener B: "Yeah, I had the same problem. Every year, my vegetables require more and more of the 10/30/20 fertilizer, but effective as it is, the plants seem to need more every year. I got fed up, and two years ago, I decided not to add any. But the soil got so hard, and bore nothing but weeds. The same thing happened to our lawn. Mind you, I used the good stuff: 30/10/10. But after I stopped using it, the lawn became hard as rock, with almost nothing but weeds and scattered crab grass. You see, now I've replaced it all with these beautiful interlocking stones. From now on, no more of this nonsense. Why don't you do the same?

Have the gardeners replaced anything they have taken from the earth? Discuss!

Box 1. A Toy Model of Opportunity Cost and Sustainable Harvesting.

Consider a logging company which plans to buy a forest region of 1000 hectares. How much is the forest worth to the company? Assume that the maximum sustainable density of mature trees is 400 per hectare, with the remaining space taken by less mature trees and other flora. In a simple forest model, assume that trees reach maturity at a rate dependent on the number of existing mature trees (i.e. by natural seeding), and mature trees survive an average of 25 years if there are no other trees around (this includes all natural death processes such as disease, struck by lightening, etc.). Survival of mature trees is dependent on the number of neighboring trees around them — the more trees, the harder it is for a tree to survive, so that at maximum density, we assume mature trees on average survive only half as long. We shall assume that the company does not do any replanting. In the absence of harvesting, the number of trees in year $i + 1$ can be expressed in terms of the number of trees in the previous year i:

$$N_{i+1} = N_i + bN_i - dN_i \times \left(1 + \frac{N_i}{400}\right).$$

Here, b is the rate at which trees mature, and d is the rate at which a tree dies if there was no competition from other trees. For a forest with a sustainable density of 400 per hectare and where the lone tree would live to an average of 20 years (this implies that $d = 1/20$ per year), it is easy to show that we must have $b = 1/10$ per year (i.e. for every ten mature trees in the forest, one tree matures every year).

What is the best rate that we can harvest the trees, so that the forest recovers at the fastest possible rate? Clearly, if we "kill the goose that lays the golden egg," and take all the trees, then the forest will not recover at all, or very slowly at least, and the company would be responsible for the full opportunity cost of 400,000 trees. If we remove a percentage of the forest, then new trees will mature every year, allowing the company to harvest the forest and maintain an income every year, while maintaining a natural resource. The chart below shows that if 200,000 trees or half of the forest is harvested, then it will still produce an additional income from up to 5000 trees every year thereafter, whereas if 90% or 10% of the forest is taken, only 1800 trees will be available per year. As long as 50% density is sufficient to maintain the ecosystem (and remember that the remaining trees are probably larger and healthier because there is less competition), provide the fruit we would eat, sustain the breathable atmosphere etc., then taking the 5000 a year is "free" because it does not reduce the total number of trees below 250,000.

This is only a very simple, "toy" calculation, designed to illustrate how we can calculate opportunity cost more carefully.

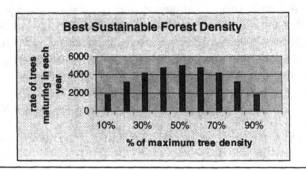

Chapter 8

People, People, People

> The following is a quote from a source unknown to the authors, but it reflects a reality in working places: how people in different levels see and feel about each other. Taken with a grain of salt, it may help brighten the day.
>
> *Life at work is like a tree full of monkeys, all on different limbs at different levels. Some monkeys are climbing up, some down and see a tree full of smiling faces. The monkeys on the bottom look up and see nothing but as... .*
>
> *(Source: circulated junk email)*

8.1 Introduction

Chapters 1 to 7 of this book were devoted mostly to the fundamentals of Entrepreneurism, and particularly how the ideology is allied to the matter of self-interest and common good. This chapter attempts to focus on people issues in human institutions. Although they are related, it will not address routine matters that involve selection, training, wages, promotion, job satisfaction, and among other things, challenges of human resources development and management, but only issues related to human value. How do we view people? As a "money-making" machine? As human capital in economic activities? Or as an agent for creativity and innovation?

8.2 The Three Perceived Views on Which People are Under Market Economy

For more than three decades, the senior author has formally or informally discussed the substance of our purpose for working, having one's own business, and/or the pursuit of knowledge. The initial response had been: to make money, and make more money. In recent years, predominantly in the blooming technologically advanced society, making money has become an obsession, as if it is the only thing that matters. However, as the discussion was carried further into the broader areas of, for example, family life, human relations and public responsibility, the subject matter, more often than not, was extended to the differences in what we perceive to be the "value," especially human value rather than the familiar conviction, money. Money is and always will be the prime drive for working, and/or having one's own business, as it commands resources, services as well as anything and everything for the satisfaction of our needs, wants and greed. Some people even believe that money can buy them a seat in heaven, if ordered in advance.

There are many thoughts and practices that can be associated directly or indirectly with human value. For our purposes, only three will be explored; to perceive and treat people as "money-making" machines in a capitalistic society, as human capital or agents for creation and innovation under Entrepreneurism. In a market economy slanted on the accumulation of private ownership society, we may find there is a mix of all three. It may be expressed as the following:

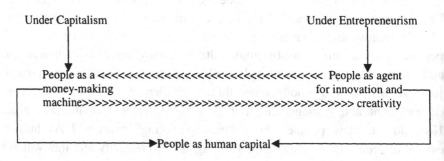

Figure 8.1 The three perceived views on what people are.

The illustration suggests the close relationships amongst the three perceptions. They have no clear separate identities, but all are viewed as human capital in any economic endeavor. A living person, be it an individual or a member of a group, is a unit of human capital, one of the three unavoidable factors of all economic activities: the natural capital, the human capital and resources available through the exchange system. Under a market economy, an individual engaged in the pursuit of making-money may progressively either be motivated by self-interest or by an influential shift to the pursuit of more creative and innovative activities to further one's needs and/or wants satisfaction. Similarly, an entrepreneur may be attracted by financial success and/or prejudiced by the power of money, consequently becoming "money-making" machine. Of course, there are a large number individuals who simply move in between the two extremes.

8.3 People as "Money-Making" Machines

Money-making model 1: the infinite craving for more

There is some truth in saying that people are perceived to be "money-making" machines. In the first place, as human capital, we are unavoidable factors in all economic activities. Under capitalism, we seem to consider, perhaps stimulated by a theme song in Cabaret, "Money, makes the world go around," everything to be a "money-making" endeavor. In our society (where reward and success are linked directly with dollars and cents), making money seems to be the only thing there is. For example, Bill Gates, is the richest man in the world at the age of 44 and is believed to have a personal wealth of US$85 billion, more than the combined total GNP of Iceland, New Zealand and Luxembourg.[1] But he still desires to have more. In the name of consumers' interest, he is practically a self-appointed government collecting tax (in the form of royalties) from every computer user in the world to further his personal wealth. Sure enough, his success in his "money-making" endeavor, is a shining example that has prompted further innovative and creative activities through others as well, thus further pushing the market economy into a fast state of growth. Unfortunately, this has not been the case. A similar situation has taken

---

[1]*ELITE*, December 1999, p. 158.

place with the automobile industry; inventions have already taken place to replace the internal combustion engine, but powerful automakers are still reluctant to consider other options. The only difference is that in the case of the auto industry, it is an oligopoly dominating a small market, whereas Microsoft is a monopoly for consumers with a craving far infinite in reality. Although Gates may be hailed as a hero in computer technology, he is nevertheless just a money-making machine.

Money-making model 2: the use of fishing tactics.
Cheat, but cheat legally

Money making model 1 illustrates how an individual can crave "money-makings", setting no limits on how much money one should and can make. Money-making model 2 attempts to demonstrate how economic entities make money by using "fishing" tactics — through advertising or other media, underpin government intervention and induce consumers to take the bait at the cost of their health and life. Consider the cigarette industry. The following is case in point:

> As it is a known and proven fact that cigarette smoking causes cancer, the government has strictly regulated tobacco industry advertising. However, this is an example how cheating takes place legally. For example, Philip Morris Inc., advertises Virginia Slims by using a total of six advertising pages portraying four young and gorgeous women in different poses, in essence, to glorify its product. The advertisement begins with the following message[2]:
>
> > 1st page: *The MYSTERIOUS POWER of my Voice ENDURES*
> >
> > (The page is emphasized with the poetry of a young beautiful black woman.)
> >
> > *VIRGINIA SLIMS REGULAR LIGHTS 100'S*

---

[2]*Ibid*, in a six-page insert between p. 182 and 183.

Then, there is one line in small print:

8 mg "tar," 0.7 mg nicotine av. Per cigarette by FTC method. The entire two pages are highlighted by a beautiful female model.

2nd and 3rd page: *MY ESSENCE GLOWS. MY HEART DANCES. My Voice SINGS*

At the bottom of the ad, a square with the following wording:

> Surgeon General's Warning: Quitting Smoking Now Greatly Reduces Serious Risks to Your Health

Further to the left, two lines read:

4th and 5th page: *THE EYES ARE THE ESSENCE OF THE SOUL, BUT THE Voice REVEALS THE SPIRIT!*

The bottom of the page contains the same message as above. But this time the two pages are highlighted with a beautiful blonde model, holding a cigarette held between two fingers.

6th page: *Virginia Slims, Find Your Voice*

A pack of Virginia Slims is displayed above the ad. This time, the page portrays women of Asian origin.

The advertisement illustrates how cigarette manufacturers view female smokers and would-be female smokers as their source of revenue, it is in fact considering females as their money-making machines completely, disregarding the fact that cigarette smoking causes cancer resulting in deaths.

On the other hand, though the cigarette industry is aware that its product is harmful to human health, it still continues to push its product on the open market for money's sake. In July 2000, a judgement was passed by the Florida District Court judge: major tobacco companies were fined US$150 billion for causing irreparable harm to cigarette smokers. In fact, are cigarette manufacturers skilfully cheating the public legally?

The senior author used the Philip Morris ad as a topic for discussion in his MBA class. One participant, mentioning that in a socialist country, people smoke cigarettes much like steam pipes blowing in every open

Table 8.1 "Fishing" tactics used in cigarette commercials.

System	"Fishing" tactics	Cigarette commercial
The right place	Finding the spot where the fish normally congregate in groups	Finding right media to match potential viewers: *The MYSTERIOUS POWER of my Voice ENDURES.*
The draw-ins	The sound, look and/or the smell, all designed to attract the fish to take the bait	The beauty, the look, the pose and the entire ad layout: *MY ESSENCE GLOWS. MY HEART DANCES. My Voice SINGS.*
The bait	The attractive lure makes it impossible for the fish not to take the bait	Alluring words, effective illustration, the viewer is drawn in step-by-step: *VIRGINIA SLIMS REGULAR LIGHTS 100'S*
Approaching the bait	What a sensation for the fish	Then: *THE EYES ARE THE ESSENCE OF THE SOUL, BUT THE Voice REVEALS THE SPIRIT*
Facing the consequences	Fish takes the bait, then struggles, and wants to be free	*Virginia Slims, Find Your Voice* Taken in by the ad, do like the lady in the ad, hold a Virginia slim in between two fingers. Then, smoking, face the consequences?

place, and there are cigarette commercials everywhere, asked: why are there no restrictions on people smoking publicly? Another person responded: "Simple, the government needs the tax revenue." And another said: "Well, if this is the case, in a capitalistic society, people cheat legally, perhaps we can also say, in some other societies, cheating also exists but the "legalized cheating" is done by the state.

8.4 People as Human Capital

8.4.1 People driven by need versus motivated by greed

All coins have two sides — the back and the front. Similarly, while people are viewed as "money-making machines" and human capital, people can also be considered as agents for creativity and innovation. Figure 8.1 illustrates that human capital is needed for innovation and creative activities, and can be viewed as a money-making machine as well. Creation, innovation and making money are driven by a need and want satisfaction, whereas innovation and creation are inner desires of an energy-driven origin — making money more likely linked with attractions of external motivations.

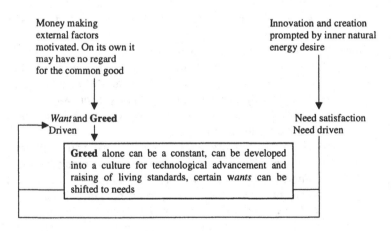

Figure 8.2 People as human capital.

8.4.2 The portrayal of human capital through tales

As one of three unavoidable factors in economic endeavors, human capital, perhaps to a lesser extent, has not been viewed fairly by those who make decisions for others. Let us imagine this conversation between a butcher and a pig. The conversation goes like this:

The butcher and the pig

Butcher: "Give me what I want and I will give you what you want."

Pig: "If I give you what you want, how do I know I will get what I want?"

Butcher: "Don't worry, you will know once I get what I want, you will know that you will get what you want. Haven't we given you what you want already, we feed you and give you shelter, at times, we even clean you?"

Pig: "Yes, you have done that, but you have done all these things because you want me to be plump and healthy, so you will kill me to feed you. You know, you will never give me what I want, because what I want from you is to let me live, but this is precisely what you can't give me."

Butcher: "Yes, you are right, but there is one consolation, we use up-to-date high technology to raise more of you. What do you think is the purpose of being a pig? So the pig generation can continue to satisfy human needs and wants."

Pig: "So you can kill more of us?"

Butcher: "Yes! Mind you, other than serving human needs what else can you do in order to make your life more meaningful? Besides, if we set pigs free in a natural environment, you will be killed by animals stronger than you anyway."

Pig: "I realize that, but at least we will be killed in a free environment, not in captivity."

Butcher: "Well, too bad, that's your problem. Have you read (or heard) what John F. Kennedy said: Our problems are man-made, therefore, they may be solved by man. No problem of human destiny is beyond human beings."

Pig: "No, I haven't read it. How could I, I am not human?"

How does the conversation between the Butcher and the pig apply to what we call the "real world?" The key idea is of course: what the butcher wants is exactly what pig does not want. Similarly, in a capitalist society such as ours, there is always a problem between those who are considered as employers, and others as employees. There seems to be an essential rift: "What you want from me is my life, and I'm not prepared to give it."

In the 1960s, farm workers in California were paid peanuts for their labor. There was no drinking water and no proper toilet facilities, and their bosses even cheated them of their meagre wages.[3] Furthermore, they had no means to claim for unfair treatment. It was only when they formed a union, were they in a position to enter into bargaining for labor relations, did matters improve. The situation then, was really no different from the pig and the butcher except in the pig–butcher tale, the butcher had to feed the pig fairly, as a skinny pig will not command a high price, thus making less or no profit.

For people in human institutions (not pig pens), there should be a common goal that everyone shares. If not, the likely case would be for someone to exclaim ignorantly "thousands of people have the qualification to work on the shop floor, but relatively few have the ability to lead a major corporation,"[4] as was stated to justify the $28.4 million compensation paid to Richard Currie, CEO of Loblaws, the giant Canadian supermarket chain. We suppose that the thousands of employees must be no better than the pigs in the pig pen who just eat and do nothing. Otherwise, how was it possible for Richard Currie to be paid $24.8 million? Surely, it was the work of workers including Richard Currie (that created Loblaw's profit). Without a shop floor, how is it necessary to have a CEO and a management? The sad thing is that despite the fact that human beings have come a long way, the treatment of people as slaves is still very much visible in human institutions.

---

[3]*CNN Headline News* Saturday, 18 August 2000.
[4]Harold Pomerantz, Why should business leaders show restraint? *Toronto Star*, 24 June 2000.

The 11 September 2001 terrorist attacks in New York and Washington D.C. not only resulted in a tragic loss of human lives, it also precipitated the loss of at least 100,000 jobs in the airline industry. But not a single highly paid corporate executive has yet to accept a pay cut which could help save a few jobs. On the other hand, the CEO of a major bond-trading firm situated in the World Trade Center that lost 2/3 of its employees in the tragedy will donate a significant proportion of the firm's profits to their bereaved families. Does it take a disaster such as this to force us to consider the human factors while making profits?

Then, there are situations where human capital was treated as disposable plastic shopping bags; once used, the brightest future for them is to be used for bagging kitchen garbage. Consider the following tale:

Let's throw away that junk jacket

A retired old man, Jack, and his wife Susan live just above the poverty line. With the change in government healthcare policy, they cannot afford to buy healthcare needs, other than those available under the public healthcare plan. Unfortunately, both suffer from aging problems — the usual aches and pains — but they have managed to survive. They have a small semi-detached house, that they can sell for some cash, but Jack refuses to do so. He said: "If I am not here, this house is Susan's security." They are relatively poor, but it has gotten worse and worse as the years go by. One of the reasons for Jack and Susan's deteriorating financial situation is that of the increased taxation implemented by the city fathers, to allow for their own remunerations to increase progressively year after year. The taxes increase annually, but not their pension income. They cannot grow money from a tree, nor would anyone hire an old person for any work, even though they are capable of doing all sorts of odd jobs.

It was Susan's idea, to buy Lotto 649 and pray for a miracle. The jackpot is $2 million, and at times, $5 or $10 million, if the six number ticket matches the winning number, twice a week. Jack did not like the idea, because he viewed the lottery as just another way of taxing the poor, but he went along anyway.

Jack purchased two tickets every week, one on Wednesday and another on Saturday. Though it was only $2 per week, he felt the pinch greatly. One day, he decided to take the plunge and bought

$10 worth. He always kept his tickets in the inside pocket of his favorite navy blue jacket. Last Saturday, he checked the Lotto 649 winning numbers from the television. To his utmost delight, he hit the jackpot of $2 million! Jack and Susan went crazy, they checked and double-checked to see if all six numbers were really there.

Jack wanted to make sure that the winning ticket was kept in a safe place, so he put it in the inside pocket of his old navy blue jacket. Though he had no money to buy alcohol, Jack bought two bottles of Blue to celebrate anyway. Over beer, husband and wife chatted and made plans for their newfound wealth. Susan wanted to use the money to buy some new clothes for both of them. In a fit of excitement, she emptied the closet and started to throw away all their old junk. Upon sieving through the unwanted stuff, Jack picked up his navy blue jacket and looked at it. Susan said to him: "Keep it, that's your favourite." Jack said: "Ah! Who wants this, it's too old fashioned anyway." He then threw it into the bag with all the other "worthless junk."

On Sunday morning, Jack figured out that the first thing he would do was to throw away all those old clothes and give them to the needy. So he drove to a nearby collection depot and dropped off the seven bags of old clothes.

On Monday morning, Jack wanted to go to Bloor and Yonge Sts. Loto center to cash the prize. It was there that he suddenly realized that his navy blue jacket was missing. Jack then recalled throwing the jacket into the bag and dropping it off at the collection depot. He immediately went to the collection agency and begged them to locate the jacket for him. Though the people at the agency checked everywhere, his jacket was nowhere to be found.

Can the above tale be true? Fact or fiction, the moral of the story is that people not only occasionally throw away a jacket worth $2 million, they also unconsciously throw away other valuables all the time.

Do we know if the fish are happy or sad?

This tale is about goldfish in a glass bowl. A loving father bought his son a large glass fishbowl. The bowl was made of a beautiful clear lead crystal that could hold about two gallons of water. The father placed several beautiful fan tail goldfish in it; one was a red cap with a clear silvery-white body, and the other was a black lion head, with an orange-red body. The son was so happy, he looked at the goldfish and said to his father:

Son: "Dad, I love them, they are so beautiful."

Dad: "I am glad you love them, they are yours, do you know how to take care of them?"

Son: "I know, and you bet I will. Ah, Dad, do you think they are happy?"

Dad: "I am sure they are happy, look at them, they swim up and down and spread their tails like fans, some like tails of the peacock, others hanging down like drapes, some short, others long, but we call them all fan tails."

Son: "Dad, maybe they are not happy, they want to get out of the bowl."

Dad: "Bill, don't be silly, you are not a fish, how would you know if they are not happy."

Son: "But Dad, how can you be sure that they are happy, you are not a fish either."

How do we know that fish are happy in the fishbowl? How do we know that fish are not happy in the fishbowl? This is the single most important question that everyone in the executive/managerial position must ask. People working on the shop floors, software developing labs and assembly lines are individuals whose working time is more than the combined time spent on all the other activities in their life. If they are unsatisfied for any reason, it would affect their performance, in particular their ability to create and innovate. Unfortunately, people at the top of the organizational hierarchy seldom bother to interact with workers on the shop floor. Perhaps the same goes for the "fish" tale, "how would I know whether they are happy or not, I am not working on the shop floor and I am not a worker."

The tale of the lantern

The tale of the lantern is a short dialogue between a mother and her son. It is about a blind man carrying a lantern in the dark.

Son: "Mom, why does this blind man carry a lantern in the dark? He cannot see what's in front of him anyway."

Mother: "You are right, Jake, he cannot see anything in front of him, but he carries a lantern, so people can see him."

Everything is useful, it depends on how we use it. The same applies to people. People are naturally creative and innovative — we take initiative, react to situations, and can be moulded if the learning environment is present. More importantly, we cannot dispose of the person simply because we do not know how to provide a suitable environment where everyone including the person can be useful. A blind person needs to see, but also needs to be seen. Similarly, a human has needs, but also needs to be useful.

Table 8.2 Summary of tales.

The tale	The meaning	The application
The butcher and the pig	Ironically, the interest and the pig are on a course of complete conflict "want." The pig can give what the butcher wants, but the butcher cannot give what the pig wants, because once the butcher gets what he wants, there is no way he can give what the pig wants, because the pig has to be killed to satisfy the butcher's wants. The butcher will not even give the pig a decent burial.	This is more common in human institutions, where there is a clash of interests between those at the top and those on the shop floor (workers). The top may want to get the most out of those on the shop floor, but this is exactly what workers do not want the top to do. There was at least one case where the top executive of a large corporation apparently stole from the workers' pension funds.
Let's throw away that junk jacket	People often unknowingly or mistakingly, based on a momentary stimulus, believe it is alright to throw away the most valuable items in one's possession.	In human institutions, there is such a thing as human value. Unfortunately, the management of human institutions too often ignore the importance of long term human value, in particular, driven by technology and immediate success, without realizing that without people there is no technology.

Table 8.2 (*Continued*)

The tale	The meaning	The application
Do we know if the fish are happy or sad?	The fish are in a confined environment. Do we know if they are happy or sad? It is a simple question and one that is not difficult to answer. First, we need not be fish before we know if fish are happy or sad. We know very well that no fish can live in a confined environment and be happy, because they die faster than they would in nature. How is it possible for fish to be happy if their movements are restricted and their environment is controlled by others?	In human institutions, when people are confined, and feel there is no room for further advancement, they are in fact in an environment that is no different from fish in a bowl. The management of human institutions may not involve the workers themselves, but instead encompasses the need to observe the "casualties" (turnover) that occurred in the past, so as to be aware of whether people are happy in their environment or not.
The tale of the lantern	The tale is about a blind man holding a lantern in the dark; while a lantern is normally used for people in the dark to see what's ahead, a blind man can also use a lantern, not to see, but to be seen by others.	A blind man with a lantern portrays wisdom, intended to make people realize that everything has its purpose. In short, every healthy human being in this world can and should be given an opportunity to be useful and to be creative and innovative, because we are energetic, and thus naturally creative. What one needs is the presence of opportunity.

We have presented only four tales, but there are countless stories, historical facts and even current happenings that can provide a wide-ranging portrayal of wisdom. They may not necessarily occupy a significant place in formal (or even informal) writing, but they nevertheless support human beings as intelligent individuals, to live and interact among ourselves in the interest of humanity.

In this age of rapidly advancing technology, with those strong waves of "IT," dot.com, www. net, on-line, E-Com, E-Trade, "E-this and E-that", etc. invading organizations, people have been made redundant, and letting someone go has become a routine practice rather than the exception. One day, out of curiosity, the senior author visited his old organization where he was once a member of the team. He noticed that the organization had tripled in size in about eight years. The receptionist, Mary, recognized him. After the usual greetings, the conversation began:

Kao (the senior author): "Now tell me, are these people still here? Peter, George, Gal, Pat and Shirley?"

Mary: "Let me see now, Peter took the package, and left three years ago, the organization let George go, Shirley also took the package, left us and started her own business last year, I have been asked to take the package, and leave next month. Next time when you come, you may not see a human sitting here to attend you, because our management has made everything "High Tech," you know, the reception area will be closed, all you'll see is a telephone with a directory. Oh! Pat's still here, do you want to see her?"

Kao: "Better not trouble her, I have not made an appointment to see her. By the way, what is happening here? The organization is getting bigger and bigger, but there are less and less people around."

Mary: "The organization is pressured from the top to cut cost, and become computerized as far as possible. Four years ago, they had this guy from a consulting firm to design the system that was to eliminate at least 20% of salaried staff, but still retain the same or even greater efficiency. So far about 15% of salaried staff were let go. Anyway, one good point is that, the management prepared quite an attractive package that allows people leaving the organization to have some sense of security until they can resettle in a new position and a new environment... .

After a short pause, Mary continued:

...I am not sure, whether or not we are more efficient than before, one thing I know is that we get a lot of complaints: complaints about not been able to get hold of a real person, complaints about how we don't respond to inquiries the way we used to, and complaints about us making mistakes but blaming it on others."

Then, she said with a relief:

"Thank God, I still have my job."

That was the end of the conversation.

During the past three years, in North America, there have been more mergers and acquisitions than any other time; all citing reasons such as: we have to compete in the world market, have to cut costs to improve profit in order to attract investment, we will all be out of a job, if we cannot compete effectively in the marketplace. What it really means is people are disposed off like discarded junk. Most business executives do not see the value in people, until like Jack in the above tale, when a "junk navy blue jacket" is suddenly worth a fortune of $2 million.

8.4.3 Human capital versus labor cost

Interestingly enough, people, one of three fundamental factors of the production process, have never been considered as "capital." Human capital is only used by scientists, and perhaps at times, economists, but never by the accountants, nor the business executives. To them, people are expired labor cost, or expense. Therefore, fundamentally people are expenses, and replaceable. What was described in Section 8.4.2 above is no surprise. Human beings are not capital, but they are sometimes perceived as disposable, and they can be replaced at the will of high-level decision makers. Human value, in retrospect, is measured by the amount of labor cost; the lower the labor cost, the greater the value. But the value of output; part of inventory value, be it finished goods, or work in progress, are all measured in dollars and cents. Under the circumstances, labor cost is certainly not an asset, therefore human capital in businesses do not exist, at least from the point of view of accounting and accounting records. For clarification purposes, an accounting method will be used to illustrate how human capital is viewed in businesses under the market economy.

To our knowledge, the frequent acquisition of any enterprise, for profit or not for profit, involves four kinds of input:

(1) Service of people (human capital or labor)
(2) Equipment, material and anything of substance
(3) Money
(4) Ecosystem services

(1) *Services performed by a human*: In general, there are two types of services. The first type of human services normally refer to the recruitment of people as permanent or period (e.g. as a three- to five-year contract) employees, who perform their services as required. This is, in effect, what human capital refers to. Unfortunately, in reality, this is not the case, because no individual involved in serving a human institution, is being considered as "capital" or "asset." Only when a payment is made, will the recording process begin, but only as an expense. For example, when a software developer is recruited, a service contract is assumed to be valid for five years. The account may be entered as follows:

(i) At the time the software developer is employed and the contract is signed. The employer usually does not sign any contract.
(ii) At the time when the software developer is paid for his work (one half of one month), in the amount of $4000. An entry to record the effect:

Dr. Salary expense	$4000
Cr. Salary payable	$4000
Dr. Salary payable	$4000
Cr. Bank	$4000

It is clear, under the circumstances, that human capital (software developer's expertise) is not recognized, only his service rendered is expensed. If on the other hand, human capital is recognized, people are an asset to the organization.

If human capital is recognized, the recording process can be arranged as follows:

(iii) At the time contract is signed. Human capital is recognized as "Human Resource" and an investment of the company/organization (five years = $96,000 × 5 years = $480,000)

Dr. Human resource (an asset)	$480,000
Cr. Human capital	$480,000

(iv) When a payment is made for his salary (semi-monthly):

Dr. Human capital	$4000
Cr. Human resource	$4000

Repeat entries in (ii).

(2) *Service performed by ecosystem*: services received from any of the following

- gas regulation
- climate regulation
- disturbance regulation
- water regulation
- water supply
- erosion control and sediment retention
- soil formation
- nutrient cycling
- waste treatment
- pollination
- biological control
- refugia
- food production
- raw materials
- genetic resources
- recreation
- cultural

No recognition for services received above, and no recording is made for the above.

(3) *If a service is required by a computer, and a computer is purchased (including software services)*: assume to be a total of $120,000. An entry will be made

Dr. Computer (asset)	$100,000
Dr. Software (asset)	$20,000
Cr. Bank	$120,000

(4) *If a capital investment is received*: assume to be $500,000, the entry would be:

Dr. Bank	$500,000
Cr. Share capital	$500,000

While the ignorance with respect to ecosystem services has already been discussed in an earlier chapter, the general view (of business management and accounting professionals) towards human resource is clearly a bias. The whole issue has not been raised in business practices or in discussions amongst professionals. However, it would be unfair to suggest that human capital is totally ignored; in cases where a company purchases life insurance for its key executives, human capital is recognized on the basis of the insurance policy.

Why human capital has not been recognized is not known; perhaps it is because "serious" readers of financial information may raise questions about the reason for doing so, or just simply to avoid unnecessary complications.

8.5 People as the Creative and Innovative Agent

People are creative and innovative by nature, and as such will further the pursuit for something new and/or something different. In essence, the creative and innovative spirit of people in all ages can be affected by four basic influences: family, society, mass media, and by an individual's perceived need and want. It may be summarized as follows:

Table 8.3 Summary of factors influencing people's innovative and creative spirit.

Influential factors	Encourage	Discourage
Family	• Provide positive support • Encourage initiatives • Teach to be self-reliant • Providing the opportunity for children to make and be responsible for their decisions • Develop risk taking attribute • Teach the need and how to respect, appreciate the sacrifice of the ecosystem to provide services to humanity • Respect self-interest and for the common good • Interact with people well	• Everything can be bought with money • Parent reliant, parents function as providers • No concern for common good • Profit, money driven family culture • No value bond in the family, everything is for money • Make it known to children or at least make them feel that they can inherit the family fortune, once the parents are dead • Greed driven culture
Workplace	• Positive support for initiative • Develop entrepreneurial culture • Remove negative subculture from the organization • A personal value–corporate value integration • An enterprise culture within the organization • A system and climate that permits individual to have a stake in the organization • A system whereby everyone shares ownership • Effective delegate decision-making (empowerment)	• Corporate culture builds on profit, not on value • There is a clearly defined and rigid relationship, and an inflexible organizational hierarchy • Environment does not encourage individuals to have a feeling that they have a stake in the organization • No ownership sharing provision in the corporate strategy. Workers encouraged to participate in ownership sharing schemes

Table 8.3 (*Continued*)

Influential factors	Encourage	Discourage
		• The organization offers no long term employment contract • Policy and "boss's" attitude discourage innovation
Society	• The environment induces healthy economic undertakings • There are infrastructures to support new and innovative undertakings • A good educational system that induces value, rather than concentrating on "profit" or "money" • Responsible government that facilitates economic growth through knowledge-based and value-driven efforts • There is a continuing enterprising culture that encourages individuals to create and innovate. Perceiving that there are always opportunities to pursue. Even in problem situations, there are perceived opportunities • The societal value builds on self-reliance, rather than government reliance • Governments that place importance in both economic as well as political democracies	• The environment induces a culture that encourages individuals to strive for short term gains, at the cost of the environment and humanity, both in the present and in the future • Under an autocratic leadership • Lacks investment opportunities • Lacks career opportunities for the individual • No business creation and growth opportunities • The societal culture tends to grow on government reliance • Conservatism: not preserving what's good, but rather resisting change, fearful of acquiring new experiences • An unhealthy mentality: no risk, no loss • In general, society as a whole makes no distinction between money and profit; between profit and value

Table 8.3 (*Continued*)

Influential factors	Encourage	Discourage
Mass media	• Promote common good • Encourage risk and the pursuit of opportunity • Promote businesses that have done well for all contributors • Provide information aiding the pursuit of innovation and creativity • Promote value-driven and knowledge-based organizations	• Promote greed • Misinform readership about wealth, money and value • Promote gambling • Promote government reliance, but not self-reliance • Promote social welfare, individuals take no responsibility for themselves
Self-motivated-perceived need and/or want	• Self-discipline • Self-reliance • Take calculated risks • Appreciate the role of being a leader • Make proprietary decisions and take responsibilities for all the decisions one has made • Determined, but with flexibility • Need to create and innovate • Desire to create wealth for oneself and for the common good • Value driven • Need driven • Optimism • Love challenges	• Selfish • Self-centered • Money is everything • A taker, not a giver • No concern for common good, unwilling to share, not even amongst partners • Destroy more, create less or nothing • Want and greed driven • Avoid risks • Interested in short term and immediate gains • Inability to manage resources; prefer to lead • Indecision • Poor listener

What has been summarized in Table 8.3 is only the tip of an iceberg. However, the basic idea is clear. For application, in a family home environment, children need to explore and make new and different things by using discarded goods, clothes or even garbage. In essence, this happens to be the simplest form of creating toys for themselves; parents on the other hand, more often than not ask them to throw away the "garbage" or "trash," and then give them money to buy new toys or buy toys for them. In institutions, new initiatives are often discouraged, simply because the administration is worried about the cost and/or failure. At least in one incident, when the senior author proposed a publication requiring no cash disbursement from the institution in the name of the university, the academic vice-president unfortunately refused to support the initiative, and said: "Who pays the cost if the project fails?" When he was told, there will be no cash commitment from the institution, he remarked: "What about those involved in the initiative, the loss of forgone revenue must also be considered." Prior to 1997, before Hong Kong officially rejoined China, Canada admitted a large number of Hong Kong immigrants who were unwilling to remain in the territory and who decided to make their home in Canada. In 1995, when the senior author visited Hong Kong, he conversed with a group of young people who had received their Canadian landed immigrant status but had returned to Hong Kong to do business. When the senior author asked why they chose not to stay and do business in Canada, they replied: "Canada is a good place for old people, but there is not enough excitement for us."

The three incidents explain the importance of how environmental factors discourage the innovative and creative spirit. Parents of the family discourage children from making their own toys; the education institution is reluctant to support creative initiatives; and the third, Canada — a nation known for its social welfare program, but regarded as — "Good only for old people, for the young, it's not enough."

Creation and innovation are human history itself. In fact, without creation and innovation, we would probably still live in caves, hunting other species for food and being hunted by them as well. Our civilization and the whole economic system is built on innovation and creativity; the beautiful part of it is, it was all created by people. It is people who make the different combinations behind all the technological and scientific discoveries. An exaggerated comparison is that of: on every American coin, there is an engraved phrase that reads "In God we trust." In so far as innovation and creativity is concerned, it is "In people we trust." However, it must be borne in mind that innovation and creativity are not the sole dominion of people in science, engineering and/or technology. The innovative and creative upper-hand can happen in any discipline and activity. Thus, we need to make the environment suitable for the pursuit of innovative and creative activities that will create wealth not only for the individual, but also for the common good as well.

8.6 The Thoughts and Guiding Principles in People Management

The ways in which people have been used and managed in the past, present and perhaps in the future, may be summarized as follows:

Table 8.4 How people have been used, and the evolution of management style in human institutions with reference to the tales.

Management practice	Management style	Remarks/with reference to tales
1. **Conqueror and slave** Do what the master wants, follow orders, or else.... Or in a modern language, do as you are told, or face the consequences	Management by fear. Mostly punishment, hardly any worthwhile reward	Conqueror and slave/*Pig and butcher conversation*
2. **Master and servant** Listen to me, if you do well, there is a reward, otherwise, you will be punished	Management by reward and punishment	Master and servant. Master assumes that's all servant needs
3. **"Me boss, you worker"** What boss says, he/she means business. There are rules, regulations and procedures	Management by rules and procedures, discretion is in the hands of the boss	Boss and workers

Table 8.4 (*Continued*)

Management practice	Management style	Remarks/with reference to tales
4. **Missionary** Listen to the gospel	Management by passion and love	Missionary and disciples/*The blind person carries a lantern*
5. **Visionary** I light and carry the lantern, just follow me	Management by the light, follow the vision	Visionary/*The blind person carries a lantern*
6. **Superior and subordinates** Builds an organizational hierarchy, emphasizes the respect for authority and responsibility	Management by hierarchy of organizational command	Superior and subordinates/*Do we know how fish feel?*
7. **Employer and employee** I pay you to do the job, so do it; if you don't, someone else will	Management by objective; management by exception	Employer and employees/*Do we know how fish feel?* And *throw away that old junk jacket*
8. **Leader and follower** Follow me. See me as your example	Management by leadership qualities, skills and persuasion	Leader and follower/*The blind person carries a lantern. If you cannot see, let us see you*
9. **Father and children** Family hierarchy, respect the command of the head of the family, what father/mother wants, he/she gets	Management by family chain of command. Juniors may air their views, but seniors make the decision	I am the Godfather, what I say counts/*Do we know how fish feel? Dad!*

Table 8.4 (*Continued*)

Management practice	Management style	Remarks/with reference to tales
10. **Team leader and the team** Team leader leads and coordinates with players	Management by leadership strategy	Team leader and the team
11. **Democracy** Majority counts, the chairperson collects group view in a democratic fashion. The majority may not be able to reach a consensus, but the chair will rule on the basis of the interest (views) of the majority	Management by the interest of majority	In a democratic forum, the chair and members relationship
12. **Fellow entrepreneurs** Encourages the individual to be innovative and creative for one's personal interest as well as for the common good	Management by developing individual's desire for personal goal attainment and sustainable growth for the organization	Entrepreneur to entrepreneurs

The above-illustrated 12 different types of relationships, between those on the top who make decisions that affect others, and those who are recipients and working based on the decisions made in human institutions, are not conclusive. Moreover, they are not clearly defined, i.e. there are overlaps, in fact, even the extremes, such as Nos. 1 and 2, may have a mixture of other relationship elements. Similarly, in the democratic form (No. 11), there are also autocratic individuals who may ruthlessly ignore the interest of the majority. They persist in doing everything their own way and for their own self-interest.

There was not much humanity in the relationships of Nos. 1 and 2 above. Conqueror and slave relationships are mostly a part of human history. The master and servant relationship described in No. 2 still exists in our society, the only difference between conqueror and slave versus master and servant is that the former had arisen from "conquest," while the other may have been from some form of contractual agreement (I pay you, and you work for me).

8.7 How People See People at Different Levels of Responsibility

In general, people at the top (the executives and the management) and their workers often have the kind of relationship that is not unlike the short little tales circulated by some office worker, as stated at the beginning of the chapter:

> *Life at work is like a tree full of monkeys, all on different limbs at different levels. Some monkeys are climbing up, some down and see a tree full of smiling faces. The monkeys on the bottom look up and see nothing but ass... .*

(Source: anonymous)

When one of the office workers showed the above to his respected superior, the "boss" looked, smiled and remarked: "Yes, we are ass...," We wonder, maybe we should computerize the whole place; robots would not care what they see, would they?

Questions for discussion

1. As a manager, you have to make decisions influencing economic variations; in particular, slowdown, technological advancement, resources supply crisis, and long term disputes, such as strike and market adjustment. What are the measures you intend to adopt in the interest of people versus "accounting profit?"
2. Businesses here are created by people, of people, and for people, how does "profit" as our accustomed notion for business success fits in with this simple reality?
3. Some 50 years ago, when his Royal Highness the Duke of Edinburgh, Prince Philip praised our technological advancement and success, he said something like this:

"While we celebrate our success in technology advancement, which contributes greatly to our standard of living, we must at the same time, remind ourselves that all technologies are developed by human and for human benefit. (These are not his exact words; the senior author assumes full responsibility for any inaccuracies in his remark.) Fifty years later, we have achieved remarkable technological advancement, and we have allowed many people to advance to the "millionaire" or "billionaire" benchmark, but the same time, we have also seen a great many people slide down the living scale to the extreme state of poverty, such as in Africa, Asia and even in North America. When will we stop seeing TV footage of starving people (in particular, infants and children), with only their skin wrapped around their skeletal bodies, and with tears and hopeless expressions on their faces? Comment!

4. In principle, the World Trade Organization (WTO) is supposedly set up to remove all barriers of trade, including goods, services, resources, technology and investment, and perhaps most importantly labor. It seems by and large, that with regards to the labor issue, it is difficult to reach any agreement, in particular between the nations of the rich and poor. Why? Do you have any suggestions that will help to lift labor movement barriers between nations of the WTO?

5. In situations where a business is challenged by market changes, technological advancement, sliding trend of profit decline, and even seasonal sales fluctuations, what can be done to meet and overcome the hurdle without having to lay off workers?

6. What do you perceive as the essential qualities required to be an entrepreneurial leader? How would you compare entrepreneurial leadership to other types of leadership?

7. Can/should computer software developers be our leaders? Why?

8. In people we trust, or in people we do not trust, but in computer we trust. Comment!

Section II. The Pursuit of Entrepreneurial Culture

Fundamentally, business is about the development of new creations and the transfer of ownership. It is about the flow of energy, just as there is a sense in which we humans are energy in a different form. The purpose of business is to ensure that business will continue, and the purpose for the living is to strive for the continuation of life. However, we must be clear in our mind that whether or not life continues depends on how we conduct our businesses. Conducting business can be a channelling of energy constructively, or it can destroy life if it is used carelessly or destructively. Like it or not, the mission of business as a whole, or in our fashionable modern day terms, the "market economy" is the continuation of life.

We must always bear in mind that we are "stewards" of the earth. What distinguishes us from the animals is that through conscious choice, we can destroy life on this earth. If we wish life to continue, we must accept this responsibility.

Chapter 9

The Creation of a New Venture

The creation of a new venture is not a highway to heaven, but it is a vehicle to economic freedom; with passion, love and sharing, that makes the creation of a new venture both for self-interest and a benefit to society.

9.1 Introduction

The creation of a new business is not a highway to heaven, but a meaningful exertion that can lead to economic freedom. To some people, it is the realization of a lifelong dream. For society, it will be considered added value as the new venture will provide the community with needed services and job opportunities. For the government, it is a good job creation strategy, equivalent to or better than that of a job training program, as the business itself becomes the training ground, and provides the job as well. Unlike training, the ventures create jobs, increase tax revenue, and consequently help to resolve the problem of unemployment and contribute more money to the treasury. As an added incentive, the saved cost of training can be re-allocated for some other purpose, hopefully a creative and innovative one, rather than just to feed the voracious appetites of bureaucracy.

There is another more cultural incentive. By encouraging people to be self-employed, it will enhance enterprising culture and make people self-reliant. A culture that supports the notion of the ideal society, will result in individuals who are more likely to be creative and innovative, providing opportunities for others rather than depending on others to make a living. Therefore the creation of new ventures has been hailed as an effective job creation strategy globally.

The above comparison only expresses the relative effect. Of course some of the contributions listed in the venture creation boxes can also be found, in effective job training programs, and if individuals are willing to upgrade themselves or become creative and innovative individuals. However, it is not an inherent feature of job training to do so, whereas it is an inherent feature of venture creation. This is similar to the way one can find examples of entrepreneurial behavior in a corporate environment, though this is rare; whereas in an entrepreneurial environment, it is more common.

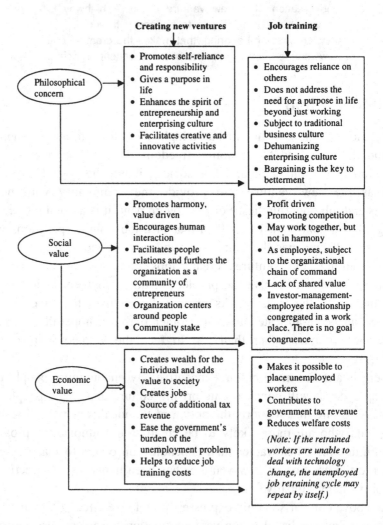

Figure 9.1 A comparison between job training and creating new ventures.

9.2 Begin With the Venture Founder

9.2.1 Who does not want to be a venture founder?

While everyone is an entrepreneur some of the time, and some people are entrepreneurs all the time, not everyone is an entrepreneur all of the time. However it can certainly be said that if you want to find someone who thinks like an entrepreneur most of the time, just look for the creator of a new venture. Others may be less inclined to do so. If you work in a 9 to 5 job, pay your union dues and look forward to your pension and your retirement, there is a pretty good chance you are not into the risk-taking life of an entrepreneur. If you like playing the stocks, looking for that gold mine in the Yukon or Indonesia to make it big, chances are you are not developing your next new idea to start a venture. If you are a politician, then you probably are not jumping around trying to find a way to fund your business start-up. If you are a professional, be it a lawyer, dentist, doctor, veterinarian or engineer, then chances are that you are looking to your income to pay the mortgage, rather than an upturn in sales. If you are praying for your lottery ticket number to come in, chances are you are not looking for your next product to hit the jackpot. Mind you, there is probably someone, or perhaps many people who fit those descriptions who prove us wrong (and we are glad of it!), but on the whole if you want someone who is trying to innovate, create and provide new jobs, look to a new venture founder. Those who endure the hardship of nursing and caring without knowing what the return will be (using Catillon's words), it is them for whom we can be certain that entrepreneurial thinking is their cup of tea.

9.2.2 Who wants to be a venture founder and create it?

It is a simple truth that people who are comfortable are unlikely to change. After all, why should they want to? Very often, people motivated to create their own ventures are influenced by negative factors more so than positive. That is, by what they do not have rather than by what they do. While forcing people onto the street might be an effective way to create a new generation of entrepreneurial thinkers, we certainly do not advocate this and we would hope that most of our readers would agree. However, there are many more fascinating and inspiring tales of people pushed to the edge who later managed to bounce back and make it big through their creative efforts, than there are of wealthy people who left it all to start a big venture. Here, we relate an interesting human experience, not a sob story, but one where a woman rose to success under rather unusual circumstances. She now owns a small software development company catering to advertising agencies, employing eight full-time software engineers and with annual sales of around five million dollars. Here is her story:

The environmental pressure and inner entrepreneurial spirit drive

The heroine enters the story as a new illegal immigrant from China, where she had earned a good quality degree in computer design. Anxious to leave and start a new life, she grabbed at the chance to move to Toronto, Canada, where she worked at a restaurant, first as an assistant cook, and then as a waitress from 5 pm to 1 am in the morning for about two years. She earned only a little more than the national poverty line income. This was just sufficient to allow her to survive on the basics of food, shelter and clothing. At times, she had to send part of her income back to her family in China. She was unsuccessful in getting a better job even though she had other skills. As she did not have a social security number, no one was willing to take the risk of employing her.

She lived in a small room nearby Toronto's old Chinatown, north of College Street close to Spadina Avenue. Though life was extremely hard, she somehow managed to get by, mostly by incurring debts on her Visa in order to supplement her cashflow. However, the situation worsened as days passed. She could not afford the bank's high interest rates, and it became almost impossible for her to make the Visa payments.

As a daily routine, she would pass by the northwest corners of two major streets, where there is a bank, a hotel with a slightly seedy reputation, a mission for the homeless and a funeral home. The setting of this commercial development had an unsettling effect on her. This haunted her all day and all night, and the message was something like this:

> *If you are heavily in debt, and circumstances make*
> *it impossible for you to cope, you may be pushed into*
> *living in a "cheap" hotel. Possibly, you may become*

---

involved in the oldest profession (prostitution), get drunk all the time, and eventually thrown out of the hotel onto the streets where you'll be reliant on the mission's free food. Finally, there will come a day when you can no longer withstand the pressures of life. You may even find it a torture to be alive. On that day you may visit the last storefront on the block, with the comfort that even if you don't have any money, at least the government will supply you with a free burial.

She could not bear the thought of this, and in particular, the possibility of being pushed into prostitution, just as she was not willing to accept the thought that one day she might end up relying on charity taking care of her. She was 36 at the time, and it was her fourth year in Toronto.

With each passing day, this little vignette strengthened her resolve to change her life. At her worst and most desperate times, she thought of suicide, but she would ultimately realize that that was not the solution. She started to deliberately avoid walking by that corner, instead taking a longer route to her workplace. Along her new route, she noticed a few computer shops on the south side of College Street, with the one attracting the most attention apparently operated by people recently emigrated from China. Driven by curiosity, she had a chat with the shopowner, who she discovered, was a new immigrant. The shopowner had also tried to secure a suitable job, but failed, and instead decided to start his own business. He told her, "I have no idea how this will go. So far, not bad! It gives me a living and a much brighter outlook on the future than I used to have!"

Recalling the computer training she received in China, and inspired by her talk with the shopowner, she then had an idea. As her fellow immigrant said: "Life is too short to complain about the circumstances. Regardless of who you are, life must continue, so let's get on with it."

First, she entered into a program at a nearby college to improve her computer and design skills. During this period, in addition to waiting on tables from 5 pm till 1 am the next morning, she was also attending computer classes from 9 am to 12 noon. In her spare time, she would approach shopowners and managers in a variety of businesses, particularly ad agencies, asking them whether they would use her services for promotion designs. She would always stress her computer skills and how they would help improve their market performance, and realize eventual growth potentials.

> Eventually, she earned the confidence of two small companies, who contracted her to do a few small jobs, which she did exceedingly well. Through word of mouth, she eventually acquired more contracts, thus allowing her to quit her waitressing job and concentrate on her business full-time. Next, she accumulated sufficient cash to engage a lawyer to help her acquire landed immigrant status. Eventually, she was able to incorporate her small, home-based venture into a respectable software development firm.

A number of research works have concluded that there are some individuals who seek venture creation opportunities. The above is only one example among many, of ventures created by individuals hungry for economic freedom. Some of these ventures are based on clever or sophisticated ideas. Other ventures involve simple ideas and appropriate technology, applied with determination and a faith in what they offer to society. With such simple tools, many persons have made livings for themselves and their families and provided jobs and useful services for others. In India, it is not unusual to see a man with a small box containing a number of strings and a small stock of beads, from which he will make some simple jewellery. He combines a manufacturing and marketing business all in one spot and

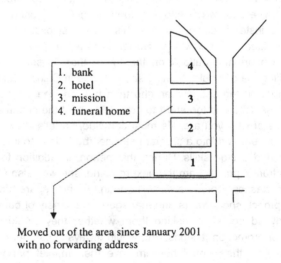

Moved out of the area since January 2001
with no forwarding address

Figure 9.2 The northwest corner of two commercial streets in Toronto, Canada.

provides a living not only for himself, but his family as well. Judging by Western standards, it is not much of a venture, a micro-undertaking at best, but nevertheless, from the point-of-view of the seller, it is a venture, and whether he knows it or not, he also contributes to India's economy. The key question to ask here, is what inspired him to create his micro-venture, or in other words, what was his motivation? The answer is obvious — he wants both himself and his family to live, and this micro enterprise is the means by which he accomplishes this.

This may not be impressive for those who only have regard for university degrees. But at the end of the day, is it not the education received, but rather the contribution made that is important? A business entrepreneur need not have a higher degree. A Harvard dropout can create a business empire, earning him the title of the richest man in the world. The founder of Federal Express is proud of the fact that he earned only a "C" grade for his business plan during his days at MIT. There is ample evidence of plenty of successful venture founders, who never even made it to the graduation ceremony.

On a global basis, there are countless people who have created their own ventures to meet the "basic needs," and who have struggled to get out of poverty. There are people who have suffered from personal setbacks, and/or are dissatisfied with the establishment or their environment. These include, in no particular order:

- school dropouts
- new immigrants
- women discriminated against for their gender
- working mothers disillusioned about 9 to 5 working hours
- people pressured by family to succeed
- homemakers bored with their lives after the children have grown up
- people with disabilities
- people desiring to satisfy their self-esteem
- pensioners who believe that retirement is just an opportunity to start something new
- persons unable to gain a higher education, perhaps because of economic reasons or possibly discrimination

Though fewer in number, there are also those who are motivated by reasons other than dissatisfaction. Some individuals have been successful in other endeavors and want to realize what seem to be impossible dreams. Others like Bill Gates, just want to prove themselves: "If he can do it, why can't I?" As noted in Fortune 500, Geoffrey Colvin made a specific reference relating to the value driven idea — " 'Entrepreneur,' which used to mean 'flimflam man' or 'unemployed,' is now the station to which millions of young people worldwide aspire."[1]

There are also dreamers such as Kanokwan Wongwatanasin who found her success by spotting a once in a lifetime opportunity and becoming the first person to offer Internet services in Thailand. She started her own Internet service venture and generated $7.5 million in sales and accounting profit of $408,000 in 1999. Similarly, Toshihiro Maeta was the pacesetter in bringing the Internet to mobile phones. His company gave him annual sales of $84.7 million and accounting profit of $7.7 million.[2]

9.2.3 Is there any lesson that can be learnt from venture success?

First, have confidence, build hope on confidence, and then build with undivided love and passion for creation

There is no magic bullet for venture success. However, there are a few simple wise words and incontrovertible facts, which if observed will increase the chances of success. In the more rational approach to venture creation, the four elements of the creation process are: get ready, get set, get planning and go. More importantly however, is that to succeed, one needs to build hope of success on confidence, effective planning, and love and passion for the business. Building a venture is much the same as giving birth and raising an infant child, everything must be rooted in love and passion or it results in naught. It involves making sacrifices whatever and whenever the need arises. If there is only $100 left in the bank, and it is a choice between using the money to buy groceries or to save the

---

[1]*Fortune 500*, 24 July 2000, p. 64.
[2]*Asiaweek*, 11 May 2001, pp. 46 and 47.

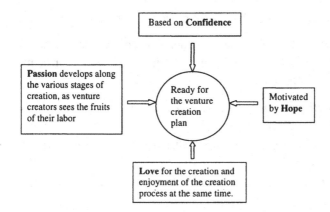

Figure 9.3 Love and passion driven venture creation initiative.

business, it is likely that the money will go towards saving the business. Passion and love are the fundamental requirements for individuals who decide to create their own ventures, building on hope for the future and on the basis of self-confidence.

Although four elemental sources of energy are identified, they are not in any particular order and are mostly inter-related. Nevertheless, it is often the confidence attribute of an individual that prompts his/her desire to pursue venture creation opportunities.

The success of a venture creation very much depends on the venture founder's self-belief and confidence in the endeavor, however business environmental factors must also be taken into consideration. An entrepreneur may be able to create a new venture successfully in Perth, Australia, but there is no assurance the same will happen in the U.S. or Canada. A variety of different factors including sociological, economic, variations in the market, buyer behavior, religious belief, political conditions and many other factors will play a role. These and other fundamentals can be found in most marketing texts and in on-line information.

Even the simplest plan, is better than no plan at all

(1) Incubating venture ideas before entering into more comprehensive planning

Selecting and making decisions on a venture type

In the traditional venture development approach, we are taught to "find a hole in the market" which means to find a niche. Put in a more concrete form, it looks like this:

Step 1: *Identify consumers in a given sector.*

Step 2: *Identify their needs.*

Step 3: *Identify suppliers to those needs, and compare what they do to what is needed.*

Step 4: *If a need is not satisfied, identify why, or if it is, can it be further satisfied?*

While successful, slavish obedience to these rules can lead to some interesting ethical ambiguities. Let us examine one. The smuggling of human cargo from China that has been occurring with increasing frequency over the past few years.

Step 1. In China, there are a large number of people who are dissatisfied with their situation.

Step 2. The reason they are unhappy, is that they cannot express their entrepreneurial desires in the communist environment, and thus they yearn to live in a free market economy.

Step 3. The only chance these people have of leaving the country is through a long legal and bureaucratic tangle, which is only accessible to a few in any case.

Step 4. The needs of hundreds of thousands of Chinese are not met, with the exception of these who are willing to take risks and skirt around the law.

This might be taken as a way out, and the smugglers might be considered to be modern day Robin Hoods or even Oskar Schindlers here, saving people from the communist oppression. The only problem is that these smuggling operators do not care about the welfare of their passengers, and are more than willing to have them die rather than allow themselves be caught. Even when they are in their new, dream countries, they are harnessed to work as virtual slaves for any number of years. What would Robin Hood think of that? What would the dutiful first year business student, so diligently copying down his notes on venture creation, think of that if he really thought about it?

Drug trafficking and other criminal organizations may promote or be the result of creation process that can be described well in accordance with the traditional approach of new venture creation. However, as we define it, they are not entrepreneurial creations, as they do not act for the common good, even when they create many job opportunities, as they are fundamentally destructive, do harm to other human beings, and thus are outside of entrepreneurial endeavors, as are any destructive entities, whether legal or not.

These would include ventures that have an unnecessarily high impact on the natural environment (e.g. excessive fishing, strip-mining or mass deforestation), perpetrate unkind acts on animals, and in general, use the land in a non-entrepreneurial way. It is these undertakings that impair the continuation of life. They may be business undertakings, but they are not creative or innovative, and thus are not entrepreneurial. Any entrepreneurial activities, although for self-interest, must add value to society too.

There are countless enterprising opportunities that will create wealth for the individual and add value to society. While there are likely to be problems, perhaps more so than business activities that are not entrepreneurial, in every problem situation, there are perceived new opportunities. As such, entrepreneurial ventures can be anything that will contribute socio-economic value to the society. They can be home-based software development, catering services for occasions, small-scale manufacturing, food processing, environmental protection, child minding, and among all the millions of opportunities, garbage disposal. Let's use the garbage disposal problem in the city of Toronto as an example, and show how it can be an opportunity for wealth creation and, at the same time, add value to society.

> *Venture idea 1: in every problem situation, there are perceived opportunities*
>
> According to reliable sources, Toronto is a dream city. The city fathers and the media claimed that it is the No. 1 city in the world to live in. However, there is another side to the story. The city residents dispose of approximately 1.4 million tonnes of trash annually. As part of the city's effort, it was planned to ship the city's trash to Northern Ontario and bury it in what is known as the Adams Mine. But the deal fell apart over a contentious clause involving liability for unavoidable costs, and

the move was met with opposition from the residents of the nearby city of Kirkland Lake.

As an alternative, the city finally signed a contract allowing for the shipping of garbage to two landfill sites in the neighboring American state of Michigan. This will involve 100,000 additional trucks on the major Ontario thoroughfare, Highway 401, every year for the next 20 years. It has been noted that, from the environment point of view, this operation is a significantly poorer proposition than the Adams mine proposal. The operation will cost the city $1 billion.[3]

The garbage dump problem is not one for the city of Toronto alone. It is becoming a global dilemma caused by the demand for higher and higher standards of living, and an economy based on planned obsolescence of products. And it will only get worse, not better. For the city of Toronto, the 1.4 million tons of trash will not end with the 20-year contract, but as the pressure of materialistic consumption continues, the trash tonnage will likely increase rather than decrease.

Situation

Mass garbage disposal: as a venture opportunity, the idea needs to transform into substance.

Current position

The city needs a short term solution; the current costs involve paying for the landfill site dumping, and trucking costs, along with hidden costs such as highway maintenance, and traffic congestion resulting in countless opportunities costs for those sharing the road with the additional 100,000 trucks. In the short term, garbage will continue to accumulate, and so an appropriate solution must be found.

The future

Within five years, as the immediate crisis abates and people become used to the additional traffic, politicians will claim credit for solving the garbage

---

[3]*The Globe and Mail*, 21 October 2000, p. 61 (similar stories in other papers: *National Post*, *Toronto Star* and *Toronto Sun*).

problem, as well as using the opportunity to increase property taxes, justified because of the additional costs involved in dealing with the garbage. Assuming that the recycle and reuse programs will continue in their present forms, the accumulation problem will continue, because recycle programs are limited, not including some types of plastics and various food wastes for example. Of course, little kitchen garbage can be reused under the current schemes.

Table 9.1 shows ways to turn a problem into an entrepreneurial business opportunity, create wealth for the individual and add great value to society, and thereby humanity as a whole. Garbage disposal is an enormous problem, it has made some of our living environments virtually unliveable. Humans ultimately must produce less waste; in the meantime, we have to address

Table 9.1 Venture opportunities derived from trash disposal problem.

Kitchen garbage classification	Administrative approach	Possible solutions	Venture opportunity
(a) Cardboard boxes, packing materials, metal containers and plasticware	Recycle	Reclassify as separate items	Set up a collection post, provide incentives for materials in reusable condition, and recondition them, make them reusable and market them as environmental friendly products to concerned users.
(b) Remains of vegetative organic matter	Trash collected for dumping into landfill or abandoned mines	Useful material as natural food for garden plants, flower bed filler, etc.	These substances can be used to create compost and/or fertilizer.
(c) Animal protein, remains including bones and leftover unwanted food etc.	Treated the same as (b) above	Same as above	Same as above, except may require more extensive processing to make it useable. In addition, may be used to make pig swill, for example, as long as it is done in a hygienic fashion.

the issue and generate business ideas. There are numerous examples of people with innovative ideas at various stages of development; some of these ideas have the potential of becoming sustainable ventures.

Turning an idea into a business opportunity depends on the would-be venturer's personal perception of the idea. The individual needs to build on the hope of making the creation a success, and have a passion and love for the idea and pursue it. A great idea is a great thing, but no enterprise, however great the idea behind it, has ever succeeded when pursued half-heartedly, especially if in competition with one pursued with vigor. It might be useful to use the following as a guide:

(2) Assess the feasibility of three venture ideas

Classification (a): Cardboard boxes, newspapers and other throwaway packaging is collected by the city and recycled, but recycling costs money, and old newspapers have limited use. Some old-fashioned shops use them as wrapping to protect breakable items, a few food shops wrap groceries in them and there may even be a few fish and chip shops that still sell you their product wrapped in old papers, but on the whole, these enterprises are few, and most shopowners would take a great deal of convincing before they would return to using newspaper wrappings.

Even if there is little one can do with the masses of useless newsprint, cardboard boxes can certainly be reused. Virtually every person who has moved house without the benefits of a moving company can appreciate the virtue of a ready stock of old boxes. And some "No Frills" supermarkets do not give out plastic shopping bags, but direct shoppers to pick suitable boxes from the pile and use them to pack their groceries.

For reuse, boxes tend to be troublesome because of their bulkiness. While the city can request that residents flatten the boxes for recycling, the reality is that residents rarely comply as it is a bit difficult to manage. Further, boxes would have to be classified and redistributed by size and strength in order for them to be reused, and this also is time consuming and costly.

The conclusion: under the circumstances, the idea listed in the box of Table 9.1 "suggesting reuse of cardboard boxes" is not immediately feasible.

Classification (b) and (c): Both (b) and (c) appear to be sensible ideas, and in fact, can be combined.

Electrically powered kitchen trash disposal mechanisms or "trash compactors" were once a popular item in many North American kitchens, but fell out of favor in the 1970s. The reasons for their decline were manifold:

- It was costly
- It caused frequent plumbing blockages
- It was hard to use, requiring separation of compactable items from those which could not be compacted
- There was low consumer awareness of the importance of minimizing garbage

However, times have changed, consumers are now much more concerned about environmental health than three or four decades ago, and technological advancements may mean that the product design can be improved. Although it is to be used by the consumer, initial marketing effort may be directed not at the consumer, but at city governments pitching the product as a way of reducing the garbage disposal cost, thus being of direct benefit to the city. For example, reduction of kitchen waste by half can help the city save several hundred million dollars. Therefore, to initiate the project, it requires at least three fundamental innovative efforts: product, initial R&D financing to build a prototype, and innovative marketing to sell it to the city administration.

Venture idea 2: government policy can lead to venture opportunities

As a policy initiative, the U.K. government encourages the single parent to return to the workforce. This initiative is aimed both at reducing some of the burden on the government, and having the person contribute to tax revenue as well as give some hope to others dependent on government support. However, single parenting is full of challenges, and locating affordable childcare facilities is practically impossible. Although not necessarily a lucrative "profit" generating proposition, childminding for working parents can be an attractive venture for those who love children. It also helps to create wealth and add value to society.[4]

---

[4]*BBC News*, 10 October 2000.

Situation

This could be a good venture opportunity especially if it offers some innovations, such as integration of an early childhood education program into the operation. Compliance with local statutes is of course necessary, but overall the entry barriers are low and start-up capital is affordable.

Venture idea 3: conservation induces venture opportunities

Conservation is a big issue in many countries, particularly for nations relying on logging as one of the major sources of national income. Even economically prosperous countries, still have a heavy reliance on lumber, both for industrial use and for the consumer market. Uses range from building needs, to pulp and paper, to making all sorts of furniture. In fact, wood remains an important resource in virtually any human domicile.

As our demand for lumber increases, reforestation and sustainable harvesting become critical issues. In cold climates, a softwood tree needs up to 30 years to reach harvestable size, and about ten to 15 years in warmer regions; in the latter case, the lumber is typically less versatile and hence less valuable. Given that trees perform a number of functions in maintaining the global ecosystem, forest preservation is of vital concern, as can be seen from the reactions to the recently derailed Kyoto accord.[5] Some logging companies are fully aware of the consequences of their activities and engage in systematic reforestation programs, usually in cooperation with local governments. However, there are many others, that ruthlessly devastate whole areas for the sake of their own convenience. Protests over logging of the Temagami region in Ontario, and the west coast of New Zealand's South Island are two cases in point. Tree planting and reforestation are needed particularly in countries that primarily rely on exporting timber as a source of income.

In the mid-1980s, a student of the senior author was inspired by the need for tree planting ideas. He secured a contract from the Ministry of Nature Resources of the Ontario Government, Canada,

---

[5]While the Kyoto accord deals mainly with reducing carbon dioxide emissions which contribute to the "greenhouse effect" or "global warming," one of the key points of the debates has been the role of preserving forests which play a vital role in reducing carbon dioxide levels.

along with logging companies contracts. He built a million dollar business within a short period of three years from a very small amount of capital investment. Although the same story may not be duplicated in other countries, the idea of working on reforestation as an independent tree planting company along with logging companies and the government is still as fresh as the daisies.

Situation

The reforestation operation initiated by the senior author's student has been written as a case and published in 1989 under the name of "Broland Enterprise Incorporated." It provides a brief operational plan and outlines some of the hurdles experienced in the venture creation process.[6]

The above offers some brief thoughts regarding how venture ideas may be generated, and opportunities may be pursued. The world is never short of venture opportunities; it is all up to the individual. The entrepreneur is always there, but it is commercialization that puts the "ship" in entrepreneur-ship, and changes an idea into an economic activity presented to serve human interests.

Questions for discussion

1. Assume that you have invented a device that generates sufficient heat to incinerate organic materials in under a minute. The object is small (about as big as a loaf of bread), weighs about 300 g, and creates a fine ash with no toxicity to the environment. What would you do to turn your invention into a viable venture?
2. What would be a business plan to market a new product? How would you prepare a business plan to attract the interest of venture capitalists?
3. Value, cash, wealth, money and profit are words that each have meanings of their own. Without referring to a dictionary, how would you define these words with respect to venture creation and managing new venture development?

---

[6]Kao R. W. Y., *Entrepreneurship and Enterprise Development* (Holt, Rinehart and Winston, Toronto, 1989).

4. Born into a well-to-do family, you were a child well-protected by your parents. In fact in your pre-teen years, you were positively spoiled. You could have anything you wanted under the sun. However, both your parents were often away on business, so you and your sister spent most of your time alone with the maid. Surprisingly however, you did not indulge in many of the vices of youth such as drugs or excessive drinking. As such, you were always viewed as a "good kid" by your parents. When you were 18, you asked your father to give you a BMW convertible. Though he bought you one, it was not what you wanted; instead of a brand new car, it was several years old. You were not totally satisfied, but accepted it anyway, and felt quite virtuous in your "sacrifice." Coming to the age when many young people wonder what they will do with their lives, you nurture the idea of one day owning a small company involved in "product innovation and development" to help those who have ideas, but due to reasons such as lack of capital you are unable to develop the idea into a viable product on their own.

Now you are 24 years old, and your father and mother still support you financially. However, you no longer live at home. You have fallen deeply in love, have lived together for more than a year and want to get married. You approach your father about getting married, and ask him to support you both financially, so that both of you can continue on as graduate students to obtain higher degrees. To your dismay, your father refuses, saying that you should get married only when you have the means to do so without parental financial support. Not heeding your father's advice, you proceeded on with the marriage plans anyway, thinking in the back of your mind that your father would never really let you down. But true to his word, he stops the steady stream of cheques you've been receiving.

Over the years, you have become completely dependent on parental support, lost all your initiative and spent all your time and energy on dating, and generally spending money in a careless manner. You have no confidence, determination and are unwilling to take risks. You know nothing about being self-reliant, but then you realize that you still have love and passion for your old venture creation business idea. You are determined to make it work, but neither you nor your spouse has any idea of how to go about doing it. But as you said to your spouse: "This is my dream, this will make me a human being that I will be proud to be, and hopefully that my parents will be proud of as well."

What will you do, to make this dream a reality? Your bank account is about to run dry and you have reached the limit of your Visa gold card.

5. Prepare a list of entrepreneurial attributes. Provide suggestions on how you would help to cultivate and develop these attributes in someone who is about to create a new venture.

6. Contact your local government or perhaps search on the Internet, to see what kind of assistance is required in the creation of a new venture that you believe will make you a wealthy "entrepreneur" in five years time or less. Your venture will be beneficial to society as well as the environment.

7. As a new MBA with a minor in Entrepreneurship, you plan to pursue further academic challenges and go for the gold (a Ph.D., that is). Your "Entrepreneurism" course professor agreed to be your supervisor, but you will have to write a plan, including the title of your dissertation, about how are you going about to complete this academic challenge. Prepare this research plan under the subject of "Entrepreneurship" or "Entrepreneurism."

8. Do you believe, that it is in the interests of an economically advanced country to encourage everyone to have a small business of their own? Why? Explain in detail. What about in a country with virtually no resources of its own, but with a well educated populace?

Chapter 10

The New Venture Creation: Planning and the Business Plan

> *Learning without thought is labor lost; thought without learning is perilous.*
>
> Confucius
>
> "Learning and thought galvanize the entrepreneurial mind, and it is the 'planning' that speaks the mind, and trans-form mind set into action." A formal plan is a guide for action. Even if it's a simple or poor plan, it is still better than no plan at all.

10.1 The Monkey Story

A group of monkeys was happily playing under a cluster of tall trees. Someone wanted to test how the monkeys would react to something dear to them, so decided to hang a banana from a transparent plastic line tied to a branch.

The monkeys saw the banana. All looked upwards, seemingly wanting the banana, and tried to find ways to get at it. They jumped and jumped, a few just simply went round and round making a lot of noise, but no one seemed able to reach the banana. Then, there was one monkey. It quietly look around the tree, climbed it, and directly approached the branch where the banana was hanging. After several attempts, the monkey got hold of the line, pulled it up and got the banana.

The objective of the monkey story is as clear as crystal. Most of the monkeys (if not all) under the tree were puzzled about what they have seen: "How is it possible for a banana to hang suspended in the air?" Some others may hope that the banana will fall onto the ground, so the fastest one will get it for a treat. But only the one who thinks, is willing to learn, and is

218

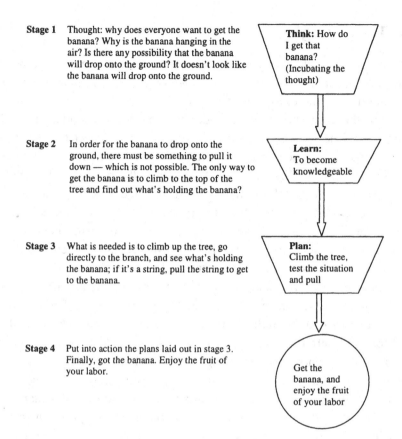

Stage 1   Thought: why does everyone want to get the banana? Why is the banana hanging in the air? Is there any possibility that the banana will drop onto the ground? It doesn't look like the banana will drop onto the ground.

Stage 2   In order for the banana to drop onto the ground, there must be something to pull it down — which is not possible. The only way to get the banana is to climb to the top of the tree and find out what's holding the banana?

Stage 3   What is needed is to climb up the tree, go directly to the branch, and see what's holding the banana; if it's a string, pull the string to get to the banana.

Stage 4   Put into action the plans laid out in stage 3. Finally, got the banana. Enjoy the fruit of your labor.

Figure 10.1 An algorithm for learning: how the monkey got the banana.

knowledgeable of the situation will be able to formulate the plan, and pursue with the appropriate action in accordance with the plan. Since gravity did not cause the banana to drop, there must be something holding the banana from above. The thought of something holding the banana stimulates the monkey, consolidates the "learning" and "thought," which is then transformed into the "get the banana" plan; the climbing, the trying, and finally the string-pulling got the monkey the banana in the end.

Whether the thinking and learning had really taken place in the mind of that monkey, the message is clear: the harvest does not fall from the sky, it is the thought, learning, planning and action that will generate the result.

10.2 The Thought

There are three fundamental requirements in creating a new venture, *the venture founder and his/her team, the product (or service) and money,* and most importantly, the existence of a plan.

Assume the would-be venture founder has a product (or products), service (or services). The thinking process takes place with respect to what to do with the product, and how to do it to make the product marketable? Testing the product idea is the first step, and testing how the product will serve the market and generate results is the next. Testing the product idea may not require financing efforts, but testing the product for the market needs financial commitment. This form of financial commitment is normally considered a soft cost. In more sophisticated terms, it is still part of research and development (R&D). Depending on the venture founder's desire and ability, it may require external financing to launch the testing. Bank financing is a source, but not desirable at this stage. Credit card loans from Visa or Mastercard are also a possibility, but they too are not desirable because these are all forms of debt financing, and the interest charged can be burdensome. There are some innovative financing schemes. For example, in the case of dealing with kitchen waste, the city government as well as other level (federal, provincial or state) government agencies responsible for marketing research grants, and other new venture creation assistance programs can be approached. All in all, if the venture founder is unable to undertake the project alone, they should try to seek out others to share the risk.

10.3 The Learning

"Thought" originated from the venture's founder. "Learning" is to know how others are doing, their knowledge, their skills and their way of doing things. Planning is both original (the idea of venture founder, the product or service offered from the venture founder) and learning from the others. The learning from what others have to offer include:

(1) Defining and affirming personal goals and the goal of the venture
(2) Appreciate the differences between value and profit
(3) Searching for and allocating resources

(4) The personal and venture's specific strategic objectives
(5) The performance standards and control

10.3.1 Defining and affirming personal goal and the goal of the venture

Each one of us has his/her own personal goals. To create a new venture is much the same as having a child; it needs care, passion and love of the creator. Therefore, the goal of the venture founder is none other than a successful launching of the new venture, and the continuation of the venture's success. This is the same goal of the venture, except that in order to clarify what it necessarily means to assure the success of the launching of the new venture and its continued growth and prosperity, the venture must earn a "profit." It is not necessary to say, however, that the undertaking is profit driven. Conventional "profit" is merely a tool and measuring device to gauge the degree of venture operation attainment. The value of the venture includes:

- The personal value of the venture founder
- The value reflected in services performed by those who work for the venture
- The public's perception and appreciation for what the venture offers
- What the public is willing to give to the venture in return

10.3.2 Value-driven venture versus profit-driven venture

In our exchange system and market economy, it appears that the fundamental difference between value and profit is seldom recognized. Profit as we know it is the end result, virtually without any challenge to the contrary, and profit is viewed as the "bottom line" throughout business culture in North America and globally. On the other hand, value places its emphasis in every process of economic activity, not just the end result or striving for the bottom line performance.

To further illustrate the differences, the following is a comparison between value driven and profit driven venture creation — the way of life,

Table 10.1 Value driven and profit driven — a venture philosophy.

The Basics	Value driven ◄	------- Profit driven
Belief	What can the venture offer	What can the venture do in order to make a profit, and more profit
Expectation	Long term sustainable growth, dictates short term financially viable	Short term result, preferably, immediate financial success
Attitude towards people	Give, if possible. Take only as it deems justifiable	Basically, take. Give only when under pressure
Value	Relationship, love one another, builds on trust and appreciation	Exchange value, basically only otherwise, anything of material substance
Vision	Shared vision. Vision used to guide operations shared by all those in the organization	Management vision imposed onto employees
Ownership	Every one has a stake in the venture. Every one is entitled to have a share of fruit of harvest, not just paid in terms of fixed wages for their labor	Ownership belongs only to the venture founder, who contributes the capital, makes sacrifices and devotes personal efforts that create the venture
Profit	There is no profit, unless all contributors receive their share of return for their contributions. Residual is not for personal enjoyment, but at least in part returned to the venture for realization of its growth potentials	Profit belongs to the owner, and it it's the fruit of the owner's labor, hard work, above all, award for risk taking
Financing	Equity plus some debt	Debt and suppliers' financing, plus equity

Table 10.1 (*Continued*)

The Basics	Value driven ◀------- Profit driven	
Attitude towards the environment health	Care for the environment. Health is a commitment, and is everyone's responsibility	It is unrealistic to place profit before environmental health
Decision-making	Empowered individuals in the organization	Concentrated in the hands of key individuals, the rest are just followers
Operational guide	Knowledge based	Niche, skill or technological based
Control systems	As feedback for improvement	As a pressure device for better performance

a business philosophy based on the beliefs of the venture founder, which may also be perceived by the public and those involved in the new venture.

Note that -----▶ ◀------- denoted in the table suggest that both value driven and profit driven philosophies are not absolutely independent from one and another. In fact, at times and under different circumstances, what is listed under "value driven" may also be found in "profit driven" firms; similarly, the "profit driven" venture philosophy can also be seen in "value driven" undertakings. In short, it is people that make the difference. At times, individuals tend to care more about "money" and "profit" than "people" and "environment," and other times and circumstances, people and environmental issues can be a priority in profit-driven enterprises.

10.3.3 Searching for and allocating resources

Money

Money to a new venture founder can be a challenge, unless the funds are readily available for use. In most cases, this is not always possible.

Start-up capital normally comes from personal savings, "love money" (loan of investment from parents and relatives), or a small bank loan. In most countries, financial institutions are available to invest in smaller ventures, but are not too keen to invest in start-ups, mainly because of the high risk involved. However, there are business development banks whose function is supposed to provide long term financing for smaller ventures. With a decent business plan, it could be a source worth considering. However, there are key factors that require the venture founder's attention:

(a) Use personal savings by all means, but consider other personal priorities. Since investing in business is a long-term financial commitment, once in the business, it will be difficult to withdraw if other needs arise. As business requires personal care, it should be freed from cashflow problems once in operation.

(b) Make a clear distinction between funds needed for building assets, and those required for operations. Over-investing in assets requires high sales volume (turnover) which may not be an easy task for a newly created enterprise.

(c) "Love money" must be repaid. Therefore, it must be treated the same way as funds borrowed from other sources. Failure to repay "love money" may cause unnecessary conflict amongst family members.

(d) Planning venture financing normally requires three sets of documentation: the cash projection for at least three years excluding the incubating period financing, the financial plan that will reflect not only financing (how to finance), but also financial management; and a long term business plan, although often it need not be quantified.

People

People are always the most important resource. Selecting good team players is not always an easy task, although it will not become a challenge until venture creation is actually taking place, when the venture founder has taxed his/her managerial capacity to the limit. On the other hand, some people involve others as founding partners at the incubating stage of the venture creation.

Two essential areas need to be considered: first, who is likely to become a working partner in the business, let's say for the entire duration of the venture? Second, who will invest their time and money into the new venture with expectations of short-term returns? At times, it is difficult to make a distinction between the two, including:

(a) Members of the family — can be a good idea, but this will be explored in the section on family business.
(b) Friends, schoolmates and people who have similar interest and devotion.
(c) Investors who are willing to join the firm as equity holders rather than money suppliers.
(d) Angels. They are different than investors. Some of them are venture capitalists with money. They could invest into smaller ventures with growth potential. Terms can be much more in favor of new ventures than normal investors.
(e) People with different background and skills that will complement any deficiency that the venture founder may have. In other words, if the venture founder is an engineer, he or she may try to find someone with a financial or marketing background. Ideally, a venture needs: a relations person, a technologist, a marketing specialist, a financial expert or accountant, and an applied generalist as general management personnel.
(f) People who are able to work and share the same vision and value as one another.

Preferably, a combination of a few of the above, e.g. (e) and (f) is good; if an angel is willing to join, it will be even better. Given the knowledge, most venture founders like to have some (if not all) of the qualities of (e), then (f) would be a logical choice. A business venture is a human institution, if there is such a "team" or "family", members of the team or family must have the willingness to have a shared vision and appreciate what value means to the individual and society. With the right people and proper financing, it is possible to consolidate all those business thoughts, and put it into a formalized plan along with marketing and operational details. As a generalization, the venture founder must always have in mind that under a market economy, we trade goods and services, but at the root of it all, business is all about people, people relations, and building relations through interactions among people.

10.3.4 The personal and venture's strategic objectives and plan

Figure 10.2 is prepared as a guide for the use of venture founders and those who work with him/her to formulate their personal and venture strategic plans and help to steer and set a course of action.

10.3.5 The performance standards and control

We have discussed extensively "big thinking," including shared vision, value among other things and personal goals. They all sound like motherhood and apple pie (a North American expression), but the thought is simply to give us the opportunity starting from the abstract, now put our feet on the ground, so as to become reality.

Standards serve two venture development purposes: as a guide and as a measuring device. But first, we need to clearly understand that human standards are artificial. They are used for measurement and as feedback indicators to reveal how resources have been allocated and for what purpose. It should not be used as a pressure device, and it is not the end of the world if standards of performance have not been met. Bear in mind that standards have been and are changing all the time.

For example, homosexuality judged by Christian standards was considered unthinkable human behavior in the past. Now, some churches allow ordained priests to marry people of the same sex. Marijuana was not too long ago completely banned as it was considered to be harmful to health, but now it is known to be useful as a form of medication. It is repulsive to know that many old inhumane acts rooted in tradition, remain acceptable in particular communities, and are still in practice. For example, incidents of killing wives and/or stove burning (now acid burning) still occur in Pakistan and some other Asian countries. The reasons? Suspicion on the husband's part that wives have had other sexual partners; a dowry perceived

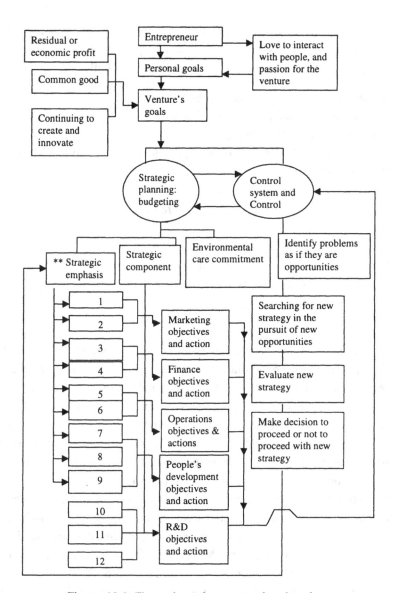

Figure 10.2 Flow chart for strategic planning.

to be too small; failure to get pregnant.[1] Any practice can become a standard, once it is commonly recognized and accepted as a standard practice, in some cases, it is even given a glorious name — "Culture."

- Know customers' wants and needs
- Co-ordinating total marketing efforts
- Short term favorable cashflow
- Long term residual (after deducting returns to all contributors from financial income)
- Efficiency: optimization input use
- Effectiveness: quality product and effective cost control
- Team efforts
- Effective board of directors
- Understanding and working with people
- Product design and utility function excellence
- Operation process
- Creativity

In business, standards must be concrete and expressed quantitatively (in units, percentages, or dollars and cents). For example, standard of performance for productivity may be established on the basis of number of units of output in relation to the number of direct labor-hours required to perform the job. For guiding marketing efforts, standards can be set in terms of sales dollars or number of units sold. Similarly, the measurement of human relations, absenteeism, labor turnover, and loss of person-hours due to accidents and strikes, can be used as standards.

There have been a lot of twists of old ideas, for example, Management By Objectives (MBO) is still very much alive, but with the addition of some new colors, such as quality control management and beyond. Except in an entrepreneurial organization, MBO, the "O" is not imposed on those who work, and those who make decisions and give orders. The performance standards are not established by people high on the top of the organization hierarchy alone, but with people who work on the job or perform tasks

---

[1] *HM Homemaker's*, November 2000, pp. 41–46.

involved. The important part of the application of the MBO concept is that those working in the shop floor offices and/or stations judge themselves on the basis of mutually established standards. They are not judged on a personal basis by the owner of the enterprise. Instead of using standards to penalize workers for their poor performance, those at the managerial level including the owner him/herself, use standards to help them locate problems, identify causes, and work as a team in dealing with the problem and searching possible opportunities conceived in the problem. Standards and control systems are essentially feedback of past performance. Certainly the existing standards themselves are not always particularly appropriate to the operation. Under the circumstances, standards should be reviewed, revised and changed if deemed necessary.

10.4 The Business Plan

It should be noted that the section on a business plan is not merely applicable to new ventures and new venture founders, it can also be used as a guide for ongoing ventures.

10.4.1 What is considered a good plan?

A good plan is a guide for action, and leads to actions that achieve the objective(s) of the plan.

There are three different ways to prepare a business plan: to use one's head, mind and heart. A good business plan needs to be prepared by using all three. The monkey story approach is about using one's head, to integrate logic, analysis and determination; only passion and love have to come from one's heart. This is not difficult, but a simple matter of expression of truth. Be true to yourself, and be true to others (the reader), and most important of all, communicate to the others. As an old saying goes: "It says what it means, and it means what it says." On the other hand, effective communication is a lot more than just what it means or what it says. Here is one story that will illustrate the point:

A family business is run by a husband and his wife, working together as a team. Unfortunately, more often than not, they do not agree on many areas of the business plan which is to be presented to potential investors. Verbally, they have argued so much that they always ended up not speaking to each other. The husband then suggested: "Let's put everything in writing." Both agreed, the plan was finished, but yet they won't speak to each other.

The meeting with investors was arranged for the next morning at 8 am. They both agreed that the husband should attend the meeting alone in order to avoid any disputes at the meeting, as everything has to go as planned. Before going to bed, the husband asked his wife: "Dear, would you please wake me up tomorrow morning at 6:30, it is important that I not be late." His wife nodded.

The next day, the husband slept till about 10 am. He was so furious, and asked his wife: "Why didn't you wake me up?" Without a word, the wife walked to the bed and pulled out a slip that was lying beside her husband's pillow. It says: "Dear, get up, it is 6:30." The message of this story is: a good business plan needs to speak for itself, even if it's lying on the bed next to the pillow.

10.4.2 The discipline of planning

Venture founders (particularly of smaller ventures) must have a business plan. Planning is a part of most human activity: people plan for what they should wear, what to buy, where to visit, whom to meet, when, and so on. But many of these plans require no formalization, rather it is only noted, and when the need arises, the details generally come to mind clearly enough, provided what's been planned is not too complicated and occurs not too far in the future. Memories are limited, and more often than not, not in the particular order that follows thought proceedings. Complex events, on the other hand, do need plans committed to writing (these days it is input into a computer).

The fundamentals of a business plan

A business plan varies from business to business. Today, with the help of computer software, a planner can be better organized by following a pre-subscribed format, but it does not replace the plan itself. Experience, however, suggests applying certain basics. Every business plan must:

(a) Have the users' needs in mind. What the readers want to know may be what the venture founder wants them to know, but their needs are often different. A business plan can be written for the need of investors, bankers, government funding agencies, last, but not least, the venture founder, or owner/manager him/herself, including members of the team.

(b) Speak the entrepreneur's mind. If the plan is to be used to guide him or her in making a dream into a reality, it must reflect the dream accurately.

(c) Show the founder's (owner-manager's) determination, commitment and competence.

(d) Be accompanied by a set of cashflow projections. Three years of month-to-month forecasts are desirable, but a good set of one-year projections is better than nothing.

(e) Demonstrate the coordination of all functions of the venture. For example, if the projected revenue is $10 million, then marketing, operations, financing, human resources, environmental care and so on must function as a team to earn that revenue, and the plan must show how they will do so.

(f) Be written so that it is clear, concise, complete and correct.

(g) Be followed with action. A plan that evokes no action is only words and figures. Even the worst-written plan, if acted upon, is better than no plan.

The following is a general outline of a business plan. Bear in mind, the outline is a simple workable guide, variations are always possible and needed to meet the particular need. The plan format, of course is available through computer software, otherwise, published samples can be secured from the marketplace.

General outline of a business plan

The business plan should begin with a table of contents.

Summary. Should be only about one page in length (two pages at the most). It should highlight briefly the key features of the business plan.

Background. Provide some description of the development of the business, with some reasons for entering the specific market. It should also include such information as date of incorporation, date of commencement of operations, and officers and directors of the company.

Management (or key individuals). State the age, education, experience, and background of the key individuals of the company.

Product or service description. Describe the company's major products or services and their contribution to the company's total accounting income and residual.

Market description. Market identification includes the size of the market, the share of the market, customers and the potential growth of the company's position in the market. The required information normally can be obtained through market research, as technological advancement has made it convenient for the search for basis information much more easily than before. Searching the Internet can provide the needed information that was not readily available in the past.

Competition. Nature and size of competition, pricing, quality, service and other forms of marketing strategies that will provide the company with an edge over the competitors (computer search may also be available).

Marketing strategy. Advertising, promotion, pricing, quality service, care for environmental health and other forms of market strategies that will provide the company with an edge over the competition.

Technology. Indication of past technology changes and anticipated advancements in the near future that may involve risks of obsolescence will indicate the company's commitment, not only to the improvement of its product (service), but also the concern for economical allocation of limited resources.

Production. Production facilities, including capacity, plant, workshop, status of the building, computer lab, machinery and equipment and production processes, and if possible, the level of technology applied (for example, for most desktop and laptop computers indicate whether there is need to regularly upgrade the technology).

Finance. A complete set of projected financial statements includes balance sheet, income statement, determination of residual and how financial income will be allocated to contributors, and cashflow projections for at least three years. Cashflow projection must be prepared on a monthly basis.

The human strength. The size of workforce, engineering force, computer programming force, sales force, administrative force, and high level decision makers. Union status should also be indicated in this section of the plan.

Risk. Identification should be made of the anticipated risk areas to be encountered and the problems to be overcome. These include: technology, production, marketing and finance, as well as human resources. If possible, describe the status of insurance in full.

Environmental care. Environmental care has always been an important factor for businesses. Only no efforts to account for it were attempted by businesses. However, during the past two decades, environmental care became a vital concern for everyone, including people in business. The vital issues involved that need to be disclosed in the plan include: garbage disposal, pollution control, energy conservation, conformity to government regulations and measures dealing with issues raised by advocates. In particular, government regulations in respect to zoning, land-use and building code; among other things, resources allocation, such as waste reduction, recycling and re-use practices.

Social responsibility. A business is a legal citizen of the community, it has a stake in the community and the community also has a stake in the business. The responsibility and commitment to matters concerning social and community welfare should also be included in the plan.

Table 10.2 Self-evaluation of a business plan.[2]

Target area	Score
	Not very satisfied ←————————→ Fully satisfied

Target area	Score
The plan format	1 2 3 4 5 6 7 8 9 10
Summary	1 2 3 4 5 6 7 8 9 10
Personal and business objectives	1 2 3 4 5 6 7 8 9 10
Product (service) design and quality	1 2 3 4 5 6 7 8 9 10
Product (service) testing	1 2 3 4 5 6 7 8 9 10
Product (service) description	1 2 3 4 5 6 7 8 9 10
Demand analysis	1 2 3 4 5 6 7 8 9 10
Marketing strategy	1 2 3 4 5 6 7 8 9 10
Risk analysis	1 2 3 4 5 6 7 8 9 10
Strategies to offset risk	1 2 3 4 5 6 7 8 9 10
Entrepreneur's competence	1 2 3 4 5 6 7 8 9 10
Human strategy (the management)	1 2 3 4 5 6 7 8 9 10
Personal financial commitment	1 2 3 4 5 6 7 8 9 10
Personal non-financial commitment	1 2 3 4 5 6 7 8 9 10
Strategies to secure non-controllable financial resources	1 2 3 4 5 6 7 8 9 10
Operation feasibility	1 2 3 4 5 6 7 8 9 10
Human resources analysis and planning	1 2 3 4 5 6 7 8 9 10
Organizational planning	1 2 3 4 5 6 7 8 9 10
Revenue planning	1 2 3 4 5 6 7 8 9 10
Cashflow planning	1 2 3 4 5 6 7 8 9 10
Cost-volume-financial income analysis	1 2 3 4 5 6 7 8 9 10
Financial planning	1 2 3 4 5 6 7 8 9 10
Overall coordination	1 2 3 4 5 6 7 8 9 10
Overall concern user's need — Information from this plan	1 2 3 4 5 6 7 8 9 10
Comforting factors from user's point of view	1 2 3 4 5 6 7 8 9 10
How well is the plan communicating with the user(s)	1 2 3 4 5 6 7 8 9 10
Concern for the environment and resources management	1 2 3 4 5 6 7 8 9 10
Flexibility	1 2 3 4 5 6 7 8 9 10
Overall evaluation	1 2 3 4 5 6 7 8 9 10

---

[2]Based on Kao R. W. Y., *Small Business Management*, 3rd ed. (Dryden Canada, 1992), p. 118, with some modifications.

The business plan format as a formalized document can be obtained from a variety of sources. There are special publications on how to prepare a business plan that are available online, thus it will not be included in this book. However, for evaluation purposes, the authors have provided a self-evaluation form for verification purpose (Table 10.2). Above all, a business plan should speak a venture founder's (owner-manager's) mind, with love and passion. A self-evaluation exercise could be a valuable process with benefits extending beyond just a "plan," because it has a human touch.

Questions for discussion

1. A business meeting is attended by a group of would-be investors (A) and three executives (B) from a large conglomerate that is in the transitional period of its economic reform. A well-prepared business plan is presented at the meeting. It is about 300 pages long but with a five-page summary. In addition, (B) makes a verbal presentation and says all kinds of impressive things about this project, with a particular emphasis on B's connection with the government. Immediately after (B) makes the presentation, one of the would-be investors (A) takes over the conversation with a smile. He says: "This business plan is simply beautiful and worthy enough to be presented to the Emperor. It reminds me of a story someone told me not too long ago." Everyone in the meeting says: "Let's hear it!" So the story goes like this:

> There was an emperor who wanted to know something about economics, so he told his ministers to work on it, and gave them one month to make the presentation. There were five on the job, and one month later, the five presented five volumes of economics to the emperor. They were ready to hear the emperor's praise, but to their surprise, the emperor was quite angry and said to his ministers: "You are out of your minds. Who do you think I am? How dare you think that I would have the time to read this? I have my responsibilities to the empire and I also have to attend to my concubines. Guards, take three of these bookworms out and behead them."
>
> The other two ministers got the message. In fear of another beheading, the two worked day and night and finally came out with

> one volume of economics. *With trembling voices, they pleaded to the emperor: "Your most gracious majesty, we have drained out every drop of our brain as if squeezing blood from a stone. This is the best and only economics volume there is in the whole empire." The emperor was not impressed, and called the guards to take one of the two for beheading. Then, the emperor ordered the one and only minister commissioned for the writing and said to him: "You know what you must do, before it's your turn."*
>
> *The last commissioned minister finally wrote a book on economics and presented it to the emperor. The Emperor took one look and smiled. He said: "This is perfect!" The book had only two sentences described what is economics: "There is no such thing as a free meal, you have to work for it." That is the end of the story.*

Referring back to our business plan issue, what is needed in a short simple sentence to convince would-be investors to consider the proposed project?

2. Assume you are in a position that requires you to prepare a business plan. In your own view, what needs to be included in a business plan for:

   (a) A banker if you are about to apply for a new venture start-up loan.
   (b) Venture capitalists if you are about to involve one of them to be your investor.
   (c) A government assistance program, if the program will assist in the marketing of your product on both the domestic and overseas markets.
   (d) Yourself as a guide for action.
   (e) A would-be business partner.
   (f) An overseas buyer who would like to test your competence in supplying his need. The gentleman is a high profile individual and an environmentalist who has great influence on major business leaders in the European Union.

3. Should social responsibility be included in your business plan? Why?
4. Discuss pros and cons for an outsider to do your new venture creation plan.
5. Design your own business plan, but bear in mind, it must include a concise financial plan with details in terms of:

- Capital investment plan
- Operations plan
- Cashflow projection
- Long term debt repayment plan
- Capital structure plan

6. Prepare a breakeven chart that will reflect your company's operation. Include your own remuneration. The chart should reflect the traditional breakeven point, the cash breakeven point, and early programmed cost recovery breakeven point. Explain why there are more than one breakeven points.

Chapter 11

Caring and Developing a New Venture for Sustainable Growth

> *Although big is better, small is still beautiful; a bold eagle gliding in the blue sky gives you a vision of what heaven can be, but it is the hummingbirds that make our Southern Hemisphere paradise on Earth.*
>
> R. W. Y. Kao 2002
>
> *We know you are getting there, but can you hang on once you've arrived?*
>
> Campaign ad for an unidentified business development center.

11.1 Introduction

A new venture is much like a newborn baby. It can do very little for itself, needs almost constant attention, provides nothing in return, and often causes a great deal of stress and sleepless nights for the parent. It needs love, passion and attention, and if it receives these things, then it will grow and eventually become just like a friend to the founder, and will help to take care of his or her needs in return. This chapter, which was inspired by interactions with a group of MBA candidates, is about those early stages of caring for a new venture. There are few big words here, only little ideas, but it is these little ideas that count. Think of it as a tool box of caring.

In his first Entrepreneurism lecture to a second year MBA class, the senior author asked the students to fill in a short questionnaire. The first question was: "Why are you electing this course?" Six of the respondents gave answers similar to the following:

"I want to have my own business, but I heard so many people with past experience say that the first three years are difficult, and the failure rate is as high as 80%. What I (we) want to know are some of the pitfalls, and tips that I (we) can acquire from this course to reduce our chance of failing."

It is on this basis that we choose to spend less time on the more philosophical issues of entrepreneurship. Rather, with our feet planted firmly on the ground, we shall outline some fundamental management wisdom and know-how — based on consulting, teaching, research and actual involvement with new venture start-ups and management. They are by no means conclusive nor complete. Rather, they are a starting point for more effective entrepreneurial management for smaller young enterprises in the interest of the entrepreneur as well as to add value to society.

Once upon a time, not too long ago, a business development center attempting to attract small young ventures to utilize their services came up with a message for an ad campaign. The message went something like this: "We know you are getting there, but can you hang on once you've arrived?" It is certainly true that any entrepreneurial inclined individual who is sufficiently determined to start up a small venture will find out that it is not as difficult as most people think. Soon, he or she could be sitting in a comfortable chair behind a big desk in the back room of their own business with a plaque in front inscribed: "Private." In some countries, you almost get the feeling that, so long as you have a decent business plan, you will make it. But one of the things that defines a great cook is the ability to look in a cupboard or refrigerators, and out of what most of us would see as nothing but a few odds and ends, put together a gourmet meal that would astound us. The same ingredients are there for us, and yet even with all the recipe books in the world, we still would not come up with the same result. There are many differences between most of us and great chefs, but certainly one thing that stands out is the passion they have for their art, and if we had that passion we would go a long way towards becoming better cooks. Similarly, the successful start-up and development of a viable enterprise largely comes from the entrepreneurs themselves: discipline, love, passion for the business and making personal sacrifices are just a few of the more important qualities required. Some of you may ask that if the sacrifice and commitment required are so huge, then what is the payoff? The answer is "plenty." It gives one the satisfaction of virtually every need outlined by Maslow, it empowers the owner to make proprietary decisions, and above all, it creates wealth for the venture founder and adds value to society. Serving people and providing jobs are just two of these higher benefits. But a good business plan, like a good recipe, is only the beginning and small part of it. The lifelong commitment is yet to come.

11.2 Becoming Disciplined and a Doer, Not Just a Talker

All entrepreneurs are primarily doers rather than talkers. Talk is good, but nothing will happen from just talk. Preparing a business plan is doing, but only provides a guide for action; without action there is no business. Talking and planning may give added motivation, but still does not create a business. Only action will generate results. And how do we proceed from talk to action? Once the mind is made up, the way of thinking must be changed. Here, we present three areas that will shape the mind towards going beyond the business plan and laying the foundation of a successful new venture.

11.2.1 Have an attitude of uninformed optimism

Uninformed optimism is fundamental to human nature. Most of us get up everyday with the expectation that at the end of the day we shall go back to bed again. We have no basis for this except for the fact that we expect it to be like every other day of our lives. We believe it because we do not know any better. It has been said before that if most of us knew what went into being a parent before we did it, then none of us would ever have children. Similarly, someone from a well-known American university acknowledged that university graduates, and in particular, MBAs grads are often averse to owning their own businesses, because they know too much. The more information they have, the less the desire they have to take risks. With a little information, we often look for more information, but there is never enough: no one can ever really have the complete information needed to ensure the creation of a sure-win situation. It makes no difference how much information we can get or how fast we can retrieve it from the Internet, still we make many decisions when confronted with a vast sea of uncertainties. The truth is, virtually all decisions and actions taken are based on limited information with a great deal of uninformed optimism. Uninformed optimism does not mean that one is ignorant, or worse stupid. Accept that we shall never know enough, and must learn as we go along. After all, that is how we do it as parents!

11.2.2 Believe in yourself

Confidence is considered by academics to be a critical entrepreneurial attribute. As a new venture founder you must have confidence in yourself, your product and your business. It is difficult to work with partners and employees without this. Real confidence is an attribute, based on knowledge and experience of yourself, and often comes from knowledge of failure and knowing that you have the ability to rise above it. Most importantly, success engenders success. Through success, you can be trained to believe in yourself, and so you should gain in confidence by aiming and achieving a series of small successes, and acquiring experience and knowledge rather than simply going for the big score and missing. Sometimes it works, but if it does not, and this happens all too often, it leads to discouragement and belief in failure. The time for the big success will come, but it will come more often to someone who has been trained for it.

11.2.3 In an entrepreneurial mindset, you have no problems, only opportunities

In life, everyday should be a blessing, and in business, all happenings are opportunities. Even in problem situations there are opportunities to be conceived. In the 1970s, the whole world was facing an unprecedented oil shortage. The crisis hit Japan severely, because with no oil of its own, its industries rely on imported oil the way a human needs blood to survive. Consequently, the crisis turned into an opportunity as the Japanese car industry concentrated on building better, more fuel efficient, smaller cars. The result was a car industry that came to rival the American giant.

11.2.4 Not just "no risk, no gain," but "no risk and lose"

Many people believe in the old adage, "no risk no gain." But a little consideration tells us, and this is not difficult to realize, that with no risk, there are many losses: the loss of opportunity, the loss of drive, and worse still, loss of initiative, and meaning of life.

11.3 The Entrepreneurial Venture Founder's Challenge: Think Big, But Put Both Feet Firmly on the Ground

Humans are strange creatures. We are basically pretty ordinary sized mammals, bigger than most but much smaller than many, and perhaps that is why we have such an inferiority complex. Sure enough, we appreciate the fact that small is beautiful, but there are plenty of individuals who think that big is always better. So many people in the business world and especially those who are just dreaming about it, want a bigger office, a bigger car, a bigger house, and it goes without saying, a bigger pay cheque. Wanting to be big may be simply a matter of gluttony. Some may say that it is human nature, while others may feel it is the environment that makes it necessary to be big and powerful. After all, they say, if we are not big enough, then someone who is will gobble us up. It is a matter of natural selection, just as Darwin said. But the truth is that Darwin did not really say so. Bigger is not always better, adaptability is more important in the long run. And smaller is often more adaptable. An entrepreneur wanting to make that giant step towards the realization of a "big dream" is better off starting-up on a smaller scale that is more manageable and does not have a high overhead. Remember that it is the small wheels that make the big wheel move. All humans started small, quite literally. The richest man in the world, Bill Gates, the leader of the most powerful country in the world, George W. Bush, the "iron butterfly" Margaret Thatcher, and the Pope, all began as the union of a tiny human egg with an even more diminutive human sperm. In short, definitely have your own business, think big if it pleases you, but make sure to plant both your feet firmly on terra firma, choosing a business start-up that requires no substantial overhead commitment.

If possible, try to land the sales before starting-up the business. This may sound unreal, but in many cases, certainly for most technically inclined new ventures, such as a customized software development company, job orders can be made on contract, requiring almost no substantial overhead commitment.

11.4 Essential Guide for New Venture Development

The following 14 points are not comprehensive, but if observed by the entrepreneurial manager, will greatly improve the chances of a new venture's success:

(1) **If you have a choice, start small, and go into business on contract rather than producing goods for stock, which you then need to sell**

If a business whose primary function is to produce for stock (a process industry), then cash is tied down in building up inventory, and uncertainty in sales must be confronted. However, in a business working for definite orders, the quoted price for the order includes all costs (variable and fixed) and normal mark-up, and there is no need to invest money in inventory build-up. In short, for a small new venture, it is better to acquire sales first and then produce, rather than produce first and then sell. The tree planting business first mentioned in Chapter 9 (page 214) was started up with virtually no capital, but secured an Ontario government tree planting contract that was to last at least 17 years. With the contract, the owners were able to secure needed finance from a bank, and create a viable business with a million dollar contract within only two to three years' time. Similarly, there is a story of a travel agent who started her business alone with nothing but a computer and a business web page; she did all her business over the Internet, and now has the whole world at her fingertips.

(2) **Do not let information about the product or worse, the product itself out of your sight, unless you are completely satisfied that it is ready to enter into the market**

New venture founders tend to become very passionately involved in what they create. They are very excited about their new product idea, the prototype, the product itself and the whole process of getting it onto the market. Perhaps the entrepreneur is eager to see success, to garner the approval of others, or is pressured to start getting some cashflow into the business. Whatever the reason, entrepreneurs are often too eager to put their products or ideas before the public. However, the entrepreneur must be aware that an imperfect prototype, once out in the open, could be copied by anyone who could improve on the prototype, and entered into the market quickly, making it difficult for an additional new entrant before the inventor even has a chance to test the market. This is a notorious problem in scientific research, where a smaller lab with innovative ideas presents early work, but a larger group with more resources is able to take it further more quickly, and eventually garners all the recognition for the discovery.

(3) **Use existing resources as much as possible**

For some people in business, the No. 1 challenge is how to acquire needed funds. In particular, how to borrow money from a bank. Yet the need for money never seems to end. It is easy enough to grasp why: like a dinosaur, it has a virtually endless capacity for food. Banks are a convenient money supplier. A business needs money to acquire resources, but existing resources can also be available, if the entrepreneur makes the effort to search for possible alternatives. Personal services can be transformed into cash by trading them for needed resources; family aid can also be utilized, both directly and in trade, and these days, virtually every government in the Western world has some form of assistance designed to help small new ventures. There is a bank that has a promotional slogan that goes something like: "The first, last and always the source for small business financing." Despite their friendly advertisements, acquisition of needed financing from a bank without a track record, guarantor's signature, collateral or other form of security can be a frustrating business. It is about as much fun as trying to reach someone on the phone and hearing nothing but their voice message, over and over again. This does not mean you will never get the bank's help. There is a good chance that you will, but you need to know how to get away from the recorded message routine and find a real human being to approach. Then you can build up a trust relationship, but you'll need a lot of comforting factors to make him or her feel comfortable about you.

(4) **Make sure costs are escapable**

Cost, by and large, can be segregated into variable and fixed, and those considered to be mixed costs (i.e. partially fixed and partially variable), can with a little scrutiny usually be separated into fixed and variable. This may be demonstrated as follows:

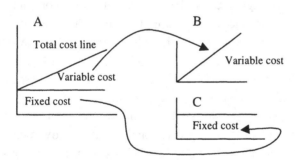

Figure 11.1 Mixed cost (A), variable cost (B) and fixed cost (C).

After separation, fixed cost goes to fixed, variable goes to variable. Although no cost is absolutely fixed nor absolutely variable, the separation is necessary for managerial decisions. For example, a sales executive's remuneration is generally considered to be fixed (in a salary scheme). But on a commission scheme, it is variable, since payment of commission is directly associated with sales activity. In short, no sales, no commission. Small and young ventures should if at all possible avoid fixed costs, and incur costs associated with activity. Of course, the situation reverses as the activity (such as sales) increases and it becomes preferable to arrange for cost to be fixed.

(5) **Avoid overhead buildup. Borrowing money to build up overhead needs a high sales volume, otherwise there will be a cashflow problem**

Referring to 11.4.4 above, as sales improve with effort and time, there is a temptation for entrepreneurs to swing away from "small" and embark on "big," going from a simple structure to a corporate pyramid, and more overhead. More overhead means more fixed commitment in cash, resulting more often than not, in a deep debt financing situation. Deep debt financing requires interest payments before "profit" is earned, putting a great deal of pressure on generating cash. When the management is pressured by cash restrictions, the priority will shift from managing the business to managing cash. Unless the business continues its growth and costs are closely monitored, so that the volume of sales is able to support the growth, otherwise, it may place the business in a very unfavorable position. Consequently, even if the company may make a paper "accounting profit," the pressure of cash requirements may send the business to the gallows.

Avoiding overhead buildup simply requires the entrepreneur to monitor business growth and cashflow; overhead buildup is only acceptable, if sales, a "profit" augment and favorable cashflow can be anticipated and realized.

(6) **If a product or business has a low entry barrier for you, it also has a low entry barrier for others**

Entry barriers involve anything from goodwill, product differentiation, advertising, R&D, technology to location. If a product has a low entry barrier for the entrepreneur, then it likely has the same for others unless the entrepreneur is in a special situation. Therefore, anyone entering the market should develop a niche. A niche is something that could attract others to buy the product you offer and/or doing business with you.

The following is an example of "niche" advertising that illustrates the point (the story was in a church minister's sermon to his congregation). He said: "In a street in an American city, there are three pizza shops. One shop advertised his product with a big sign that read: *We have the best Pizza in the United States of America.* The next shop then put up a bigger sign that read: *We have the best Pizza in the world.* The third one, a new entrant, but smaller outlet, put up a not so big, but bright sign that read: *We have the best Pizza on this street.* That's the idea."

(7) **Use a break-even analysis to guide** *action*

A break-even analysis is a simple tool to relate cost, profit and volume. More so, it is a planning tool to control costs and help to exercise self-discipline. Here is how it works:

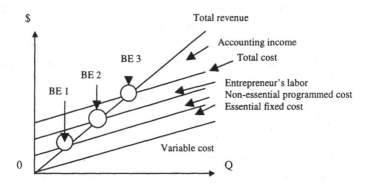

Figure 11.2 BE chart for control.

The simple break-even chart serves not only to reflect the cost, volume and accounting profit relationship, but also indicate that it has three "break-even" points where the user can visualize sales volumes required to meet various cost obligations. BE 1 shows sales volume needed to meet immediate variable cost incurred,

BE 2 on the other hand requires a high sales volume to non-essential programmed cost in addition to sales requirements needed to meet other pressing obligations. BE 3 sales will give sufficient reward to compensate the entrepreneur's efforts to run the business.

(8) Focusing on favorable cashflow

Cash in a business is much the same as blood in a human body. Without a minimum circulating blood flow, the consequence is simply death. The same can happen to a business, and in particular to smaller enterprises. To focus on favorable cash management means the entrepreneur must always reconcile their bank account and do a cashflow analysis of their business (or empower someone to undertake the task). Regular checks will serve as an additional guide to caution that cash movement is in a safe direction.

(9) Always cost the product or service with full costing

Full costing is to cost the product/service on the basis of the total sacrifice the entrepreneur makes to produce/sell the product. Full costing means the product inventory value carries both the variable cost of the product/service, as well as a portion of fixed factory overhead. Full costing is needed for long term survival and growth, and all costs must be realized from the sale of the product/service. However, for short term promotion and competition reasons, it is still possible to proceed with a lower selling price, so long as the selling price is greater than the variable cost. On the other hand, one must be cautious when playing with price, as however much lowering the normal selling price is good, it may discourage further sales if customers are aware of the "lowering price" policy.

(10) Understand the meaning of profit, and adopt "Residual Income" for operational guidance and planning

Until we can successfully venture onto another planet, our resources are limited by the capacity of our planet earth, and this is true for ourselves as well as for our children and all other living beings now and in the future. Not only the non-renewable resources, but even the renewable resources are limited because they all depend on the limited resource of the sun's energy, and there is only so much of that, that we can capture. Our creativity and innovation can make different combinations and extend the utility function of the "renewable resources," but there is ultimately a limit. One might ask if it matters that we have been misguided into believing that there is a "profit" without appreciating where this "profit" is coming from. Our Mother Earth is all we have. Since we cannot really add anything to it, but merely change its face, what profit can we really have? Therefore, what we claim to be profit processed through the accounting system is in fact a residual of unpaid costs including perhaps the entrepreneur's own entitlement. As we realize the reality of paying all these unpaid costs, it is necessary to abandon the whole idea of "accounting profit."

As a start, the entrepreneur should recognize two things: the opportunity cost or imputed interest as a going rate of his or her investment in the business, and the full recognition of his or her own efforts and sacrifices for running the business. If it is possible, recognition must also be given to other contributors to the business, whose contributions are not recognized. As an example, assume that accounting profit before deducting your full salary is in the amount of $550,000.

Accounting profit		$550,000
Opportunity cost of entrepreneur's investment $1,000,000 @ 6%		$60,000
Full salary for the entrepreneur	<u>$150,000</u>[*]	<u>$210,000</u>
Operation residual before deducting recognition of environmental preservation, and employees' share of entitlement of the fruits of their labor[†]		$340,000

[*]If an outsider is engaged to run the business, this would be his or her remuneration

[†]No cash disbursement is involved at this stage, just residual allocation

(11) **Know where you want to go and have a rough idea how to get there**

Properly defined this means

Vision: How you see where you want to go.

Strategy: The vehicle that will take you where you want to go.

Plan: Establishes the road map (make sure you read it!) to guide you to the place you want to go.

In action terms: Set your venture objective, and prepare a business plan that will guide you to reach your destination.

(12) **In business, there is no enemy, only the competition**

Some people draw a parallel comparison between business strategy and war strategy. This is terribly wrong. The trouble is they cannot see the difference between killing and competition. In business, you compete and also make friends, but in war, you fight and kill. In business, you cannot afford to have enemies, and never have enough friends.

(13) **If possible, make friends before doing business**

Friendship before business is wisdom as well as sensible business practice. In Turkey, business acquaintances are treated as true friends, and even if the business deal does not go through, the friendship remains. In China, once the other party is aware of the presence of friendship, the business deals will most likely proceed much more smoothly and people tend to be more helpful.

(14) **Profit is not for you to spend on luxuries, but residual after full costs are deducted from revenue. It is new blood needed as a return to business for sustainable growth**

Accounting profit is not what it seems to be. In a true sense, all of us are entitled to be paid for our labor, and accounting profit is the fruit of this labor, but there are others who have contributed to making it possible to yield the fruits of human labor. If there is anything left it would be "residual," supposedly used for reinvestment into the business to sustain it and help it to grow. It should not be spent on a lavish spending spree, or to build that ballroom in your new "mansion" you always wanted.

Spending lavishly (of the fruits of everyone's labor) is as bad as killing the goose that lays the golden egg. The residual is the lifeblood of the business. It is a simple idea that everyone should be able to appreciate: we all live for today as well as tomorrow, not only for ourselves, but also for our children and children's children. Residual is more than what is for the future after we have received our entitlement for the present, it is part of the whole calculation.

11.5 This Matter of Managing. ...No, We Mean Caring

In a family, which would you prefer — a father who is a manager of his family, or one who cares for it? It is the same in business. Fundamentally, caring for one's own enterprise as compared to managing someone else's business is a matter of ownership, and ultimately decision-making. There is also a difference of objective. Put simply, caring for one's own business is for the business and for self-interest. In traditional corporate management philosophy, making money in the name of satisfying the shareholders' return on investment is the corporate life. It is reflected in policy, particularly in attitudes towards people. In an owner managed business, people are viewed as valuable assets, whereas in corporate life, people are part of the money-making machine, diposable and replaceable. This is what is happening now, as computerization and automation remove many of the lower skill jobs. Everything is programmed, a mere click or a scan away.

11.5.1 The Caring of People

Compared to just a few decades ago, the miracles of technology appear mind-boggling. It seems that virtually anything is possible. Yet despite this, we still cannot make a machine that thinks like a man, or that can replace people's minds. Therefore, the traditional theories of X, Y and Z still make the classroom rounds, and we still very much rely on Maslow's theory of need to explain what makes people tick. So we shall begin with "Motivation."

(1) **No one can serve two masters. Either he will hate one and love the other, or he will be devoted to one and despise the other. You cannot serve both God and Money.**[1]

Whether you believe in God or not, there is a fundamental truth here: money can be an effective motivator, but you cannot let money be your guide. It can only corrupt your desire for achievement, and moreover, money can blind a person who then becomes a slave to money, rather than its master.

In one seminar, the senior author distributed two coins to each participant and told them to use the coins to cover their eyes. He asked: "What do you see?" Some said: "Money," others said: "Nothing, nothing at all." He then asked them to let go, and of course the coins dropped to the ground because of the natural force of gravity.

What does this tell us? If all you see is money, then you see nothing else. But if you let go of money, then you can see again. Money has no power except the power that we give it — let go of it, and it drops like scales from your eyes. The driving force of Lee Kuan Yew, the founding father of modern Singapore, was definitely not that of money, since he could have been a lot wealthier if he had continued to practice law as he was trained to. Nelson Mandela, jailed for 23 years, was also certainly not in politics for the money. The great achievers who have made huge contributions to humanity were all motivated by other factors rather than by money.

Life is about sharing: for self-interest as well as for others. Sharing ownership, decision-making authority and/or the fruits of labor can motivate to a greater extent than just money. The great motivating factor is the appreciation of sharing common interest, as well as satisfying the individual's desire for self-interest. Money is important to everyone, but there is a lot more in business and in life than money.

---

[1]New Testament Matthew, 6:24, New International Version.

(2) You cannot make a person a member of the team, if he or she does not share in the fruits of the team's labor

Individuals who work for the entrepreneur and get paid only for their labor cannot be initiated as members of the team. "They work **for** me" is how it was in days past; today's reality is: "they work **with** you," sharing a common dream, attempting to achieve the same goal, carrying the same burdens, earning their part of the glory, and experiencing the thick and thin together. How can this be accomplished? How does one get such "super-employees?" Among other things, sharing in decision-making and delegation are effective means of motivation. Nowadays, this concept carries a fancy term: Empowerment. Although it's easy to say, it is often hard to do. The hard part is if something goes wrong, who pays for the "wrong?" The answer becomes much easier, if we stop viewing wrongs as an expensive mistake, but as an investment. After all, the payoffs for the future are very handsome!

(3) Managing your vision

Vision is not about whether we perceive the earth as round or flat, or how we fit ourselves into the square or circle. It is the realistic target that beckons the organization. An entrepreneurial vision must be shared with those around you. It must be stable over time, but dynamic enough to respond to the changing situations. Above all, it must raise the enthusiasm, and empower the members of the enterprise.

(4) Planning for human resources before you decide to expand the business

Most people tend to think that money comes first before business expansion becomes possible, and this may be true. However, money without competent people may result in loss of money and the business. Plan and assemble the needed human resources first. Money will be a good complement to make the business expansion achievable.

(5) Competing for good people

Large corporations have all the muscle to attract able young individuals. For smaller firms, the strategy has to be different from those large companies.

This includes providing opportunities in management, personal growth, ownership, participation in important business decisions, flexible time and opportunities for community involvement, family care service, not just for babies, but elders as well. And above all, to treat people, not just as analytical machines, certainly not as potential deadwood to "weed" out of the organization and "net" them into the "volunteer army of unemployed" in the words of Milton Friedman.

(6) Competent board of directors

Every incorporated entity needs a board of directors. It is a statutory requirement, and more often than not, entrepreneurs that are also sole shareholders will form a board consisting of their friends and family, just to fulfill the requirements. The board of directors is then treated as nothing more than a paper entity. But this is wrong. Engaging retired accountants or other professionals can create an effective board of directors who will act to provide advice to the entrepreneurs who may be lacking in some areas of expertise. Although this may incur some minor expenses, in comparison with the benefit entrepreneurs may receive, it is certainly worthwhile to try.

(7) If possible, avoid a pyramid type of organizational structure, instead have a flat leader-follower related union

This is appropriate for a very small organization, involving no more than half a dozen people working as a team. Under the circumstances, it will be justifiable to organize in a way where each individual relates directly to the entrepreneur as follows:

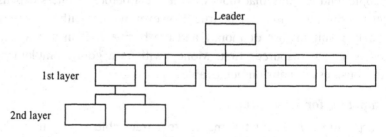

Figure 11.3 Pyramid organization illustration.

However, as the enterprise becomes larger and the operations get more complicated, a second layer (creating more boxes) may change the flat, "one top decision maker" structure to a pyramid organization, ultimately resulting in multiple layers of organization with a lengthy communication process chain. It is much more effective and facilitates empowerment and delegation if the enterprise is structured as a multiple leader follower type of organization, not placing the leader on the top, but in the center of people, so everyone can relate and interact, as shown in the following:

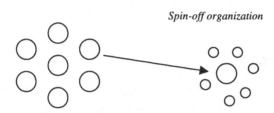

Spin-off organization

Figure 11.4 Leader-follower organization illustration.

(8) Staff function re-defined

Staff in the enterprise, such as an accountant or human resources manager, are important to the organization. Among other things, they perform two distinct functions, control and support. More often than not, the staff tend to lean more towards the control aspect rather than the supportive. This hinders initiatives, and makes the support function persons the sore thumbs among colleagues, as they are often viewed as a burden to the rest because they do not generate revenue from outside. However, steps should be taken to ensure that staff in the enterprise also perform the supportive function and offer their expertise to explore opportunities rather just solving problems and troubleshooting.

(9) Communication and negotiation

Some inflight magazines on airlines in North America carry an advertisement with a person in his 50s, unsmiling and with a general air of success about him. The ad carries this short message: "In business, you do not get what you deserve, you get what you negotiate." Negotiation and communication skills are needed by virtually all business persons. The senior author once told his nephew, a very successful businessman with wide international connections, about this ad. He responded: "Uncle, he is right, but you have to watch yourself carefully when you complete the negotiation and shake hands across the table to seal the deal — you have to make sure that you still have your arm with you."

Table 11.1 contains some general guidelines about communication and negotiation. They are by no means complete, but they should be observed carefully. They are intended to enhance one's knowledge, and to improve awareness. If carefully used, they will increase the chances of success in dealings through negotiation.

11.5.2 Finance

In the business world, the minute finance is mentioned, people tend to think it is all about money. This is true enough; whether it is to finance a venture, or manage a company's finance, finance is all about money. When the senior author was serving on the Consultative Committee to the Canadian Minister of Small Business, there were two words that were on everyone's lips all the time: "Money" and "Management." Some people say that if you have money, you can hire experts to manage the business. However, "experts" do fail; they probably fail even more miserably than non-experts. Of course, some others were saying, if you have good management, money is not a problem. Nevertheless, dealing with the topic of "Finance" should not be divorced from management, because everything in business is management.

Table 11.2 contains a group of "general guidelines" concerning financing and financial management for entrepreneur managed small young ventures.

11.5.3 Marketing

In business, marketing is where the excitement is, because marketing is the functional area that brings in revenue from outside. Without revenue (sales), there is no business. And the entire market economy is built on the concepts of buy (demand) and sell (supply), even in this day of one-click shopping and the Internet.

Table 11.1 A general guide for negotiation skills.

Category and guide	Explanatory notes
Needs: continuation	Develop a carefully planned tactic.
Belonging and esteem	In negotiation, it is no longer about you or your team and their team, but about sharing a common objective.
Achievement and fulfillment	The accomplishment of a mutually satisfying agreement
Attributes: discipline	Exercise self-control at all times.
Attractive personality	A negotiator should be clear-headed and modest, sympathetic and have common sense, with a natural concern for good relations, and have a good command of the language of negotiation.
Manners	Manners are associated with heritage, scholastic achievement, expertise and specialization. A negotiator must have a specialization, but must be versatile. Culture makes a person rich in spirit and confident in manoeuvrability.
Communication skills	Communication refers to both listening and speaking. Communicating is not about making impressive speeches, but about getting feedback and results.
Actions: preparation of mind	Be sincere, and willing to negotiate in good faith. Alertness is only a small part of presence of mind. A negotiator should be relaxed, but be able to react and respond quickly, and offer direction when the need arises.
Setting the objective	The objective should be in response to all the background factors and all the reasons for the negotiation. One should not overstretch the objectives, attempting to do too much, and accomplishing little.
Organization	Organize the team and material. Study the opposing point of view as well as their team's.
Preparation, summary and presentation	Carefully study all documentation relating to the matter to be negotiated. Consult experts on anything you do not understand. Prepare simple, easy-to-understand audio-visual aids needed to support the presentation.

Table 11.1 (*Continued*)

Category and guide	Explanatory notes
Setting the environment	If negotiation is conducted on your turf, a meeting place should be equipped with all the essential presentation aids, in a comfortable and friendly environment, away from all disturbances, and conducive to free interface between the two parties.
Ensuring punctuality	There is no excuse for late arrival. To reschedule for another meeting reveals a weakness in the negotiator, and may be misinterpreted as lack of interest to negotiate.
Divulging information. Grouping the negotiation package.	Do not volunteer information unnecessarily. Negotiation is a long process. At times, it is difficult to break the deadlock. For the purpose of achieving the objective, it is better to break the whole package into parts, so partial agreement can be attained, permitting the interaction to continue.
Making personal contacts with the other party	It is always better to develop a good rapport with your business partners. If possible, be friends first before business.
Have confidence in your translator	International negotiations are an important part of today's global economy. If a foreign language is used and translation is necessary, make sure that you have confidence in the translator and be certain that he or she translates faithfully; no more, no less.
Establishing the groundwork for the negotiation	An agenda for the meeting is a must. It is always good to start with a smile and enthusiasm. Minutes must be kept in detail and approved by both parties. Keep spirits high, and be constantly aware that negotiation is for both parties and it has to be mutually beneficial.
Preparing the agreement	An agreement should be prepared from approved minutes, then drafted into a formal agreement, which should be signed and amended if necessary.
Taking care of human relations	Keep a friendly atmosphere throughout the negotiation, and keep personal feelings out of the negotiation. Remain friendly, even if the deal does not go through as expected.

Table 11.2 General guide for financing and financial management.

Function:	Areas of concern and general guidelines	Explanatory notes
Financing	Finance the new venture using "debt" instead of "equity."	Although the cost of debt is normally less than the cost of equity, in the early stages of operation, most firms operate on a breakeven or even planned loss basis, and therefore cost of equity is not an immediate concern, but cashflow is. Thus, debt financing imposes cashflow restraints which a young firm may not be able to withstand.
Cost of capital	The cheapest cost of capital is accounts payable.	Warning: If a firm is unable to take a 2% ten days payment term offered by suppliers, the cost to carry payables can be substantial. The cost of not taking 2% ten days' offer is 36.72%. The calculation: $$= \text{discount rate}/(1 - \text{discount rate}) \times 360 \text{ days}/(\text{Final due date} - \text{discount period})$$ $$= 0.02/(1 - 0.02) \times 360/(30 - 10)$$ $$= 0.0204 \times 18 = 36.72\%$$
Use of working capital	Do not use working capital for expenditures that will not generate immediate revenue.	Working capital is for short term financial obligation needs. Long term investment needs long term borrowing or additional equity.
Financing your operation through your customers	Ratio analysis.	It is a common practice to finance your operations through your customers by asking them to leave a reasonable amount of deposit, or in the form of instalment.
Financial management		A ratio analysis gives some idea as to how you are doing with resources under your trust. In general, there are four types of ratio more meaningful to new and smaller enterprises than others:

Table 11.2 (*Continued*)

Function:	Areas of concern and general guidelines	Explanatory notes
Financial management (*Cont.*)		Liquidity ratio: currents/current liabilities Activity ratio: receivables/average sales per day Profitability ratio: net income after tax/sales Profitability ratio: net income after tax/net worth
Budget		Consists of: • A statement of objective • Review of past performance • A list of priorities • A set of pro-forma financial statements • A monthly cashflow projection • Schedules and departmental budgets
Control		Costs should be separated into fixed and variable. The controllable costs (could be either variable or directly related fixed costs controllable by certain individuals, or both) should be clearly assigned and defined. If possible, establish a standard cost system. At the end of each operational period, make a comparison between actual spending and standard cost allowed or budgeted, locating discrepancies between the two, which can then be discussed with those responsible for the cost, in order to improve performance.

There are countless marketing and marketing management texts in the market. The idea of the 4 "Ps," product, price, promotion and place are still as fresh as daisies, and are known to everyone who knows even a little bit about business. The following are some of the pitfalls that are common to new ventures and younger enterprises:

(1) Improper pricing (too high or too low).
(2) Lack of knowledge about costing the product or service costing.
(3) Inability or unwillingness to plan.
(4) Poor communication among partners and/or members of the management team, particularly in respect to important sales decisions.
(5) Poor retail location.
(6) Lack of self-discipline.
(7) Dishonesty.
(8) Management incompetence, lack of marketing experience or ignorance about the market.
(9) Failure to interact with people in the marketplace.
(10) Non-controllable environmental factors, such as government regulations, taxes, high occupancy costs, market shifts, consumers' choice, preference changes, inability to compete, and difficulty to acquire needed finance to support market efforts, especially advertising and promotion.
(11) Entrepreneurial failings, such as bad judgement, lack of entrepreneurial value, no drive, and/or risk aversion.
(12) Unwillingness to make a commitment that involve uncertainties about the company's future.

Entrepreneurs of smaller enterprises should be aware of these common pitfalls. Some of these pitfalls can be either directly avoided or are easily underpinned. Other pitfalls may present more difficulties, such as choosing a poor retail location.

Ventures start up small, but with the venture founders personal care, passion and sacrifice for the newborn enterprise, they can gradually develop into sizeable operations. But as the firm grows beyond the entrepreneur's solo mental and physical capacity, the expansion is often an even greater challenge than the starting-up. As mentioned in the beginning of the chapter: "It is easy to get there, but can you hang on?" Caring for and managing a growing firm without losing its entrepreneurial drive is a real challenge.

11.6 Government Assistance Programs

All countries differ, however the following are some examples of government assistance programs.

11.6.1 Canadian Government efforts

In the name of creating jobs and economic growth, the Government of Canada provides approximately 13 different programmes designed to assist smaller young ventures in the area of financing, including:

- Small Business Loans Act
- Business Development Bank of Canada
- Financial support through the Regional Economic Development
- Atlantic Canada Opportunities Agency
- Canada Economic Development for Quebec Regions
- Federal Economic Development Initiative for Northern Ontario
- Western Economic Diversification Canada
- Community Futures Development Corporations
- Canada Community Investment Plan
- Sources of Financing
- Agriculture Financing Farm Credit Corporation
- Financial Assistance for Canadian Cultural Organizations
- Community Economic Development Program
- Resources Access Negotiations Program
- First Nations and Inuit Youth Business Program

Then, there are programs for international trade, tax services, management and skill development, science, technology and innovation, and many other things. The bottom line is, it is at least worth looking into doing business with the government. To access these and other programs, you may wish to browse through the appropriate Internet addresses. It has approximately 100 addresses listed in "Your Guide to Government of Canada Services and Support for Small Business Services (1999)."

Table 11.3 Avoidable pitfalls.

Pitfalls	Guide to avoid pitfalls
Improper pricing	Price should be determined by demand, competition and cost. Among the three factors, only cost is controllable. Therefore, you should control cost while at the same time adjusting price in accordance with demand and competition, and focus on niche marketing.
Lack of knowledge about product costing	Prepare a specification and cost sheet, listing all costs (variable and fixed), and cost allocated to the product; determine unit cost of a product before you determine the price.
Inability to plan	Acquire a good computer planning software package, sit in front of the computer and learn to plan, or enrol in a short course and learn how to do a business plan.
Poor communication among partners	Hold short, weekly, formal meetings with partners. Prepare an agenda and have all essential documents distributed to all participants before meeting.
Managerial incompetence	Take a short course on "Small Business Management" from a local educational institution, join a trade association and attend some of its management seminars. Learn to listen as well as talk, to interact with people. You can also learn from other business owners as well as online.
Inability to acquire needed finance	Improve management skills: do cashflow analysis, ratio analysis, learn how to raise funds from the balance sheet (convert other current assets into cash, such as from accounts receivables, inventory etc.), have a good relationship with your bank manager, or look for a business partner.
Inability to compete	Niche marketing, develop a good relation with your customers. If you can, do not compete on price, but on personal service.
Lack of entrepreneurial value	Learn to develop entrepreneurial attributes. For example, learn how to take risks. Much like learning how to swim, almost no one does it naturally, but it is easy once you do. The basic entrepreneurial value is to be honest, and always caution yourself: a good business deal is one where both you and the other party have to be totally satisfied.

Table 11.4 Pitfalls difficult to avoid but can be underpinned.

Pitfalls	Guides to underpin pitfalls
Lack of discipline	Crucial especially in spending. Monitor both personal and business spending habits. Stay within an established budget allowance, do a variance analysis, pinpoint the causes of variances, and follow with action to underpin the causes of undisciplined spending. It is a matter of discipline, discipline and discipline.
Dishonesty	Think of others as if the others were yourself: Do you like someone cheating on you? Dishonesty is a bad habit, and it can only be overcome with effort.
Unwilling to plan	Engage an outsider to help you do a business plan. It can be very costly, which might make you think about the consequences of not planning, and then plan.
Poor communication within the management team	Have an open door policy, or have regular lunches together with team members. Start with casual conversation, then talk about business.
Bad judgement	Think before you act. Acquire more information before making a decision. However, do not overload on information, as it does not matter how much information you have, a decision has to be made in time for action.
Risk aversion	No risk no gain, but not no risk no loss. There is a loss of opportunity and loss of personal drive. Appreciate the reality that life itself is a risk, so take calculated risks, and maintain and nurture the entrepreneurial risk-taking attribute.

11.6.2 European Charter for Small Enterprises

Under the motherhood name of job creation and fostering economic growth, other governments also offer *assistance* to their smaller, newer and younger enterprises. At the European Union Summit in Portugal (June 2000), the EU member nations adopted the following principles:

- Acknowledge the dynamic capacities of small enterprises in answering for new market needs and in providing jobs.
- Stress the importance of small enterprises in fostering social and regional development, while behaving as examples of initiative and commitment.
- Recognize entrepreneurship as a valuable and productive life skill, at all levels of responsibility.
- Applaud successful enterprise, which deserves to be fairly rewarded.
- Consider that some failure is concomitant with responsible initiative and risk taking and must be mainly envisaged as a learning opportunity.
- Recognize the value of knowledge, commitment and flexibility in the new economy.

Besides abiding by these principles, the member nations are also committed to targeting the following ten areas of action. These include:

(1) **Education and training for entrepreneurship**

Member nations will encourage and promote youngsters' entrepreneurial endeavors, and develop appropriate training schemes for managers in small enterprises.

(2) **Cheaper and faster start-up**

(3) **Better legislation and regulation**

Small enterprises can be exempted from certain regulatory obligations.

(4) **Availability of skills**

To ensure that training institutions, complemented by in-house schemes, will provide lifetime training and consultancy of skills needed by smaller enterprises.

(5) **Improving online access**

Online registration should be increased.

(6) **More out of single market**

Member nations must pursue the reforms aimed at the completion in the union of a true internal market; user-friendly for small businesses, including electronic commerce, telecommunications, utilities, public procurement and cross-board payment system. At the same time, European and national competition rules should be vigorously applied to ensure that their small businesses have every chance to enter new markets and compete on fair terms.

(7) **Taxation and financial matters**

Three key areas, with respect to taxation and financing are identified. They include:

(i) Identify and remove barriers to the creation of a pan-European capital market and to the implementation of the Financial Services Action Plan and the Risk Capital Action Plan.

(ii) Improve the relationship between the banking system and small enterprises by creating appropriate access conditions to credit and venture capital.

(iii) Improve the access to the structural funds and welcome initiatives by the European Investment Bank, to increase funding available to start-ups and high-tech enterprises, including equity instruments.

(8) **Strengthen technological capacity**

Member nations will foster the involvement of small enterprises in inter-firm cooperation, at local, national, European and international levels as well as the cooperation between small enterprises and high education and research institutions.

(9) **Successful e-business models and top-class small business support**

Member nations will coordinate among themselves and through EU activity to create information and business support systems, networks and services which are easy to access and understand, and relevant to the needs of business; ensure EU-wide access to guidance and support from mentors and business angels, including through websites, and exploit the European Observatory on SMEs.

(10) **Develop stronger, more effective representation of small enterprises' interest at Union and national level**

Member nations commit themselves to progress towards these goals using the open method of coordination of national enterprise policies.

The multi-annual Programme for Enterprise and Entrepreneurship, the Cardiff Process on Economic Reforms, the Luxembourg Process on Employment Policies and other Community programs and initiatives will be used to this end.

Source: *www.europa.eu.int*

11.6.3 Australia and New Zealand

Some countries, such as Australia and New Zealand, have smaller enterprise support programmes in line with their own national enterprise and entrepreneurship development policies. The development in Australia is similar to that in Canada at both the national and state level. For example, at the national level, efforts are concentrated on legislative matters affecting all states and territories of Australia, including:

- Legal Issues Guide for Small Business — Internet based
- Small Business Adviser Training Program — on legal issues
- Working With Contracts — practical guide (available free on the Internet)

At the state level, for example, Queensland has a network of 16 state development centers which offer help to prospective and established businesses, including:

- Tools for self-help — business start-up kits
- Workshops — cash, customers, managing, marketing, networking, etc.
- Business information — bookshop, licences, resources, support, etc.
- One-on-one consultations — special small business officers
- Women in business — Special events, training grant scheme
- Management skills development
- Fostering innovation and expanding the market — financial support

Source: *www.smallbusiness.qld.gov.au*

New Zealand, on the other hand, has 20 community-based centers offering support to new and existing businesses through the following services:

- Practical business facilities
- Referral to other help agencies

- Introduction to government department, local businesses and consultants
- Business courses, seminars and workshops
- Ongoing support and networks
- Helpful leaflets and guides for owner/managers

E-mail source: *mail@csbec.org.nz*

Questions for discussion

1. What do you perceive as being: "Owner managed venture sustainable growth?"
2. Develop a new venture growth strategy. You may wish to begin with:
   - Venture purpose
   - Entrepreneur's personal and business vision
   - Commitment
   - Venture sustainable growth strategy
   - Implementation plan

3. Think about some niche marketing strategies. How do you develop such a strategy?
4. In an earlier chapter, there was a butcher and pig conversation. The butcher said to the pig: "If you give me what I want, I will give you what you want." For an entrepreneur managed firm, is it possible to use a similar approach to stimulate the motivation of people working in the entity? Why?
5. Develop a venture growth strategy based on cashflow management, building up valuable assets, disposing of outdated assets, developing new insights and high-tech technology. And then, why not go public?
6. It is an unfortunate reality that some venture's financing strategy is to use accounts payable. Some venture's customers do the same to their suppliers. One day, the manager of the company received a note from its supplier. The note reads:

   "We have carried your account longer than your mother
   has carried you!"

   What must you do?

7. Would you place environmental health and workers' interest before profit? Discuss.
8. Assume you decide to admit a partner into your business. What would be the pros and cons for such an initiative? How would you take necessary measures for a good and smooth relationship?
9. Would you share ownership with those working in the venture? If not, how would you create an environment whereby all those working in the entity have a stake in the company?
10. What is your personal value or the value of your business? How can such a value be shared within the firm?

Chapter 12

Family Business: The Home Based Community of Entrepreneurs

The family is a natural human institution. Motivated by entrepreneurial drive, family members may work and stay together. Their elevated creative spirits build businesses that serve their multiple purposes of: creating wealth for the individual, promoting harmonious family relations and adding value to society. Members of the family share family value, vision and purpose — stimulating business growth and enjoying nature's gift — the beautiful relationship of human interaction. If on the other hand, due to an individual's desire for a greater part of interplay or the pursuit of personal interest, family business can then be the cause of family conflict, resulting in deterioration of the entrepreneurial spirit, conflict of interest and disintegration of unity, bankrupting both family relations and business, and at the very extreme, resulting in crimes and even capital offences.

12.1 Introduction

Family business is perhaps the earliest and simplest human institution among economic activities, perhaps second only to formalized marriage. However, while cooperation and coordination have social and economic benefit, as human interactions become more intense, there will be increasing unsatisfied needs and wants among family business members. If these issues are unresolved, it would inevitably lead to disaster not only for the business, but for the members of the family and society as well. The following short passage describes how the family business evolves:

The first generation creates the business, the second generation may build the business, but when it comes to the third generation, there may not be any business.

There are, however, exceptions to the above (the U.S.-based Marriott family chain of hotels is an example). Unfortunately, some family businesses cannot even survive after the first generation. A family-run retail giant, "T. Eaton's of Canada," failed after the third or fourth generation. Although the Eaton's name remains in the shopping malls, the new departmental store now identifies itself as "eatons," instead of "Eatons." Another family-owned departmental store, "Simpson's," changed from the family ("Simpson's") to in-laws ("Burton"), then finally was taken over by another family-owned business, "Thomson's," known as "The Bay," the real retail giant in Canada, which has branches all over Canada.

12.2 Family Business Defined

For practical business and the purpose of this book, we extend the search from the desk (called secondary or desk research), and define:

A family business is an economic entity, created by a member or members of a family, thus owned and operated by family members.

However, this simple definition can have a number of variations, including:

- A business created by a family member, controlled by a family member or members, but managed by non-family members.
- A business acquired by a family member (or members), owned by family member/members, but managed by non-family members.
- A family business, whose share holdings consisting of both family members and outsiders, but controlled and managed by family members.
- Members of a family have controlling interest in a business, but managed by non-family members, the management can be external shareholders or non-sharing holding outsiders.

In essence, although a family business clearly signifies that ownership is the sole criteria, the weight is placed on whether or not the family is able to retain controlling interest of the business. Although the variations listed above are only the "substance" of a family business, variations also exist in the "soul" of family business.

12.2.1 Family, business and family business

A family business is an economic entity functioning in the marketplace, but it has three separated, yet interrelated characters in the entity — they are the family, family business and business. In order to distinguish the characteristic variations from the substance variations, we consider the "soul" of family business to vary in accordance with their characteristic differences as perceived by us.

Figure 12.1(a) suggests that both family and business are entities, whereby family is an entity consisting of family members who love and care for each other, share family values and chores. Business is, on the other hand, unrelated to family. It operates as a separate unit, with its own set of operational guides and purposes. For example, the family value is to abstain from vices such as smoking, drinking and gambling, but the business is in selling cigarettes and alcoholic beverages.

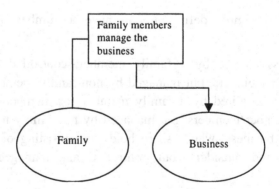

Figure 12.1(a) Category A: family, business. The first generation business: when the venture founder business may survive, but will not be a family business. It has no family value or founder's value.

There are certain distinctive advantages to keeping family and business as two distinct entities — family is family, business is business, so to speak. Under the circumstances, a family business is in fact conducted as in any other corporation. It will not have the advantage of sharing a family value. If the board members of the business can remain independent from their family influence, the business then has its own identity, not influenced or benefited from what the family owns. This model reflects a practice in human institution, similar to "common-law live-in," which is different from the official marriage.

Family business of this nature has no particular characteristic that will sustain the family value and purpose, instead it concentrates on making "profit" or financial success. Consequently, members of the family will focus only on their personal share of the earnings of the company. After the first generation, successors will likely be more interested in the question "What can I get out of this business?" rather than what can they do for the business.

Figure 12.1(b) illustrates a characteristic that puts "family business" in a position with family and business in the background. It means at times the family and business remain separate, as a unified identity but integrated into the business as a family business. Using a similar example as before: when the family value is to abstain from drinking, it remains as the family value. But members of the family responsible for the policy decisions will bring family values into the business, which means that the business still involves the selling of cigarettes and alcoholic beverages, but at the same

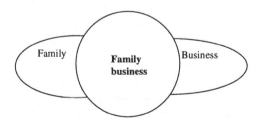

Figure 12.1(b) Family business, category B: family, business and family business. Second cohort family business: family values reflected in the family business, the business may continue as a family business with family value.

time, also gets actively involved in anti-smoking and anti-alcoholism promotional and educational schemes or other forms of public awareness programs. These activities are, to a certain extent, regulated by the government, e.g. the banning of unlicensed sale of cigarettes and the passing of the law preventing sale of alcohol to persons with past criminal records. Violation of these laws is punishable by fine or other forms of control. This family business model reflects family values, but continues with its business activities the same way as in other businesses. This form of family business is similar to marriage, where each partner has his or her own personal identity, but is presented to the public as a couple. A family is initially constituted by a man and his wife.

Large family businesses of this category will likely have longer life expectancies. Integrated family values, the founder's entrepreneurial drive and committed management on the part of the family to place business well-being before family members' self-interest, will allow the business to carry on with appreciable growth beyond the second generation.

Figure 12.1(c) features a family with its own identity and its own family business value. By and large, this is the ideal type of family business, similar to that of a child, conceived from love. It has an entrepreneurial spirit of business whose purpose is to create wealth and serve people. The moral fiber of the family value is filled with love and passion.

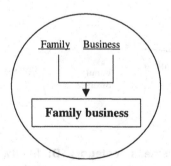

Figure 12.1(c) Family business, category C: family business has its own value and identity.

A family business with its own identity is a human institution in its own right, and will not be directly affected by the individual's or small group's behavioral variation. It is a natural assembly of people who share the common goal of family continuation, for self-interest and common good, a democratic process within the family, but expressed through family business. Category C family business can have a much longer life expectancy than both categories A and B.

12.2 Reasons for a Family Business' Success and Causes for Its Failure

In its entrepreneurial context, both success and failure factors of a family business are difficult to obtain. A closely held family business that tends to keep all vital information in the hands of a few, or perhaps one person, it is extremely difficult to trace its reasons for success and failure. A family business had partners who were the senior author's students. They responded to two sets of questionnaires designed to single out family problems related to their businesses (the members of the board are all brothers). The first set of questions asked the respondents to address problems areas. Virtually all answered that they do not have any problems, except one who wrote a sentence at the end of the questionnaire: "We don't have problems, only situations." Unfortunately, the situation had forced one partner to leave the business. Three years later, the partners sold all their holdings to an outsider. There was also another "situation" where criminal wrongdoing was suspected. Though the partners did not press criminal charges, the family business still could not be saved.

The more publicized troubled family businesses (including cases where ownership was given up to outsiders), e.g. T. Eaton's of Canada, Yeo Hiap Seng and Scotts Holdings of Singapore are cases where information was made available to the media (though without the detailed statistics). Based on these published information, personal observations through early consulting work and teaching experiences of the senior author, common reasons for their success or failure are identified.

12.2.1 Common successful factors

Bearing the risk of generalization, there are at least five common reasons for family business success, and similarly common pitfalls are also evident.

Factors contribute to family business success and some are found in practice:

About people: *the venture founder*

(1) The venture founder has assumed the role of the head of both family and business. Although there are exceptions where one member may assume the role of the head of a family business while the other earns his/her respect for making decisions that matter to the welfare of the business. Thus, it is possible to separate business decision-making from family matters.

(2) The venture founder has a strong sense of duty. Has earned his/her respect through his/her love and passion extended to all members of the family, and to others as well.

(3) The venture founder is true to him/herself, true to others, and true to his/her beliefs, and has a good understanding and practice about relationship and people.

(4) The venture founder is an entrepreneur and has a strong relationship with other members of the business, both as a parent and a friend.

About people: *members of the family working in family business*

(5) In the event that differences of opinions in any respect related to the business occur, family members working in the business must air their grievances openly with those involved and seek solutions to deal with the issues. Above all, it is necessary to place business' interest before personal concerns.

(6) All members working for the business must learn from each other, respect others, earn respect from others, and support each other in times of need.

(7) Family members respect the right of the company as outsiders do.

(8) There is no privileged class for family members.

(9) All family members working for the business must keep family differences, if any, away from the business; similarly, any differences on the business level must be kept from interfering with family relations.

The family value

(10) It has a strong family value. For example, if it is a Christian family, Christian values are part of the family and commitment to uphold this lifelong value is ingrained into the family member's mind. To illustrate what is a family value, we may consider the following:

> A friend of the senior author told him about his family value experience. He said: "I lost my father when I was two years old, my mother occasionally told me about my father, what he did, how he lived his life, and specifically how he successfully managed to resist temptations." His mother said: "Your father was a government auditor, whose work often called for him to leave home for wherever demanded his expertise." During one of his trips, he returned back to the hotel (after having a drink with some of the company's employees), to find a beautiful young woman naked in his bed. At first, he did not know what to do, but later he decided to grab a handful of bills from his pocket, handed them to the woman and asked her to leave. She not only did not comply, she continued to pursue him and even attempted to undress him. It was only after your father went down on his knees and begged her that she finally left with the money.

The above short story represents a family value. Confucius said more than 2000 years ago: "Food and sex are human nature." Resisting free sex is not an easy decision. But the gentleman made that decision, a decision he perceived to be "right versus wrong." To him, to cheat was wrong, even though no one would have known that he cheated on his wife and children.

At times, we are confronted with a situation when we have to make a difficult decision: "War or peace," "take the money or not to take the money," "to lie or not to lie." When a choice is made, we are sure, that some values, in particular family values, will have a role to play. This is the true meaning of civilization.

The declaration of rights and obligations of the business

(11) Officially and unofficially, the business has its own charter of right, including such declarations as:

- The business is an entity; a legal person that has its own right and obligations.
- The business is entitled to its own properties, and all members of the company must respect the property rights of the business. This includes all assets tangible and intangible.
- The business must assume all obligations to its contributors, including consumers, shareholders, individuals working in the company at all levels, suppliers, governments, and ecological services in general.
- The business is a devoted business citizen, it has a stake in the community where it conducts business — locally, regionally, nationally, and/or globally.
- The business serves the public, in the interest of the public and earns the respect from the public.
- The business commits itself to exercise extreme discipline in allocating resources for protection of the environment.

The continuing drive, creativity and innovation

(12) The business is structured to induce and encourage the individual's continuing desire and need for creative and innovative activities.

The management essentials: general

(13) Customers' satisfaction must be the top priority, and it must be guaranteed clearly in documentation used to communicate with customers and the public.

(14) All members of the family business share a clear vision of the business, and the role of each member is clearly defined.

(15) There is a free flow of business information.

(16) Remuneration system is based on efforts and results, each and every member is entitled to have a share of the harvest, based on residual concept.

(17) Although the functions of family members working for the business are clearly defined, flexibility must remain the theme.

(18) Human resource development must be in place for clear specification of the purpose, not just for the company but also for development of the individual's growth potentials.

(19) If there is no outsider on the board of directors, a third person must be appointed to mediate any disputes arising from members of family for matters concerning the well-being of the business.

(20) Every individual who associates with the company in any capacity and who uses any asset of the company must assume the stewardship responsibility, i.e. use in the interest of the company.

(21) Business decision-making is a shared responsibility. Thus, the organization must be structured to induce empowerment. All decisions made by the lower level are respected by high-level decision-makers.

The management essentials: finance and financial management

(22) The management of the family business must respect cashflow as the most important financial management function, much like the blood flow in the human body. A comfortable position is a key for good management.

(23) No cash shall be withdrawn from the bank, removed from the cash box register or petty cash box without proper written authorization.

(24) Definite financial ratio must be maintained at all times.

(25) The management should not use funds generated for long term projects for short term financing purpose; similarly, short term funds must not be used for any long term projects.

(26) The business adopts the residual approach for its performance determination.

(27) The residual is determined on the basis of the following formula:

Financial income (the same as the traditional accounting profit)
− (capital charge + allocation for environmental care + ⋯)

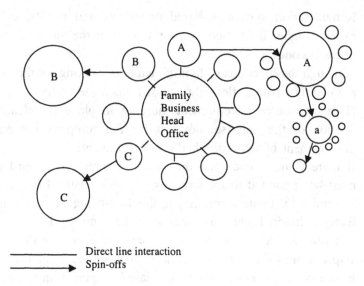

_____ Direct line interaction
———————▶ Spin-offs

Figure 12.2 Satellite organization: three layer spin-offs.

(28) Any non-budgetary spending must seek approval from responsible people in a managerial position.

Managerial essentials: organization

(29) Satellite organizational structure should be adopted (Fig. 12.2).

Family business head office
Venture founder: 1st generation

Satellite
First layer spin-off A: 2nd generation, second daughter
Second layer spin-off A: 3rd generation, first grandson
First layer spin-off B: 2nd generation, nephew, maternal
First layer spin-off C: 2nd generation, cousin, paternal

It should be noted that before the re-organization takes place, it would be wise to organize all operation units from the box pyramid type of organization with a central command into various profit centers. A profit center has the following characteristics:

- It must have operational independence.
- It must have a separate revenue.
- It must have a separate cost accumulation and responsibility reporting system.
- It must be created as a center that can become a financial profit center.
- It must allow an individual in charge of the center the right to conduct business with whoever he/she prefers.
- It must have a transfer price system in place.
- It must provide an annual capital charge at a market rate of interest for corporate investment. The amount is determined by a joint effort between the corporate executive and persons in charge of the centers.

The idea of beginning with a "profit center" and progressively elevating the center into a spin-off entity is to allow family members to be involved in business for business, not just for money. The individuals earn their places; they are not simply given by venture founders or a person in charge of the family business.

Management essentials: recognition and support

(30) There is a spin-off opportunity for family members to pursue their own ideas, yet allow them to receive a company's support financially and technologically.

(31) Family members working in the family business receive the same recognition as outsiders, both financially and in all other matters.

Plan for succession

(32) Design a succession plan. If possible, every member of the family has the right and obligation to participate in the design of the plan, and learn from the plan.

(33) All family members participate in the design of succession plan, and declare their support and respect of the plan. They are obligated to see that the plan is implemented in accordance with its intent to the letter.

12.2.2 Common causes for failure

As noted earlier in the chapter, searching for causes for family business failure is a difficult process, since most family business holdings are closely held corporations. However, through consulting and personal experiences involving family businesses, we are able to assemble some common pitfalls that have been incurred in family businesses, some of which originated from fundamentals. Although we can easily identify failure factors by simply referring to the success factors in reverse, failure causes are in actual fact far more complicated human experiences.

Common causes of failed family businesses include the lost of controlling interest or ownership (even though the names of those businesses remain unchanged, both the ownership and the management are completely new).

About people: the venture founder

(1) The venture founder may be the head of the business, but not necessarily the head of the family.
(2) The main purpose of creating the family business is to make money for him/herself, using family members as cheap labor.
(3) The venture founder has not earned the respect of other family members working for the business.
(4) The venture founder is not true to him/herself, true to others, or true to his/her belief.
(5) The venture founder is more of an opportunist, rather than an entrepreneur.
(6) Parents are not involved with the children.
(7) Venture founder(s) become tyrants in their families and in business.
(8) A strong-minded founder prevents anyone else from having a stake of the business and only delegates pieces, which makes it impossible for the development of the successor.
(9) Venture founder has a big ego with delusions of grandeur. Typically, some owners think that success in their business can be duplicated in politics or entirely different endeavors. Therefore, they tend to be distracted with new off-track undertakings which take them away from running their business properly.

About people: members of the family working in family business

(10) Family members working for the business have no commitment. In the event that there are differences in opinions or grievances relating to the business, family members do not solve problems through the normal channels within the organization.

(11) Members working for the business dislike each other, maintain a superficial relationship, are jealous of each other and backstab one another.

(12) Family members give no respect to the rights of the company.

(13) There is a privileged class for family members.

(14) Family members working for the business make no distinction between family and business, and more often than not, bring family differences into the business.

(15) As working members of the business, they act as if they have more rights than others.

Family value

(16) No family values. The only family value (if it can be considered as such) is to make money and only money. They might be interested in power; since with greater power, there will be a bigger share of money.

Creativity and innovation

(17) The business is structured in such a way as to discourage initiative. Stealing the ideas of others is a matter of routine rather than the exception. Perhaps there are schemes designed for making money, but these have no moral foundation, ethics or consideration for public interest.

The management: general

(18) Customers receive priority preference, only if money can be made.

(19) Information is the source of power and must be controlled.

(20) Remuneration system and promotion are based on the desire of those in the decision-making position. Preference is given to the favorites.

(21) Although the roles of members of family working for the business may be defined, no one seems to treat it seriously. "Passing the buck" is a common practice.

(22) No human resource development policy nor practice.

(23) Members of the family working for the business have no respect for the company's assets. They take as they please without regard for the general well-being of the business.

(24) Corporate credit cards used for personal expenditures.

(25) Business decisions are made by only a few. There is seldom any feedback; if any, it will land in the hands of those who make the wrong decisions in the first place anyway.

The management: money and profit

(26) More often than not, the business enters into a downturn, incurring excess debt. The management depends mainly on banks and suppliers. May do bank reconciliation or cashflow analysis once in a while, but there is seldom any follow-up.

(27) Stealing from company's cash reserves often occurs. Petty cash money is often disbursed without proper authorization.

(28) Financial reports are produced by the computer but seldom used or followed up.

(29) There is no distinction between management of funds in the short or long term. More often than not, committed funds are used for different purposes.

(30) Cheating on government tax.

(31) Major transfer of funds or goods from the company to private accounts.

(32) Though there is a budget, no one seems to care very much about over-spending, nor provide any meaningful analysis.

Managerial: organization

(33) Traditional organizational structure: a triangle pyramid defines functions between line and staff. But the structure (as shown below) puts people in boxes, with multiple layers of reporting. In terms of chain of command, it looks clearly defined, but in fact, it is bureaucratic and unsuitable for entrepreneurial organizations.

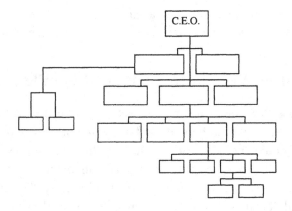

Figure 12.3 The pyramid organization structure.

(34) No clear-cut decision-making system for members of family working for the business.

(35) There is no spin-off opportunity. Any suggestions of this nature would be considered as splitting up the family business and a crime against the family.

(36) Technology is absolutely safeguarded by those members in the control position. It is unthinkable to transfer technology out of the company.

(37) In the event that there is an opportunity to invest in an entity, it normally seeks the controlling position.

(38) The company is governed by a leader, particularly in the hands of the founder of the company who largely secured his/her position through practising "management by fear, suspicion, game play, back stabbing, and possibly even through criminal activities.

Passion, love and care

(39) The company is viewed as a money-making machine.

Plan for succession

(40) Children are not educated, or not even oriented to take over the business, but they are sent to the university to pursue a professional and/or high academic degrees anyway.

(41) There is no such thing as a succession plan on the part of the venture founder; there may not even be a written will.

12.3 Social and Economic Value of Family Business

Family business has a long history, in fact, its strong foundation provides an economic future for members of the family and offers important benefits to society. Although people tend to aim for "providing jobs" as the key contribution, cooperating to build, create and innovate can also certainly provide inspiration as well as contribute to family unity. "Family", as used in some ethical "business" communities means a great deal to people in the "Family." It is a social unit, an economic unit, and of course extended further, a political unit as well. Successful family businesses normally have all the characteristics described above. On the other hand, ill-gotten gains motivated by greed can result in a poorly managed business. Money can be a source of corruption, and a seed-bed for the incubation of crimes. These are the tragedies and the glories of family business.

In some cases, the effects of a failed family business not only does harm to family relations, it can affect society's morals and cause economic losses to both the business and others associated with it.

12.4 Conclusion

There are countless family businesses worldwide; some are extremely successful, while others just fade into thin air. To further understand what happened to these failed businesses, we use five real-life family businesses, presently operating in a country outside North America, as examples. On the basis of factual information and the senior author's experience of over 40 years in examining family business, we can shed some light on why some family businesses can continue serving the family and society, while others may not continue after the second and/or third generation. Hopefully, it can help us to better understand how entrepreneurship is involved in these businesses and how they exist in society to serve society and how they create personal wealth; why some have succession problems, while others are right on track. These will be explored in Chapter 13 "The Tragedies and Glories of Family Business."

Note: Chapter 12 is written based on the senior author's work and teachings. The senior author is personally involved in family business and consultation, as well as Family Business Management programmes held in Canada (Faculty of Management, University of Toronto, 1989), and in Singapore (ENDC, Nanyang Technological University, 1995). His knowledge is also reinforced by extensive reading of the following works: Gibb, Allan A. (1986–1987), *JSBE* 4(4/3); Dana, Leo Paul, *The Last Days of Companero Model in Cuba, Entrepreneurship and Innovation* (5/2), recordings from an Ontario forum, "The Transition to Younger Management in Family Business," *Family Enterprise* (27); and *Proceedings of Family Business Seminar* (ENDEC, Nanyang Technological University, Singapore, June 1996).

Questions for discussion

1. Family value, venture founder's entrepreneurial drive and desire to create are often reasons for the success of family business (measured by its sustainable development and growth potentials). What can be done in order to make this part of the inheritance package?

2. Assume you are a venture founder, ignoring differences in qualifications and ability, who would you prefer to have as the person involved in your business?

Family member	Pros	Cons
Spouse Son(s) Daughter(s) Brother(s) Sister(s) Brother(s)-in-law Sister(s)-in-law Cousin (first) Cousin (second) Cousin (distant) Other relations		

Give reason(s) to support your choice.

3. Well-educated children of a family business normally do not prefer to work for the business created by their parent(s). However, this may not always be the case. Based on the following, evaluate each with respect to the involvement of family members in business from the point of view of a well-educated individual who has an MBA, a Ph.D., an M.D., a C.A., an LL.B., or an M.Sc. (Engineering).

   Use the 0 to 10 scale (see below) to indicate your choice. For example, an MBA holder would place 0 for returning to his/her parents' fish and chip shop, but 10 for a five-star hotel and resort chain.

$$0 \quad 1 \quad 2 \quad 3 \quad 5 \quad 6 \quad 7 \quad 8 \quad 9 \quad 10 \longrightarrow$$

Low preference   High preference

   0 = Not interested at all
   10 = Definitely will return to the family business

If your response is 0 to 2 or 8 to 10, please provide your reason(s).

	MBA/ MA M.Sc.	Ph.D.	M.D.	C.P.A./ C.A.	LL.B. (Lawyer)	B.A.,Sc. B.Eng (Eng.)
Fish and chip shop						
Small retail store						
Department store chain						
Five-star hotel and resort						
Software developer						
Professional office						
Furniture making						
Car dealer and rental						
Real estate and property management						
Construction and home building						
Bookstore chain						

4. Under what circumstances will a family business involve outsiders:

   - To be a member of the board
   - To be an advisor to the board
   - Join the management team as the CEO
   - Join the management team as the COO (based on his/her expertise).
   - In other capacities, such as: marketing manager, R&D director, new product development manager, or manager of finance.

5. Entrepreneurial attributes are important to an entrepreneur-managed family enterprise. What can be done, if family members working in the business have a negative culture of relying on their personal relations with the venture founder, they have no drive and absolutely refuse to take initiative?

6. If a family member cheats on his/her traveling expenses, what should be done?

Chapter 13

The Tragedy, Glory and Succession of Family Business

> "Family" is a magical word, especially in some ethnic communities. It means a great deal to people in the family. It is a social unit, an economic unit, and at times even a political unit as well. At its best, successful family businesses typify all the best characteristics of an entrepreneurial entity, motivated by love and passion and a desire to help others. On the other hand, a family business that is poorly managed, ill-founded, motivated by greed and in which the objective is only to make money, can be a tragedy and a seed bed of corruption, incubating crime. This is the glory and the tragedy of family business.

13.1 Introduction

Here we continue the search for family business issues explored in Chapter 12, but with an emphasis on the human factor, the grey areas of this all too human institution.

As the case itself is rich in content, the authors have decided not to make a lengthy discussion or evaluation of the situation, and allow the situation to speak for itself. The case is of a family business built on the basis of the founder's personal values and self-reliance, a business built both for the family and the nation and to create jobs for himself, his family members and people around him. With his determination, and a vision described not so much in big words but in actions, he weathered through thick and thin, and the business survived and grew from virtually no equity to an estimated value of US$60,000,000. However, from the pinnacle of success it took a mere eight years before the very success of the business was to cause unbelievable hardship for the family. Indeed, this story involves a death under tragic circumstances, a death clouded in an uncertainty which perhaps will never be resolved.

A family business is a unique institution. It can be, not just an economic entity, but an expression of the collective love, care and passion of an entire family. Each family business is unique, and its story is rarely written in dollars and cents. The success and failure expressed in traditional terms can be deceiving, but a story told descriptively can have long-lasting lessons for us all. Here, we use one such story, which has many lessons to tell. The story is based on real events, but the characters and location have all been changed.

13.2 The Story of Golden Tiger

In the beginning

The Shin family was founded in Garden State, South America in the late 1800s. Mark Shin, is now the head of the family. It is the 1950s and he has lived in the capital city of G.S. for many years, supporting a family of ten, including his seven children and his parents. The Garden State is beautiful, full of natural wonders, but the economy is poor, and life is hard in the 1950s. However, Mark and his wife, Naomi, have managed to send three of their children to North America, with hopes that they will find a successful and happy life there. The three sons, however, have remained at their side. The two elder sons have managed to make their own way in life, while Mark, Naomi and the youngest son, Shawn, work in the family trading business. However, times are very hard, and they have started to drain the little savings they have from their years of hard work.

Motivated by the need to survive, Mark has been having thoughts of starting a new venture, using local material to manufacture consumer goods both for domestic and exporting purposes. Although "free trade agreement" is a meaningless phrase at this time, world trade is opening up, and many countries in Southeast Asia are actively engaging in a trade amongst themselves. Pressured by the need to provide food on the table for the family, Mark is ready to try anything, and he gets the idea of using the countries vast resources of natural rubber in new ways — by integrating it with new polymer compounds to create a flexible, hard-wearing material to be used for floor covering, tabletops and for other possible purposes. Mark has had only seven years of formal education, and had no idea what can or cannot be done. However, after discussing it with Shawn, they both feel confident enough to take up the challenge.

Golden Tiger: *incubation and start-up*

Like his father, Shawn had little formal education. However, he had a keen interest in science; his reading of science magazines had provided him with some basic knowledge and also encouraged him to experiment making "different combinations" from natural and man-made materials. Eventually, he was confident enough to ask his father to equip him with a small chemical lab, where he began experimenting in a big way. Basically, he combined different proportions of natural rubber compounds and polymers, first reducing the raw rubber to an ash, then combining it with the polymer in powder form and re-liquefying it with a form of natural resin. After much tinkering and hard work, the experiments produced a hard-wearing, flexible material. They soon found an application for this material — as a component in the soles of running shoes. Mark Shin discussed the idea with an old friend, Joe Johnston, who advised him to pursue the shoe sole angle. Joe also introduced one of his friends, a local banker, who helped Mark secure a small bank loan to start this business of making shoe repair materials. After several trial and error experiments, Shawn happily showed his father the final product samples. Mark approved them, and took them to a local cobbler, who agreed to buy them. Thus, they made their first sale, and the whole family was filled with joy and hope.

The birth of a tiger

For the next five years, the Shin family worked as a team; everyone had their share of work in the small factory, with the mother working on the mixing machine, the eldest son, Derek, working as a foreman, and the second son, Scott, also working in the factory (performing office duties in his spare time, even though he had already qualified as a medical doctor).

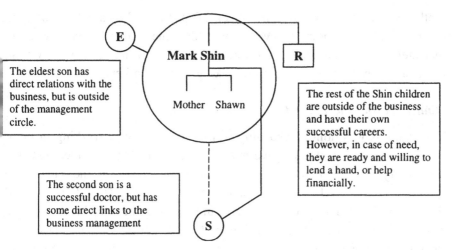

Figure 13.1 GT stage 1.

Shawn devoted his efforts towards improving the existing product and new product development. Everyone seemed to have a purpose; that purpose was to build the "factory" as well as build better lives for everyone. The second son had no real financial interest in the "factory," but he helped nevertheless.

Who owns the tiger?

By the early 1960s, the factory, now known by its brand name "Golden Tiger" (GT), had been incorporated as a "non-registered name limited liability company." (This means that no one is a shareholder of the company, only those who hold registered share papers are owners of the company.) Mark Shin had the shares locked away in the company safe and assured the family that everything was taken care of. All his children thus assumed that the company had four shares: the father's, the mother's, Scott's and Shawn's. Then, Scott got married and moved away from the Shin family. But by this time the business was really starting to take off. It seemed that Mark had firmly put the business on the road to prosperity. With Scott gone, the structure of the company simplified somewhat. Mark was president of the company while Shawn became vice-president, and the mother's role appeared to be the "Jack of all trades." In addition to being president of the company, Mark was also the finance and marketing manager as well. The eldest son did not do much in terms of supervision, but instead spent most of his time talking to the workers.

Dinner, music and beyond

The business was doing reasonably well, with two things working in favor of GT: one was that the government of Garden State granted GT the proprietary right to manufacture sporting shoes, while at the same time prohibiting imports from the East to compete with GT; and the second thing was that a major U.S. manufacturer sub-contracted GT to produce soles for their shoes in accordance with their specifications. These two facts gave the Shin family a great morale boost, and almost instantly GT became a household name throughout the Garden State. Meanwhile, Shawn was still a bachelor. Some families in other parts of the State had their eye on him and view him as a potential catch; Anita Wong was one of them. She decided to take the aggressive approach, asking Shawn out on a date. She went all out to impress him, even made dinner for him at her house, where they spent many hours discussing their mutual interest in music. They hit it off very well, and soon Anita's mother, Lisa, and the Shins were talking about marriage.

In no time at all, Anita Wong and Shawn Shin were married. The Shin family was not particularly happy about the express marriage, but accepted the union anyway. They only hoped that the young couple would be happy. Soon after the honeymoon, Anita announced her desire to learn about the business. She received one year of psychology training at the local university, and she wanted to make good use of what she had learnt. She thought that a psychology background plus a few business courses would make her qualified enough to run the Shin family business one day. This was also about the same time as when the business took off. Sales increases were manifold. Mark ambitiously used this opportunity to purchase a piece of vacant land located just outside of the capital city center, at a low price. While the area was currently underdeveloped, Mark saw its potential, and he was sure that there would soon be substantial capital gains on the property. However, after purchasing the land, there was a sudden drain of

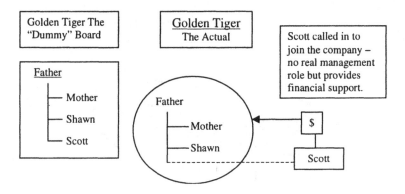

Figure 13.2 GT stage 2.

company cash. As a drastic measure, Shawn requested that his mother take an early retirement without pension. Shawn also pensioned the elder son off, as in Shawn's opinion, his role in the business did not amount to much anyway. This freed up some needed cash, but it was not enough. The cashflow problem persisted, largely because of excessive debt financing for expansion to meet the unexpected demand, together with the large cash layout used to purchase the land. Ironically, fuelled by its success, the company was being driven by the need for cash nearly into the ground.

Mark persuaded all their children, except Shawn, to give financial support. Between them, they managed to come up with an undisclosed sum. There were no receipts, acknowledgements, or records, as it was understood that every cent was going into the business. They felt that they were doing this out of filial piety. Thus, the business was saved, and harmony was restored in the family, with the exception of only a few minor squabbles. However, things were about to change.

It was the late 1970s and Lady Luck was smiling on the Shin family again. Business was steadily improving, further boosted by government incentives for companies in the exporting business. In order to encourage export, only one-tenth of export dollars were required to be brought back to the country, and exporters like GT were allowed to keep the rest. In the early 1980s, Shawn and Mark set up a U.S. bank account for GT, and started to accumulate funds there. Of course, this practice again limited the

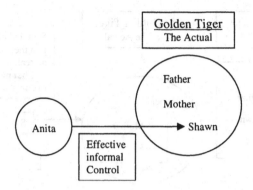

Figure 13.3 GT stage 3.

flexibility of the company's cashflow. And at this point, Shawn's wife, Anita started acting upon her wish to get more involved in the business. However, she was well aware that Mark Shin was still in control of the company, and so chose to act only as Shawn's advisor, never directly interfering in business affairs, but nevertheless getting more and more involved in financial matters. It was also at this time that Scott relinquished all of his duties in the business, due to his burgeoning medical practice. However, he continued to provide financial support whenever required. Despite the improved GT financial position, none of the money loaned to the business was ever returned to the family members, as everyone treated the loan as a means of financial aid to their father.

The tiger pounces

As a developing country with an island economy, Garden State needed hard foreign currency to enable its people to buy things such as petroleum, new cars, televisions, stereos and various luxuries for the rich. Therefore, the government did everything to encourage exports. In the 1980s, export is the name of the game as far as the country is concerned, and Shawn Shin played the game well.

He hired an accountant, who knew how to handle the government taxes. On record, GT started up with zero assets which had grown to over US$10 million in holdings, though with capital gains tax of unknown amount that would have to be paid if the acquired land (supposedly for the new plant) was to be sold at the early 1980s current market price. In addition, other than required remission of 10% export dollars taken back into the country, Shawn managed to keep US$10 million+ in a U.S. bank under the name of Royal Tiger with Shawn and Anita as the signing officers. On the advice of Anita's brother, Richard, they also created a dummy company to handle the U.S. taxes. Mark gradually began to lose control over the business, other than the signing of a few cheques. Instead, effective control lay with Shawn and a few individuals around him, including Richard and Joe Karnia, a friend of Anita's and Shawn's in Garden State. At this stage, GT really had two boards, the official board in Garden City, and a second unofficial board which held all the cards.

The GT activities meant that for every US$100,000 shipped out of Garden State, almost US$200,000 was added to the Royal Tiger account in the U.S., with only US$10,000 returned to the Garden State (their legal requirement). The fruits of the labor of the people of Garden State were being drained into an American bank account, with no benefits to them, at a time when the poverty-stricken country badly needed an influx of foreign currency. It was the early 1980s, a time of recession in the Americas, but for Shawn Shin and the Wong family, every day was the 4th of July.

Even while keeping their reservoir of money in the U.S. bank account, Anita and Shawn were still able to rapidly raise their standard of living in the Garden State. They moved from their modest home to a much grander estate in a high priced district of the city. In addition, Shawn sold their old Honda Civic and replaced it with two 300 series Mercedes-Benz sedans. Anita also travelled frequently. She would take their two children at least two or three times a year to New York, Toronto or Miami to shop. Her no spending limit American Express Gold Card certainly gave her the convenience to shop extravagantly.

Who wants a bargain?

The Shin family was good at many things, especially in negotiating with the government and in looking for loopholes in the market. But no one seemed to be capable of managing money. In fact, from day one, the company had done nothing to manage their finances other than through

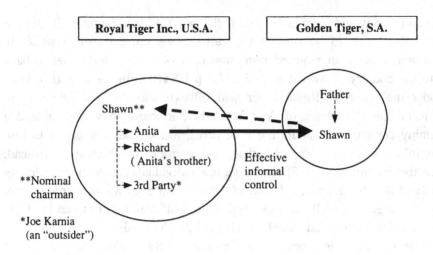

Figure 13.4 GT stage 4: The Royal Tiger.

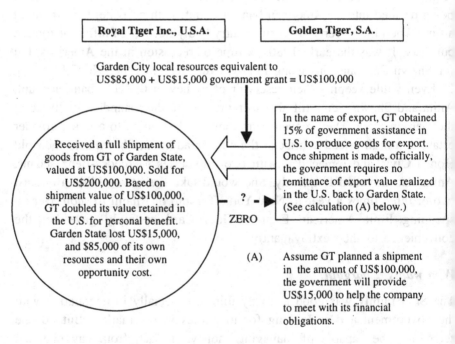

Figure 13.5 The accumulation of Royal Tiger U.S. bank account.

debt. Borrowing from the bank, mortgaging practically anything, asking for help from their children — these were the ways in which the company got itself out of difficult situations time after time. Fortunately, because of government protection, the company was able to enjoy continued growth. Unfortunately, however, for every inch that the company grew, the problems of financing and cashflow grew two inches. By the mid-1980s, despite years of good sales, Golden Tiger was about to meet its Waterloo.

Cash was slowly being drained out of GT into the Royal Tiger bank account in the U.S. Despite the continued help from the Shin children,[1] cashflow became so bad that the suppliers were pressing for payment, and the banks threatened full closure of the company. Out of desperation, Mark asked his son-in-law, Allan, who is a professional, whether he knew anybody who would buy the business for US$15 million? Allan responded positively, and asked his father-in-law about sales figures, and for possible profit and loss reports for the past three years. When Mark asked Shawn: "Can you inform Allan of our past three years' sales and profit or loss? Shawn's face turned red immediately, replying: "Who is going to tell him sales and profits? That's crazy!" before exiting from the room with an angry face. Mark, by this time an old man in his 70s, regrettably looked at Allan, and with a sad and weary expression on his face, shook his head. That was the end of the conversation.

A gift from heaven

Perhaps it was the Shin family luck, but instead of being forced by the bank to put the company into receivership, the "East Clock" Company's lawyer from the U.S. approached Shin, and expressed interest in buying the GT land. The clock company was willing to pay US$5 million for one-half of the holdings. The news came like a gift from heaven. The mother, Anita and a few other Catholics all went to church to pray and thank God for their good fortune. The land deal was completed at the end of 1983, and GT's financial trouble was temporarily over.

Mostly from Scott, the doctor, with some contribution from the daughters. The eldest son contributed only a small amount, even though he continued to draw a pension from GT.

With the additional US$5 million in cash, everything changed. The banker's attitude was completely different, and instead of pressing for repayment of the loan, they encouraged Mark Shin and Shawn to consider expansion. So, expansion it was, and GT expanded almost immediately. But they never returned a single penny to Scott who had been paying the interest on a US$300,000 guaranteed loan. The issue of repayment was never raised, not even by Scott, as he felt that he was doing it "for his father." Once, Scott asked Shawn why the company could not give any money back to him. Shawn replied that they had no money back in the Garden State, which was the truth, but what he failed to say was that all the money was in the U.S. bank account of Royal Tiger Inc., USA.

The outward prosperity continued. Shawn travelled to Europe, looking for new machinery and technology. Meanwhile, Mark Shin was building a new residence in the ambassadorial area at an estimated building cost of approximately US$500,000. Scott and his family were very uncomfortable about the whole thing, and the question always remained in the back of their minds: "You seem to be doing so well, so why don't you pay back the money we guaranteed?" Anita's spending became even more outrageous. She started to do her Christmas shopping in the U.S. She also became more aggressive, pushing for official membership on the GT board. As time passed, Mark Shin's health was beginning to deteriorate, and it was becoming increasingly difficult to put up any struggle against Anita's ambitions. The Shin family was becoming very uneasy, largely because Shawn held all the company's shares, or at least, so they all suspected. Nevertheless, Mark Shin continued to support Shawn. In truth, Mark Shin knew little about GT's financial condition, nor the power struggles that were going on. The organization remained the same, except that Mark asked that everyone give up any share in the company to him, with the exception of Shawn. They all did it, because it was, again, "for father." Paradoxically, while bringing more of the official ownership into his own hands, Mark let go of it in reality, essentially becoming semi-retired. He visited his children in North America and stayed with them a lot. Even when he was back at the Garden City, he would only visit the office once in a while. As Shawn said: "Papa really isn't doing much, when he comes to the office, he just sits there, drinks his tea, reads the newspaper, and takes a catnap."

The reorganization effectively transferred proprietary ownership of GT to the Wong family from the Shin family.

It is not clear what role Joe played at this time, but he was part of Anita Shin's decision-making team.

Golden Tiger, Stage 5

Organizational note:

Mark Shin:	Father, founder, titular head. No power
Shawn Shin:	Nominal head of the business, but controlled by Anita
Anita Shin:	Actual head of business, supported by her brother, Richard and Joe Karnia
Peter, Rose and Hugh Shin	Support Anita

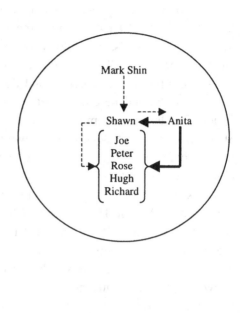

Figure 13.6 GT stage 5: Wong or Shin?

The new board

Without the knowledge of anyone outside of his own family, Shawn restructured the board. It consisted of six people, with himself as chairman, Anita as CEO, and their three children and Richard (Anita's brother) as the other board members. Though officially still a Shin business, GT in all but name now belongs to the Wongs.

The beginning of the end of a family business

Garden State is a small country, and the people in the country know each other. There, the grapevine can pass news faster than the information highway. Soon enough, everyone in Garden State seemed to know what was happening. Mark Shin (now in his late 70s) had also heard the rumors relating to "his" company. He thought if he could move his grandson Isaac (his eldest son's first child) into the company, all could be saved. Mark felt strongly that Isaac could save the situation, as he had the perfect qualifications to run the company: an engineering degree combined with an MBA. Despite all his wheeling and dealing, Shawn still had some respect for his family, and he did not really want to make things difficult for his father. So, Isaac was moved into the company as the senior engineer. Shawn and Isaac got along well. Shawn was so pleased with the arrangement that he told everybody: "Isaac really helps me a lot, we work as a team. He is just like my brother."

Mark Shin was also taking steps to secure his legacy to his children. For example, he told Hamlet, one of his sons-in-law, working in Africa for the UN at the time: "Why do you have to go so far to work? If you need money, we have it. Just tell me, how much do you want?" Hamlet was moved almost to tears by his father-in-law's offer. What Mark Shin did not know was that he could not get a cent of GT's bank account. He had no personal savings at all, and was no longer drawing his old salary as Chairman of GT. So, in actual fact, he had no means of preparing his own will. Thus, he thought of asking his youngest son (Shawn) to sell his Golden Tiger upon his death. His intention was to use the money realized from the sale of the company, to pay all debts to the various children; one-half of the remainder would go to Shawn to start up a smaller business on his own, and the balance, his and his wife's share, one-quarter to the two elder sons, one-quarter would likely go to support his wife, the mother, and the remainder would be given as a gift to be shared amongst the four daughters.

Only five months after Hamlet's conversation with Mark, his wife Alice received a call from the Garden State home, informing her that her father had passed away.

Mark Shin died just three days before they (the old couple) were due to move to the new residence. (The couple was living with their elder son during the time.) Days before he died, he wanted so badly to go to the office, and told Shawn "I must go to office, as I have some important things to attend to." Shawn would not let him go, saying: "Papa, everything is fine, there is no need for you to go, in three days, you will be moving into your new house; meanwhile enjoy staying with Derek (his elder son)." The night before the move, Mark Shin was dancing and laughing with his children. Before the night was over, he told Derek's wife: "I pray that God would let me have ten more years, so I can dance and enjoy life with all my children, grandchildren and great grandchildren." Less than 24 hours after he said those words, he left all his children, grandchildren, great grandchildren, and his Golden Tiger, permanently.

Upon hearing the news, Hamlet and Alice immediately boarded a plane for Garden City, but it was too late for the funeral. The family in Garden City who took care of the funeral arrangements had decided not to wait for all of Mark's children to come and pay their last respects to their father. When Hamlet and Alice arrived, they heard someone in the family say: "Joyce suggested reading father's will." Shawn had heard his father's last wishes, and had intended to tell the family about them. However, Joyce, perhaps feeling that it would be inappropriate at the time, told him not to. She said: "This can wait," so Shawn waited.

About five days after Mark's funeral, Shawn drove Hamlet and Alice to the airport, and in the car, he told Hamlet: "I plan to sell the business, but not now. The business is doing so well, it is best to wait a while until we can sell it for more money. Then, we'll sell, and I'll start-up a new business by myself." However, while Hamlet was at the check-in counter paying the airport tax, Anita screamed at Shawn: "How dare you talking of selling my business!"

The firing of Isaac

The informal board created by Anita and Shawn became official after Mark's death. Now Shawn was the only member of the Shin family with official ties to Golden Tiger. For no apparent reason, one of the decisions approved by the new board was to create a small factory in Pointer, a town south of Garden City. Golden Tiger rented a warehouse with minimum investment, no plant assets, but piles of inventory. Isaac was appointed as manager of the factory, even though it was not the best use of his talents.

One day, while Hamlet and Alice were in the U.K. and Scott and his wife were in Italy, Alice received a call from Scott informing her that their mother had had a fall, was admitted to the hospital where she soon passed away. Six months later, Isaac was fired, and the last of Shin's family members (with the exception of Shawn) was kicked out from a once highly successful family business.

Postscript

In November 2000, a press reported visited Golden Tiger asking to interview Shawn. She was told by the receptionist that there was no such person. Then, she asked to speak to anyone from Mark Shin's family. Joe Karnia and Richard Wong told the reporter to get lost. They told her that there is no one in the company with the family name of "Shin."

Questions for discussion

1. What contributed to Golden Tiger's success?
2. Shawn had a limited formal education. If he had more, would it have made any difference?
3. How would things have been different if Mark Shin had prepared a legally binding formal will? Keep in mind that one could argue that a will is only as good as the intentions of the executors.
4. In a partnership situation, shares of one partner can be legally transferred to another partner or partners if the method of transfer is written into the partnership agreement. Would this have been possible for Golden Tiger case, where most of the contributions had been unrecorded and informal? What if the contribution of the various partners had been more transparently recorded?
5. Give an account of the history of Golden Tiger as Shawn Shin might put it. Speculate on his transformation from the loyal, hardworking family son to what he became in his later life? Did Golden Tiger contribute to this?
6. Golden Tiger is still in business, but it is no longer the "Shin" family business. The tragedy is not just for the Shin family, but also for Garden State as a whole, with so much of their money siphoned out of the United States. What benefit did Golden Tiger have to the people of Garden State under Mark, and then Shawn? Is it part of the market economy?

Chapter 14

The Succession Challenge and the Glory of Family Business

> The success of family business is one where family and business can be proud of each other, with the purpose of stressing family harmony as well as achieving a high level of business success.
>
> The chapter is created on factual information, but the names and places of origin were changed and restructured into three scenarios for the purpose of this book as learning and reading references. Families in all three cases are considered to have been running successful family businesses, all with the prime objective of being in business to strive for success rather than just to make profit. Their success is not only in terms of building respected institutions but that of family harmony as well. Therefore, it is possible to suggest that a family business should not only set its objective for making profits and financial success, but more importantly, for harmonious relations among all members of the family. Although some members of the family may desire not to return to work for the family business, at least one member of the family is the key decision-maker, maintaining financial control of the business.

14.1 Family Business and Family Value

Scenario 1: *No operation, no pay. A family business builds on family value.*

Charles Lee was born in Rio de Janeiro but received his early education in Japan and Hong Kong. He returned to Rio at 18 and continued his education in a local university. Graduating with an MD degree, he further specialized in medication to alleviate symptoms of human bone and joint degeneration. Upon completing his specialization, he paid his dues to the government for the sponsorship of his studies and then opened a small clinic in Rio. He worked hard for two years (80 to 90 hours a week) with little success; he could not establish a clientele and faced some financial difficulties. On one occasion, his old professor visited his office and talked about his plans for the future. They concluded that he should advance himself into both the prevention and treatment of bone and joint degeneration, and extend his services to patients of all ages. The professor helped him to obtain a special grant from a hi-tech company and provided him with a computer for diagnostic analysis in Japan (used for the implementation of procedures based on the repair and replacement of bone tissues without operation, sensible diets and preventive medicine from the cradle to the golden age, for both men and women). With his professor's recommendation and the support of the hi-tech company, Charles was able to spend four years of his youth in Japan. Prior to leaving for Japan, Charles got married and subsequently had two children, a boy and a girl, with his wife, Gloria. Charles worked and studied hard, lived a very simple almost monk-like existence. He graduated with an advanced diploma from a renowned institution in Japan. He again returned to Brazil to set up his own clinic, but this time with an added responsibility: the technological company asked him to be the company's technical advisor, and empowered him to represent the company in South America.

With this new responsibility, Charles positioned himself and his clinic as a possible center to help people with body degeneration problems, in particular, kidney degeneration and associated pains. He decided to treat anyone, rich or poor, following the standard fees schedules. With each treatment, however, he would take out a portion of his income for a fund to help those unable to pay the full amount of the service.

Charles is a physician and a surgeon, but the improved technology has relieved him from conducting traditional surgical techniques. He perfected a painless micro drilling process and fine instrument insertion technique into the body to remove or repair any partial damages. The procedure had become so successful that Dr. Charles Lee suddenly became a legendary name in South America, as well as the U.S. In one case, a woman came all the way from Taiwan to get Charles to repair her partially damaged spine. After the operation, she refused to pay, and she told Charles "Sorry, Doctor, I cannot pay you, because our insurance will not pay me for the operation. The truth is, I don't have the money to pay you myself." She made no payment, and Charles did not pursue this. Charles' colleague asked him why he did not press for payment? He said: "Well, if her insurance doesn't pay her and she has no money, what can she do? Anyway, our business is in helping people to reduce pain, and recover from degeneration. I have done that. Don't you think we have served our purpose? Money is secondary, we have money to meet our overheads and pay staff. I am not worried about it."

By this time (approximately 25 years after the inauguration of his clinic), Charles and Gloria have had four children, two boys and two girls, three of whom wanted to follow in their father's footsteps. Two of them are already licensed medical doctors, they had gone to Japan to earn their advanced diplomas and are now working in their father's clinic, and the third one is just about to leave for Japan to pursue his studies. The two older children plan to specialize in the same field as their father while the youngest son plans to enter into the field of genetic diseases. All four, however, have the same commitment as their father, that is to abide by the mission of healing people of pain and body degeneration. Charles is a likeable person, everyone addresses him by his first name, and the clinic has now more than ten staff and doctors, functioning like a real team. There is no communication problem and only a simple one-to-one organizational arrangement. Above all, it is small and manageable.

Dr. Lee is now 62. He said to his children and colleagues: "I have plans to set up an institute dedicated to body degeneration problems with all our colleagues from the Pacific region. I anticipate it will take five to ten years, thus I have no desire to play golf, or travel just yet.

Remark:

The Lee's Clinic of Medication and Prevention for Body Degeneration is an institution created with the mission of helping people to ease pain and recover from degeneration. Money is of secondary importance to the clinic. It appears that the clinic will pass on to the next generation, not just as an institution, but its values as well. Although the planned succession is not visible, it is obvious; Lee's children have developed the same love and passion for the profession. The influence of their father's practice and education has allowed the family business to continue to serve humanity, the same way as Charles has committed himself to do so. Charles has earned and thus enjoys his success.

There is no Lee's clinic in Rio, but the story and the moral behind it are real, only the name, place and practice are changed. It is for us to understand why a family business can continue after the first generation, perhaps even the second generation and beyond. The answer for this illustration is clear: to make money alone will not sustain a family business to continue. It needs a "family value" to go along with the succession, and successors of the business must be educated along the same path, but by their own will and with the same value and commitment as the founder of the venture.

14.2 A Successful Family Business May Not Necessarily Attract Children Back to the Business

Scenario 2: Making money and extravagant living may prove family business success, but not necessarily for succession.

As in any other large cities in the world, London, New York, Toronto, San Jose, Rio and Paris all have a large population of people of Chinese origin. In the early days, migrants from China started small businesses as a means of livelihood. Consequently, a large number of settlers were operating small shops, restaurants, trading companies, and food supplies companies, providing dry goods, fish and poultry. (Although in later days, more opportunities opened up for the younger generation, including an appointment as Governor General of Canada!)

First generation immigrants are pushed by the need to survive and establish themselves in new places, motivated by the desire to escape from poverty, make a living and earn their place in society; many of them sought retailing and trading as a means to support their families. A large number of them became successful only after a long and gruelling struggle. On one occasion, the author visited several families, five of whom were related to the author. Almost all of them enjoyed comfortable living, through operating retailing stores, selling shoes, clothing, furniture, as well as retailing fish products and seafood. They all possess large luxury living quarters, well appointed furnishings, and have chauffeur-driven expensive automobiles. When they travel, they fly first class, and stay in five star hotel accommodations. To them, business is just about making money; with money, they can have everything and anything they want. Thus, making money seems to be the sole purpose of all five of the family businesses that the author contacted.

Among those families, all of them have sent their children to the U.S. or Canada. Almost without exception, the children are holders of advanced degrees such as MA, MBA, MSc, PhD, LLB, LLM, MD or Bachelor of Dentistry. Most of them land positions as managers, engineers, lawyers, computer programmers, analysts and marketing representatives. They have no intention to return to their country of origin (such as Malaysia, Costa Rica, Brazil, or Indonesia). At least one family out of the five interviewed said that each of their children requires at least US$40,000 to US$50,000 to support one child annually, and this particular family has four children, so their education needs in the U.S. amounts to approximately US$160,000 per annum. One may wonder, how can a small retailer afford such expenses. Yet, the children are not returning home to assume the responsibility of running their family businesses. Why?

Both parents and children of the five families were asked the same questions. Basically, the objective was to find out why parents worked so hard to support the next generation and sponsor their studies in expensive universities, without guarantee of a suitable business successor. They are obviously only concerned with providing a first class education for their children.

Remark:

Scenario 2 clearly shows that family business with the objective of making money alone does not necessarily mean that there will be an easy succession.

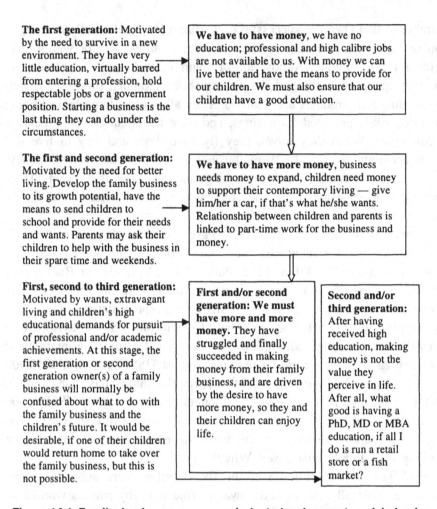

The first generation: Motivated by the need to survive in a new environment. They have very little education, virtually barred from entering a profession, hold respectable jobs or a government position. Starting a business is the last thing they can do under the circumstances.

We have to have money, we have no education; professional and high calibre jobs are not available to us. With money we can live better and have the means to provide for our children. We must also ensure that our children have a good education.

The first and second generation: Motivated by the need for better living. Develop the family business to its growth potential, have the means to send children to school and provide for their needs and wants. Parents may ask their children to help with the business in their spare time and weekends.

We have to have more money, business needs money to expand, children need money to support their contemporary living — give him/her a car, if that's what he/she wants. Relationship between children and parents is linked to part-time work for the business and money.

First, second to third generation: Motivated by wants, extravagant living and children's high educational demands for pursuit of professional and/or academic achievements. At this stage, the first generation or second generation owner(s) of a family business will normally be confused about what to do with the family business and the children's future. It would be desirable, if one of their children would return home to take over the family business, but this is not possible.

First and/or second generation: We must have more and more money. They have struggled and finally succeeded in making money from their family business, and are driven by the desire to have more money, so they and their children can enjoy life.

Second and/or third generation: After having received high education, making money is not the value they perceive in life. After all, what good is having a PhD, MD or MBA education, if all I do is run a retail store or a fish market?

Figure 14.1 Family business owners mindset development and behavior.

In fact, without family value, the business can pass on to the next generation without a willing successor to run the business, because there is a clear difference between those who are interested in the money and those interested in the business. In scenario 2, the owners of the family business will undoubtedly continue running the business, and the business may remain successful, but once the older generation retires, the continuation of the business will be a matter of concern. The following comparison of two scenarios of value and management differences will perhaps explain the factors involved in easy family business succession.

Table 14.1 Value and management comparison between two family business scenarios.

Categories for comparison	Scenario 1	Scenario 2
Value	Healing people of body, bone degeneration and pain problems, making money is secondary	Making money, although the business also has other economic values to society, but not known to children
Nature of the business	Professional, and academically related	Retailing, fishery and similar businesses
Challenge to successor	To explore the unknown, search for the cure to human illnesses, etc.	Working day in and day out on how best to provide service to consumers
Satisfaction	Interact directly with people in need of medication and treatment — gives satisfaction beyond what words can describe. People with the same interest and dedication working harmoniously together	Customer satisfaction. To obtain more money in cash register and bank account
Management	Simple organization, mostly one-to-one. Business value professional conduct as a vehicle to link human relations	Depending on size of the operation, money issues are usually involved. It may have employee turnover challenge from time to time. Money matters are real management headaches, particularly when sales targets are not being met. Inventory, and cost control are also some of the management problems

Table 14.1 (*Continued*)

Categories for comparison	Scenario 1	Scenario 2
Successors' education	No problem. Working in the same environment, with same interest and training, self-motivated in a sharing environment	Not self-motivated, but sometimes imposed. The purpose of learning the trade is to make money, learning itself has low or no motivation
Succession	With a gradual pace, smooth transition	There might be an inheritance problem. Among other things, personal interest conflict is rooted before the "succession" day

The comparison provides some fundamental issues and challenges involved in family business. In short, the following essentials should be observed:

(1) There has to be a "Value" associated with a particular family business, and the successor must make an early acquaintance with such a value, and what it means to him/her.
(2) The successor should be involved in the family business; he must work and earn his salary like a normal employee of the business.
(3) The successor needs to develop his/her personal interest, love and passion for the business. Ensure that the successor's interest is in the business and not just the money.
(4) The successor's managerial or professional competence is important for success in the business, and further education should be relevant to the business. Unrelated higher education may push a would-be successor away from the business.

　　Under the circumstances, the business owner must choose and decide what is the priority — the successor's self-interest, career choice, and his/her future expectation of the family business?

(5) It may come to the point whereby the owner of a family business must realize that the family business succession is the choice of the

successor and not of the parents. Because the real succession takes place after the parents retire from the business, not when they are still in charge of running the business.

(6) While it is necessary for the successor to familiarise himself with business operational and management details, it is also important for the successor to appreciate the business culture in addition to business and management knowledge.

The above are thoughts directly related to illustrated scenarios 1 and 2. The topic of family business succession will be explored in a later chapter.

14.3 The Glory of Family Business

Scenario 3: Small is beautiful, but "Simple" is better. A family business built on shared value within the family.

Linda Snow, has an MSc degree, and has been holding a corporate executive position for the past four years. In her leisure time, she would visit her grandfather in the mountains where he has a business in trout farming, which serves both as a tourist attraction and as commercial fishery for the regional market. Linda describes him as a person who loves to live a simple life. She recalls him saying to her more than once: "Small is beautiful, but simple is better." He once told her a story about his experience in Tobago, a small island in the Caribbean: "Linda, what I'm about to tell you may seem strange at first, but if you think it through and try to decipher the meaning of it, you will eventually understand it." This is what he told her:

> I was on a government mission in Trinidad and Tobago, where I had been assigned to help with regional development. After I completed my work in Trinidad, my host gave me a short holiday in Tobago, where he put me up at the Turtle Beach Hotel. The following morning, after I had settled in, I decided to take a walk along the beach where I saw a young man (about 18 years old) fishing. The next day and the following days, thereafter, I would always find him fishing there. So I approached him and our conversation began:

Linda's grandfather:	How old are you, young man?
Young man:	I'm 17.
Linda's grandfather:	Why aren't you in school?
Young man:	What for?
Linda's grandfather:	If you go to school, have a better education, you will be able to get a good job and earn more money.
Young man:	What for?
Linda's grandfather:	I guess you are not married yet? Do you want to get married?
Young man:	What for?
Linda's grandfather:	When you have a good job, you will have some money to get married, and then you will have a good life.
Young man:	What for?
Linda's grandfather:	Then you can raise children and have a good family.
Young man:	What for?
Linda's grandfather:	After your children have grown up, you can use your savings to retire to a nice, warm place and do some fishing.
Young man:	That's what I am doing.

Linda did not quite understand this story at the time (around the early 1970s). She was only a young teenage girl then; Linda is now in her early 40s and a vice-president of an auto manufacturing company. Her busy corporate life sometimes caused her to neglect her other responsibilities to family, relatives and religion, but she maintained a good relationship with her grandparents and visited them often. As she observed how her grandparents live, she began to realize the meaning of the story her grandfather told her. It is a story of being simple. Live a simple life, enjoy the process and find happiness from it. Then, she asked herself, why is she contributing to the auto industry? Virtually every car company tries to promote an environmentally friendly image to the public, yet every one of them wants to sell more cars. More cars need more petroleum, and more roads are needed to accommodate more cars. China is still very much a developing country, yet there are auto manufacturers in every major city. Every year, more and more cars are being put on the road. Korean-made cars are already competing on the Western market. Soon, China will also enter and compete for their share of the market, how then is it possible for auto makers to still claim that they care for the environment?

Linda now understands what it means by a sustainable economy. In some ways, Linda and her grandfather think alike, though both pursue different goals in life. Her grandfather leads a simple life, while she chooses almost the opposite. More often than not, she wonders if she should join him? Linda greatly respects her grandfather, not just as an elder but as a dear friend as well.

14.3.1 The beginning of the beginning

George Snow (Linda's grandfather) is in his 80s. He lives in the mountains where he has a trout farm business, employing about 20 people, eight of them are his children, grandchildren and two nephews. George holds a PhD degree in urban planning, and has worked as a chairman for land use of a large Canadian city. The federal government frequently assigns him to assist other countries in their urban and regional development. Linda knows him as a person who believes and practises a simple life. For example, he once visited a Caribbean country where he was assigned to provide consultation for the country's tourism development. At the first meeting with the minister in charge of tourism, the minister listed the objectives: to increase the country's tourism revenue by at least three-fold during the next five years, and to develop the industry into a leading tourist attraction, with Japanese and U.S. visitor numbers doubling every year for the next three years.

George said to the minister: "Carlos, before you have these expectations you should first assess whether the airport is capable of handling the traffic, and also take an inventory of all the major attractions and events in this country. A booming tourism industry may be beneficial for the economy but it has its ill effects as well. Thirty years ago, 80% of the land was green, but now, less than 50% is green. At this rate, the country will have nothing but highrise hotels, with brown patches everywhere and the beaches overcrowded. I agree that tourists' dollars are good, and the industry helps promote better human interaction, creates job opportunities, and facilitates cultural exchange. In fact, in the old days, people claimed that it is a clean industry without the chimney. Unfortunately, however, this is not true anymore." The minister asked him why.

George replied: "Carlos, most people think that the tourist industry is an environmentally friendly industry. Though this may be true to a certain extent, in reality, it's one of the worst enemies to the environment, especially if we follow the traditional way of developing the industry. Five star hotels, beach resorts and other tourist attractions will attract "big tourist money" but all of them are environmentally unfriendly, since you need land to build hotels, not to mention cutting down trees and clearing out beaches just to allow people to swim, boat and surf. These human activities will of course destroy marine flora and fauna. Tourists may also damage the environment unconsciously, as their mere presence disrupts the natural ecosystem, affecting insects, birds and other living creatures in the area.

Carlos smiled at George and said: "George, if I listen to what you say, I might as well just resign from my post as our country's minister of tourism." George replied: "No Carlos, that's not necessary, you just have to remember that you can work with the environment, and keep it simple. It may not be the best solution, but it is certainly better than the way some other places are developed. Besides, the tourism industry is a crazy one, you can never satisfy your tourists for too long. First, there may be just one or two resorts offering a package deal — that's fine. But very soon, competition kicks in, and the operators themselves will find that their business has become saturated. They would then have to close down the operation or find new places offering greater attractions and then promote the older place as a bargain basement for low budget-minded tourists. How many new places can you offer? Soon enough, your green land will change its color and shape. However, you can still develop the industry by changing the emphasis, focus on something that will work with nature. Although tourists must be treated like royalty, they should and can be educated to learn how to protect the environment at the same time. We can educate tourists by making everything simple, help them to learn from simple things, and provide the opportunity for them to enjoy what they experience. The whole idea is based on "Simple." Schumacher said small is beautiful. But really, I think simple is better." Carlos asks George: "Tell me how are we going to do it?"

George told Carlos: "Before I design a model to show you what can be done, can you please let me know what's available?" Carlos responded: "In addition to our beaches and shopping attractions, we have mountains, waterfalls, rainforests, cultural festivals and many other features waiting to be developed. What we need is a master plan to outline what we have, what needs to be done and how can it be done." George reacted favorably, and said to Carlos that it is possible. He would like to consider how to develop the mountains, waterfalls and hot springs in a way that they can be regenerated. This will be unlike other developments where you have to destroy first before you build. Carlos agreed, and told George: "Why don't you give me a formal plan, so I can see what is possible and what can be done."

George also suggested using natural water from the falls to feed both man-made and natural ponds for the rearing of fish, specifically "trout." Carlos then encouraged George to take up trout farming, and promised him that he would do everything he can to help.

George had in mind a simple trout farm which uses running water from the waterfalls. During the past seven months, George actively went about to see what can be done. He planned on devoting all of his time on trout farming. After weeks of searching, he finally found the ideal place by Green mountain, where there are several falls flowing in a 100-meter wide area, all the way down to the foot of the hill. The mountain is about 1200 meters above sea level, and is on government land. It has a sharp slope on the south side and a gentle one on the north. Along the slope, there are several abandoned shelters, a paved road leads to the mountain, and a mature footpath running all the way to the peak.

George talked with Carlos about his plans. He had even prepared a mini plan for the proposed undertaking.

The concept:

To develop a tourism industry through education and participation, so that one can appreciate and enjoy the environment. Trout fishing is only one part of a total involvement, the others may involve activities taking place in the country's protected areas, including sports like white water rafting, horseback riding, as well as riding on inflatable kayaks into the tranquil waters of the lower rivers. In George's case, his interest lies in trout fishing. His farm also offers inexpensive accommodation for visitors.

14.3.2 The natural waterfall feeds trout farm: to transform an idea into a family business

George's basic idea is illustrated in Fig. 14.2.

George's plan is to create a clear area with waterfalls freely flowing in three tributaries. The area has approximately ten cabins, originally built as living quarters for coffee pickers. As a rough estimate, it is possible to have approximately 20 to 30 fish ponds, fed by fresh running water from

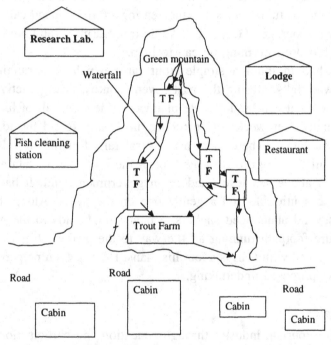

Fresh water flow into the pond from the top, and flow out from the pond, back to the stream, then to another pond.

Figure 14.2 Natural waterfall feeds trout farm.

the top. After filling the pond, the water will flow out to the lower area and feed another pond. This water is absolutely clean.

Carlos told George that he can have the area on a renewable 90-year lease. Within this period, George can build the industry as planned, on the condition that it is friendly to the environment. Besides refraining from the cutting down of trees, the establishment also has to find ways to dispose of its own garbage, preferably using an environmentally friendly method. It was also suggested that George should contact a few tour operators about joining the venture. George liked the idea, and with Carlos's support, he successfully started the trout fishing business.

14.3.3 The shared value

The Snow family members are mostly well educated, love nature and devoted to the pursuit of knowledge. The two sons work with George; Ian and David both have had impressive careers. Ian was a trade officer and a country representative for the bilateral trade negotiations during the period (before the creation of the World Trade Organization) of Trade Liberalization in the Uruguay Round. As a fishery expert, he is often concerned about people's ignorance of marine life, especially with regards to how fish reproduce or how the ocean regenerates. They continue to poach from the sea just to satisfy their need for "profit." He believes in focusing more on fresh water fish reproduction rather than that of reproducing salt water fish. He said: "Our technology can be used for the development of fresh water fish — which is controllable. In the case of salt water fish, however, we have no knowledge on how they reproduce themselves, or how long the stock will last, given the rate at which man keeps taking from Nature." Dave has an MBA in marketing, but like George and Ian, he shares the same fundamental belief:

> We have the choice of either work, live with nature, or ruthlessly exploit against nature. But if we stay on course and live in accordance to what we need, rather than want, then in fact, nature provides us with more than we need. It is the simple lifestyle that will deliver our hope for peace and economic sustainability.

Ian's value of pursuing for need satisfaction and working and living with nature coincides with George's idea of "small is beautiful, but simple is better." This unknowingly becomes the shared value in the family, and is also the value shared by all those working in the trout farm.

Trout farming is a very successful family business by any standards. It was created based on the shared value of simplicity, productivity and, innovatively, without infringement of nature and the environment.

The employees of the farm consist of three generations all working in the same environment. They learn from each other, and share both working and family life experiences. Everyone is a leader of his/her interest and expertise. There is no boss, only decision makers of each and every task. They earn money to live, not live to make money. These nine key individuals make up an unconventional organizational structure described below.

14.3.4 The trout farm organizational structure

The three parts of the organization do not form a formal structure; it is based on needs, and no unit is superior that the other. There is no president, CEO, or any job title, structured from the basics (bottom up so to speak), not top down. All contributors are equal; it makes no difference if some contributed money (start-up capital or continued financing) or labor, they are all on a first name basis. The farm provides complimentary staff residence to employees, but they need to maintain the place and pay all expenses by themselves. Those who prefer not to stay in the farm, will be provided with a small subsidy. Parking is free, and the farm provides free transportation from farm to the town three times (return trip) a day. All major decisions will be made at a general meeting conducted as democratically as possible. As a rule, issues will be discussed in general. If resolved, no detailed discussion is necessary, otherwise, a limited time is set aside for discussion, then a decision will be made either by the person involved or on a voting basis. No unresolved issues are left to the "next meeting." As David said: "In a democratic process, there are differences in opinions, but a decision has to be made. Over the past 30 years, there have not been any problems that members of the farm could not resolve.

Note on organization: Trout production

Each box has one decision maker. The smaller box inside functions like the bigger box.

People in the box make decisions with no interference from people outside of the box.

The farm has two ponds; they are used to incubate the fish, and are everyone's responsibility.

Everyone is responsible for his/her own pond. All are jointly responsible for the two large ponds.

Although there are ponds assigned to each individual, everyone will chip in to help if one of them is in need.

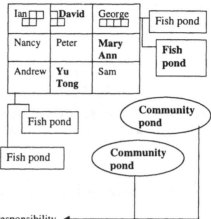

Joint stake and joint responsibility ◄─── for fish spawn and breeding, nurturing and care, until the fish grow to the adult stage, then transferred to the small ponds, where they then become the individual's responsibility.

Square organization means more rigid in responsibility and decision making, oval suggests flexibility among decision makers.

Figure 14.3(a) The trout farm organization: trout reproduction.

Note on organization: Administration

Round organization means flexibility:

All administrative positions can relate to one another.

All positions can be rotated, if individuals prefer.

Nine positions on the left include:

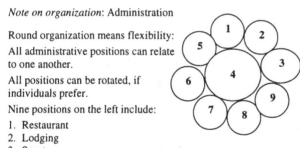

1. Restaurant
2. Lodging
3. Sport
4. Finance and Accounting
5. Family coordination
6. Transport
7. Marketing
8. Tour operator's coordination
9. Facilitation and coordination

Figure 14.3(b) Trout farm organizational structure: administration.

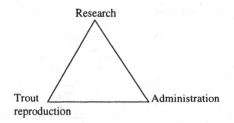

Figure 14.3(c) All trout farm organization positions can be rotated amongst all individuals who have decision-making positions.

14.4 As a Community of Entrepreneurs

The trout farm characterizes itself as a community of entrepreneurs. The entire farm is a community, and everyone in the community shares two sets of values.

The fundamental value: They all believe that sustainable economic growth is possible, if everyone can live and work harmoniously in the same environment. Living and appreciating a simple life is a continuing process. By leading a simple life, one can enjoy every process, and find happiness in the process.

The entrepreneurial value: As we appreciate that life is a continuing process, we make every process meaningful. We are creative creatures by nature, capable of "making different combinations." We create wealth for ourselves and add value to the community.

Based on these shared values, every member of the farm works and enjoys nature, the fruits of their labor (the trout), as well as the human interactions within the community. It has a very small staff turnover and no labor union. Pay equity is a fact, not just a verbal statement. Members assist each other in every way possible. As creative and innovative individuals, their goal is to improve fish health (there are virtually no health problems, as the water is always free flowing and free from pollutants) fish quality, and hospitality to tourists and their own members. There is practically no such thing as management, as they believe that no "management" is management itself.

Community life involves the sharing of cooking duties for community members who use restaurant facilities. The restaurant is originally designed to entertain tourists who wish for their catch to be prepared according to their own personal preferences (such as deep fry, steam or grill). Individuals are encouraged to practice their gourmet cooking skills to entertain other members of the farm. They can also choose to have meals on their own, since the staff quarters have cooking facilities too.

14.5 Financing and Ownership

The Trout farm is financed by its members in the form of a venture. Investment is in terms of cash or labor. Shares of the farm are not to be sold to outsiders; in other words, if any member of the farm wishes to leave, he/she may do so but must sell his/her shares to other members of the farm. The price of a share is determined by a professional estimate. Those who wish to purchase shares, but have no means of doing so may be financed by the farm and will be committed to a repayment plan. The system is designed to encourage individual members to maintain the shared value of the farm.

As agreed by all members, the farm's objective is to maintain an operationally manageable size without seeking external help. If growth is inevitable, then the aim is only for sustainable growth, not maximum size or profit. Growth is only necessary if current facilities are unable to support the farm's objective of serving people, and of caring, living and working with nature. Since it has no financial objective to expand, debt financing and leverage are therefore not part of the consideration — Grow only if absolutely necessary.

14.6 Succession and Inheritance

Succession has not been a problem in this 30-year-old family business, for the following reasons:

(1) "Succession" applies only to the shared value. It is the shared value in the farm that holds members together as a family.
(2) Inheritance does not apply, since every member is given the opportunity to take part in community life. And shares of the farm must be earned, not given.
(3) Members of the farm are part of the farm, no outsider can join the farm, unless he/she is a member of the farm.
(4) There is no such thing as inherited money or business, since all members are shareholders and/or stakeholders.

During her last visit to her grandparents at the farm, Linda decided to leave the corporate life and join the family business.

One final note: George's success in changing the tourism focus from luxury five-star hotels, beach resorts and big shopping malls to "live and enjoy with nature" has made Green State re-focus its promotional efforts, calling it: "We are turning over a new leaf…" as a result.

14.7 Conclusion

It is a natural process for a family to start a business and share the responsibilities of creating and managing the business, and normal for a member of the family in the business to crave recognition for his/her contribution and for rewards that meet with his/her expectations. It is also natural that all those involved in the business feel that they should have a piece of it when the founder (owner in charge) departs from the business. However, a distinction must be made between individuals who are genuinely committed to the business and members of the family whose primary objective is that of money and/or power. Under these circumstances, it is not just the business that fails, family relations will break down as well. There is no reason why any successful family business cannot survive and pass to the third generation and beyond. To do so, the following should be observed:

• A family business must have a family value. This value should also be extended into the business; it must be a value driven entity. A profit driven motive is insufficient to sustain a family business. More often than not, the pursuit for greater profits is the cause of family conflict and dissolution of the business.

• A family business must have shared responsibilities. It is insufficient to have only a few making business decisions, with the rest as willing followers.

• Family members must share the fruit of harvest in addition to their share of compensation for their labor.

• A family business should have a simple organizational structure. Even if the business expands in size, communication among family members working for the business should be maintained on a one-to-one basis.

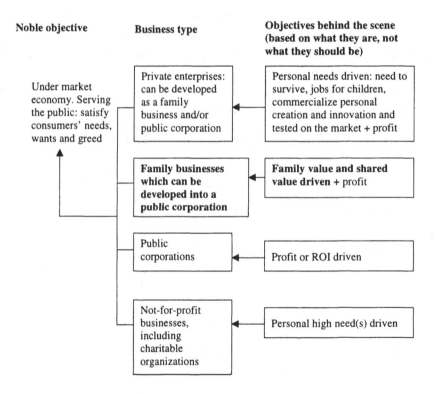

Figure 14.4 Business objectives among private enterprises, corporations and family businesses.

14.8 Common Success Factors

The trout farm is a case based on fact. We seldom realize that all businesses have two sets of objectives: the noble objective and the objective(s) behind the scene. Figure 14.4 shows businesses differentiated on the basis of their objectives: the private enterprises which do not solicit financing from public, the corporations which secure their financing from the public, and the family business, essentially owned and controlled by its family members (irrelevant how a family business is financed).

Questions for discussion

1. Name some family businesses that have integrated their family values into business values and say how such values have contributed to the success of their businesses. (Success is achieved when the business has realized its sustainable growth potentials and has gone beyond the second generation.)
2. List the factors contributing to the success of the three scenarios from your point of view on the basis of:

   (a) business, and (b) family relationships. Comment!

Scenario 1	Scenario 2	Scenario 3
Business success	Business success	Business success
Family harmony success	Family harmony success	Family harmony success

3. Comment on the following:

   The disappearance of a family business as illustrated in Chapter 13 was not coincidental. It was the lack of value in the individual and the business that sent a family business, the Golden Tiger of Shin, along with the family relations into its grave. People seldom realize that the sustainability of life and human civilization is built on values, and everyone has his/her own personal values. Money may make us rich, but it is the values that gives us the harvest, the joy and happiness to receive the fruit of our labor — physical, mental, emotional and spiritual.

4. Suggest some ways to assist venture founders in the preparation of successful family business challenges.

5. The fishing story illustrates what living and enjoying a simple life is about, and shows how to find happiness from simplicity (the idea of "If I can enjoy life now, why should I wait until I retire?"). Is it possible to raise children in a successful family business environment to learn from this wisdom? If yes, how? If no, why?

6. Comment on the following. In your opinion, would Irene be a good family business successor?

   The senior author was once a business partner in a family business dealing in the selling of English bone china, with well-known names such as Wedgwood, Crown Derby, Spode and a few other international names. One day, a wealthy young lady visited the shop and started to admire the well-planned China display. She was interested in quite a few pieces, particularly a pattern named "Spode's Renaissance."

   Irene, the shop assistant started to chat with her about the piece. Irene said: "If you like this piece so much, why not order a starter's set?" The lady smiled and responded: "Well, my mother has this pattern, I can hardly wait to inherit the set."

7. Almost without exception, parents would do what they can for their children's education. In the case where someone is both a venture founder and parent, the venture founder-parent(s) would have to make a choice: Educate children so they can make their own decisions on what to do with their life, or train them to take over the family business, i.e. to assume the right to make decisions for their children?

Of course, the win-win solution is to educate children in the interest of the family business as well as that of the children and the children's children. A family business is not limited to a human lifespan. A venture founder-parent would normally have love and passion for both business and life, even if they are somewhat different. What is your opinion?

Chapter 15

Corporate Entrepreneurship: Corporate Power and Issues Concerning Corporate Profit

Entrepreneurial Corporation: *The corporate entity, regardless of its size, is a community of entrepreneurs. Individuals in the entity are there by their own right. They are all agents for change working together as a body dedicated to the creation of wealth for every individual within the entity while adding value to society.*[1]

"Profit" and "ROI" (a ratio between profit and investment) are powerful tools used to stimulate and motivate people to behave and act for their own self-interest. There is no doubt that self-interest must come first before we can have concern for the common good. The same is true in business, any business in any form. It is perfectly justifiable for any business to make a profit, except we must recognize there is no profit unless all costs are accounted for. The current practice in the determination of profit seriously overlooks the importance of legitimate costs, and consequently, misrepresenting profit. Therefore ROI is a major contributor to the erosion of resources for humanity of the future. The sad part of it all is that ROI is like a prison that has captured business management and "B" school education in a lifelong sentence with no chance for parole. Lord help us!

---

[1]Kao R. W. Y., *An Entrepreneurial Approach to Corporate Management* (Prentice-Hall, 1997), p. 124.

> Lastly, even though we cannot predict the future, we must recognize that what is in the future belongs to the future. Our stewardship responsibility does not extend us the right to steal what belongs to the future, just because we need and want them for the sake of our pleasure and enjoyment.

15.1 Corporate Power

15.1.1 The bigger you are, the bigger your wants

Corporate entities in the Western market economy, have taken hold of the individual's life. Banking and financial institutions, information and telecommunications, motor vehicles and parts, meat packing, petroleum refining, brewing, canning and preserving, computers, electronic products and parts, food preparation, bread and bakery, newspaper, hotels and tourism, soap and glycerine, footwear, retailing organic chemicals, prepared meat, tires and tubes, paints and varnishes, prepared animal food, refrigeration machinery, aircraft manufacturers, woollen fabrics, flour and meal, cotton fabrics and fashion are just a few of the countless businesses that, through the form of limited liability, have made their presence felt in the marketplace, and that impact the life of every human being on earth. They buy, they sell, they provide jobs and take them away. It is also undeniable that in today's world that we live in, no government can realistically claim to hold the balance of power, even in the few states which still proclaim themselves communist. Now, particularly in the Western developed countries, they must always deal with the multinational corporations: they are the emperors and empresses, the princes and princesses and the dukes and duchesses of today, tied in a holy knot with the stock exchanges through which they run most of the world.

The economic model of the oligopoly[2] that we are well acquainted with is no longer applicable; the idea of competing for market share which

---

[2]A competitive balance amongst a limited number of business entities.

persisted through the 1980s is almost a thing of the past. Today, dominance through merger and acquisition is the theme of banks, corporations, and even charitable-based not-for-profit organizations. They grow from big to bigger, and flirt with the status of monopolies, always staying just the right side of the legal restrictions (Microsoft's problems notwithstanding!). Many governments are willing collaborators in these schemes, and even if the government has the desire to oppose them, they are often powerless to do so. Thus, the corporate giants will do what they will. They act in the name of competition while destroying all competition. They give the consumers not what they need, but what they make the consumers think they need. They are profit driven, with no desire for anything but to get bigger, and ultimately be the biggest. They are virtually untouchable. However, regardless of how powerful corporations are, they are still composed of people, people who serve them, and of course people who govern them. Although it may seem to be a meaningless question, nevertheless we ask: "Who are these people that govern powerful corporations?" They are normal human beings like everyone else, no doubt with the same wants and needs, the same urges, but at the same time they are driven by the concept of "ROI" and the search for profit. And the only question we really have to ask them, is when they have everything to live for, why should they live for this?

15.1.2 ROI, the stock exchange and the "B" schools

There have always been two related but sometimes conflicting challenges which beset the minds of those who govern corporate entities: on the one hand to be the biggest, and on the other, to earn the highest (maximized) rate of return on investment or ROI. The question of which one comes first has never been clear, though of course some obvious principles are involved. And what is obvious is that in order to become big, a corporate entity must have an attractive ROI to bring the investors in. Therefore, ROI becomes the thing, and the only thing that corporate executives care about. Naturally, it is the stock exchange that provides the funds that corporations need. The stock exchange and corporations both require funds for expansion,

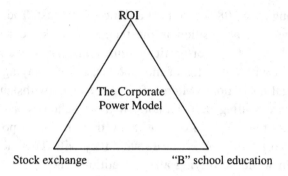

Figure 15.1 The corporate model.

and are like two sides of the same coin, with the corporations being the fuel on which the stock exchange runs, and the stock exchange giving corporations their needed funds to achieve the ROI attainment objective. However, it would not be possible for the corporate entities to flourish, develop, grow, expand and grow big, bigger and biggest without proper management. In particular, this includes the "B" school where young executives are developed before they enter into the corporate world. Therefore, the triangular relationship amongst the corporate entities' desire for adequate ROI, the stock exchange and the "B" schools make an impressive model that portrays the economic reality of today's business world.

With the infusion of managerial talent from higher educational institutions, and funds generated by the stock exchange, achievement of ROI has become more than a reality — it is a virtual certainty, at least for some. The B schools keep turning out the graduates, the stock market keeps going up and up, and corporations are getting bigger and bigger. This trinity of business success also gives the corporations impact in every aspect of the life of every individual. Through the ROI driven economy, people, and in particular the "developed" Western nations have enjoyed the great benefits of what this world can give, but at the cost of unprecedented pollution, depletion of non-renewable resources, and the theft of our children's heritage.

15.1.3 Signs of second thought: can business be about more than just profits? Could it be a force for good?

As stated in the previous section, ultimately, corporate bodies are made up of people. And while the circumstances of corporate power plays and power struggles can affect the common good through their unconcern, there are some people working within the corporate environment who have had many a serious second thought about making profit with a concern for long term impact on the future of humanity, as well as the meaning of ROI and the role of ROI as a motivator for business executives and managers. The following are two examples taken from commercial productions that portray a significant departure from the corporate "ROI only" mentality. This may be one financial sermon on the mount which has lost just a bit of its gospel.

First half of a Shell Oil Ad:

There was a time when oil and gas reserves seemed endless. But with the world's population continuing to increase, and developing countries seeking energy at exponential rates, fossil fuels will eventually fade. And so, the likely question is: will oil companies just sit there and fade away as well?

National Geographic (2/198 August 2000)

Note that the ad claims that the causes of energy drain are: (1) "the increasing world population" and (2) "developing countries seeking energy at exponential rates." These are at best only part of the story, and the smaller part. First World countries are far and away the biggest users of fossil fuels, not just on a per capita basis, but also in terms of total usage. While it is easy to name the United States as the major culprit, there are certainly many other countries whose level of guilt only seems small because of the massive American consumption. Most developed nations have nearly stable populations, and while the populations of developing countries may be increasing, most of them are still in poverty, and thus their ecological impact remains small.

From a BP advertisement:

Beyond Petroleum

Can business be about more than just profits? Could it be a force for good?

We think so, and the employees at BP, Amoco, ARCO and Castrol are forming a new company to try.

National Geographic (November 2000)

While some might claim that these advertisements are simply a cynical grab for good public relations, both Shell and BP clearly realize that the environmental issue is important.

Corporations can no longer take the earth for granted by exploiting it wantonly to satisfy human desires; solutions must be sought in order for both the corporation and life to continue. Corporations recognize the need to turn over a new leaf, and even for selfish reasons, look beyond profit and acquiring power for economic dominance.

15.2 The Perception of Corporate Power

The acquisition of economic power by the big corporations has been the result of a long evolution of the market. It is based on the motherhood idea of economics: supply and demand. On the demand side, consumers look for satisfaction of their needs, wants and greed. Corporations, through informative advertising, supply goods and services based on these demands, and then further manipulate consumers through pervasive advertising and promotion. Based on their success as suppliers they then further expand their operations, building-up their market power through merger and acquisition while claiming to be "customer driven," in the "battle for survival" and in the spirit of "healthy competition." This perception may be illustrated as follows:

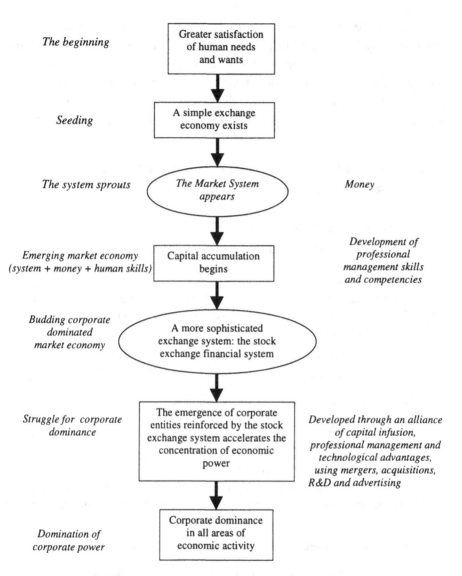

Figure 15.2 Corporate power: its development to the state of economic dominance.

What can be clearly seen here is the progression from a market which was originally intended to help to provide goods and services to satisfy the consumers' needs and wants to becoming a system that fuels the exchange system. Of course, the relation situation is only caricatured by this simple picture. What remains simple though, even when all the complexities are added, is what lies at the center of the issue: corporate profit.

15.3 The Drilling and Extraction of Petroleum Reserve: Cash and Profit

Consider the following example:

Assume a petroleum company has discovered oil in Alaska, or perhaps Canada's far north. It is estimated that the value of the deposit is approximately $500,000 billion. The deposit is expected to last approximately 50 years, based on current rates of extraction. To simplify the recording process, assume the following entries have been established.

Dr. Petroleum deposit (Alaska)	$500,000 billion
Cr. Common shares	$500,000 billion

Additional shares issued for cash and paid:

Dr. Cash	$50,000 billion
Cr. Common share stock	$50,000 billion

The drilling operation is run by the book — no illegalities or improper activities. The petroleum extraction takes place smoothly, and based on the estimate of a 50-year lifespan for the operation (i.e. annual production of 1/50 of the deposit), we have the accounting entry:

To record the depletion of petroleum deposit:

Dr. Depletion-petroleum deposit	$10,000 billion
Cr. Petroleum deposit	$10,000 billion

Further assume that the operational cost including all expenses recognized in accordance with accounting postulates amount to $5000 billion, with the oil sold on the market at a price of $15,000 billion, the entry would be:

Dr. Cost of oil production	$5000 billion
Dr. All cost measurable	$2000 billion
Cr. Cash	$7000 billion

The oil sold in the market of the above production is estimated to be worth $25,000 billion.

The entry would be:

Dr. Cash	$25,000 billion
Cr. Sales	$25,000 billion

The above will be concluded as:

Sales	$25,000 billion
Cost of sales	$17,000 billion
Accounting profit	$8000 billion
Taxes 50%	$4000 billion
Accounting profit after tax	$4000 billion

The company's cash position would be:

Cash

Share capital	$20,000 billion	Production cost	$5000 billion
Sales	$25,000 billion	Other costs	$2000 billion
		Income tax	$4000 billion
Total	$45,000 billion	Total	$11,000 billion
Less	$11,000 billion		
Ending cash	$34,000 billion		
– Bargaining cash	$20,000 billion		
Net cash gain	$14,000 billion		

Concluding: Operational gain (accounting profit)	$4000 billion
Cash gain	$14,000 billion

In virtually all cases, the realized cash of $14,000 billion would be considered "profit" for distribution, mostly to a few. Surely, we must all realize all of those $14,000 billion are cost (or capital). Where is the "Profit," if the mining company cannot put more deposits back into the ground? We can hear the protests already. How can one put anything back the way it was? Does this mean that we cannot use even solar energy, because we cannot put energy back into the sun? Of course over the long term there is no answer, all energy must disappear eventually, just as we all must die. But there is the answer, in that the method used to calculate "Profit" measures all input according to a common denominator, dollars and cents. What does the oil company do with $14,000 billion? The drilling and exploitation will continue for another 49 years. In other words, the petroleum reserve will be completely depleted in 50 years and all the estimated value of $500,000 billion will be re-allocated to who knows whom. After all, entitlement has been paid to its shareholders, or distributed among key executives and members of the board, some might even go to charity. But what has been given back to the earth? The millions of years it took to create that petroleum deposit — should it all go to the pockets of private individuals?

It is corporate power, with all its financial and human resources, with all its technological and management expertise that is able to uncover and exploit the oil reserves, and it is corporate power that produces petroleum and other crude oil products that are so vital to today's First World economy. It is corporate power that employs thousands of people, trains them, gives them their salaries and healthcare and benefits and improves their standard of living. But it is also corporate power that takes from the future without giving anything back, that will ruthlessly end a town's lifeline of jobs when they become unprofitable, that will pay employees the lowest wages they can get away with, and that will walk away from the people when the oil runs out. But it is not all bad; to paraphrase Desmond Tutu: the corporate entity has tremendous ability to do evil, but it also has even greater power to do good.

15.4 The Mystery of Corporate Worth: The Classic Case of Nortel's Stock Price

Nortel had been a leader on the Toronto Stock Exchange for a number of years, and was considered one of the bright lights of the telecommunications

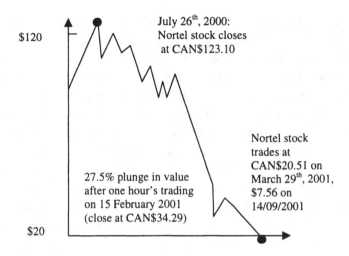

July 26th, 2000:
Nortel stock closes
at CAN$123.10

27.5% plunge in value
after one hour's trading
on 15 February 2001
(close at CAN$34.29)

Nortel stock
trades at
CAN$20.51 on
March 29th, 2001,
$7.56 on
14/09/2001

Figure 15.3 Stock price movement of Nortel stock traded on the Toronto Stock Exchange between 26 July 2000 and 16 February 2001.

industry. But Nortel's stock value plunged 27.5% in an hour's trading, following the news on 15 February 2001 that the bellwether technological company's performance would fall well short of forecasts that year, confirming the worst fears of a sharp slump in the telecommunications sector. For the record, this technology giant's stock, which traded at CAN$123.10 per share as of 26 July 2000, was worth only CAN$34.29 on 15 February 2001. By the end of March 2001, Nortel shares were traded as low as CAN$20.51 per share, about one-sixth of the trading value eight months earlier.

- Granted that Nortel's reported accounting profit did not meet with expectations, this does not explain the drop in its stock value by over one-quarter of its worth in a matter of hours. What really happened is the result of market perception. Who created that perception? Media, stock analysts, managers of the company, and more often than not, people on the street, eventually reaching the investors. Gossipers and the grapevine spread rumors and speculations based on real share information plus their opinions — this affects the investors who begin to sell and starts a chain reaction of selling. None of this has any effect or is affected by what **actually** happens at Nortel. Of course, some of this speculation is primarily based on ROI, profit etc. It may seem unreal to those of us who live outside this particular reality, but more often than not, managers do not really manage the company, rather they watch the movement of stock price, and attempt to manage the stock values instead. The chairperson (CEO) of the board of the Pacific operations of a large U.S. company had been performing well over the years, but recently (early 2001) he decided to step down and seek a position in the academic world instead. As he said: "Believe it or not, I spend more time monitoring our stock value than running the company. I watch the price fluctuate, but I cannot change the force of stock trading on the market. At last week's board meeting, our parent company put a lot pressure on me and asked me to trim down the operation by retrenching about 2000 people in the region to cope with the slump stock price which has nothing to do with my operation. What kind of life is this? I just can't take it any more…. I guess I'd better seek greener pastures while I still can, rather than watch what's going on in the stock market all the time."

15.5 What's the Meaning of ROI to Stockholders?

Ironically, virtually all investors are aware that "ROI" has little impact on the shareholders' desired return on investment, but stock price does, although a great deal of speculation is based on stock analyst's analysis of stock value, and ROI is one of many factors considered. In fact, shareholders do not always receive the "return on their investment." Even when a huge profit has been earned in the last year, dividends may not be declared, and even if declared, they may not be paid because of the company's need for cash for expansion, or they could be declared, but converted into shares added to the existing shareholders' holdings. What the shareholders could do is to sell shares in the market, and making gains from selling existing holdings rather than anticipate cash dividends from the company. To corporate executives and the directors of the board, the excuse that "we need to earn superior profit or highest ROI for our shareholders" is nothing more than a convenient excuse with a nice ring for the publicity department. Meanwhile, they satisfy their own desire to grow big, and make more money for themselves. At times it can even be a useful pitch to lay off workers, and an easy underground railway to escape their inability to deal with public pressure. Often, it is not in the interests of the common good.

15.6 Corporate Profit, Stock Price, ROI and the Power of Perception

15.6.1 Perceptions: a force forging stock price

In Western society, everyone is interested in making a profit, but at the same time is also interested in environmental issues. This is expressed to different extents depending on the context. For example, the media are interested in generating sensation. It is their perceived role to inform the public of events that affect corporate profit as well as other events related to matters of the common good (the environment, science, charitable events, etc.) as well as things that people are just interested in, such as sports, entertainment and gossip. The modern media are armed with an unprecedented ability to disseminate information quickly: through electronics, newspapers can turn around new stories in hours, and TV, radio and more recently the Internet almost instantaneously. From the media's point of view, the balance of issues is strictly one of which grabs the most attention. Relevance to the world of investment is only important because it is something some people want to hear about. On the other hand, people involved in investment may have the same concerns as the media and the public at large, but at least in their professional role they tend to have a one track mind, concentrating on the highest return on their investment. The three different related forces originating from perception may be illustrated as follows:

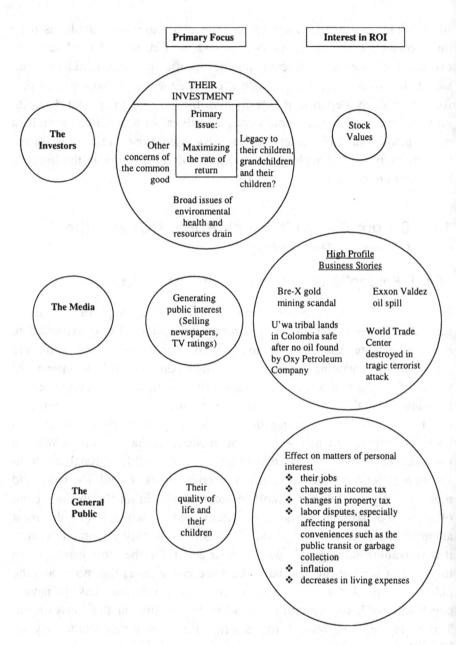

Figure 15.4 Three perceptions of ROI — investors, the media and the general public.

These three illustrations show that, far from being the center of the universe as some would place it, not everyone is interested in ROI. Even those that have some interest in the matter, may also be influenced by other economic activity. On the other hand, everyone in society can be a source of rumors that can spread rapidly to alter any investment situation. For example, though many large Southeast Asian corporations were superb performers for many years, the devaluation of the Thai baht caused the Asian stock markets to crumble. The real cause originated from the manipulative behavior of the currency traders, pushing the markets over the brink of destruction. In a matter of months, Malaysian corporations for example, lost stock trading value amounting to US$367 billion. Did this have anything to do with corporate performance? Whatever the "true" value of those shares, it certainly did not.

ROI certainly provides some basic information that can be valuable when weighed in the balance of all other information available. However, the emphasis placed on it is unhealthy. Moreover, ROI is susceptible to manipulation of accounting practices, and thus it is a far from reliable source of information with respect to a firm's performance.

15.6.2 "Profit driven" corporate mentality and the big breasted chicken

Growing corporate power and corporate dominance of the market economy has provided people in the developed, industrialized West with a high standard of living. But making great profits and the continued increase in the size of corporate operations also creates insurmountable hardship for people and other living things, due to uncontrolled and senseless pursuit for greater profit. Technology has created many problems. Mad cow disease, global warming and ozone layer destruction — these are all results of our shortcuts and attempts to manipulate the world around us to our satisfaction. This is one example: In January 2001, on a number of news programmes, a story was aired about the poultry industry. In recent years, chicken breasts have become overwhelmingly popular. Perceived as a healthier alternative, and in a poultry market already driven sky high by the demand for McDonalds' "Chicken McNuggets" and similar items, producers are in the position of never having enough chicken breast meat to sell, but too much of everything else. A farmer and breeder speculated that as the push for faster growing, bigger-breasted chickens reached its logical conclusion, soon we would have chickens that are unable to walk and unable to fly, and the old-fashioned self-ambulatory chicken would then go the way of the Dodo.

15.7 The Real Challenge of Corporate Profit, ROI, Corporate Power and Common Good

The market economy has evolved from economic activities that were generated to provide goods and services to satisfy human needs, to a corporate profit-oriented beast, that creates consumer wants. Near universal acceptance of the profit notion is now the basis for perception, resulting in speculation that is to the cost of the common good, and impairs the future of human interest and the world's.

The truth about profit is that it is not what we have known and practiced through the centuries. The crucial omission is our ignorance of "cost," even while recognizing the difficulties involved in measuring those costs that involve no cash transactions or commonly recognized market values. However, it is not impossible to do so. It is a lack of entrepreneurial drive for those involved in designing the model systems on which we base our economy, and on our educational system. Profit is applied only to individuals, but this is really only a way of taking from Peter to pay Paul, because we are limited by the resources available on planet earth. In truth, we cannot make any true gains as long as we add nothing to the Earth but only take from it. At best, what we have is only a "Residual," the result recognized from making different combinations.

Traditionally, corporate profit is based on accounting practice, drawn on a set of postulates laid out by accounting professional organizations, including the American Institute of Public Accountants (AIPA), the Canadian Institute of Chartered Accountants (CA) and similar organizations in most other countries. Indeed, they have served and continue to serve the business community well. However, until this day, the professional organizations have yet to provide guides that move away from the traditional measurements to consider opportunity cost, or environmental cost, especially as it relates to our legacy to future generations. Corporate profit using existing accounting methods will never be meaningful, as long as only part of the cost is recognized.

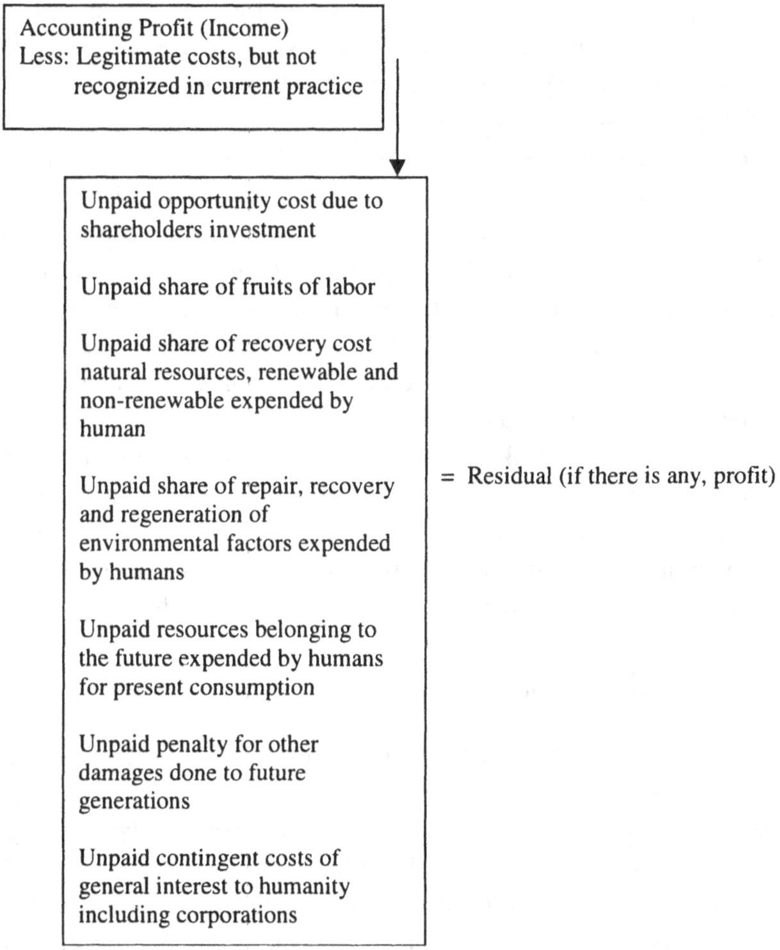

```
┌─────────────────────────────────┐
│ Accounting Profit (Income)      │
│ Less: Legitimate costs, but not │
│        recognized in current    │
│        practice                 │
└─────────────────────────────────┘
```

Unpaid opportunity cost due to shareholders investment

Unpaid share of fruits of labor

Unpaid share of recovery cost natural resources, renewable and non-renewable expended by human

Unpaid share of repair, recovery and regeneration of environmental factors expended by humans

= Residual (if there is any, profit)

Unpaid resources belonging to the future expended by humans for present consumption

Unpaid penalty for other damages done to future generations

Unpaid contingent costs of general interest to humanity including corporations

Figure 15.5 The nature of a meaningful profit: residual.

15.8 Corporate Profit, the Fruits of Labor of Many Contributors

"Profit" and "ROI" are powerful tools used to stimulate and motivate people to behave and act for self-interest. There is no doubt that self-interest always comes first before we can have concern for the common good. The same is true in business, and for any business in any form, it is perfectly justifiable to make a profit. However we must recognize that there is no profit unless all costs are accounted for. The current practice in the determination of profit seriously overlooks the importance of legitimate costs. Consequently, profit, and therefore ROI are responsible at least in part for the erosion of our future.

"Can '*corporations*' be more than profits? Could they be a force for good?" The answer is "yes." With the demise of communism in Eastern Europe and the Soviet Union, all the world is looking to capitalism to be their Holy Grail. Unfortunately, in its present guise it is more likely to be a cup of poison, sickly sweet, pleasant at first, but ultimately deadly. However, with a change in focus, and in combination with an entrepreneurial outlook, corporate entities can become a force for good. Indeed, so they must, for there is now no alternative.

To do so, decision makers must understand the nature of profit and make a clear distinction between cost and profit. They must come to a realization that a corporation is not a money-making machine for a few, but a community of entrepreneurs working to harvest the fruits of their labors for the benefit of all its contributors, including the earth.

Questions for discussion

1. "Can business be about more than just profit? Could it be a force for good?" Comment!
2. Alternative energy powered vehicles have been in the development stage for ages. Rechargeable batteries, propane fuelled, natural gas fuelled, fuel cells, solar power — you name it, someone has tried it. And yet despite all this development and the occasional hyped product, still the internal combustion engine, burning non-renewable petroleum,

is king. We have all heard the claims of the petroleum companies to explore new energy sources, and of the automakers to make more efficient cars, but isn't it ironic that the fastest growing car segment of the past ten years is the sports utility vehicle, the over-sized, big-tired, gas-guzzling 4×4 vehicle (one wonders how many of those cars are used for anything more than getting to work or doing the weekend shopping). And as the auto-manufacturers continue their effort to make bigger cars, politicians continue to build roads to accommodate cars in the name of meeting consumers' demand and provide jobs. Sure, they are giving the people what they are clamouring for, but who is being a leader? Who is showing the people what they need? There are solutions that can be found, but unfortunately, rather than working together to find them, we are all working towards short term wants and greed satisfaction rather than long term sustainable economic growth. Why?

3. Re: Figure 15.5. In your opinion, is the model workable in the current working environment? If yes, what can be done to make it work? If not, why not?

4. Economists are fully aware that our resources are finite. Why is it then, that they advocate "profit maximization" for the firm? How can profit be maximized if it is not taking from the future or underpaying the value of labor?

5. The price of petroleum will continue to rise. The petroleum companies count their profits on the basis of current accounting practice, and of course the cost to the planet earth is not part of the calculation. Meanwhile the oil producing countries set the price of crude oil on the basis of what they feel is justifiable. They certainly profit from the transactions, so where do the profits go? Profit generated by petroleum companies, profit made by refineries: is it profit created simply by selling birthrights? Discuss!

6. How does a corporation build its power under the market economy? Rank the following in terms of their importance for this purpose and explain your reasoning:

   - Creativity and innovation
   - Ability to acquire existing technology

- Entrepreneurial management
- Financial backing
- Marketing strategy
- Networking with the government and/or other public institutions
- Others (please specify)

Chapter 16

Corporate Governance, Responsibility and Profit

> In essence, the function of management is having a "Stewardship" privilege in the caring of people and resources, in the interest of humanity for now and the future.
>
> However, according to the American Petroleum Institute (API) (*www.api.org*), there is a 95% possibility that the world's remaining oil resources will last for 63 more years, and a 5% chance that the oil reserves will last another 95 years. Yet, we have more cars on the road, car makers are still making more cars, and there are plans that oil drilling may take place in Alaska, the last frontier of human inhabitants.
>
> Is this how our corporate executives execute their stewardship responsibility?[1]

16.1 The Traditional View of Corporate Governance

The key to corporate governance is to govern responsibly. However, corporate governance is not as simple as a concept or practice, because corporate activities involve virtually every segment of the economy: the shareholders, the public, those who supply resources either through trade, or just on the whole "taking."

---

[1]Based on the API finding, we (our oil and auto industries) have in fact exhausted a million years' worth of natural petroleum reserves for humanity in a matter of less than a decade. Is it in the name of humanity? Or in the name of profit?

Traditionally, the answer is as simple as one word: "Shareholders," or those in the equity position. Through the shareholders' right to vote, a board is selected that in effect governs the corporation. But in reality, this has not been always the case. A corporation is really governed mostly by individuals who hold a block of 30+% of outstanding and paid shares. They in turn choose executives, particularly a CEO to run the corporation. More often than not, the CEO him/herself is a block shareholder as well. There appears, therefore, to be a block of 30+% shareholders, who, through a CEO, actually governs the corporation, unless this practice is challenged by the rest of the shareholders whose cumulative votes (through proxy at times) is greater than the 30+ block shareholding. Therefore, a corporation is in fact governed by a minority. The people in power can stay and govern the corporation as long as "God" is in no hurry to have their souls. And the most effective means for the governing group to maintain their power is to publicize the need to serve our shareholders' interest and reward them for their trust in us with the highest rate of return to their investment. Very noble, indeed!

In the political democratic process, as one person has only one vote, it does not matter if he is rich or poor. But in corporations, voting right is based on the number of shares held, with the use of proxy for voting which makes it convenient to secure power through acquired proxies with a combined strength of personal holdings to gain power in corporate governing. The economic democracy under the circumstances ensure only the rich (based on shareholdings) govern, therefore, it would not be a surprise at all, if the corporate objective is set to what we so often hear: "maximize the rate of return on shareholders' investment," or politely, "shareholders' desired rate of return on their investment," the ROI. As such, corporations are governed by humans — the members of board of directors who empower the CEO to preside over the entities. ROI is however, the supreme of all. Corporate entities, therefore, are governed by ROI or financial benefit of their shareholders as the supreme goal typically reflected in the following mission statements:

Imperial Oil: *The mission of Imperial Oil is to create value for its shareholders through the development of hydrocarbon energy and related products.*

Sears Canada: *Our vision is to be Canada's most successful retailer... providing total satisfaction for our customers, opportunities for our associates to grow and contribute, and superior returns for our shareholders.*

Federal Express: *To produce superior financial returns to our shareowners as we serve our customers with the highest quality transportation, logistics and e-commerce solutions.*

16.2 From Primary Shareholders' Governance to Consumers' Focus

The claim of shareholders' supremacy in corporate governance received no challenges for a long time, until people like Ralph Nader and other advocates raised the banner of safeguarding consumers' interest and placed it high on the corporate altar, which made it necessary for corporate executives to have one eye on money and the other on the geese that lay the golden eggs. Perhaps it is even more pressing than the need for earning ROI for their shareholders. Because if consumers do not buy the product(s) the corporation sells, it will not have any earnings at all. It is therefore, another force to be reckoned with in the executive offices and in the boardroom. The importance of consumers surpassing shareholders' interests in corporate management is also evident during interviews conducted by the senior author with a consumer product development manager of a multinational consumer products company. He related his experiences as a product development manager:

"As an employee of a major multi-national consumer products company I would like to think that I can provide a personal perspective to the question of how we focus our major efforts in the marketplace. The interest of shareholders is always a factor that is taken into account when a new product is developed but I truly believe that the consumer is the most important factor in a new product launch. This belief is preached throughout our company from the CEO on down. There is two "moments of truth" for a product that determines if it wins in the marketplace. The first is the time in which a consumer selects our product from the shelf at a store. The second is when the consumer uses it for the first time in their homes. These two moments are crucial to winning lifelong consumers. With this philosophy in mind it is clear that the marketers are focused on the consumer. If the consumer is not the focus then the product will be unsuccessful and, in the end, the company will not prosper. Therefore the shareholders won't be happy either. As a product development manager of a consumer products company we cannot focus on making shareholders happy with what product we introduce. It will be the consumers who determine our success and this success translates into happy shareholders."

Consumers' interest becoming the priority concern is particularly visible in the retailing business. For example, as stated by the company Canadian Tire in its mission statement:

Canadian Tire: To be the first choice for Canadians in automotive, sports and leisure, and home products, providing total customer value through customer-driven service, focused assortments and competitive operations.

Shell, on the other hand, combines consumers' need satisfaction with the need for discovering new energy sources (through R&D efforts), and makes it a public commitment:

Shell: Shell plays a major part in the move from oil to gas. We are also currently planting the seeds of renewable energy with Shell International Renewable — a new business committed to making renewable energy commercially viable. In Uruguay, we are exploring the great potential of "biomass" energy from fast-growing forests, and we are developing biomass-fuelled plants in the South Pacific to bring electricity to remote areas. It is part of our commitment to sustainable development, balancing economic progress with environmental care and social responsibility. In 2050, half the world could be powered by renewable energy, so we're focusing our energies on developing these new solutions.

(Note: The above is not Shell's mission or vision statement, rather, it is the second half of its advertisement (see p. 333), placed with *National Geographic*, in the inside cover and the first ad page 2/198, August 2000.)

In addition to consumers, there are governmental and non-governmental organizations such as environmental advocates and environmental watchdog groups, such as Greenpeace and the Sierra Club. Consequently, corporate governance is no longer a simple matter of the "vote" of shareholders, since many others have some influence on corporate affairs. The corporate vision or mission statements show that these other groups have an impact on corporate governing through two important forces: the consumer (customers) and corporate investors (shareholders).

16.3 Views of Would-be Business Managers and/or Executives

As a matter of personal interest, the senior author made an effort to solicit opinions of those just about to embark on their corporate careers, namely the MBA, commerce or business graduates in several universities for a period of approximately 13 years. In the earlier years, virtually all respondents indicated that corporations are governed by shareholders who are responsible for using their funds and earning desirable returns to their investments. There were a few who noted that consumers should also have a say in corporate governing. In recent years, it is found that some others may have a stake in corporate affairs, even though they may not be directly involved, e.g. workers (or employees), advocates for environmental health, and among others, the general public. Along with shareholders and consumers, their influence may not be direct, but can be semi-direct and/or indirect. They may be illustrated as follows:

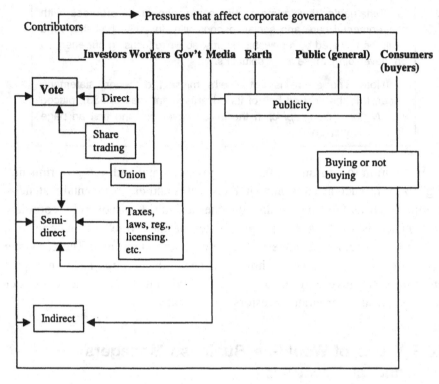

Figure 16.1 Pressures that affect corporation governance.

Figure 16.1 suggests that virtually all members of society, including silent members such as resources and environment have a stake in the corporation. They may air their views and displeasure for corporate wrongdoings in different forms, but all their actions and opinions have some impact on corporate governance. In short, despite the fact that corporations are a powerful instrument affecting everyone's life in the market economy we currently live in, there seems to be a growing concern about how they behave and act in the marketplace. Consequently, it is no longer an assumption that corporations can only serve shareholders' interest. Others have their claim as well.

The following are some specific examples that undermine corporate governance by various groups:

(1) *Consumers*: Consumers always have a say in corporate governance, except they say it quietly. For example, in a letter dispatched by Robert Milton, CEO of Air Canada to pilots about a need to launch a discount airline to compete with low-cost competitors. The letter specifies that "...in just four years, short-haul routes in the West have become the most unprofitable in our system. This is not due to too few passengers; rather, our customers are simply not willing to pay higher prices when they have lower-cost alternatives..." Not to purchase goods or services from any particular company or group of companies is a simple indirect governance by consumers.

(2) *Industrial buyers*: It also has become evident that some companies refuse to purchase from suppliers who do not abide by the conservation code, and/or their products do not meet environmentally friendly standards. Companies such as IKEA and some hotel and resort tourist operations also express their unwillingness to do business with companies who do not observe and practice these requirements.

In Chapter 15, the stock price decline of Nortel Networks was used to illustrate how stock price relates to a company's real worth.

> ...*Paul Sagawa, a high profile New York analyst whose influential 28 September 2000 report sent the first major ripples of fear through the telecommunication equipment market and defensive rebuttals from other major brokerages at the time. At one point in January 2001, a senior investor relations official at Nortel beefed about a coverage during a phone call. "She said: "Do you have something against us?"*

> Steven Chase, Report on Business, *Globe and Mail*,
> 23 February 2001, B1

This is a clear indication that suggests how media (stock analysts) influenced the public view that impacted on the company's management and indirectly on the governance of the corporation.

(3) It is a known medical fact that smoking causes cancer. Therefore, the tobacco industry as a whole has been under close scrutiny by the government, media and the general public. Such scrutiny and

closer monitoring in its operation affects the governing of the industry and every tobacco corporation as well.

(4) An autoworkers' union strike against General Motors in the late 1990s illustrates the role of Unions in corporate governance. The reason for the strike involved the company's desire to take work offshore, contracting out to countries where labor costs are low. The union held their position, firmly claiming that "These are our jobs, don't take them away from us." Consequently, the management backed down. This signifies that the power of the union is in place to claim workers' stake in the corporation.

(5) The environmental activists, lobby groups disenchanted about corporate behavior in the marketplace at the cost of animals, and above all nature, through their protests, demonstrations and boycotts are more often than not curtailed by corporate activities that impact their governance.

Those who make use of their clout to influence corporate governance have, in fact, assumed corporate responsibility, although earning superior profits (or returns) on shareholders' investments will always be an important part of corporate responsibility. It is the total responsibility at stake that is at the root of the management challenge.

16.4 A Breath of Fresh Air: Multi-Responsibility

Towards the end of the 20th century, the general public progressively acquired needed information and knowledge relating to our environmental health. Corporate entities can no longer blindly seek profit without having considerations for matters relating to the common good. BP's advertisement contains a two-part question that reads: "Can business be about more than just profits? Can it be a force for good?" The pressure for corporations to assume their responsibility has been ignored for perhaps too long. It is no longer just about corporations having social responsibilities, it is also about other stakeholders contributing to the corporate well-being. It is obvious that the business community, by and large, is gradually adopting technology to enhance our living standards. Corporations are no longer just money-making machines. There is also a need to develop the entities as communities of entrepreneurs. This awareness has prompted a change in corporate vision or mission to be in business.

In a recent study by the senior author, six groups of MBA candidates in three universities responded to the question of corporate responsibility. In the order of importance, the shareholders' interests rank first, followed by customers, workers, the earth (including environment and resources); government, media and the general public are also included, but to a much less degree than the first four categories. The information is summarized as a percentage of each and plotted as follows:

Table 16.1 Corporate responsibility as seen by participants (expressed as a percentage of corporate executives time and energy).

Investors	Workers	Gov't	Media	Earth*▲	Earth*▼	Public	Consumer
10	10	5	0	10	–	2	20
15	20	10	5	20		5	5
15	30	5	12	10		5	21
15	10	0	0	20		20	5
10	10	0	0	5		5	10
100	0	0	0	0		0	10
40	15	20	0	20		5	10
20	10	5	5	30		10	20
40	15	20	0	15		0	10
25	5	5	5	40		20	10
80	20	20	0	0		0	18
30	22	15	4	3		20	16
25	30	15	5	10		10	15
15	30	20	10	11		14	10
35	20	15	10	10		5	15
10	20	20	0	40		10	10
40	30	10	5	10		0	15
30	50	10	2	5		3	10
5	10	0	0	20		10	17
5	15	0	0	5		5	50
10	20	0	0	5		10	50
10	20	0	0	30		5	15
20	15	0	0	5		10	30
26.3	18.5	8.3	2.7	14.1		7.6	18.6

*▲ Earth above the ground: land usage, water, air environment in general.
*▼ Earth underground: resources deposit, underground water, energy such as petroleum, natural gas, mineral deposits. Although participants made no distinction in their responses.

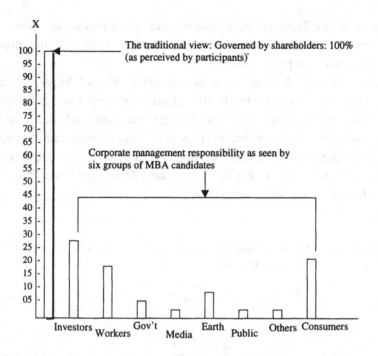

Figure 16.2 Corporate management responsibility as seen by future managers (based on Table 16.1 data).

The four largest groups identified by participants are: shareholders, workers, consumers and earth.

16.5 The Sweeping Change: Ethical Funds

A responsible corporate management does not only strive for "ROI" for its shareholders, rather, they seek a balance of human interest, environmental care, resources utilization and investors' interest. They are dedicated to serve humanity, or more specifically, consumers, employees, environmental health and also those who have a stake in the corporation. "ROI" will not disappear from the altars of corporate entities, because regardless of how a corporation operates, shareholders' investment must earn its just return, equivalent to the opportunity of funds that will not be kept in the treasure chest of public corporations. What is important is that corporate management makes a commitment to assume multiple responsibility for the good of all its contributors. Even though corporate entities are still officially governed by shareholders through their elected members of the board of directors, consumers have been gaining ground, as a large number of consumers are also investors (through mutual funds) and their opinion affects the direction where funds should be invested. In recent years (a little more than a decade), there has been a powerful movement pushing the need for environmental care. "Ethical Funds" is a mutual fund that has been around for over 15 years. This fund family has criteria that exclude companies participating in the generation of nuclear power, manufacture of military weapons, or production of tobacco products. This is a proven record that people are concerned about public issues of a common good, including investors whose prime objectives are supposedly for "making a profit."

16.6 The Entrepreneurially Responsible Management

Recent years have seen the emergence of many corporations that assume multiple responsibility and recognize that contributors other than share-holders also have a stake in the corporation, reflected in their mission/vision statements:

Sandals Hotel and Resort: *To offer the ultimate Caribbean vacation experience by innovatively, reliably and consistently providing the safest and highest quality services and facilities to guests, while attaching a premium to our human resources and being among the most environmentally responsible and community friendly groups in the hospitality industry.* To support its mission statement, the hotel participates in and supports the Caribbean Cares program, adopted and practising the following environmentally friendly procedures:

(1) We are choosing suppliers whose manufacturing processes and products are environmentally sound.
(2) We are offering our guests the options of re-using towels and bed linens to conserve water and energy and use less detergent.

---

(3) We recycle as much as possible in our locality.
(4) We have set aside smoke-free guest rooms for our guests who are sensitive to smoke.

Mountain Equipment Co-op: *The Mountain Equipment Co-operative is a member owned and directed retail consumer co-operative which provides products and service for all propelled wilderness oriented recreational activities, such as hiking and mountaineering, at the lowest reasonable prices in an informative, helpful and environmentally responsible manner.*

3M: 3M integrates vision into strategy by adopting what is called "Strategies for continuing improvement of ideas into reality." These are:

(1) Continue improving compliance assurance systems to meet and exceed government and 3M standards.
(2) Maintain emphasis on Life Cycle Management, considering environmental, health and safety opportunities and issues for all stages of a product's life cycle — from development and manufacturing to customer use and final disposal.
(3) Meet 3M's aggressive goals for environment, health and safety and move as close to zero as possible for environmental releases, injuries and illnesses (*http://www.3m.com/profile/careers/working/html*).

Sleep Country Canada: *Sleep Country Canada's mission is to exceed our customers expectations when they purchase a new sleep set and to earn their trust.*

Our customers' assurances of value and service will be provided by offering a comprehensive assortment of quality sleep products, staffed by a knowledgeable, helpful and friendly sales force, that is supported by a dedicated team of customer service and delivery associates.

Sleep Country is committed to being environmentally and socially responsible, while providing a caring and rewarding work environment where our staff can achieve their individual potential.

Last, but not the least, The Body Shop, a retail store that was created for body, and body healthcare has a mission statement as follows:

The Body Shop: *Our reason for being*

- *To dedicate our business to the pursuit of social and environmental change.*
- *To creatively balance the financial and human needs of our stakeholders: employees, franchisees, customers, suppliers and shareholders.*
- *To courageously ensure that our business is ecologically sustainable: meeting the needs of the present without compromising the future.*
- *To meaningfully contribute to local, national and international communities in which we trade, by adopting a code of conduct which ensures care, honesty, fairness and respect.*
- *To passionately campaign for the protection of the environment, human and civil rights, and against animal testing within the cosmetics and toiletries industry.*
- *To tirelessly work to narrow the gap between principles and practice, whilst making fun, passion and care part of our daily lives.*

Accompanying the mission statement is the Body Shop's trading charter. This charter asserts that company trade relationships will:

- Be commercially viable, mutually beneficial based on trust and respect.
- Aim to ensure human and civil rights are respected throughout their business activities.
- Support long-term sustainable relationships with communities in need.
- Use environmentally sustainable resources wherever technically and economically viable.
- Promote animal protection.

In 1996, the United Nations Environment Program declared the Body Shop a "trailblazer," scoring highest marks for its first Values Report, a self-evaluation to grade the Body Shop on how well it puts into practice its stated values.

There are also some negative publicities surrounding the company, such as the one revealed by a Consumer's Report, that the Body Shop uses petrochemical ingredients and their contribution to environmental and social causes were less than half that of the average percentage of pre-tax profits being spent by U.S. corporations. Bear in mind though that what the Body Shop has committed to and attained are far greater than fot typical North American corporations.[2]

These and many other companies have not, in any way, failed their performance in the marketplace, nor are they being put into a financial straightjacket. They have been in business for years and have proven themselves to be viable operations that promote sustainable economic growth.

It must also be emphasized that our human tragedies, environmental disasters and resources drain are the responsibilities of humanity. Sure enough, individuals can work for the attainment of self-fulfilment, self-interest and for the common good at the same time, but are limited by numbers and by our physical and mental capacities. The government can also play an extremely important role in dealing with the challenges, but governments are generally re-active rather than pro-active, even in the countries that claim to be most democratic. But it is the corporations who have the resources, manpower, technology, power and network, and above all the deepest "self-interest" to dedicate to the betterment of environment and human interest now and in the future. The root of every problem today is caused by the failure to recognize legitimate costs and appreciate the true meaning of profit.

16.7 Innovation and Creativity are All For Profit

Without innovative and creative activities, humanity is probably still living in caves; similar to Plato's story of a man chained next to a fire, imprisoned but warm. Plato told him to break the chain and come out into the "real world." As we have been chained by the traditional notion of profit, it would be difficult to escape unless we break the chain of the tradition. We do not need a cannon to break the chain, but simply try to begin making an attempt to appreciate the meaning of cost and profit with a little "push."

---

[2]Jon Entine, *Shattered Image, An Icon Tumbles* 1994 (http://www.betterworld.com/BWZ9512/cover2.htm).

The fixation on corporate profit is similar to the mindset of the caveman sitting in the cave and chained next to the fire. All we know and care about is the almighty traditional profit, or accounting profit or financial income (i.e. all that is in the box).

In fact, as intelligent humans, we can allow our mindset to push the traditional profit idea out of the box, much the same as the caveman breaking the chain and leaving the cave and entering into the "world." Surprisingly enough, the box is not empty, any more than the world outside the cave is empty.

Traditional profit, accounting profit or financial income

Push the Traditional Profit out of the box, we will realize that the box is not empty, but contain costs that contributed to the making of traditional accounting profit, which are not recognized and compensated. This is the root of our problem.

Traditional profit, accounting profit or financial income (out of the box)

Unrecognized and not compensated costs** + Residual

**Unrecognized and not compensated costs which contribute to corporate entities.

The box contains unrecognized and not compensated legitimated costs:

- **Shareholders' investment opportunity cost.** This is part of total cost: same as labor, and other forms of contribution that support the corporation and provide inputs for production and operations.
- **Environmental contribution.** Ecosystem in general.
- **Employees' portion of the fruit of their labor.** This is wages for their labor, but the harvest, the fruit of their labor.
- **Depleted non-renewable resources and waste and/or contaminated renewable resources and environmental damages.** Mining companies, in particular, petroleum; recently even renewable resources such as fish, marine life, plants and among other things, animals.
- **Community at large.** This includes the concern for the betterment of society, local, regional, national and to some extent globally.

The above are only a few notable items that have contributed to corporate growth yet have not been compensated. Only until these costs are accounted for, and funds are allocated to restore the damage and seek new sources of supply and repayment, can there be such thing as profit. Under the circumstances, it would be more appropriate to designate it as "Residual" rather than as "Profit."

17.8 Corporate Philosophy, Profit and Sustainable Economic Growth for Humanity

Capitalism is a means by which human and other natural activities (animals and plants are also used by corporations) are conducted on the basis of private ownership of financial (money) wealth. Corporate entities are the instrument of capital accumulation. Therefore, the corporate philosophy has to be the accumulation of financial wealth; or put in another way, making "Profit." If it were a living organism, "profit" would be a parasite; it lives on Planet Earth and on everything above and below its surface, human beings in particular. When a corporation makes a profit, it is in effect taking from humans and/or a visible and invisible substance of the planet. This parasite is a greedy beast that will never be satisfied. It will continue to take what it takes without killing its life support, unless the parasite depletes its food source and dies when the supply is completely exhausted. The only way that the parasite can continue to take what it needs to grow is to replenish what is needed by the parasite's food suppliers (human as well as visible and invisible substances of the earth). Through creation and innovation, both the parasite and its food suppliers can live. Therefore, creation and innovation, the making of different combinations, is required to sustain profit-making endeavors, except it has to be both for corporate (and individuals in the entity) interest as well as for the common good. Unfortunately, the current practice of generating profit is not "Profit," but a capital impairment, and taking without putting it back.

The making of profit for corporations can only be a "Profit," if what has been taken from the capital is restored back to it origin — if this is at all possible.

Making profit based on the traditional notion of financial income or accounting profit is not the corporate philosophy, but a parasitic act of selfishness to feed itself without concern for the need of its food suppliers. It is through innovation and creativity that adequate "financial income" to repay what is indebted to people, the environment and other contributors can be generated. Only the earning of "Residual" can be the philosophy of corporate entities.

Questions for Discussion

1. A corporation is a legal entity. A legal entity is much the same as a natural person; it has its own identity, character, culture and responsibility, and should not be owned by any single group or person. Why is it that, in practice, shareholders assume the ownership of the entity? Explain!
2. Assume a democratic principle applicable to all human institutions where all adults are able to make a decision and exercise the right to vote. How can such a right to vote be used in the corporate governance? Explain.
3. Following your response to Q.2, in the Western nations, there are double standards of democracy — one person one vote in the political process, one share one vote in corporate governance. Under the circumstances,

is it fair to say that in the corporate world, there is no democracy, only money?

4. In the corporate world, shareholders have the right to vote, consumers have the power to cast their vote through "to buy" or "not to buy;" workers are given the right by the government to form unions and exercise their right to bargain or strike to secure their position and right in the system; then who would represent the environment and resources supplier to exercise their right to live and continue to serve humanity? More importantly, who should represent those who were pushed out of the system and those in the poverty and below minimum survival line? Discuss.

5. Economists often refer to our world as the forest, where there are large trees, tall trees and trees which have to struggle to grow and reach for sunlight. In addition, there are also many smaller trees in their infant stage, which continue to struggle to get more "life support" in order to survive and grow. Some of these smaller trees may eventually live and realize their sustainable growth potentials, while others will die, thus providing nutrients for other trees to grow. Do you think that this is how the marketplace in the human environment should be? Comment!

6. The growth of corporate power is in fact the result of growth of the stock exchange, where a corporate entity can be traded as merchandise. Our "market economy" has developed into a state where everything is merchandise, including the "human body," "money," even the "human spirit and soul." What could be the possible result to humanity? If only "money counts," can we sell our children and their body parts for experimental purposes? Comment!

Chapter 17

Corporate Management

> In the interest of humanity, on behalf of all corporate entities in the world, the authors would like to convey this message to all citizens of the world:
>
> We would like you to buy our products and use our services. We are here to serve you, your children, children's children and their children. When they are here, we will still be here to serve them the same way as we have been serving you. We have pledged ourselves and visualized this to be our mission, commitment and purposes of being in business.

17.1 Introduction: The Fish Quote and the Entrepreneurial Corporate Management

There has been some interest generated with regards to the application of a quote: "To give a man a fish or teach a man how to fish." The question is aimed specifically at how the quote applies to the idea of entrepreneurial corporate management as compared to the traditional way of managing a corporation. Figure 17.1 illustrates the answer to the question, which is further amplified by the comparisons in Table 17.1.

With the fishing story in mind, it is possible to make a comparison between what we call responsible entrepreneurial corporate management and conventional practised corporate management.

Part 1 of the quote: "When you give a man a fish, you feed him for the day."

What will happen to the man tomorrow and thereafter?

This is charity. There is no management. (Part 1)

Part 2 of the quote: If you teach a man how to fish, you will feed him for life."

However, as the man acquires knowledge and techniques on fishing, he is able to catch many fish, big and small. Then, in order to catch more fish, he uses fish nets with smaller holes. When he wants an even bigger catch, he graduates to hi-tech fishing. Consequently, he catches more and more fish, faster than they can reproduce, soon endangering the fish population.

This is the traditional management model: It teaches people how to maximize, with no regard to the long term impact on people, and the damage to the future.

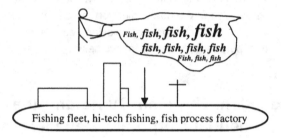

Part 3 of the quote: "If you teach a man how to fish responsibly, not only do you feed him for life, but for the rest of villagers as well."

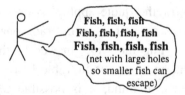

Use a large fish net with larger holes, so the smaller fish can escape. And fish only after the fish spawning season, so the fish can reproduce and future generations can continue to have fish as a source of food.

This is the entrepreneurial management: For self-interest as well as for common good.

Figure 17.1 The fish story and models of management.

Table 17.1 About the fishing and the management.

About fish	About corporate management
If you give a man a fish, you will feed him for a day	Charity, incorporated charitable organization management, sometimes *no management. Possibly managed the same way as any "normal businesses," or* just simply give
If you teach a man how to fish, you feed him for life	"B" school type of management, may be called a "General Management Model." The entire corporate management tradition is based strategically, it looks like a triangle: The ROI, the "B" school's teaching and the Stock Exchange. The spiritual love triangle of capitalism
If you teach a man how to fish responsibly, then not only do you feed him, you also feed the rest of the village, and future generations as well.	The entrepreneurial model: a corporation is a community of entrepreneurs, not just a money-making machine

17.2 Human Problems Created by Humans Can Only be Solved by Humans

The oil drain signifies that our corporations, specifically the petroleum and auto industries as a whole, have been "fishing irresponsibly." The same goes for many other industries, and mining in particular. A basic economic text informs readers that if capital is impaired, there is no profit. Yet since before the last century, oil and mining companies have been

Table 17.2 Responsible corporate entrepreneurial management versus traditional management practice.

Responsible entrepreneurial corporate management	Traditional corporate management
• Based on wealth creation for the individual and add value to society. • View innovation and creation as the way of life — the making of different combinations in all economic endeavors. • Increased individual and corporate responsibilities to society. • Value driven, improving performance to serve a large constituent, instead of narrowly focused serving shareholders' interest. • Ownership and stakeholder structure, people are responsible for themselves and have assumed stewardship responsibility for resources and environmental health at the same time. • Committed to long term sustainable development for both the entity and economy. • A corporation is a community of entrepreneurs, dedicated to create and innovate for self-interest and common good.	• Based on meeting ROI requirements, bottom line management so to speak. • View every economic activity as an event. Measuring success based on short term goal attainment. • Stock performance is primarily the benchmark. • Management separates from ownership. It is ROI driven management rather than enterprise interest driven management. • Ownership belongs to shareholders, everyone in the entity is an employee. • Short term, financial income (or accounting profit) driven management. • Status quo: "I get paid every two weeks. Five years down the road, I do not know where I would be? Let the future be taken care by those who take care of themselves, just like what I do for myself." • Everything is for money. Money makes the world go round.

making "profits," and those profits have all been distributed to God knows who. Although it is a consumer and capital driven world, nonetheless, they have not used resources responsibly. Since the depletion of oil deposits has been addressed more than 30 years ago, no suitable alternatives for car fuel and other industrial purposes have been found. And car manufacturers are still making more cars. Even if the petroleum industry finds a new source of energy, the car makers still continue to manufacture their petroleum fuelled internal combustion engines and their big 4×4's, mini-vans and long limos. Do we expect them to suddenly shoot all these cars into space? Or push all of them onto the market, and then pressure politicians to build more super-highways, motorways and autobahns? In John F. Kennedy's words: "All our problems are caused by people....." So, let's talk about people, namely corporate managers.

17.3 Corporate Managers and Entrepreneurial Corporate Managers

In a seminar on entrepreneurship, the discussion topic focuses on the differences between a corporate manager and an entrepreneurial corporate manager. Here is a comparison submitted by one of the participants. It is the opinion of a very highly educated engineer with considerable business experience:

Corporate manager	Entrepreneurial corporate manager
A corporate manager makes decisions that are in the best interest of his own personal wealth and the company. His goal is to dominate the industry by maximizing ROI and eliminating competition. He is ruthless and cares only that his employees achieve the corporate goals at the lowest possible cost. The corporate manager cares only about community when the press is present and gives nothing back to the community or environment that is in excess of the legal requirements he is forced to abide by. His idea of the future consists of a 3-month calendar and cannot justify putting in the effort to look beyond that because of the fear of losing his generous salary and enviable social status.	The decision made by the entrepreneurial manager will show responsibility to society and the earth and subordinate those demands put forth by greedy investors. He will care about his employees and their concerns. The employees will be paid fairly and will have responsibility within the firm and the community. The entrepreneurial manager also cares about customers and their children. He has an interest in the future and not just short term achievements. He looks to add value to the community and society and realizes that he can make a difference.

The manager concludes by saying: Clearly, there are distinct differences between entrepreneurial corporate managers and corporate managers. But these are often not as evident as is displayed above. Both groups can often hide their personalities well enough to fool most people. His comment was further tested on six mixed groups. It reflects an opinion that individuals may move from one end to another, depending on circumstances. At times, some managers can be very entrepreneurial, but at other times, may display their traits as a typical corporate manager, the company person.

17.4 The Commitment

17.4.1 Begin from a mission statement

Consider a hypothetical situation: Alternative Energy Corporation, a hi-tech company mainly dealing in the business of energy exploitation and delivery for users worldwide. In the past, the company has been earning handsome accounting profits. As an energy source company, its operation is primarily in underground mining, permanently removing from the source and never replacing. Through this depletion, the energy deposits are turned into cash. Instead of distributing entire cash (may be profit) as dividends, executive salaries, bonuses and incentives, a large after-tax residual was committed to the continuing innovative and creative efforts in making new and different combinations. At the turn of the 21st century, inspired by R&D efforts of companies such as Shell (development of "biomass" energy from fast-growing forests), the company investigates (a) extracting geothermal energy, (b) using solar energy from the Sun, and (c) the combination of geothermal and solar energy. Using new storage technology and microwave transmission, energy can be delivered directly to users. It is anticipated that with this new discovery, all other forms of energy supply, including hydro, nuclear, petroleum and natural gas will be outdated. All the company's products can be used for heating, cooling, power engines and other uses. This company, in addition to its new product line, also has a traditional corporate commitment to people, through its innovative and creative search for alternative sources of energy. The corporation identifies itself through its vision/mission statement:

We would like you to buy our products and use our services. We are here to serve you, your children, children's children and their children. When they are here we will still be here to serve them the same way as we have been serving you. We have pledged ourselves and visualized this to be our mission, commitment and purpose of being in business.

The statement signifies that the corporation anticipates the continuation of serving people as long as humanity continues to be on this planet. Its desire to sustain itself is clearly revealed in the statement. Humanity as a whole will continue infinitely, and this is environmentally possible so long as resources are available to support the continuation. At the same time, the corporation will continue receiving the support needed, as the company will continue to pursue creative and innovative activities, so that resources, people and environmental health prevail, to allow for corporate growth. Under the circumstances, the traditional financial income is, in effect, a part of the process, rather than the end itself, and only the economic residual becomes meaningful to both the corporation and society.

17.4.2 The corporate philosophy and operational deed

The corporate philosophy is fundamentally about earning a "Profit," but it is not the accounting profit, which we traditionally use to calculate the ROI. It is also important to recognize that making a "Profit" is not the same as "Making Money." "Profit" must contain the element of value and must reflect, at least in some way, economic reality.

Almost without exception, business is for profit. As an economist said: "A corporation will fulfill its society objective. The only trouble is that the profit is not necessarily a profit, if it has no value in that profit." Companies that create products or services through processes that add negative value to society (pollution or killing the goose that lays the golden eggs) are not creating value in a positive sense, therefore not a "profit." A profit that adds value to society cannot be determined in vacuum using only monetary standards. Profit derived at the expense of something else, such as the environment or human misery, must be discounted to reflect the harm done to society over the long term. Therefore, corporate profit or earnings must be re-addressed to take into consideration the "debts" due, and only the economic residual is regarded as a more meaningful measure for corporate performance.

On the basis of its mission statement, and economic profit making philosophy, the company formulated the following deed both as a commitment and a guide for its business conduct:

(1) Be economically sustainable, viable and mutually beneficial to all our dealings, including people, environment, resources, and among other things, the community at large wherever we operate.

(2) Aim to obey human rights and respect the earth. Support organizations dedicated to developing sustainable development principles into practices; conventions and biological diversity and climate change; and/or other undertakings in the interest of the planet's health, and sustainable economic future to humanity.

(3) Support long term sustainable relationships with global communities in need.

(4) Empower all individuals working in the company to make discretional decisions, and categorize the cost of decision empowerment as a corporate investment.

(5) Develop all individuals working in the corporation as entrepreneurs committed to the continuing creation and innovation for their self-interest, interest of the corporation and humanity.

(6) Pursue innovative and creative activities, as these are the only means of sustaining humanity.

(7) Promote a partnership program with related industries and/or corporations where possible, to jointly coordinate R&D efforts in the interest of environmental health and sensible resources utilization.

(8) Promote stakeholdership program aimed at all individuals who are stakeholders of the corporation.

(9) Use environmentally sustainable resources wherever technically and economically viable.

(10) Promote environmental protection.

(11) Recognize contributions made by contributors other than share-holders. Their contributions will be recognized and compensated accordingly.

17.4.3 The program

As a strategic measure, the company has further integrated 14 deeds into four programmable action groups:

The environment care group	The resources and earth care group	The innovation and creation group	People and networking group
• Be economically sustainable, viable, mutually beneficial to all our dealings including people, the environment, resources, and among other things, the community at large wherever we operate • Promote and adopt models of utilizing resources, production and reproduction • Respect and safeguard regenerative capacities of the earth	• Promote a partnership program with related industries and/or corporations where possible in joint efforts to coordinate R&D efforts in the interest of environmental health, and sensible resources utilization ⊛ Use environmentally sustainable resources wherever technically and economically viable • For all corporate involvement, to protect and restore the diversity, integrity and beauty of the planet's ecosystem	• Aim to ensure human and earth rights are respected, support organizations dedicated to sustainable development practices, and/or other undertakings in the interest of planet health, and a sustainable economic future for humanity • Continue in the pursuit of innovation and creative activities, as these are sustainable by humanity	• Empower all individuals working in the company to make discretionary decisions, and categorize the cost of decision empowerment as a corporate investment • Promote stakeholdership program aimed at all individuals who are stakeholders of the corporation • Recognize contributions made by contributors other than shareholders. Their contributions will be recognized and compensated accordingly

(*Continued on next page*)

(Continued)

• Respect Earth and all life. The corporation as a whole committed to respect independently of their utilitarian value to humanity	• Where there is risk of irreversible or serious damage to the environment, take precautionary action to prevent harm		• Support long term sustainable relationships with global communities in need

To implement the strategic measures in these four groups, the company has committed itself to four fundamental areas of management innovation:

(1) Abandon the traditional boxed pyramid type of organization, and adopt the round satellite type of organization, so each group becomes a self-governed entity with inter-locking directorship within the corporation.

(2) Use the economic residual concept approach, replacing the current accounting approach for income determination.

(3) To systematically recognize all costs and compensate all contribution to the corporation.

(4) To develop all individuals to be entrepreneurs in their own endeavor, and make the corporation as a community of entrepreneurs.

17.5 The Round Satellite Type of Organization

The satellite entity organizational structure features self-governing, and the entity has complete operational freedom under the corporate mission and operational deed. The satellite entity has the obligation to remit a capital charge of equivalent market interest rate to the corporation. With an interlocking directorship, the corporation and satellite entity maintain an entrepreneurial working relationship to cooperate and coordinate R&D, marketing and administrative efforts.

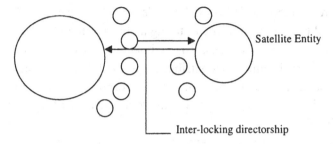

Satellite Entity

Inter-locking directorship

Figure 17.2 The round satellite type of organization.

17.6 Cost Recognition and Required Compensation from Corporate Earnings

We further assume that there are five major contributors to which corporations are indebted, yet are not recognized nor compensated. In particular, the five major groups are: (1) The investors' opportunity cost for their investment, (2) the fruit of labor outside of workers' wages paid for their work, (3) environmental contributions, (4) depleted resources and environmental damages, and (5) through people and earth care to replenish sacrifices experienced by people and the planet in general, as a result of technological advancement and rapid economic growth.

(1) Investors' investment opportunity cost:

Of all debts, only the investors' investment opportunity cost is possible to establish since there is a going rate, the market rate of interest. In fact, investors should receive their compensation for funds invested in the corporation, at least equivalent to a market interest rate.

(2) The fruit of labor due to workers are used and are popular among corporations that have a profit sharing plan. There are many forms of such plans, depending on the board's decision. Normally, companies allocate 10% of earned accounting profits.

(3) Environmental cost is difficult to estimate; although an estimate given by a research group was approximately US$35 trillion for ecosystem contribution, and humanity as a whole experiencing

approximately a US$17 trillion deficit (Costanza *et al.*, 1997). It would be extremely difficult to tag a cost assumed by the corporation. Under the circumstances, it is estimated that corporate responsibility for the environmental contribution to be 1% of corporate earnings, measured in accounting terms. If the corporate earning for any fiscal year is $1 billion, the environmental costs will be estimated at $10 million.

(4) Depleted resources and environmental damages are also impossible to assess to corporate responsibility. However, similar to (3) above, 1% of earnings in accounting profits are provided.

(5) People and earth care. Provisions are used to find solutions for retrenched workers of the company. In addition, there must be support for earth care programs and other programs to aid the neediest at home and in developing countries. As a matter of judgement, 2% of corporate earnings in accounting profits will be provided for the purpose.

Funds allocated from corporate earnings expressed as accounting profit may not be re-allocated for any other purpose.

The above is merely an illustration. The idea is mainly to demonstrate to corporate decision-makers what can be done to ensure sustainable economic growth, where corporations still play the most important role, summarized as follows:

Scheduled environmental debt, people and earth care[1]:

(1) Shareholders' investment opportunity cost:
Assume the market rate of interest is 6%,
therefore, the corporation recognizes it
as follows:

---

[1]Earth care as part of operational cost has been seen in businesses such as Patagonia (see Patagonia Inc., *Louder Than Words. Ventura, Defining Quality Ventura Patagonia*, also *http://www.patagonia.com*. An earth tax was charged to the company — either add 1% of sales or 10% of profit, whichever is greater.

Paid share capital $15 billion +
Capitalized R&D $10 billion =
$25 billion. $25 billion × 6% = $1.5 billion

This amount is to be deducted from
corporate accounting profits. If, on the other
hand, there is no accounting profit or it is
insufficient for such capital charges, it will
be shown as a deficit.

(2) Fruit of labor for workers: 10% of corporate
earnings based on accounting profit.
$10 billion × 10% =   1.0

(3) Environmental cost: 1% of corporate earnings
based·on accounting profit.   1.0

(4) Resources depletion and environmental damage:

3% of corporate earnings based on
accounting profit   .3

(5) People and earth care: 2% of corporate earnings
based on accounting profit (1)   .2

Total accounting profit after tax allocation $3.0 billion

17.7 The Corporate Economic Residual

17.7.1 Economic residual reserved for sustainable growth

The economic residual earned by corporations is a simple computation; it does not deviate from the traditional financial income intelligence, except that it is extended further to accommodate other uncompensated costs. The format is based on what has already been explored in previous chapters.

Assume the Alternative Energy Corporation has a paid share capital of $1.5 billion with a further long term debt of $1.5 billion, and capitalized research and development cost of $1 billion, constituting a total equity plus long term debt of $4 billion. As a corporate policy, the $1.5 billion

R&D expenditure will be amortized in a period of ten years on a straight-line basis. The company's operating costs, measurable by an accounting method (the annual charge as scheduled), amount to $150 million. The following is assumed to be the company's fiscal year performance report:

Alternative Energy Explore Inc. Performance Report for the Year Ending 31 December 2005	
Revenue	$100,000,000,000
*Costs expensed for the year's operation	$60,000,000,000
Direct contribution from revenue	$40,000,000,000
Administrative and financial charges	$20,000,000,000
Traditional accounting profit before taxes	$20,000,000,000
Taxes	$10,000,000,000
Traditional accounting profit after taxes	$10,000,000,000

Reserves for environmental responsibility:
  People and earth care cost and
    compensation for other contributors
	$3,000,000,000

Economic residual for shareholders and for sustainable development and growth	$7,000,000,000

It is inaccurate to label the economic residual as real profit, since real profit must be taken into consideration when determining "capital." Underground resources, fish in the ocean and the ecosystem are all important economic capital, yet we still have no adequate way of quantifying their existence and the amount used for our purpose. However, the process described above is at least one step ahead of what we have done in the past. Moreover, the allocated amount ($10 billion) in all requires no cash outlay, although in due time, it may be necessary to do so. For example, additional allocation for shareholders contribution in addition to reimbursing their investment opportunity cost, may require cash payment; only at that time, a disbursement will be made. The same applies to other allocations. For example, assume that the company's operation requires some restructuring either on a temporary or relatively permanent basis. Then some adjustment may be needed. The payment required for such an adjustment can be made by leasing funds reserved for people and earth care. Similarly, in the case of an environmental clean-up, an adjustment can be made as it is for the care of people and earth reserve funds. Economic residual is therefore, in effect a residual after commitments to the environment; people and long term sustainable growth are materialized, and corporate earnings are not affected in any way.

17.7.2 The matter of ROI and corporate worth

ROI will still be calculated on the basis of traditional accounting profit. The only difference is that previously (and now), accounting profit was assumed to belong to the shareholders. Under the economic residual approach, part of the accounting profit should be returned to other contributors, and a portion of it will still be available for the shareholders. But two calculations are needed instead of one:

The traditional ROI: $10,000,000,000/$100,000,000 = 10%

Now, it needs another calculation for the economic residual allocated for shareholders. Assumed to be 50% of the residual, another 50% is reserved for sustainable economic development and growth.

Economic residual return to shareholders investment: 50% of $7,000,000,000 or $3,500,000,000/$100,000,000 = 3.5%.

In fact, shareholders' expectations have no direct relationship though it may affect stock prices on the market. The real ROI is not how much of the corporate earnings are returned to its shareholders, but rather, how much they can make by buying and selling the company's stock on the stock market. Human interest as well as care for the environment and resources may increase the company's stock value; or at other times, decrease, depending on judgement of the individual, stock analysts' report, macroeconomic performance, plus at least another half dozen factors, which may or may not be relevant to the value of the company, e.g. CEO of Alternative Energy Corporation just re-married to the corporation's number one competitor CEO's daughter.

17.8 Developing Individuals in the Corporation to be Entrepreneurs

From corporate philosophy to corporate culture

Corporate philosophy, as described earlier, is nothing more than "making economic profit, or economic residual" — a meaningful commitment as a way of life for individuals in the corporate entity. Unlike "accounting profit," the economic residual has a value that can be identified by individuals in the entity, thereby, possibly developing the link to the corporate enterprise culture supporting individuals' entrepreneurial attributes for the continuing pursuit of innovative and creative activities — the individual's enterprising culture.

Entrepreneurial attributes and their development

There is a general comment about entrepreneurship development: "Entrepreneurship cannot be taught." Then, there is another observation: "Entrepreneurial skills should be taught."

During the past three decades or so, virtually all the entrepreneurship research has been focused on entrepreneurial attributes. If attributes are required for an individual to be creative and innovative, then entrepreneurial attributes must be cultivated, nurtured and developed so that the entrepreneurial spirit can flourish. However, before continuing with Alternative Energy Corporation's strategic program with respect to developing individuals as entrepreneurs, we shall first discuss two rather unique and real-life situations that relate how entrepreneurial attributes are prevented from flourishing:

> *Situation 1: "I have to ask my mother."*
>
> During his past 22 years, a mother's son was constantly nursed and cared for. It was his mother who told him what to wear, what to eat, what to do in the presence of people, and what to study. He was well-liked by his peers as he had a pleasant personality and he always had a ready smile on his face. Furthermore, he did well in school, because he was such an obedient student.

After graduating from college with a degree in computer technology, he had a job offer, but was required to be interviewed. The interview was just a formality, as the company had already decided to employ him. But, at the interview, when the interviewer (possibly his future manager) asked him: "When can you start?" He smiled and replied quietly: "Oh! I have to ask my mother!" That was it, he was never called to take up the job offer.

Situation 2: "It's up to you!"

For more than 30 years, the senior author had been involved in teaching and research activities in universities; this included giving term paper assignment topics to students, with the following instructions: "Here are a list of topics from which you can choose one to prepare a term paper to fulfill partial requirement for the course. You have the freedom to do as you like; use your discretion to write the paper and submit it two weeks before term ends, so I will have the time to read and evaluate properly." Surprisingly enough, one week after the announcement was made and written instructions were given out, the students had already begun asking questions like: "How long should the paper be?" "Should I just do some desk research or primary research?" and "Should it be a conceptual paper or should it be tested empirically?" Each time a student asked any of these questions were asked repeatedly, the response to them was always (without exception): "It's up to you."

In both of the above situations, the individuals involved need to have opportunities to develop their self-confidence. Situations differ from one incident to another. To build the individual's confidence there is a need to remove fear from the individual, and prove success in decisions made by the individual.

Motivation, confidence, achievement and job ownership

In a corporate environment, as well as in the technologically advanced society, creativity, initiative and a desire to achieve (these are all entrepreneurial attributes) may be irrelevant to a typical corporate employee who works on a 9-to-5 basis. They may not see the need for creativity as work is routine to them (based on numerous efficiency studies). They may think that employees do not need to take initiative. They just need to work and follow the rules — a programmed process. There is hardly any motivation to achieve success or take initiative in an organization where promotions are typically based on seniority as opposed to performance.

This complacency about entrepreneurship is still a questionable practice in today's corporate environment. Corporations can and should develop entrepreneurial attributes in employees working for the corporation. One way to develop these attributes is through job ownership programs. These programs give the people who perform the work responsibility and control over decision-making. Workers develop entrepreneurial attributes, as they are responsible for problem solving, opportunity identification and implementing ideas in the job they own. Creativity is stimulated, as employees must search for solutions to problems. They also are encouraged to take initiative and make decisions based on their knowledge as opposed to based on the authority of a superior. Successfully implemented job ownership typically produce employees who take pride in their accomplishments and who have a drive to succeed.

These are the types of entrepreneurial attributes that corporations should strive to develop. More importantly, there is a need to develop an entrepreneurial culture. In essence, such a culture can be based on: "Decision making (empowerment) and a matter of ownership." Perhaps, we can use Southwest Airlines in the U.S. as an example.

Southwest Airlines

Southwest is the fifth largest airline in the U.S., operating more than 2100 flights per day and carrying over 44 million passengers a year. Its success is owed to its corporate philosophy of caring for its people:

(1) Employees are No. 1. The way you treat your employees is the way they will treat your customers.
(2) Think small to grow big.
(3) Manage in the good time for the bad times.
(4) Irreverence is okay.
(5) It is okay to be yourself.
(6) Have fun at work.

(7) Take the competition seriously, but not yourself.

(8) It is difficult to change someone's attitude, so hire for attitude and train for skill.

(9) Think of the company as a service organization that happens to be in the airline business.

(10) Do whatever it takes

(11) Always practice the Golden Rule, internally and externally.

To support their belief that people take better care of things they own, and that this special care is ultimately passed on to the customer, Southwest created profit-sharing with stock option plans which manifests the priority they place on employees initiative and responsibility. Southwest is built on the principle that employees are expected to take on an entrepreneurial role in being proactive owners who are cognizant of corporate values and confident enough with their empowerment to participate in decision-making and continuous improvement. This entrepreneurial spirit provides employees with the freedom and responsibility to take effective action and financial participation through ownership which allows them to benefit from the company's overall performance (Southwest Airlines at *www.southwest.com*).

The proposed Alternative Energy Corporation entrepreneurial culture development strategy

Many entrepreneurial attributes have been identified by researchers and practitioners; the list can be as long as one wishes to explore, but the essential ones commonly acknowledged are: risk-taking, confidence, determination, perseverance, passion, flexibility, communication, initiative, etc. Some people may feel one is more relevant to him/her, but the reality is that all attributes contribute to the strengthening of the entrepreneurial drive, and one individual may be inclined to have some attributes more than the others. But the fundamental attribute in the authors' opinion is "passion," passion leads to a person's dedication in his/her endeavor and strive to work beyond one's realized potential to generate value for him/herself, the corporation and the society.

Alternative Energy Corporation acknowledges all entrepreneurial attributes to be important to the continuing efforts of the company's desire in the pursuit of long term sustainable economic growth through innovation and creativity. Only a few can be directly linked in the company's efforts in strengthening the development needed. These are: moderated risk taking, flexibility, confidence, and above all, assuming entrepreneurial responsibility. To do so, the company adopts the following strategies:

- To put value in "Profit," and establish that earning economic residual is the corporate life, and the company's philosophy.
- Through policy and personal contact, the company's philosophy is to be integrated into personal value, thus building corporate value on the basis of personal value of those working in the corporation.
- The company will devote its efforts to eliminating subcultures, such as: "No risk no gain, no risk no loss"; "be strong to show them who is the boss"; and among other things, "It is none of your business, let someone else take the blame."
- The company designates a portion of Economic Residual for Sustainable Development and Growth reserves for the support of employees at all levels to allow them to make discretionary decisions with respect to innovation, creativity, and added value undertakings of any project and/or undertakings.
- Develop entrepreneurial attributes as identified by all members of the corporation as part of corporate culture.
- Take responsibility for the creation of a support system to allow the development of entrepreneurial attributes through individuals, so they can be free from fear of failure. Cost of failure in the course of attributes development will be considered as part of corporate investment.

There are other attributes that are useful for the development of individuals in the organization that will help to transform a money-making machine into a community of entrepreneurs. In short, a suggested scheme should consist of: (1) empowerment, (2) support, and (3) recognition. It is crucial that individuals are given authority to act in entrepreneurial ways. Of course, this is not something new or exciting, some large corporate entities have their own scheme to encourage employees to make entrepreneurial decisions. For example, in the Ritz Carlton Hotel, the management allows employees to make whatever necessary decisions amounting to $1000 for appropriate services to hotel guests.

An entrepreneurial corporation should be built on the strength of its philosophy and the people in the entity. Ideally, needs of people in the entity are linked with the corporate philosophy. Corporate philosophy as such is the "economic residual"; this philosophy must be part of the corporate culture — welding the corporation and people in a united body where everything — decision-making, responsibility, fruit of labor, and above all, a common dream — are shared. The dream as specified at the beginning of this chapter: serve humanity now and in the future.

A proposed entrepreneurial corporate management model based on the above is summarized in Fig. 17.3.

Questions for discussion

1. Management is a stewardship function. Its responsibility is essentially to use the resources under its trust efficiently and effectively to achieve the entity's objectives. In your opinion, what are these objectives? Would for self-interest and common good be sufficient as corporate objectives? Why?
2. What's wrong if a corporation's objective is solely to serve investors' interest? After all, they are the ones who provide needed money to sustain corporate development and growth.
3. Towards the end of the 20th century, the pension fund trusts turned out to be one of largest investors in corporate holdings. In essence, today's capitalism is not quite the same as in some 50 years ago. Does this mean corporate responsibility and management should also be changed as well? Why?
4. Perhaps the way to go is to have the largest home service department store whose corporate purpose is to service everything that is needed for the home, at the same time caring for the environment, including selecting its suppliers on the basis of their commitment to conservation requirements. In early May 2001, there was a plan to create a giant store in the Garden City, which would consequently result in a Garden City without a garden. Comment on the plan, make any assumptions

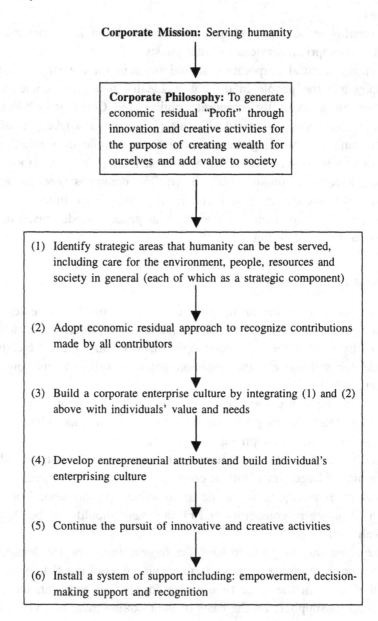

Corporate Mission: Serving humanity

Corporate Philosophy: To generate economic residual "Profit" through innovation and creative activities for the purpose of creating wealth for ourselves and add value to society

(1) Identify strategic areas that humanity can be best served, including care for the environment, people, resources and society in general (each of which as a strategic component)

(2) Adopt economic residual approach to recognize contributions made by all contributors

(3) Build a corporate enterprise culture by integrating (1) and (2) above with individuals' value and needs

(4) Develop entrepreneurial attributes and build individual's enterprising culture

(5) Continue the pursuit of innovative and creative activities

(6) Install a system of support including: empowerment, decision-making support and recognition

Figure 17.3 Entrepreneurial corporate management model.

necessary. Pay a visit to a store anywhere in North America. It may help you to get some idea what is meant by balanced long term and short term economic sustainability, corporate responsibility and management.

5. As a corporate strategy, some large corporations may find themselves in a straight-jacket with the environmental protection and conservation regulations. As a business decision, they move their production facilities to a Third World country, as the facilities can be unfriendly to environmental health. The argument is simple enough, these countries need cash and people need jobs. After all, no job means no money. Even if there is a promised land, it can never be reached. Comment on the business decision.

6. In your own way, find a corporation of your choice, and assume that you are the CEO of this not-so-new company. Your board of directors expects you to prepare a set of practical statements, including corporate philosophy, purpose, mission, strategy and a plan for implementation.

7. Continue with your response to Q.6, what is your plan to take the corporation from the traditional corporate entity to a community of entrepreneurs?

8. In every U.S. coin there is an inscription: "In God we Trust." In other words, it is our belief that generates the value, as in democracy, market economy, and other political ideologies and economic doctrines. Is it the same in the case of corporate profit? If so, what happened in the 1997 financial crisis? Failing stock prices, inflation (currency value in particular)? Does it mean: "In God, we do not trust anymore?"

Chapter 18

Should/Can the Government be Entrepreneurial?

> As humans, we are all governed by two sets of natural laws: one governs the individual in the pursuit of self-interest and the other compels all of us to look out for the common good. Without the pursuit of self-interest, individuals cannot survive. Devoid of the common good, we will have no society.
>
> It is the common good that gives us status as humans and builds our civilization, so we can have a society that allows individuals to be a part of the group. On the other hand, it is the excessive pursuit of self-interest that erodes human value, subsequently bringing us closer to the obliteration of our civilization.

18.1 Introduction: Let's Begin With the Idea of "Value"

"Value" is a word frequently used in recent years. The notion of value has been explored, studied, researched and applied, particularly with regard to how "value" affects individuals' behavior, business conduct or human actions in general. In fact, the idea of "value driven" has long been associated with our thoughts, overseeing our conduct and the way a business should be managed. It is only recently, with the accelerated pursuit of personal wealth accumulation, "high living standards," and profit driven business culture fuelled by the "Who wants to be a millionaire?" mentality, that "Value" seems to be a bit old-fashioned, maybe even an empty shell with no substance. Perhaps not even good enough for the birds, since to attract birds, food and not just words is needed. Even to this day, we seem to live on money alone, though like it or not, to a large extent, we still are governed by "value." This is applicable not only to the individual but also to the family, and is of national importance as well. Consider the following:

> Paul is over 80 years old. He has not worked a single day in his life since he was 58. Between the ages of 58 to 65, he claimed sick benefits as he was unable to work due to health reasons. With unemployment insurance benefits and social welfare payments, he lives normally like a middle (perhaps lower middle) class individual. He lives all by himself, although his sister sometimes stays with him. Prior to his unofficial retirement at 58, he worked periodically as a bartender. He enjoyed his work, as he said: "I met a lot of interesting people during my days of working in the bar. Besides, tips were very good."
>
> In good weather (summers and springs), Paul would sit in the front porch of his home and wave at passers-by. Quite often, he would engage in idle conversation with neighbors about: Who is divorced, who is hospitalised, whose children is getting married etc.; on colder days, he would dress up and take a stroll around the nearby commercial area, acknowledging people he knew along the way. Although Paul needs medical attention, he receives free treatments under the Canadian Medicare system. He only needs to pay $100 a year for medicine prescribed by his attending physician.
>
> Some six years ago, Paul discovered that he was suffering from advanced deterioration of his bone structure, spinal cord, leg and arm joints, and also experienced pains all over his body. As he is under Canada's Medicare system, he continues to receive free treatments.
>
> Since contracting bone problems, Paul has not been able to walk normally, but on a sunny day, with the aid of a cane, he would walk very slowly (at a snail's pace) along the sidewalk, greeting any familiar faces along the way. He would say to them: "You know, George, I must be a very important person to Canada, the government sends two nurses to my house to take care of me, at no charge since it's all under Medicare." Then he emphasizes. "They must feel I am important enough to send not one, but two nurses to take care of me."

Why is Paul an important person to Canada? He does not work, earns no income and pays no or minimum taxes and yet claims maximum benefits on everything that the Canadian social welfare system has to offer.

He produces nothing and provides no service to anyone. Why then is Paul an important person to Canada?

Paul is an important person to Canada, because he is a citizen of this country and is therefore important. It matters not how much taxes he has paid, or what he has contributed to the economy, this is what Canada is and these are its value.

Each country has its own value system. For example, Singapore though a small country, as an initiative undertaken on the part of its government, has become the first country which expresses its values by legislating that the caring of parents is the responsibility of the children instead of the state. Along with the legislation, the government also gives an incentive to provide grants to any citizen who purchased his/her/their dwelling nearby where the parents live. If, on the other hand, parents are neglected and left without care, the children responsible will be brought to court, and the matter is resolved through conciliation, rather than through a judicial process.

Both the Medicare system in Canada and the parental care in Singapore are not exactly programmed vocabulary in a market economy and capitalistic system. In some countries, there are old and disabled people living and then dying alone. Only recently, the media reported several such cases, where their bodies were discovered only many days after they died.

18.2 Entrepreneurial Initiative for Self-Interest versus Common Good

The Medicare system in Canada and parental care legislation of Singapore are entrepreneurial initiatives on the part of the government. They are for the common good, although also in the interest of the government, since both governments, thereby governing parties, are expected to be re-elected when the next general election takes place. The main difference in the government initiative as compared with the private sector entrepreneurial initiative is that, in the case of the private entrepreneurial sector initiative, its prime reason (even if there are exceptions) is mostly for self-interest and benefit to society is secondary. More specifically, self-interest is the prime motive stimulating the private initiative to act; while in the case of a government initiative, it is the common good that comes first, and "self-interest" is the result of the good deeds. Similarly, if you ask anyone in business, why he/she is in business, it would not be a surprise if the answer is simply "for profit" or "making money." If a similar question is addressed to a politician: "Why are you working for the government or why be a politician?" It would be unthinkable, if the party responded by saying: "I am in politics for the money, or working for the government is to make a profit." They would most likely say: "I am in politics, or I work for the government to serve the public, people and/or the country." The question remains: While it is the function of the government to work for the common good, how well can a government's entrepreneurial initiative fit with the idea of the individual's pursuit of self-interest under the market economy? This is the major concern under the market economy and continues to be a challenge.

18.3 Let the Enterprise be Free

A little more than two decades ago in Canada, the Liberal government under the late Prime Minister Pierre Elliot Trudeau, acted swiftly, and vehemently limited business activities in the marketplace, and the Foreign Investment Review Agency (FIRA) was created as a watchdog to review all major foreign investments in Canada in the interest of Canada's economy. The insurance industry for example, bought a one-page ad in all the national newspapers; the ad showed a big bird flying in the sky, with a note: "Let the enterprise be free!" It was about the same time that one business association leader openly expressed his disenchantment on government intervention in a public forum: "As far as the government is concerned, they do nothing, but just stand there." That was in the early 1980s when interest rates went as high as 16 to 18% with double digit inflation and unemployment rates, and businesses were protesting loudly against the high rate of interest. Smaller businesses and mortgage borrowers, (the rate was about 20%+) were practically pleading with the government to do something. There was a great cross-country debate involving two courses of action: let inflation go on (if control is needed, do so moderately) for the sake of jobs, or both interest rate and inflation must be in line, otherwise the consequences will be unthinkable.

It was clearly evident that the Canadian government's entrepreneurial initiative limiting business activities designed for the common good appeared to be a direct confrontation between self-interest (particularly business interest) and the common good functions of the Canadian government. To paraphrase Trudeau; for the Anglophones and Francophones it was one or the other — business and government. For those who have had the opportunity to observe the political movement at the time, the change of government was inevitable. Big businesses seem determined to vote the Liberals out of power, and so it happened. The defeat of the Liberal government did not mean that its initiatives to limit corporate market activities were not in the interest of the people of Canada.

Like it or not, government intervention in the marketplace towards business activities is inevitable. Contrary to the "free enterprise" belief, both market economy and free enterprise should not be absolutely free without guide for directions. As they are both man-made, and the man-made economy and the man-made free enterprise embrace the imperfection of the behaviors of man. True economic growth that is of benefit to mankind cannot be attained by free enterprise alone. What matters is the degree of government intervention and how it intervenes. If on the other hand, government intervention is of any value to the economy, it has to be judged on the basis of the long-term objective of broad human interests and the common good.

Unfortunately, by and large, from the private sector businesses' point of view, the government's entrepreneurial initiative for the common good is not particularly appreciated, especially by the larger enterprises of the economy. And under the market economy, to reconcile the differences between self-interest and the common good is always a challenge to the government. While recognizing that Bill Gates was able to make himself virtually the No. 1 richest man in the world, through his pursuit of self-interest, it was in the name of serving the consumers' need that made him and his organization a power entity next to the government. Through his "monopolistic power," he was virtually levying "taxation" on computer users, as if there was a royalty paid to Microsoft for every computer sold on the market since almost all are bonded to Microsoft software. Similarly, the banking industry in Canada (going as far back as two decades ago when the country was under a conservative government), has made attempts to develop the concept of "one stop for shopping for financial needs" or "financial supermart" for Canadians. At the time, this was not very successful, but the powerful bankers have never given up on the idea. Instead of lobbying the government to "liberalize" Canada's banking industry, they made a great attempt by themselves through merger. There were plans to combine existing major banks (Royal, CIBC, Montreal, Nova Scotia and TD), resulting in only two (or three), so as to create "near monopolistic financial institutions" in the name of competition and to better serve the public. Although the banks had already made their move to streamline the operation, close down branches, takeover trust companies, and add insurance to the list, the bank merger proposal was turned down by the government. However, near universal computer and touch button banking have given the banks what they want: one stop shopping for financial needs, financial supermarket, and even the names were changed. Instead of just "Bank," it became: "Bank and Finance Group," all for free enterprise, competition, and of course, the good of the consumer. Or is it?

18.4 Entrepreneurship versus Entrepreneurial

Would government intervention in the marketplace be viewed as "entrepreneurial," or may the franchising right of government given by people be viewed as a discouragement for the private sector's entrepreneurial initiative? This is however, largely dependent on two factors: one specializing on the need for making a distinction between entrepreneurial and entrepreneurship, and the other is a matter of how the government enters into the market, commonly known as an issue of government policy.

The distinction between entrepreneurial and entrepreneurship

In the private sector, in the conventional view, there is no difference between entrepreneurial and entrepreneurship, so long as one engages in running a profit-making business. The person is an entrepreneur, owning and running a business that is viewed as an entrepreneurial activity. The whole process of incubating, creating a new venture, and managing it are christened "entrepreneurship." However, a broader application of the term is in essence to accommodate entrepreneurial activities assumed by individuals in business entities, including corporations, spin-off subsidiaries, family businesses with different labels and terms not found in the dictionary, such as "Intrepreneurship" (used in corporate entrepreneurship), "Entrapreneurship" (spin-off companies), "Intrapreneurship" (subsidiaries), and "Interpreneurship" (entrepreneurship within a family business structure). Under the circumstances, there is no reason that government initiative cannot be viewed as "entrepreneurial," if such an initiative is for the common good, and a benefit to the "government." Self-interest for the government, therefore, is a way to sustain itself in the economy for the acceptance of people (consumers).

18.5 Government Initiatives: In the Name of Common Good, Some "Entrepreneurial Undertakings" are Questionable

All government initiatives are supposedly for the common good (Fig. 18.1). In principle, no initiative should be in competition with businesses in the marketplace, simply because the use of public funds to engage in commercial undertakings in competition with those enterprises whose financial sources are from private individuals are considered to be unfair. Nevertheless, state operated enterprises do exist, and many of them operate in the market no differently from other private sector enterprises. In accordance to critics, such undertakings not only use public funds as their sources of financing, but they also lack profit responsibility. The following concerns, even though they are for the common good, can be entrepreneurial.

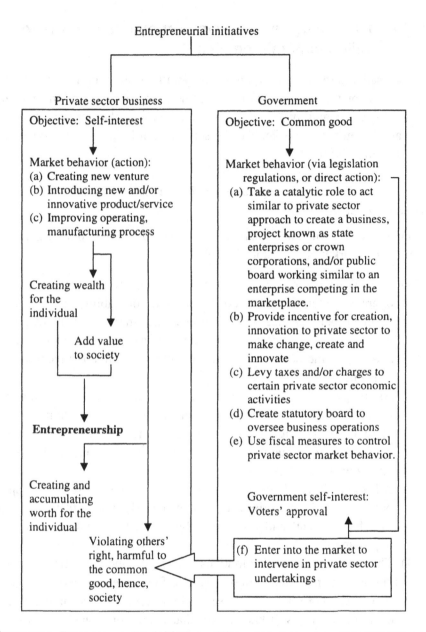

Figure 18.1 Entrepreneurial initiative differences between government and private sector businesses.

18.5.1 State enterprises, crown corporations and other public economic entities

State owned enterprises and/or crown corporations are common worldwide. The reason for the state to create a commercialized organization or board is due to a demand pressure for services, where the private sector is reluctant to enter into the field where services can be provided, for reasons such as shown in Table 18.1.

Further comment on state operated or financially supported business practices

In general, state owned and operated or supported business practices in any form in the marketplace is questionable:

(1) The public perception is that the management of state owned and operated enterprises has no apparent accountability, in particular financial performance, since it is not measurable in terms of profit; in most cases, classified as cost centers, as all cost centers are, by and large, measured on the basis of operation effectiveness, not efficiency.

(2) As all publicly owned and operated business entities are financed by public funds (mostly government taxes collected from people), there is no justification for any government entity to use public funds to operate businesses which compete in the marketplace with privately owned businesses.

(3) All funds have their opportunity cost. If funds used to support public owned enterprises are not efficiently and effectively used to achieve social and economic objectives, there will be a loss of opportunity.

(4) There are government initiatives found to be not specifically in the public's interest, and countless public funds are invested in projects which do not particularly serve long-term societal interest. For example, it is a well-known fact that automobiles are the worst air polluters, and large sums of public funds are required to support the construction of highways to accommodate large volumes of cars on

Table 18.1 State enterprises/crown corporations in practice in non-socialist countries.

Created for:	Sample businesses	Remarks
Category 1: There is a monopolistic nature, of a national interest, and it is unsuitable for the private sector profit-taking entities to care about public interest.	Hydro, and/or nuclear power generated electricity, water supply, space exploration, port administration, in some cases, communication and transport services, and medical or health services.	State enterprises of this category can all be privatized, on the other hand, . privatization can suffer unthinkable consequences. The British rail disaster, and Canada's Walkerton water pollution tragedy (*The Globe and Mail*, Tuesday, 9 January 2001, A3) that killed seven people are cases in point.
Category 2: The service is required by certain sectors of the economy. Yet, the nature of such a business, cannot provide desired or sufficiently certain returns to attract private capital investment. Consequently, it became the government's responsibility to provide the service through a business entity created and operating for the public interest.	Publicly funded garbage disposal operation, road construction in remote regions, public transit services, particularly in developing countries. Similar operations such as, basic research undertakings, are provided on a cost recovery basis, others with planned loss are subsidized through public funds. All of these can be privatized, but not for short term profit.	Since all these operations do not provide short term profits (even though they can all be privatized on the basis of their financial feasibility), the government retains them as public corporations. As an alternative, some governments award contracts to the private sector to undertake the task, but remain as the public's responsibility. However, the economic benefits for both the public and private sectors are difficult to measure.

Table 18.1 (*Continued*)

Created for:	Sample businesses	Remarks
Category 3: For reasons such as control, regulation and/ or monitoring of consumers' behavior, making of profits and using them to meet other social and economic development responsibility requirements.	Liquor control board, state lottery operations, licensing bodies, among other things, financial (including insurance) banking institutions.	Similar to Category 2, all these state owned and/or state operated business activities can be privatized. However, the social and economic benefits to the public of these government initiated undertakings cannot be easily dismissed.
Category 4: To sustain cultural identities, educational needs and other long term social benefit responsibilities.	Operating entities of amateur sports, art galleries, educational institutions, museums and other culturally related establishments.	The ideal situation of these public supported initiatives: activities should be based on a long term sustainable basis, and should not be operated to generate profit or surplus, nor incur any deficit over a period of time.

the road, whereas the public transit system, if properly managed, can be a much more efficient means of transporting people, and are lesser polluters than the massive movement of private vehicles. However, auto makers argue that they are serving consumers' need for cars, particularly new cars. Thus, new cars continue to rapidly roll off from the assembly lines all over the world; the rate of accumulation of automobiles is far greater than the population problems encountered so far. The following are only some of the concerns:

More cars and bigger cars in the name of "that is what people want"

It seems that auto makers have no concern over the number of cars on the road. All that matters to them is to produce more cars and to sell what they produce.

In one of the large automakers' mission statement: "Our cars are made to be friendly to the environment for people who will be proud to own it and take pleasure from driving it," no reference was made to roads.

Why should they be concerned about building roads? Should not the statement be: "Give us more highways and super-highways because these will complement our cars."

Build more highways and super-highways to accommodate the car makers' policy of making more and bigger cars (mini vans, 4 × 4's, etc.) in order to satisfy their bottom line needs?

Politicians who are eager to please the public and car-makers make no mention of what cars can do to the environment and Planet Earth, particularly the issue of availability of land to be used for building highways. As we have witnessed throughout the world, everyone seems eager to build super-highways, first with four lanes, then six, then eight, and in major metro cities, the major motorways are extended to as many as 16 to 20 lanes.

What they do not realize or simply do not appreciate is the reality that it does not matter how many motorways are built, the rate of car production and number of cars on the road are much more than the roads can ever handle.

Although there will always be the argument that the auto industry and other related support systems provide jobs, it cannot change the fact that it is at the cost of the future.

Traffic congestion is only a small part of the problem

During peak hours, the loss of time and fuel makes driving a less efficient means of transporting people from one place to another. In the greater London area, near and around airports, traffic tie-ups are the rule rather than the exception. In Los Angeles and other North American cities, it is normal to sit and wait in the car for three hours on the highway. This is needless waste, yet governments continue to deal with the problem by building more super-highways.

Building more super-highways to accommodate the increasing number of cars is not an entrepreneurial initiative on the part of the government for the common good, but rather a form of politically motivated expediency at the cost of the future, in the name of satisfying consumers' need and job requirements.

The traffic congestion problem is not an unsolvable problem. There are two basic measures which have been in the public administration agenda for quite some time: one is city planning, and the other is to build up an efficient public transit system for moving people around smaller centers, from one point to another, rather than focusing on city core areas. However, there are more effective ways of limiting the amount of cars on the road, instead of building more roads to accommodate cars; for example the following measures used by the Singapore government to limit the amount of cars on the road:

- Require car buyers to purchase a Certificate for Entitlement (COE), a measure used by Singapore to limit the individual's right to purchase a car, unless a certificate is issued before the purchase can take place.
- Issue different license plates to users with different needs separating non-essential and essential car users. A number of countries in Europe have also adopted this policy.
- Limit the number of older cars on the road and differentiate by issuing different license plates and/or increasing registration fees for renewal of road privileges.
- Encourage car sharing through imposing of restrictions on driver only cars on the roads.

There are other measures taken by other countries to limit the individual's right to use roads without hindering them from using vehicles for business purposes (including to and from workplace). These are entrepreneurial initiatives on the part of the government. The building of more highways and super-highways is not only non-entrepreneurial but also morally irresponsible, as it involves the use of limited and valuable land space just to satisfy the auto makers' need to meet their "profit" objectives, although often, in the name of employment and meeting consumers' need. Instead, we should seek alternatives which can move people effectively and efficiently at much lower costs to the environment and create jobs through other means.

Other government initiatives are listed in Fig. 18.1, shown as (b) to (f). Some of them are entrepreneurial in nature, while others may have other state objectives, as further explored below.

18.5.2 Provide incentives to encourage new venture creation: loan guarantee and other entrepreneurial private sector initiatives

People involved in the running of smaller enterprises generally have to deal with two sets of problems, which hinder their development and prevent them from realizing their growth potentials; management capability is one, and the other is finance. Consequently, countries such as Canada, the U.K., Singapore and France all have their own entrepreneurial initiatives, e.g. programmes designed to strengthen the management capabilities, such as the Enterprise Development, Growth and Expansion program (EDGE) in Singapore, or financial assistance including the Small Business Loans Act in Canada, Loan Guarantee Scheme (LGS) in the U.K., and Société Française de Garantie des Financements des Petites et Moyennes Entreprises (SOFARIS) in France. These are all designed to help small and/or young enterprises to overcome financing difficulties.

As a measure to gradually reduce the government's guarantor's responsibility to the bank, the guarantee's amount assumed by the Canadian government regressed from 100% in 1961 to 85% in 1985. In the U.K. the Loan Guarantee Scheme (LGS) gives the bank a guarantee of 70% (85% in disadvantaged areas). In France, the loan guarantee assumed by the government is generally 50% of the loan, and 70% of the borrowing for start-up of new ventures.

In the U.S., the efforts of the U.S. government have been concentrated on facilitating the development of private equity markets for small and young enterprises. The initiative was in place as early as 1946; the Congress took steps to promote venture capital investments by individuals through the Small Business Investment Companies (SBIC), with subsequent efforts designed to seed for future growth. In the 1970s, through to the 1980s and

1990s, the evolution of the limited partnership in combination with the favorable regulatory and tax changes spurred the flow of capital to the private equity markets.[1]

As a job creation strategy, governments taking an entrepreneurial initiative to assist smaller and younger enterprises with financial assistance is not limited to developed countries. However, financial assistance schemes used by the government to stimulate economic growth and create jobs are not limited to small and young enterprises, often if not always, in the opinion of the public, these are not necessarily entrepreneurial, but questionable practices. For example, in early 2001, Canada's pride, Bombardier, known as a small executive jets builder had reported earnings of $70 million, yet the Government of Canada gave the company a $2 billion loan with much lower than market interest rates, in the name of creating jobs. This has since been seen as a questionable government initiative. Not only is there a question of whether or not an entrepreneurially motivated government initiative is backing the winner in the so-called "free enterprise market economy," but there is also the question of opportunity cost for the billion dollar allocation: how many jobs can Bombardier create with $2 billion as compared to other economic undertakings? Then, Canada became a member of the WTO — such an undertaking would certainly be difficult to justify in the name of "fair trade" practice.

It has to be a standing policy that the government provides R&D grants to private sector enterprises to encourage creative and innovative ventures. In Canada, the Human Resources Development Program and the Technical Assistance Program are designed to facilitate job creations and to assist in R&D undertakings, respectively.

18.5.3 Taxation and government direct subsidies

Taxation as a means of providing incentives for the private sector is a measure commonly used throughout the world. Lower income tax rates for small enterprises, direct subsidies out of rights grant, and interest free

---

[1]Fenn G. W., Liang N. and Prowse, *The Economics of the Private Equity Market, Board of Governors of the Federal Revenue System* (Washington, D.C., 1995).

or lower interest rates to corporations are just some of the government initiatives — both entrepreneurial and questionable. It depends on "what motivates the government to do what and for what purpose." To offer lower interest rates to a company who is already profitable is a questionable undertaking. On the other hand, offering lower tax rates for smaller enterprises encourages them to use tax incentives to build their enterprises in the interest of common economy and for the benefit of the common good. This is thus considered favorable.

In Canada, small enterprises have been offered lower income taxes, from somewhere around 20 to 25%, as compared to normal business income rates of approximately 50% on earnings. However, there is a ceiling for the smaller corporations; if their accumulated earnings exceed $5 million, they are required to pay normal taxes at the same rates as their bigger cousins, the large corporations. The ceiling idea may be a necessity but is also, on the other hand, a questionable policy, since the purpose of giving lower rates is to encourage the business to reinvest its tax savings into the business for growth and expansion. However, as most of us are aware, any expansion needs money, and $5 million accumulated earnings give a favorable margin to a firm to continue with capital investment and to grow, thus more jobs. Why then stop at this point? On the other hand, if there is no ceiling limit, where and when should we stop the lowering of tax rates?

Governments are not considered to be "entrepreneurial," basically because governments are not pro-active entities. They react to the public's need, but the truth is they do not know what the public needs. For example, consumers and voters need a better environment, no traffic congestion and energy-saving alternatives, and a better economic future for their children. At the same time, they also want to have all the luxuries: maybe own a motor boat, speed along the beach fronts, drive bigger cars, fish for sport, etc. What will happen if the government starts to set policies and conducts lunch programs with messages such as:

- We do not want to build anymore highways.
- We do not allow you to use speed boats along beach fronts, because they are the worse polluters.
- We do not allow you to catch fish for fun.

- We will limit the number of cars, the size of the car, and ration gas purchase.
- We will regulate TV programs so the media can only promote common good, rather than promote "Greed."
- We want to limit the size and number of pages of newspaper ads.

If the government was to do as described, how long before there will be chaos. This is not a democracy, but a dictatorship, perhaps even with a dangerous color of "Red." Seriously, who can afford that? But this is what consumers want: a good living environment, no traffic congestion, plenty of resources, and all of which must lead to a better economic future. But, at the same time, they also want every luxury imaginable, for their immediate consumption and enjoyment. What then should the government do? Politicians have a four- or five-year job (if they consider this to be their job) security. Will they risk their "job security" for a future which they will not live to see?

18.5.4 The use of statutory board to oversee common good

The use of statutory boards to oversee market performance by the private sector, and guide consumers' behavior were included in Category 3 of Table 18.1. Some of these government initiatives may be viewed as direct government intervention in the marketplace, such as Canada's Common's Finance Committee created to oversee banking and the insurance business. Nevertheless they are not necessarily entrepreneurial but for the common good.

18.5.5 The use of fiscal measures

Typically, the use of varying interest rate as a policy initiative is also not necessarily entrepreneurial, and generally considered to be used for the control of market performance, through governing money supply · and demand — a measure frequently used by the U.S. Federal Reserve Board and Canada's central bank, the Bank of Canada. As a leading indicator, high interest rates suggest government's intention to stimulate the economy, whereas lower rates intend to control economy overheating and prevent further economic growth towards inflation.

18.5.6 Direct intervention

Stopping Canadian bank merger applications and launching action against Microsoft's monopolistic market behavior are in the intervention category. These too, are actions taken by the government in the interest of the common good, and may also be considered entrepreneurial initiatives.

18.5.7 Tax policy, for the common good or for special interest?

In the market economy and democratic voting process, it is believed that a government is mainly supported by voters who believe that the government will be effective and efficient. The people give the power to the government to levy taxes to be used for the common good. At the regional, provincial and/or municipality, each level of government has its right to levy certain taxes and spend the money collected in accordance with the desire of those who are elected to represent them. In the case of the Canadian governing system, the provincial government collects income taxes (through the federal taxation system) and other taxes such as sales tax, as well as levy users for government services as user's fees, such as through licensing. At the municipal level, the city government has the right to levy property tax and other forms justifiable either as subsidized service (such as public transportation) or no charge services in the interest of common good (such as public security or policing). Although education at the primary and secondary levels have always been the responsibility of the municipality (school boards) it is under the watchdog eyes of the provincial government. Throughout the years, the provincial government had the right to levy income tax from its residents and other tax levy privileges. This policy was set up in the name of promoting the use of the public transit system (both to minimize traffic congestion and encourage environmental friendliness) and caring for the needy. The province had been using some of the tax money collected from tax payers to subsidize those and other socially related initiatives. However, this has recently been changed; instead of assuming those responsibilities, they are now downloaded to the municipality. As a result, in order to maintain the level of services required, the cities would have to seek revenue from the residents, mainly through increasing property tax — in effect to shift the burden to individual home owners. This is how the city government of Toronto, Canada informs its tax payers about the situation:

Downloading: What Is It?

Here are a few simple facts — the Toronto experience

Toronto has been forced to assume financial responsibility for services that used to be paid for by the Province. But we have not been given enough resources to meet those financial responsibilities.

Worse, we cannot do anything about it. Toronto does not have constitutional status. The Province dictates what services we should provide and where your tax dollars should be spent.

Downloading is not just a Toronto problem; it has caused property tax increases all across Ontario. *Elected officials and ordinary citizens from Windsor to Ottawa, Oshawa to North Bay have complained about downloading and its impact on the quality of life in their citizens.*

Public transit
The biggest problem

How does downloading hurt Toronto? The biggest impact comes from the downloading of transit costs. The Toronto Transit Commission (TTC) needs about $400 million a year to purchase and maintain the buses, subway cars and street cars that move more than a million riders a day. Everyone in Ontario reaps the rewards of good public transit. The Province used to pay 75% of the TTC's capital cost and 50% of the TTC's operating costs accordingly.

No more. Not only has Queen's Park (provincial government) stopped subsidizing the TTC, it has also downloaded 50% of GO Transit costs onto Toronto's tax payers — a responsibility that is expected to average an additional $52 million a year over the next five years.

The city simply cannot afford this. Toronto is the only major city in North America that is forced to fund transit exclusively through a combination of property taxes, fare box revenues and borrowed money. The interest on that borrowed money alone increases by more than $55 million a year.

Social housing
$232 million

Social housing provides over 200,000 people with homes in Toronto. This is an important part of our city's social safety net as many residents are provided housing based on their ability to pay.

The Province of Ontario used to be responsible for funding social housing. This is no longer the case. Queen's Park has downloaded its responsibility for social housing onto Toronto tax payers at a cost of $232 million annually. Against its will, the City of Toronto now has administrative, legal and funding responsibilities for over 95,000 social housing units and apartments. We can't afford them. A significant number of the buildings the City inherited from the Province are in need of capital repairs and, as many rents in social housing are geared to the income of residents, it is not possible to increase rents to cover increasing costs.

Bill 140
Hurts Toronto residents

Although downloading is a major problem, it isn't the only one facing Toronto. The Province has taken away the City's ability to increase taxes on commercial and industry property owners through Bill 140 — meaning residential property owners must bear the burden of tax increase without assistance from commercial and industry property owners. Bill 140 limits Toronto's access to its entire tax base, causing any future tax increases to fall only on the residential property owners.

Here is the question: Is the shift of tax burden entrepreneurial or not entrepreneurial?

To subsidize the public transit system, education and certain social services is largely in the interest of the common good. However, the recent provincial government, with a banner of building a health economy through private initiatives (it does sound very much entrepreneurial), advocates and practises privatization, from safety drinking water inspection, road building, to property assessment.

18.6 A Government Entrepreneurial Challenge: A New Model for GNP and GDP for the Nation and the World

The GNP and GDP are about 50 years old, but nothing was changed since the day someone from the United Nations created an accounting model on the basis of calculating a nation's productivity as an indicator for economic growth. As it is an accounting model, it is subject to limitations of accounting capability and governed by accounting postulates. It has no concern for opportunity cost, environmental deterioration, resources drain, and technological change, consequently, it has been quite derisory to measure cost appropriate against revenue, and among other things, the shift in currency value. The 50-year-old model is not new any more. In fact, what this old model gives to the public with respect to a nation's productivity is misleading, and at times even deceiving. What happened in 1997, the currency crisis in Southeast Asia, is a case in point. How can a country like Malaysia, with a promising economic future prior to 1997, with at least an 8% growth rate, plunge into the negative and lose stock values of US$140 billion in a matter of one year? What happened to the GDP and GNP measurements?

It's time for a change, and time to be entrepreneurial. Either throw away the 50-year-model or at least give it an overhaul (but not a new coat of paint). The challenge is in the government. Would any government be willing to take this entrepreneurial challenge?

Questions for discussion

1. The United Nations Human Rights Commission members voted and ousted the U.S. from the Commission, with three Western nations in (Sweden, France and Austria). On account of this, the U.S. House of Representatives voted to block the final overdue payment of its debt in the amount of US$244 million, which was cleared by the Clinton Administration, until such time when the U.S. regains its seat in the Human Rights Commission (*Singapore Sunday Times*, p. 16, 13 May 2001). Is this how democracy works? Discuss.

2. Under the market economy, private enterprises are there essentially for self-interest. In fact, cost saving revenue maximization is the gospel that will help achieve the corporate profit objective. Yet, these undertakings are vital to public interest. Comment!

3. How does a government promote Entrepreneurism without interfering in market operation?

4. It is the opinion of some that politicians are, by and large, a mouthpiece, while the real movers behind the scene are public servants. Therefore, it is these movers who are in the position to promote entrepreneurship. Do you agree?

5. A common complaint relating to government policies is that it has no "profit responsibility." Unfortunately, the profit referred to here is not economic profit or real profit. Under the circumstances, is it still valid to suggest that the government should go with the "trend" of making "surplus" (a term used for the government to reflect their financial gain) as the government's operating objective? On the other hand, no government should generate any surplus, because surplus means that the government must have cheated the tax payers on government services. Do you agree? How should we measure government? Entrepreneurial or not entrepreneurial?

6. In your opinion, how must GDP, GNP be modified to reflect a nation's sustainable economic growth?

Chapter 19

Charitable and Not-for-Profit Organization Entrepreneurship

> The great success of the market economy is that it creates human wants and then fulfills them, thus becoming an instrument of self-justification. It is not clear, however, that it gives us what we need. Different forms of market economy exist. First, we have the market economy of the developed countries, then we have the transition market economy for the developing countries, and the survival market economy for the poverty-stricken nations. Last but not least, is the fourth category, the *benevolent market economy*.

19.1 Introduction

The market economy and capitalism occupy the highest position on the economic altar, and their advocates seem to believe that in them, humanity has found the road to paradise: political democracy to look after the public interest, and the market economy to promote the individual's economic freedom. With money in one hand, and the electoral vote in the other, we have the tools to put the socialist dream into its dark dungeon, but also to call upon the messiah of capitalism, armed with the shield of "profit" and the sword of "ROI." How nice this is. However, market economy or not, things are not always as easy as they appear. Unlike Jesus Christ, this messiah can only reach those who can afford to pay the price. For the others, well, tough luck. They can only afford to live in the sewers, sleep on the sidewalk or on rotten straw, and earn their living by carrying buckets of water. Well, what else can we do? If you are reading this book, then there is a good chance that you form part of the 25% of the world that accounts for 75% of world energy and resources consumption. Or perhaps even the 10% that accounts for 90%. For many of us, the images we are bombarded with, of suffering and hardship, of heartbreak and misery, the things we see on the streets, in the news, and through charity appeals, tug at our heartstrings, and make us want to do something to help. Charitable organizations form the linkage between the haves and the have nots: for those who give, it is an opportunity to express our concern and passion, to those who are at the receiving end, it is an opportunity to survive, even if survival means a continuation of misery. And yet, as Jesus Christ himself said: "The poor will always be with us." It is true that there will always be poor people, just as there will always be the unlucky, the unhealthy and the infirm. Yet what we ask is that there will be a ray of hope for them, a chance to get what you the reader has, so that they can live with dignity, like us.

19.2 The Charitable Organization as Part of the Market Economy

The market economy is based on the exchange system. At the simplest level, it is expressed in the utility function to satisfy human needs, but on a more sophisticated level, it is expressed in the exchange value, or the value something has in exchange for something else that directly satisfies human needs. Charitable works, once the sole preserve of the church and other religious organizations, are now the function of many secular organizations and government bodies which similarly minister to the physical needs of the underprivileged. It seems that the market economy has grabbed every single economic activity under its wing, including charitable works.

Why this growth in charitable work? Is it a better means to care for others? Or is it a better awareness of the troubles of others? Or is it that the market economy has actually increased the need for charitable aid? Or even that it has increased the number of people who simply want it?

On one occasion, the senior author and a friend saw a middle-aged man begging on the street with his child. He was in his 40s, and looked as if he had not had a meal for days. His child was saying to him, almost whispering: "Dad, I'm hungry." The child was obviously undernourished. At least, a few passersby (including the senior author) were moved enough to drop a few coins in their hat. As the two of them left, they began to ask the question of why does the man need to beg? And why do people respond to begging? After all, this incident took place in Canada, a country with an excellent social welfare system. In the end, there seemed to be no answer, except that it is simply a form of market economy. Begging performs a service to the giver as well as the receiver; as humans, we experience empathy with others to a greater or lesser degree, and we all carry emotional burdens resulting from our witness to social injustice. Charity gives us catharsis. Charitable organizations and not-for-profit organizations act in a similar fashion, giving us an outlet for our passions and relief from our emotional burdens.

19.3 Contributions of Charitable Works are Two-Fold

19.3.1 To restore human dignity

Charity is perhaps one of the finest expressions of human dignity. Where once a man cared only for himself, or perhaps his family, and at some point in the development of civilization, his tribe, his city, or his country, here it is expressed as a different thing: the belief that all men are brothers, and all women are sisters, and that it is not acceptable for anyone to die on the ground, for any aged persons to live alone and helpless, waiting for their final days, for children to starve on the streets for the sick or helpless to be unattended, for women to be assaulted or men to be degraded. The basic things that we expect, which we now can say all men expect, and it is through the work of charity that this idea is expressed. Like it or not, the market economy of the first category cannot and will not help the poor helpless souls of the world. On the contrary, more often than not, it is the cause, because "common good" is not a phrase in the Category 1 dictionary. It is all about self-interest. When the market makes its adjustment, there is no rescue for the losers. Relying on the government is also a hopeless dream, and so it is left only to the charitable organizations to bridge the gap. It is the charitable organizations that carry the banner of the Goddess of Mercy to help humanity restore at least in part human dignity, help those who are helpless, and eventually help them to help themselves.

19.3.2 As job providers

As noted from an Organisation for Economic Cooperation and Development (OECD) study, charitable and not-for-profit organizations are important job providers. In 1996, non-profit organizations (including charitable organizations) provided 6.8% of total employment in the U.S., 4.2% in France, 3.7% in Germany, and 3.5% in the U.K. In terms of their operating

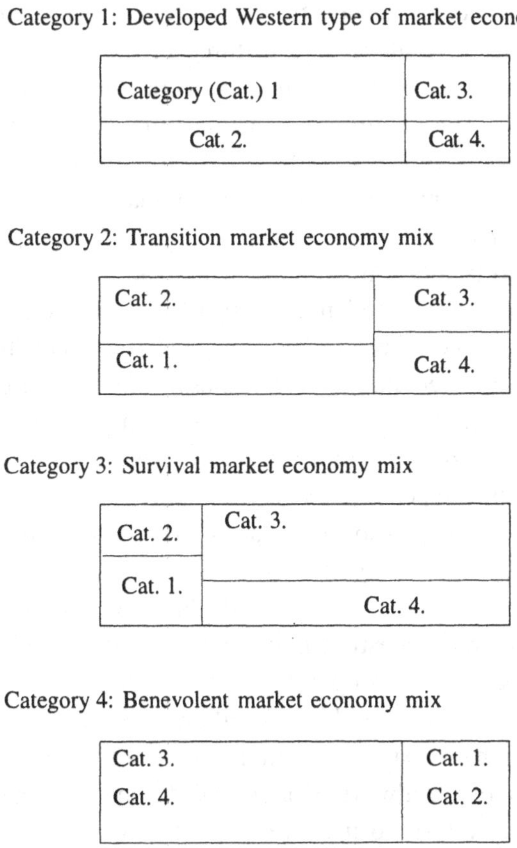

Category 1: Developed Western type of market economy mix

Category (Cat.) 1	Cat. 3.
Cat. 2.	Cat. 4.

Category 2: Transition market economy mix

Cat. 2.	Cat. 3.
Cat. 1.	Cat. 4.

Category 3: Survival market economy mix

Cat. 2.	Cat. 3.
Cat. 1.	Cat. 4.

Category 4: Benevolent market economy mix

Cat. 3.	Cat. 1.
Cat. 4.	Cat. 2.

Note: The above is for illustration purposes only.

Figure 19.1 The scale of market economies.

expenditure, the U.S. ranked first with 6.3% of GDP. Other examples are 4.8% for the U.K., and 4.0% for Sweden. There has been rapid growth in Europe, and the European Commission has a vast horizontally integrated work program, which seeks, among other things, to link local development and employment initiatives to the not-for-profit organizations. Charitable and not-for-profit organizations are an important, large, diverse and economically influential force in our society. Canada is considered to be one of the world richest nations, and even with a total population of under 30 million people, it has more than 76,000 registered charities and approximately 100,000 other non-profit (or not-for-profit) organizations. It is also significant that in Canada, one in three in the nation's population volunteered at least some of their time to work for charities or other organizations in 1997. This represents donating time equivalent to 578,000 full time jobs, approximately 9% of the labor force. They also received over $90.5 billion in revenue, equivalent approximately 12% of Canada's GDP (*http://www.civicus.org*).

Though these efforts are admirable, it would be a mistake to believe that the growth of charitable and not-for-profit organizations reflects the triumph of the market economy. Rather, they are a response to an illness conceived in the market economy — an illness which requires a market adjustment. They are not what we would normally consider to be a traditional value adding process, rather they are a bandage to deep human suffering caused by the imperfections of the market economy. One of the fundamental issues is the question of opportunity considerations: if funds were not spent on dealing with social ills, but redirected into more directly innovative and inventive activities, would this be more beneficial to humanity? A more pointed question is the extent to which the benevolent market economy encourages people to rely on "hand-outs" that erode their entrepreneurial attributes and reduce their self-reliance, rather than encouraging its growth to make them more contributory members of the society. Of course there are always people who do need that helping hand, just as there are many efforts to increase self-reliance rather than give out handouts, but the question of reliance on charity remains a valid one, especially as it plays an increasing and troubling role in the market economy.

19.4 The Growing Pressure for Accountability in Charitable and Mission-Based Not-for-Profit Organizations

In response to upheavals in the world (technological advancement, corporate restructuring, the move to the cities, the aging of the population, the general heartlessness of the "rat race," and the incapacity of the government to look after many unfortunates), individuals and community groups have taken the initiative to form charitable and mission-based not-for-profit organizations (CMBOs) to attend to their needs. Many of these noble initiatives certainly add value to society, but on the other hand, there are also some questions of the extent to which these organizations act in the interest of the common good, and how much is in fact for self-interest. The truth of the matter is, in any situation there is always someone, and often more than one, who will act on their own greed and take advantage of a situation; in this case the target is the wallets of the good-hearted general public. One TV talkshow about charities focused on the question: "Where did the money go?" In one incident that was mentioned, the executive of a CMBO traveled first class and stayed in five-star hotels. Questioned as to why he spent so elaborately, he responded: "The clients I visit are top corporate executives and VIPs. How would they have any confidence in me if I were to portray myself as the same kind of people who are in need of charity?" Similarly, not-for-profit organizations housed in gleaming new buildings of glass and steel, lushly carpeted and well-appointed with all the modern amenities are not the best advertisements for any organization which claims to be devoted to helping the less fortunate. Indeed, the question of "Where did the money go?" is a relevant one. In reaction, there is now a great deal of pressure placed on CMBOs to be customer driven, and morally and fiscally accountable. Meanwhile, decreased government funding and competitions amongst these proliferating bodies has created a survival type market economy, making it necessary for these social enterprises to use the same business practices and level of professionalism found in private "profit" oriented corporations. This has created the irony of CMBOs which exist in the survival market economy but operate in the benevolent market economy.

19.5 Entrepreneurial Culture and CMBOs

19.5.1 Growth and accountability

CMBOs are human institutions, and all human institutions are essentially created for self-interest first and then to add value to society. CMBOs are no different from any other human institution, except that their success should not be measured by their growth. The simple reason is that growth implies more people in need. Ironically, if they are truly successful as a whole, then they will disappear. If we consider the lack of individual self-reliance to be a social illness, then the growth of CMBOs simply suggests the illness is progressing to the advanced stages, which in effect undermines the capability both of the vaunted market economy and the impotence of the government. However, despite the fact that there are increasing numbers of CMBOs, the challenges confronted by these organizations are to serve as many people as possible, to serve them well and for as long as possible. The ways in which to serve however, and the methods to do so have changed dramatically. The pressures on these organizations today are daunting. Costs continue to climb, traditional sources of financial support have become increasingly unstable, the number competing for funds from both private donations and government support has risen dramatically, the ranks of people in need are escalating and the demand for accountability from donors and others are more demanding than ever. For example, the Children's Aid Society has been the center of a scandal in which several children under their care were found to have been abused, in some cases resulting in death (15 March 2001, 6:30 pm news report on the local Toronto Television Station, CFTO). Because these organizations exist in a highly advanced, highly competitive survival market economy, survival itself necessitates innovation and creativity on their part, as they serve the needy and seek funds to support their activities.

19.5.2 Entrepreneurial for their own survival

Living in a market economy, CMBOs must be entrepreneurial in order to survive and serve their causes. For example, the Canadian Cancer Society (CCS) was founded in 1938 with the mandate to search for all possible means to eradicate cancer and enhance the quality of life of people living with cancer. Despite the fact that CCS is a charitable organization, it is still competitive by nature. It competes in its pursuit of funding and sponsorship by large corporations. It also competes with people's other time commitments by asking people to volunteer their time to work for the society. Obviously, the one more touched by the situation is more likely one is to give up his/her time to volunteer or to donate money to a cause, and so publicity of the right kind becomes very important. The CCS's solution to this has been to build close ties with a single large, corporate sponsor, the Canadian Imperial Bank of Commerce (CIBC). This high profile involvement benefits both the CCS, by giving them the clout of one of the biggest banks in Canada, and the CIBC by giving them a no-lose boost to their image. The prime relationship that links with this profit pursued banking institution is the "CIBC run for the CURE." This is the largest fund raising event for breast cancer research, education, diagnosis and treatment in Canada. This event is sponsored, organized and managed by CIBC (*http://www.cancer.ca/gen/missione.htm*). Of course, there are other examples of crossovers between the Category 1 market economy and the benevolent market economy.

19.6 The Social Enterprises

CMBOs operate under a variety of guises as social enterprises (i.e. improving the lot of individuals in society). They are usually reliant on government support, but at the same time they act in the competitive economy in a number of very different ways:

(1) Activating hitherto unused or under-used material and conceptual resources, they generate new skills and new jobs.

The growth of large corporate-like CMBOs has been coupled with the development of new mini CMBO enterprises. These enterprises are often initiated and managed by people coming from the survival market economy environment. They, themselves are seeking the means to be self-reliant, while at the same time recognizing a social need. These need driven "social entrepreneurs" make a living for themselves while at the same time helping others. For example, there are enterprises that adopt the reuse, recycle and repair philosophy to take underused, discarded materials such as clothing and home furnishings, refurbish and resell them to people at a price well below the retail value of the items when new. Thus, they prevent waste and also provide a service to the less fortunate. They collect their "inventory" from households and use a simple market strategy of cold calls and personal visits. An important part of the business is the ability to provide official receipts for charitable donations. First, it legitimizes the organization, and second, in many countries the official receipt can be use to claim income tax deductions.

(2) Create new and high quality services at prices affordable to as wide a section of the community as possible.

This group of social enterprises originated from a relatively small number of CMBOs that have grown as a result of demand from contributors and those who require assistance. These organizations evolve through alliances with similar organizations to form network links, much the same as other businesses form business associations. One example is Goodwill Industries (GWI), which runs retail stores just like any other clothing stores. Clothes are collected from donors, cleaned, repaired and refurbished then sorted and put on display.

Formalized as a social enterprise entity, GWI funds their mission by collecting donated clothing and household goods, and then selling these items in more than 1700 retail stores throughout North America. It has 38 international associate members in 27 countries.

As an innovative strategy, both to sustain the organization and attempt to optimize the opportunity, rather than directly giving money to the needy, GWI uses the funds generated from retail sales to set up training programs to train individuals who are able, but not properly prepared for the job market. As a social enterprise, GWI is in its own way, an entrepreneurial social enterprise that builds on its ability to blend business and human development disciplines.

(3) Fostering local development by pooling information, skills and financial resources through formal or informal networks of affiliated organizations with the help of community support and, in particular, large corporate entities.

The United Way organization provides assistance to individuals on a worldwide scale. It was formed in Denver, Colorado in 1887. In Canada, the United Way funds more than 4300 agencies/programs and has directed gifts to more than 10,000 organizations. Individual United Way agencies are independent from other agencies. As a social enterprise, the United Way provides assistance for numerous services that will assist communities throughout the world. It seeks out information on the various groups and the threats associated with the group's existence. The knowledge retrieval and utilization assists the United Way in deciding upon the appropriate amount of aid necessary to help particular groups.

Self-fulfilment occurs for both the individuals within the United Way and the donors to the cause. The gratification felt by the donors of the funds helps them to meet their basic self-actualization needs. This is alluded to in the mission statement of the United Way: "To promote the organized capacity of people to care for one another." Its creativity creates wealth for individuals involved in the process and adds value to society, as reflected in the organized support drive. Private individuals play a major role in helping the United Way fulfil its mandate. Individuals are recruited from major corporate entities to target their fellow employees. In this way, United Way operates in multiple niches, targeting the workers of the company to raise funds. Moreover, it is also at the forefront of a technological advance in fund-raising through electronic pledges. An electronic pledge will simplify the whole process of raising funds, making donations and the whole accounting process.

Apart from the growing societal need for charitable and mission-based organizations to fill the gap created by the market economy, large organizations are not alone in serving the Goddess of Mercy. For people living in poverty or even possibly at the edge of survival, the market economy often seeks and sometimes finds solutions both for themselves and for others.

Social enterprise is a phrase suited to our times. It combines the passion of a social mission with an image of business-like discipline, innovation and determination commonly associated with the business pioneers, and the time is certainly ripe for an entrepreneurial approach to today's social enterprises. For charities, wealth is not just to show a "surplus" for stake-holders or as a measure of value creation (as is generally used in business), it is also a means to an end for charities. Social enterprises are looking for long term social returns, and an entrepreneurial, value driven, knowledge based approach[1] may be part of the answer to the illness problems of our society.

19.7 An Entrepreneurial Approach to Reaching Clients

In essence, a properly created and managed CMBO should be entre-preneurial, because the idea of serving the needy is creative in itself. However, the creative idea of a benefit to society and the individuals involved is not necessarily an easy task in the developed Western market economy, because their services confront two issues. One of the services is to draw resources from others; donations and contributions and other services are to "give," in most cases, to the needy and find those who are in need. For example, the primary objective of the "Rape Crisis Center" is to help victims of sexual assault with handling the various issues they face after the experience, yet by and large, victims of sexual violence are usually unwilling to be in the public eye. Therefore, promoting the services available and encouraging the victims to come out for the service is not an easy task. Advertising campaigns have to be especially eye-catching since there is little opportunity for word of mouth to spread the message. For example, a shocking photograph of a victim and a slogan such as:

We are open 24 hours a day. Rape can happen anytime.

This can catch people's attention, and hopefully stay in their minds for when they or someone they know might need the service.

---

[1]Creation, innovation, wealth and value, meaning wealth for the individual and value added to society.

Organizations such as World Vision, and the Christian Fund for Children typically have impressive advertising messages televised on the TV networks, consisting of moving messages supported by a visual heartrending presentations.

19.8 Charitable and Mission-Based Social Enterprises are Here to Stay

As part of human economic activities, social enterprises and their charitable works will be with us as long as the market economy is here, and that looks to be a very long time. As long as the market economy dominates our life, there will always be winners, and therefore there will always be losers, those who are unable to cope with the market economy's merciless ways. The "market," "government," "labor unions" and "charitable and mission-based organizations" are all parts of this society of ours; just like one very big family, even though sometimes we are more like the Mafia than the Waltons of television fantasy.

Managing a CMBO is not easy, As one charity worker said: "We looked very welcoming with big smiles all the time, but life is never easy on anybody, and particularly on us. At times when we stand next to a person or a group of people in need, I really want to have a good cry, but there is nowhere I can cover my face. Hold back my tears, do what I can do to attend to their needs. But the task never ends. Unlike other enterprises, social enterprises have to find ways to generate funds to meet "not our needs," but the needs of others. How I am supposed to describe the plight of hungry children crying for food, shivering in the bitter cold at a street corner? Can the rich and famous understand that after I save a nine-year-old boy from hanging himself, he said to me: "Let me die, I have nothing to live for, my life is worse than a rat's?" Yet, I had to move on. I have my own worries. Money? I have no magic without money.

The challenges facing CMBOs are ever-increasing. Costs are escalating, resources diminishing, the competition for such resources increasing and people in need are increasing almost at a compound rate. Technology brings wealth to a few, according to a recent report from the televised news.[2] The bottom 20% of people living (or surviving) below the poverty line in

Canada have seen no changes to their situation in the past two decades. What has technology done for them? The market economy has brought glory for a few, and misery to who knows how many?

If it is the market economy that has created the social illness, or the cracks in society, then who is it up to, to fill the cracks? There is no evidence that the governments will fulfill this role, nor labor unions, and certainly it does not seem to be the corporations. In our minds, and the minds of many others, it is the CMBOs that have been entrusted with this mission. Can they do it?

In Europe, a wave of new financing organizations has emerged. The International Association of Investors in the Social Economy (INAISE) network is supposed to meet the challenge of financing social enterprises. Will something similar emerge in North America, Association of Southeast Asia Nations (ASEAN), China and elsewhere? Perhaps some countries just do not have such a thing as a benevolent market economy.

In principle, any charitable or mission-based not-for-profit organization must operate at the breakeven point. If it has a surplus this means they are cheating on their services; if they have a deficit, this means that they are inefficient.

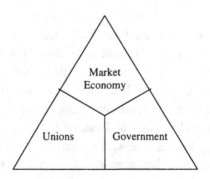

Figure 19.2 The ideal market economy: no cracks — the perfect triangle.

---

[2]*CTV National News*, broadcast in Canada, 17 March 2001.

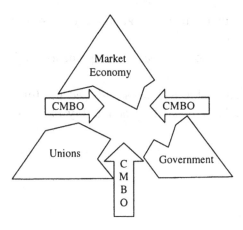

Figure 19.3 The cracks in the market economy and position of charitable and mission based organizations (CMBOs).

Questions for discussion

1. Should the government provide financial assistance to charitable organizations such as grants and low interest loans for special purposes, so the society can narrow its gap between those acting for self-interest and the need to serve causes of the common good?
2. Recall the CMBO executive, who was found to be living the high life on company funds (first class travel, five-star hotels), interviewed on the TV talkshow. Recall also his justification, saying that he could not meet up with top executives and VIPs without emulating their lifestyle. Discuss.
3. Four key words contained in the definition of entrepreneurship are creation, innovation, wealth and value. Apply these to a CMBO, and draft a mission statement for the organization.
4. Based on an OECD study, there is an increasing number of CMBOs. Some of these organizations also grow in size to become something like large corporate entities. Assume these organizations are here because of societal need. How would they contribute to GDP? More

importantly, do their creative and innovative initiatives make a better society for all of us?

5. In your opinion, who are social entrepreneurs? What is social entrepreneurship?

6. To whom are charitable and mission-based not-for-profit organizations accountable to? How is such accountability measured?

Chapter 20

Conclusion: A Model of Gross Planet Productivity

> With finite resources on earth, humanity can only be sustainable if we continue with the pursuit of innovation and creative activities, and not merely for self-interest. For without the presence of the common good, self-interest alone can sustain nothing.

20.1 The Introduction to the Conclusion

This conclusion feels like the end of the sowing of seeds with hope that some will take root, germinate, sprout and exponentially grow to enhance ideas of entrepreneurial thoughts. It is intended that the idea to create and innovate, would not merely be for self-interest, but for the common good as well. Self-interest is the motivation we need to create and innovate, but it is the common good that gives us civilization, and economical sustainability is needed for humanity to survive on this planet. Although obstacles for economical sustainability are many, some of them we may not even be able to identify, they are all rooted in the ignorance of the nature of "profit." The way we determine "profit" is what has led us to cause impairment of Earth capital, unnecessary abuse and waste of resources, as well as the sacrifice of people, and worse, the life support system of the future.

21.2 The Life Support System on Earth is on Its 29th Day of 30 Days in the Water Lily Pond

There is an illustration projected in the senior author's early publication, based on the foreword in Clifton and Turner (1990), which suggests that our life support system is on its 29th day of its 30 days in the water lily pond, which means that unless we realize fully the unfortunate impending reality will come to us sooner than we might imagine.

If a lily pond contains a single leaf on the 1st day and every day the number of leaves doubles, when is the pond half full, if it is completely full in 30 days? The answer is the 29th day.[1]

Where are we now? Are we on the 29th day, the day before, or the day after? It cannot be the day after, because the 30th day is the end of it all. Perhaps we are still on the 29th day or the day before, but indications are clear that we are just about running out of petroleum reserves, have polluted countless lakes and rivers and have cleared out almost unimaginable numbers of forests. Worst of all, our automakers, in the name of employment and the economy have not shown any signs of slowing down their production. Many more new and bigger cars are being churned out like the spring run of salmon up a narrow stream; it is not so much a matter of low or high fuel consumption, but it is the total consumption that is of concern. Sure enough, petroleum companies are engaging R&D to search for new sources of energy. For example, Shell Petroleum Co. claims that through their efforts in research and development, they are committed "to making renewable energy commercially viable. In Uruguay, we're exploring the great potential of 'biomass' energy from fast growing plants that can be turned into fuel in Peru."[2] But there is no sign that car makers have in any way attempted to coordinate new energy search efforts by developing technology that will replace the internal combustion engine with cleaner alternatives.

The potential sacrifice of what is considered "profit" or "ROI" is what makes the powerful corporate giants unwilling to do the right thing. Of course, there is always the usual claim about employment and difficulty to make adjustments since it is too involved. However, with the clear sign that cheaper cars will soon be on the road, the car makers seem to have settled their minds on making the driving and owning of cars affordable, so what else can be said?

---

[1]See Kao R. W. Y., *Entrepreneurship, A Wealth Creation and Value Adding Process* (Prentice-Hall, Singapore, 1993), p. 120.
[2]*National Geographic*, inside front cover and the first page ad., 198/2 August 2000.

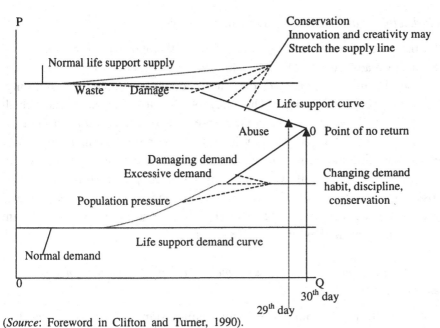

P

Conservation
Innovation and creativity may
Stretch the supply line

Normal life support supply

Waste   Damage

Life support curve

Abuse

0   Point of no return

Damaging demand
Excessive demand

Changing demand
habit, discipline,
conservation

Population pressure

Life support demand curve

Normal demand

0

Q

30th day

29th day

(*Source*: Foreword in Clifton and Turner, 1990).

Figure 20.1 Graphic expression, life support system

20.3 The Encouraging Signs of Restraint and Realization

The Earth Charter

Figure 20.1 lists six of the causes for excess demand or a decrease in supply. It was published just over a decade ago, and during the past 12 years some changes have been made, and progress has been seen with respect to environmental care. In particular, the Earth Council proposed the recognition of the Rights of Earth, or "The Earth Charter." Presented by the President of Costa Rica, it is hoped that the Charter, subtitled "Values and Principles for a Sustainable Future," will be adopted by the United Nations as a commandment for us to take care of the planet earth.[3]

---

[3]The senior author attended the presentation ceremony in Costa Rica, 7 November 2000. Maurice Armstrong of Canada shared the podium with Costa Rica's President.

Self-discipline and monitored population growth

The pressure of population growth, while still important, is beginning to decline. Already growth of the wealthy Western European nations is being sustained by immigration, with the native populations either growing only slightly or slowly declining. This may be due to changes in individual perception of lifestyle, or government pressure (such as found in China). Certainly one no longer sees families of 12 anymore. By and large, two seems more like the norm. In China, it is a state policy that only one child per married couple is allowed, and only those couples in rural areas and those belonging to racial minorities may have more than one. They hardly ever have three. Moreover, the state also made it a law that a couple can only get married if they are over 18 years of age.

To protect, conserve, reduce waste and 3 "R" pledge culture of the general public

Travelling in rural China, there are visible signs everywhere, worded simple enough to understand: "Managing the economy is the business of the government, but taking care of the environment is on us." In fact, to protect, conserve, reduce waste and "recycle, reuse and repair," have gradually penetrated into the minds of people and has virtually become a culture for living, even though there is still much to be improved. The unfortunate part of this culture is that it has not yet surpassed the continuing waste and over consumption and abuse of resources due to corporate entities pushing and overselling through skillful promotion and advertising, that has led consumers to want more than what they need. The rapid accumulation of garbage in major cities is a transparent indicator of this trend. There is also a sad reality that some developing countries in need of "hard cash," open their doors widely to attract investors into their countries. Opportunists then seize the opportunity to grab whatever they can with no regard for their people and the environment.

The corporate response

There are always two sides of a coin; in the business world, there are people who care, have passion for their business, people and the environment, and there are also those who have total disregard for humanity, who don't give a damn about anything apart from profit, ROI or money. However, there are corporations that are committed to the care of the environment and people; this includes Home Depot, the largest home needs supplier in North America, and 3M, a company known for its innovative and environmentally responsible approach. For example, here is how Home Depot commits itself.

Home Depot: The company uses the following as its operational guide.

> One of Home Depot's core values is "Doing the Right Thing." As an extension of our values, our actions must help sustain the environment and strengthen our business. We must face environmental issues today, so that we can help ensure that the world is a "greener" place for future generations.

Accordingly, the company takes the following actions:

(1) Home Depot will give preference to the purchase of wood and wood products originating from certified, well-managed forests wherever feasible.

(2) Home Depot will eliminate the purchase of wood and wood products from endangered regions around the world by year-end 2002, unless certified.

(3) Home Depot will promote the efficient and responsible use of wood and wood products.

(4) Home Depot will promote and support the development and use of alternative environmental products.

Home Depot also informs the public that the company recycles 113,334 tons of cardboard and paper a year which translates into 1,926,678 trees, 45,333,600 gallons of fuel (manufacturing process) or 12,466,740 cubic feet displacement in landfills.[4]

---

[4]Home Bloom into Spring catalogue 2001 p. 3.

3M: 3M integrates vision into strategy by adopting what is called "Strategies for continuing improvement, idea into reality," these are:

(1) Continue improving compliance assurance systems to meet and exceed government and 3M standards.
(2) Maintain emphasis on Life Cycle Management, considering environmental, health and safety opportunities and issues for all stages of a product's life cycle, from development and manufacturing to customer use and final disposal.
(3) Meet 3M's aggressive goals for environment, health and safety and move as close to zero as possible for environmental releases, injuries and illnesses.[5]

Of course, there are other companies worldwide who are responsible corporate citizens that think about more in the corporate life than just ROI. There are definitely more to strive in addition to the conventional idea of "profit."

20.4 The Focus is on "Entrepreneurship" and "Fish Responsibly"

When the definition of "Entrepreneurship" was published in 1993, there were comments that it was too broad, but nonetheless it was subsequently adopted by the International Small Business Congress held in Jakarta in 1994 as the official definition for the Congress. Recently (in 2001), one of the discussants in a Corporate Entrepreneurship seminar, Dave Manning, imparted his views on the following:

> "These definitions struck me as very broad the first time I read them, perhaps too broad. However, the more thought I put into them, the more I really begin to understand their depth and the reasons for the breadth. These definitions can only be practised if there are the associated attitude changes, for the changes in attitude are the core of the definition. These definitions expand the limits of entrepreneurship

---

[5]*http://www.3m.com/profile/careers/working/html*

> and causes one to take a profound look at their places in society.
> Most overwhelmingly, through your definition of entrepreneurship,
> everyone can participate not only economically, but also socially."
>
> Dave Manning, Eng., M.B.A.

As an ideology, the broad definition of entrepreneurship is intended to be considered as an alternative to the two extremes in our time; socialism or communism on the left, and capitalism on the right. It consists of three subdefinitions.

(1) "Entrepreneurship" is the process of doing something new (creative) and something different (innovative) for the purpose of creating wealth for the individual and adding value to society.

(2) An entrepreneur is a person who undertakes a wealth creation and value adding process through incubating ideas, assembling resources and making things happen.

(3) Entrepreneurs are individuals or groups who engage in economic activities for the purpose of creating wealth responsibly for self-interest and add value to the society.

If sustainability is our life, then we must continue to create and innovate for self-interest and to add value to society. Entrepreneurial activities must be the cultural food for the individual; as a force of motivation, it must have broad applications. In essence "entrepreneurship" is property of ten words: Innovate, Create, Wealth for the Individual and Value for Society.

20.5 Where Do We Go From Here?[6]

Broadly, as we see it, there are seven areas of challenge that we should address, rooted in entrepreneurial drive, plus six guiding principles, including:

---

[6]Dennis Tito made history by being the first human tourist to fly into space (price ticket for the trip was $20 million). Profit-minded people may think of selling insurance for travelers to space within the foreseeable future. In any case, if the Americans don't, the Russians would (20 April 2000, *CNN 16:00 news*).

The root:

To instil value driven, knowledge-based entrepreneurial culture and develop entrepreneurial attributes that will allow individuals in every sector of the economy to pursue creative and innovative activities for self-interest and common good.

The guiding principles for strategic actions:

    (1) To use clean technology for all innovation and creative activities.
    (2) To observe and assist wherever we can for nature to regenerate itself.
    (3) To remove any unfavorable measures taken by humans that will affect environmental health.
    (4) To educate and make learning possible — anything matters to pollution prevention.
    (5) To protect life support systems for future generations.
    (6) To develop entrepreneurial attributes where possible in all segments of society.

Guiding principles for our commitment with respect to the rights of the earth:

In addition, there are at least four strategically important measures which can be integrated into the system that would allow better information for decision-makers, in particular those in corporate entities having the responsibility of allocating finite resources and interacting with people, and are in contact with the natural environment. They are: (1) Revamp GDP and GNP, (2) Institute compulsory full disclosure of corporate environmental responsibility, in corporate reporting, (3) Adopt "Residual" concept for corporate accountability, and last, but not least, (4) Creation of a Gross Planet Productivity (GPP), and use the model to measure our economic performance against the planet productivity of natural resources available to us.

(1) Revamp the GDP and GNP models currently in use
Re-formulate the GDP and GNP models, to include nature's contribution to productivity, and depletion of finite resources, as the present model used

to derive at a nation's GNP (and GDP) is essentially an accounting process with no regard to environmental health and finite resources utilization. What we claim as GNP may in fact be a declaration of destruction of the environment and depletion of finite resources — which means the higher the GNP, the greater the destruction to the environment.

As declared by 12 organizations that participated in a seminar on the cost of the ecosystem, the identified 17 services provided by the ecosystem was estimated in the amount of approximately US$33 trillion on average.[7] This does not include other resources outside of the ecosystem. The new GNP model must consider environmental factors and the use of the resources as well as the waste.

(2) *Make full disclosure for environmental responsibility compulsory for corporate reporting*

Stock exchange commissions throughout the world require that all corporate entities listed with the exchange fully disclose their environmental responsibility, including measures for caring of people and resource usage.

(3) *Adopt "Residual" to replace accounting profit or financial income*

Formally adopt "Residual" as a viable concept, and further reconcile the difference between accounting profit and economic profit leading to the recognition of economic value and contribution of business activities.

(4) *Create a Gross Earth Planet Product (GPP) model*

The simplest and most ideal way to explain a model of GPP or Gross Planet Product is that the GPP should be equal to the sum of all nations' GNP or Global GNP. Consequently, in accordance with the Baltimore study reported by *Nature*,[8] Global GNP is in debt of US$15 trillion annually, therefore, measured by total input against total output, the GPP would have to include all contributions taken from the planet. This will include:

---

[7]*Nature*, Vol. 387, May 1997, p. 254.
[8]*Ibid.*

   (a) Seventeen identifiable ecosystem services (Ecs), plus
   (b) Depletion of non-renewable resources, including petroleum deposits, basic mineral substances such as iron, silver, nickel and others (Nr), and the ozone layer, plus
   (c) Lost utility function of earth substance, including forest, alternative land use, among other things, polluted rivers, lakes and loss of coral reef (Elu).

Where

$$GPC = A + b + c,$$

or Gross Planet Contribution to all human economic activities.

    Therefore, to attain a natural equilibrium for human economic activities, the GPP can be defined as:

> Gross Planet Product
>   = Global Gross National Product
>   + Depletion of non-renewable natural resources
>   + Lost of partial planet utility function of earth substances
>   + US\$17 trillion

or,

$$GPP = Global\ GNP + Nr + Elu + US\$17\ trillion.$$

In order for us to improve our performance, to attain equilibrium, we would have to continue pursuing innovation and creativity to increase Global GNP, which appears to be impossible at least at the present time, or reduce:

The depletion of non-renewable resources to 0	(Nr = 0),
The loss of utility function of earth substances to 0	(Elu = 0),
Plus elimination ecosystem deficit equivalent of	US\$15 trillion

Therefore, if we are to look at our human economic activities closely, we are in fact living our life in debt to the planet. Then where does "profit" come from?

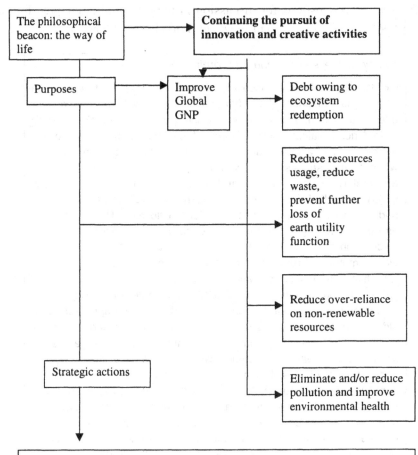

Figure 20.1 Entrepreneurism: the philosophy, economic and social value of entrepreneurship.

There are no questions for discussion in this concluding chapter, but let us go back to the little orphan elephant story from Chapter 5:

Revisiting the story of the little orphan elephant

On 12 May 2001, the Discovery channel televised a story about a little orphan elephant (hereafter named "he"), who lost his mother after birth, but had a strong will to live. He wandered alone in the wide African plains, a little orphan refugee frantically looking for his mother (maybe also the father) — walking and calling for his parents without any success. He was completely exhausted and was desperately in need of milk and shelter from the sweltering heat. When he finally found a herd of elephants, he went towards a female and attempted to reach her breast for a little milk. The adult threw him out of her sight, but he approached the group once more, only to come into contact with a male's private parts whom he thought was a mother's breast. The male adult used his powerful trunk to toss him like a saucer away from the group. He got up in pain, struggled and regained his balance, and continued, dragging his small body on the endless burning ground, finally he approached an old tree where he rubbed his body on the bark thinking it was his mother's leg. The disappointment did not kill his courage, as he continued his search for anyone who would give a little shade or spare a drop of milk. His need for food and shelter drove him to continue wandering under the scorching sun, the possible source of relief or the only means that can help to give him just a little more strength to continue, unfortunately failed. There seemed very little chance that he will receive any mercy from anyone. He grew weaker and weaker, but he continued calling for help. His efforts were in vain and all seemed hopeless.

Finally, he came to a pond of mud water where there was a large number of elephants. He approached them, but was trampled, kicked and thrown away, as expected. On land again, he persisted, and met a group of young ones like him, but they are the children of a herd of matured elephants. These adults protect and care only for their young ones, and he was once again kicked out of their group.

It seemed that the orphan elephant cannot accept the reality that he will not get any help or relief from anyone. But he continued in his struggle and search for his "family." He found a large group of adults whom he thought would help. But, when he tried to get close, they not only rejected him, they turned violent against him. However, the little orphan did not lose hope, in his mind, he believes that there was a "Goddess of Mercy." Alas, instead of mercy, he encountered danger in the form of vicious hyenas. The little orphan sensed the danger and tried to escape, but failed. The hyenas caught him, one of them used its sharp teeth to cut into his little trunk: As he struggled, the others tore apart his legs, and the whole gang then moved in for the kill. The little orphan elephant soon died, his body completely mutilated by his killers.

Our market economy and democratic process have left many little orphans out in the big wide "jungle," but going nowhere through no fault of their own. We might learn from the elephant story, making an effort to try to be better than adult elephants, sharing a little shade and sparing a little hope to those who cannot help themselves. We must accept our role as stewards of this planet, not the owners, since the helpless and the unfortunate little orphan elephants are also part of this world. With finite resources, the rich and wealthy didn't fall from the sky, they must have acquired their wealth from somewhere. Sure enough, in fact elephants in nature take care of their own offspring but only their own. On the other hand, we are not elephants, but humans; does this not speak for itself?

The little elephant story presented here and in Chapter 5 is not a plea for charity, but a sensible decision for us to assume our stewardship responsibility.

We must be aware that the market economy has no direct affiliation with democracy, but is a vehicle to facilitate the movement of resources. It is a beautiful dream of the World Trade Organization to advocate free trade among nations. However, without free movement of labor, free trade only facilitates accumulation of wealth for the rich and therefore contributes to a greater "poor." It cannot fulfill the dream of economic democracy globally. Political economic fairness will make this world a better place for human beings and other living beings so we can live as it should be. The market economy can only be of benefit to humanity if we observe the simple wisdom mentioned earlier in this book:

> *In case of oxygen loss in the cabin, an air mask will drop in front of you. Put the mask on yourself, and assist the person next to you who may need help.*

Make no mistake, even if the market economy alone does not turn human beings into hyenas, it certainly creates more little orphan elephants, and it only makes it possible for the hyenas to have an even greater feast. If government intervention inhibits the spirit of enterprising whereas enterprising is the foundation of market economy, Entrepreneurism is still our alternative to the extremes. But entrepreneurship cannot be simply creating an enterprise and/or economic endeavor for self-interest; it has to add value to society and more broadly for the common good.

Postscript: The Search for Answers

> *In memory of those who lost their lives to terrorists in the U.S. (11 September 2001). The victims of this inhuman act will never know the cause of their death.*

The subheading of a CNN 13 September 2001 news telecast —: "**America Under Attack**" — was flashed on TV throughout the day, it read: "**The Search for Answers**."

> "Unknown enemies waged war against the United States yesterday, killing thousands, quite possibly tens of thousands of people, sparking unprecedented fear and calls for revenge."
>
> *Toronto Star*, A1 2001, 09 12

> "A nation's confidence is among the casualties after unspeakable bloody attacks on the proudest symbols of U.S. power (piteously vulnerable to the whims of madmen)."
>
> Rosie DiManno, *Toronto Star*, B1 2001, 09 12

The First War of the 21st Century (President George W. Bush (13 September 2001); **America's New War** with a subheading: **Why America is Hated** (*CNN*, 14 September 2001)

We share the sorrow, fear and sadness of the American people, in particular, those who have lost their loved ones. We are touched and moved as witnesses through our TV screens, watching those who held up pictures of their loved ones, while standing in front of the collapsed buildings and hoping for miracles. But more so, we are deeply troubled and wonder how those, who have so innocently lost their lives in the tragedy, will ever know the cause of their deaths. Will they ever be able to rest in peace?

What has caused this tragedy? While CNN calls for "**The Search for Answers**," as the living, can we ever really know?

References

Adler A. *Understanding Human Nature* (Premier Books, New York, 1959).

Alcorn P. B. *Success and Survival in the Family-Owned Firm* (McGraw-Hill, New York, 1982).

Alkhafaji A. P. *A Stakeholder Approach to Corporate Governance: Managing Dynamic Environment* (Quorum Books, New York, 1989).

American Accounting Association. *Committee to Prepare A Statement of Basic Accounting Theory* (American Accounting Association, Chicago, 1966).

Aoki M. and Kim H. K. *Corporate Governance in Transitional Economics: Insider Control and the Role of Banks* (World Bank, Washington, DC, 1955).

Archia M. and Tropp S. (eds.) *Environmental Management: Issue and Solutions* (John Wiley, New York, 1995).

Babbage C. *On the Economy of Machinery and Manufactures* (Charles Knight, London, 1932), reprinted by Augustus M. Kelley, New York.

Baumol W. J. *Entrepreneurship, Management and the Structure of Payoffs* (Massachusetts Institute of Technology, Massachusetts, 1993).

Berkhof L. *The Doctrine of the Decrees in Theology* (The Banner of Truth Trust, London, 1958).

Birch D. *Job Creation in America* (Free Press, New York, 1982).

Birley S. "Succession in the Family Firm: The Inheritor's View," *Journal of Small Business Management.*

Blair M. M. *Ownership and Control, Rethinking Corporate Governance for the 21st Century* (Brookings Institute, Washington, DC, 1995).

Brown H., Bonner J. and Weir J. *The Next Hundred Years* (Viking Press, New York, 1958).

Bruges J. *The Little Earth Book*, 2nd ed. (Alastair Sawday Publishing, Bristol, U.K., 2001).

Bruton G. D., Keels J. K. and Scifres E. L. *Corporate Entrepreneurship versus Financially Driven Buyouts, Indications for Restructuring and Performance Century* (1998).

Chell, Haworth and Brearly. *The Entrepreneurial Personality, Cases and Categories* (Routledge, London, 1991).

Chichilnisky G. "The Economic Value of the World's Resources," in *Trends in Ecology and Evolution*, Vol. 11 (Elsevier, 1996), pp. 135–140.

Churchill W. C. and Hatten K. J. "Non-Market-Based Transfers of Wealth and Power: A Research Framework for Family Business," *Family Business Review*, Vol. 10, No. a (Spring, 1997).

Clifton C. and Turner T. *Wild by Law* (Sierra Club Books, San Francisco, 1990).

Costanza R. *et al.* "The Value of the World's Ecosystem Services and Natural Capital," *Nature*, Vol. 387, pp. 253–260 (May 1997).

D'Arge R. C. and Kneese A. V. "Environmental Quality and International Trade," *International Organization*, Vol. 26, No. 2 (1972).

Dacin M., Beal B. D. and Ventressc M. J. "The Embeddedness of Organizations," *Journal of Management*, Vol. 25, No. 3 (1999).

Danco L. A. *Inside the Family Business* (The University Press, Cleveland, Ohio, 1980).

Dawkins R. *The Selfish Gene*, 2nd ed. (Oxford University Press, 1989).

Dearden A. and Vancil. *Management Control Systems* (Richard D. Irwin, Homewood, IL, 1972).

Dunkheim E. *The Elementary Forms of the Religious Life* (Free Press, New York, 1995).

European Commission. *Green Paper on Innovation, Bulletin of the European Union* (Supplement 5/95, Brussels, 1995).

European Venture Capital Association. *A Survey of Venture Capital and Private Equity in Europe* (1997 Yearbook, Zaventen, Belgium).

Flood R. L. "Entrepreneurship, Intrapreneurship and Innovativeness," *Entrepreneurship, Innovation and Change*, Vol. 1, No. 1 (Plenum Press, 1992).

Fock S. T. "The Impact of Family Conflicts on the Development of Chinese Entrepreneurially Managed Family Business: The Yeo Hiap Seng Case in Singapore," *Journal of Small Business and Entrepreneurship*, Vol. 15, No. 2 (1998).

Francis B. C. "Family Business Succession Planning," *Journal of Accountancy* (August, 1993).

Frederick W, "The Next Step in Management Science. A General Theory," *Journal of the Academy of Management*, Vol. 6, No. 3 (1963).

Freedman M. *Capitalism and Freedom* (University of Chicago Press, Chicago, 1962).

Fritz B. *The Race in the Year 2000* (Doubleday, New York, 1962).

Fukuyama F. *Trust. The Social Virtues and the Creation of Prosperity* (The Free Press, New York, 1995).

Gersick K. E., Davis J. A., Hampton M. M. and Lansberg I. *Generation to Generation: Life Cycles of the Family Business* (Harvard University Press, Boston, 1997).

Gibb A. A. "Education for Enterprise: Training for Small Business Initiation-Some Contrasts," *Journal of Small Business and Entrepreneurship*, Vol. 4, No. 3 (1986/87).

Giddens A. *Capitalism and Modern Social Theory* (Cambridge University Press, Cambridge, 1992).

Gough L. *Asia Meltdown, The End of the Miracle* (Capstone, Oxford, 1998).

Grady P. *Inventory of Generally Acceptable Accounting Principles for Business Enterprises* (American Institution of Certified Public Accountants Inc., New York, 1965).

Grahm K. K. *Karl Marx: Our Contemporary Social Theory for a Post-Leninist World* (Harvester, Whitest, New York, 1992).

Grandori A. (ed.) *Interfirm Networks: Organization and Industrial Competitiveness* (Routledge, London, 1999).

Greiner L. E. "Evolution and Revolution as Organizations Grow," *Harvard Business Review*, Vol. 50 (1972).

Griffiths A. *Small and Medium Enterprises and Structural Change in the 1980's: The Case of Japan's Manufacturing Industry*, The Study of Business and Industry, No. 6 (The Research Institute of Commerce, College of Commerce, Nihon University, Japan, 1989).

Gujarati D. *Government and Business* (McGraw-Hill, New York, 1984).

Gulati R., Nohria N. and Zaheer A. (eds.) "Special Issue: Strategic Network," *Strategic Management Journal*, Vol. 21, No. 3 (2000).

Halal W. E. *Capitalism* (John Wiley, New York, 1985).

Halal W. E. *The New Capitalism* (John Wiley, New York, 1986).

Halford G. S., Maybery M. T. and Bain J. D. *The Development of Thought* (Lawrence Erlbaum Associates, Hillsdale, NJ, 1988).

Hamel G. and Prahalad C. K. *Competing for the Future* (Harvard Business School Press, Boston, 1994).

Hammer M. *The Soul of the New Organization* (adapted and edited from: "Beyond Reengineering. How the Process-Centred Organization is Changing: One Work and Our Lives," Harper-Collins, 1996).

Harrison G. "Culture and Management," *Australian Accountant*, Vol. 64 No. 10 (1994).

Hawken P. *The Ecology of Commerce* (Harper Business, New York, 1994).

Hicks J. R. *The Mainspring of Economic Growth*, Nobel Memorial Lecture, in Nobel Lectures, 1969–1980, ed. Lindbeck A. (World Scientific, Singapore, 1992).

Hitt M. A. "Twenty-First Century Organizations: Business Firms, Business Schools, and the Academy," *Academy of Management Review*, Vol. 23, No. 2 (1998).

Hofstede G. *Culture and Organizations* (McGraw-Hill, London, 1996).

Holt D. H. *Entrepreneurship: New Venture Creation* (Prentice-Hall, Englewood Cliffs, NJ, 1992).

Hornaday J. A. "Research About Living Entrepreneurs," in *Encyclopaedia of Entrepreneurship*, eds. Kent C. L., Sexton D. L. and Vesper K. H. (Prentice Hall, Englewood Cliffs, NJ, 1992).

Huey J. "Managing in the Midst of Chaos," *Fortune*, 3 April (1992).

Jacobs L., Gao G. P. and Herbig P. "Confucian Roots in China: A Force For Today's Business," *Management Decision*, Vol. 33, No. 10 (1955).

Jarillo J. C. "On Strategic Networks," *Strategic Management Journal*, Vol. 9 (1988).

Jones T. F. *Entrepreneurism* (Donald I. Fine, Inc., New York, 1987).

Journal of Small Business and Entrepreneurship, Vol. 15, No. 2 (1987).

Kao J. J. *Entrepreneurship, Creativity and Organization* (Prentice-Hall, Englewood Cliffs, NJ, 1989).

Kao R. W. Y. *Strategic Issues in Financial Management for Starting and Managing New Small Ventures* (Canadian Treasury Management Review, The Royal Bank of Canada, Toronto, 1986).

Kao R. W. Y. *Accounting Standards Overload: Big GAAP versus Little GAAP* (Accounting Standard Authority of Canada, Vancouver, 1986).

Kao R. W. Y. "From Entrepreneurship to Professionalism," *ICSB Bulletin*, Vol. 24, No. 4 (International Council for Small Business, 1987).

Kao R. W. Y. *Entrepreneurship and Enterprise Development* (Holt, Rinehart and Winston, Toronto, 1989).

Kao R. W. Y. "Who is an Entrepreneur?" in *New Findings and Perspectives in Entrepreneurship*, eds. Donkels R. and Miettinen A. (Gower, London, 1990).

Kao R. W. Y. *Small Business Management*, 3rd ed. (Dryden Press, Toronto, 1992).

Kao R. W. Y. "Defining Entrepreneurship: Past, Present and?" *Creativity and Innovation Management*, Vol. 2, No. 1 (Blackwell, Oxford, 1993).

Kao R. W. Y. *Entrepreneurship, A Wealth Creation and Value Adding Process* (Prentice-Hall, Singapore, 1993).

Kao R. W. Y. *Family/Home Based Business and Its Challenges*, Proceedings of the International Small Business Congress, Jakarta, 1994.

Kao R. W. Y. *An Entrepreneurial Approach to Corporate Management* (Prentice-Hall, Singapore, 1997).

Kao R. W. Y. and Tan W. L. *Entrepreneurship and Enterprise Development in Asia* (Prentice-Hall, Singapore, 2001).

Keirstead B. S. *Capital, Interest and Profits* (Basil Blackwell, Oxford, 1959).

Kendall N. *Good Corporate Governance: An Aid to Growth for the Smaller Company* (Accountancy Books, Central Milton Keynes, 1994).

Keynes J. M. *The Theory of Employment, Interest and Money* (Macmillan, London, 1964).

Kirby D. A. and Fan Y. "Chinese Cultural Value and Entrepreneurship: A Preliminary Consideration," *Journal of Enterprising Culture*, Vol. 3, No. 3 (1995).

Koontz H. "The Management Theory Jungle," *Journal of the Academy of Management*, Vol. 4, No. 3 (1961).

Koselka R., Meeks F. and Saunders L "Family Affairs," *Forbes*, Vol. 144, No, 13 (1989).

Kurlansky M. *Cod: A Biography of the Fish that Changed the World* (Jonathan Cape, London, 1998).

Lansberg I. "The Succession Conspiracy," *Family Business Review*, Vol. 1 No. 2 (1988).

Leavitt T. "The Dangers of Social Responsibility," *Harvard Business Review*, Vol. 36, No. 5 (1958).

Lutkin J. C. F. *Foreword in International Corporate Governance*, eds. Lutkin J. C. F. and Gallagher D. (Euromoney Books, London, 1990).

Marshall A. *Principles of Economics*, 8th ed. (Macmillan, London, 1920), first published in 1890.

Martin H. "What Do Bosses Do?" *Review of Radical Economics*, Vol. 6 (1974).

Maruyama M. "Mindscapes, Workers and Management: Japan and the U.S.A.," In *Japanese Management, Cultural and Environment Consideration*, eds. Lee S. M. and Schwendiman G. (Praeger, New York, 1982).

Meek V. L. "Organizational Culture: Origins and Weakness," *Organizational Studies*, Vol. 9, No. 4 (1988).

Mintzberg H. "Who Should Control the Corporation?" *California Management Review*, Vol. 27, No.1 (1984).

Mohamad M. *A New Deal for Asia* (Pelanduk, Selangor Darul Ehsan, Malaysia, 1999).

Morrison P. and Morrison E. (eds.) *Charles Babbage and His Calculating Engines* (Dover Publications, New York, 1961), a reprint from Charles Babbage (autobiography), "Passages from the Life of a Philosopher" (Long & Green, London, 1864).

Murayama M. "The Japanese Business Value System," in *Japanese Management, Cultural and Environmental Consideration*, eds. Lee S. M. and Schwendiman G. (Praeger Scientific, New York, 1982).

National Commission on the Environment. *Choosing a Sustainable Future* (World Wildlife Fund, Washington, DC, 1993).

OECD. *Fostering Entrepreneurship* (1988).

OECD. *The Polluter Pays Principle: Definition, Analysis, Implementation* (Paris, 1975).

OECD. *The OECD Jobs Study* (OECD Publications, Paris, 1994).

OECD. *OECD Economic Surveys — United States* (OECD Publications, Paris, 1997).

Oliga J. C. "Editorial: Toward Enterprising, Innovative and Interventionist Social Practice," *Entrepreneurship, Innovation and Change*, Vol. 1 (Plenum Press, New York, 1992).

Overy R. (ed.) *The Times History of 20th Century* (Time Books, London, 1999).

Pang Y. H. (ed.) *Contemporary Issues in Accounting* (Addison Wesley, Singapore, 1995).

Paton W. A. and Littleton A. C. *An Introduction in Corporate Accounting Standards* (American Institute of Certified Public Accountants, Iowa City, IA, 1940).

Peck M. J. "The Large Japanese Corporation," in *The US Business Corporation: An Institution in Transition*, eds. Meyer J. R. and Gustafson J. M. (American Academy of Arts and Sciences, Ballinger Publishing Company, MA, 1988).

Peilly W. K. Foreword in *Are Environmental Regulations Driving U.S. Industry Overseas?* ed. Leonard H. J. (The Conservation Foundation, Washington, DC, 1984).

Perrings C. "Economics, Ecology and the Global Biodiversity Assessment," *Tree*, Vol. 11, No. 6 (1996).

Peters J. S. J. and Waterman R. H. *In Search of Excellence* (Harper & Row, New York, 1982).

Pierson F. C. *The Education of American Businessmen: A Study of University-College Program in Business Administration* (McGraw-Hill, New York, 1959).

Pinchot G. I. *Intrapreneurship* (Harper & Row, New York, 1985).

Polak F. I. *The Image of the Future*, Vol. 2 (Oceana Publications, New York, 1961).

Sandberg W. R. and Holfer C. W. "Improving New Venture Performance: The Role of Strategy, Industry Structure, and Entrepreneur," *Journal of Business Venturing*, Vol. 2 (1987).

Schroeder R. *Max Weber and Sociology of Culture* (Sage, London, 1992).

Schumpeter J. A. *The Theory of Economic Development: An Inquiry into Profits, Capital, Credit, Interest and the Business Cycle*, translated by Poie R. (Harvard University Press, Cambridge, MA, 1934).

Seager J. (ed.) *The Corporate Way* (Simon & Schuster, New York, 1990).

Shollhammer, H. "International Corporate Entrepreneurship," in *Encyclopedia of Entrepreneurship*, eds. Kent C. A., Sexton D. L. and Vesper K. H. (Prentice-Hall, Englewood Cliffs, NJ, 1982).

Simon H. *Economic Theory*, Vol. 3 (Macmillan, New York, 1967).

Smith A. *The Wealth of Nations*, Vol. 3 (Richard D Irwin, Homewood, IL, 1963).

Smith A. *An Inquiry into the Nature and Causes of the Wealth of Nations*, eds. Cannon E. (University of Chicago Press, Chicago, 1976).

Smith, L. "The Boardroom is Becoming a Different Scene," *Fortune*, 8 May (1978).

Steiner, G. *Business and Society: Environment and Responsibility*, 3rd ed. (McGraw-Hill, New York, 1975).

Stern M. H. *Inside the Family-Held Business* (Harcourt Brace Jovanovich, New York, 1986).

Tann J. *The Development of Factory System* (Common Market Press, London, 1970).

Tapscott D. *Strategy in the New Economy, Strategy and Leadership* (November/December 1997).

Taylor D., Wayne W., Allan A. and Baetz M. C. *Business and Government in Canada* (Prentice-Hall, 1999).

The Social Responsibility of Business is to Increase Its Profit, *New York Times Magazine*, 13 September 1970. Baron, Chap. 17, pp. 110–113.

Timmons J. *New Venture Creation* (Irwin, Homewood, IL, 1977).

Turner R., Kerry D. P. and Bateman I. *Environmental Economics* (Harvester Wheatsheaf, Hertfordshire, UK, 1994).

Usher P. *Putting Something Back* (The Planning Exchange, Glasgow and Manchester, 1989).

Vesper K. H. *New Venture Strategies* (Prentice-Hall, Englewood Cliffs, New Jersey, 1990), revised edition.

Von Hayek F. A. "Economics and Knowledge," *Economica*, Vol. NS4 (1937).

Von Mises, L. *Human Action: A Treatise on Economic* (Henry Regnery Company, Chicago, 1966).

Water I. *Environmental Management and the International Economic Order: An Agenda for Research* (D. C. Heath, Lexington, MA, 1973).

Weber M. *The Protestant Ethic and the Spirit of Capitalism*, translated from German by Parsons T., G. Allen & Unwin (London, 1930).

Weber M. *The Theory of Social Economic Organization*, translated from German by Parsons T. (Oxford University Press, New York, 1946).

William J. J. *Positive Accounting Theory: A Synthesis of Method and Critique* (Addison-Wesley, Singapore, 1995).

World Commission on Environment and Development. *Our Common Future*, Report of the World Commission on Environment and Development (Oxford University Press, Oxford, 1987).

Index